LANDMARKS

The public art program of The University of Texas at Austin

This publication was made possible by the generosity of Sara Carter and the Still Water Foundation.

Distributed by Tower Books, an Imprint of the University of Texas Press

TOWER
BOOKS

LANDMARKS

The public art program of The University of Texas at Austin

2008–2025

EDITED BY Andrée Bober

ESSAYS BY Rainey Knudson
Kathleen Brady Stimpert
Kanitra Fletcher

WITH TEXTS ADAPTED FROM CONTRIBUTIONS BY

Sana López Abellán
Ombretta Agró Andruff
Andrée Bober
Kanitra Fletcher
Valerie Fletcher
Rudolf Frieling
Alex Grimley
Lauren Hanson
Linda Henderson
Lynn Herbert
Catherine Zinser Mandel
Alexandra Mendez
Timothy Morton
Christiane Paul
Florencia Portocarrero
Nancy Princenthal
Veronica Roberts
Gwendolyn Dubois Shaw
Lumi Tan
Robin K. Williams
Stephanie Sparling Williams

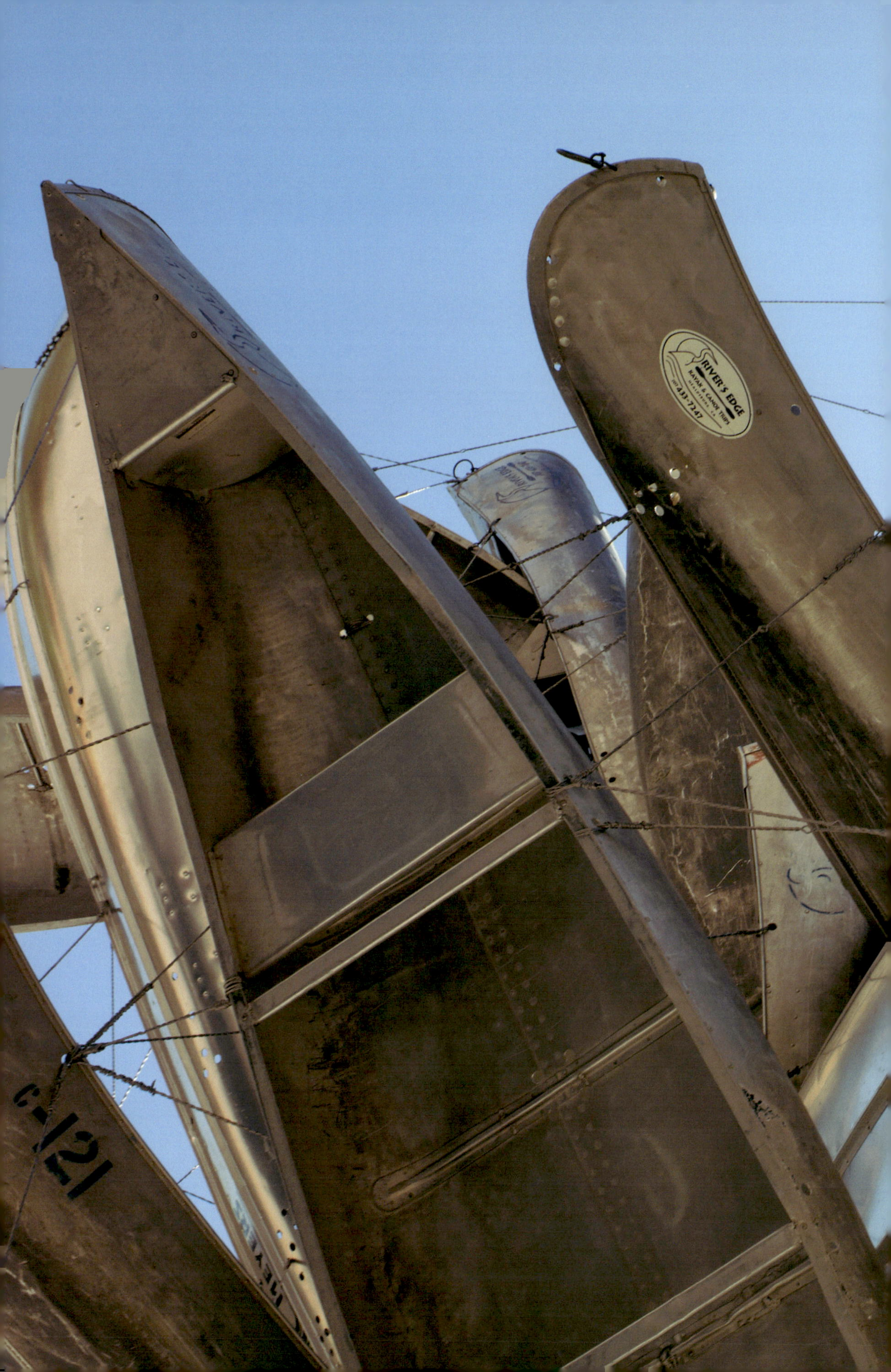
RIVER'S EDGE
KAYAK & CANOE TRIPS
HEALDSBURG CA
707 433-7247
C-121

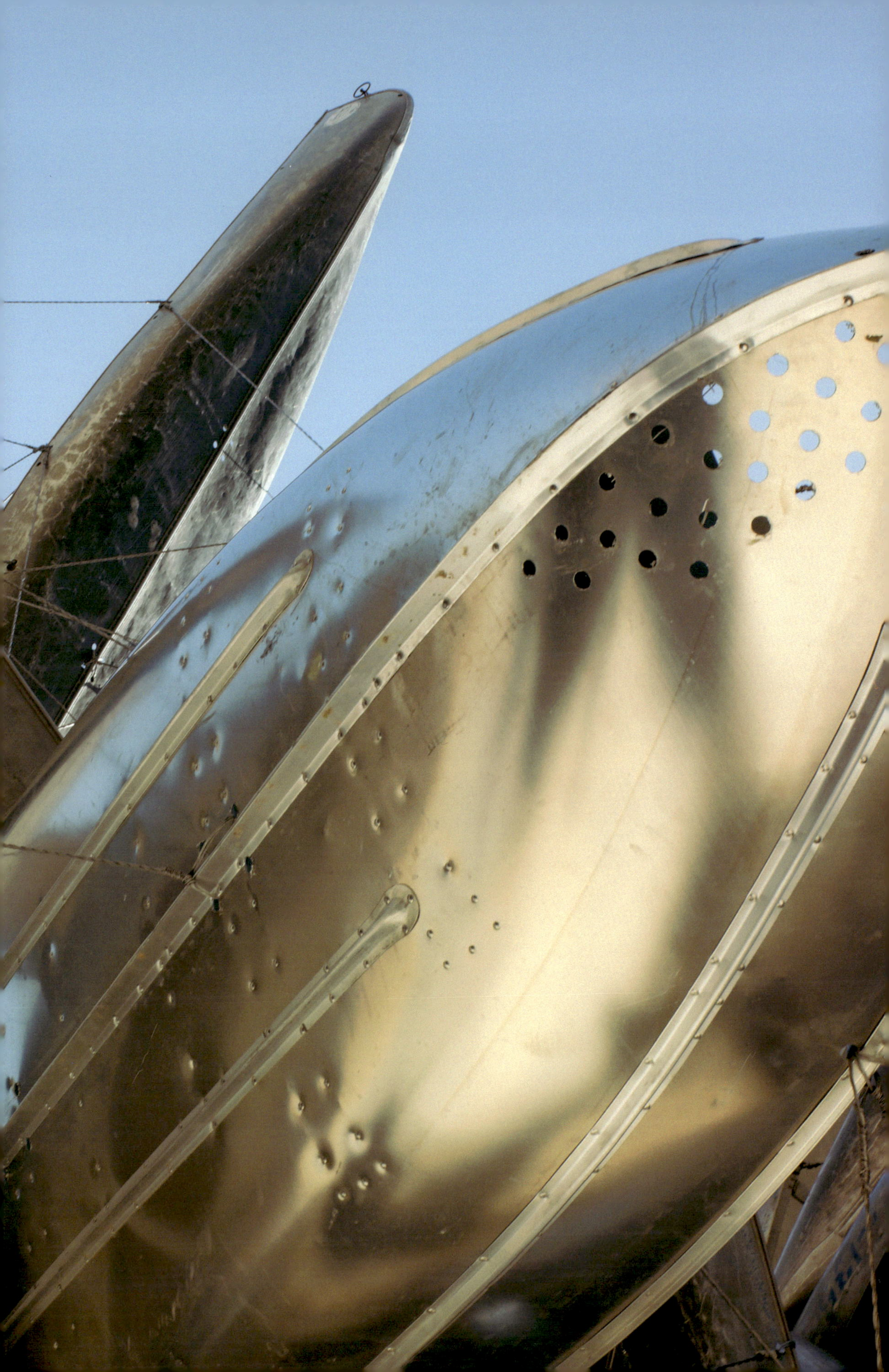

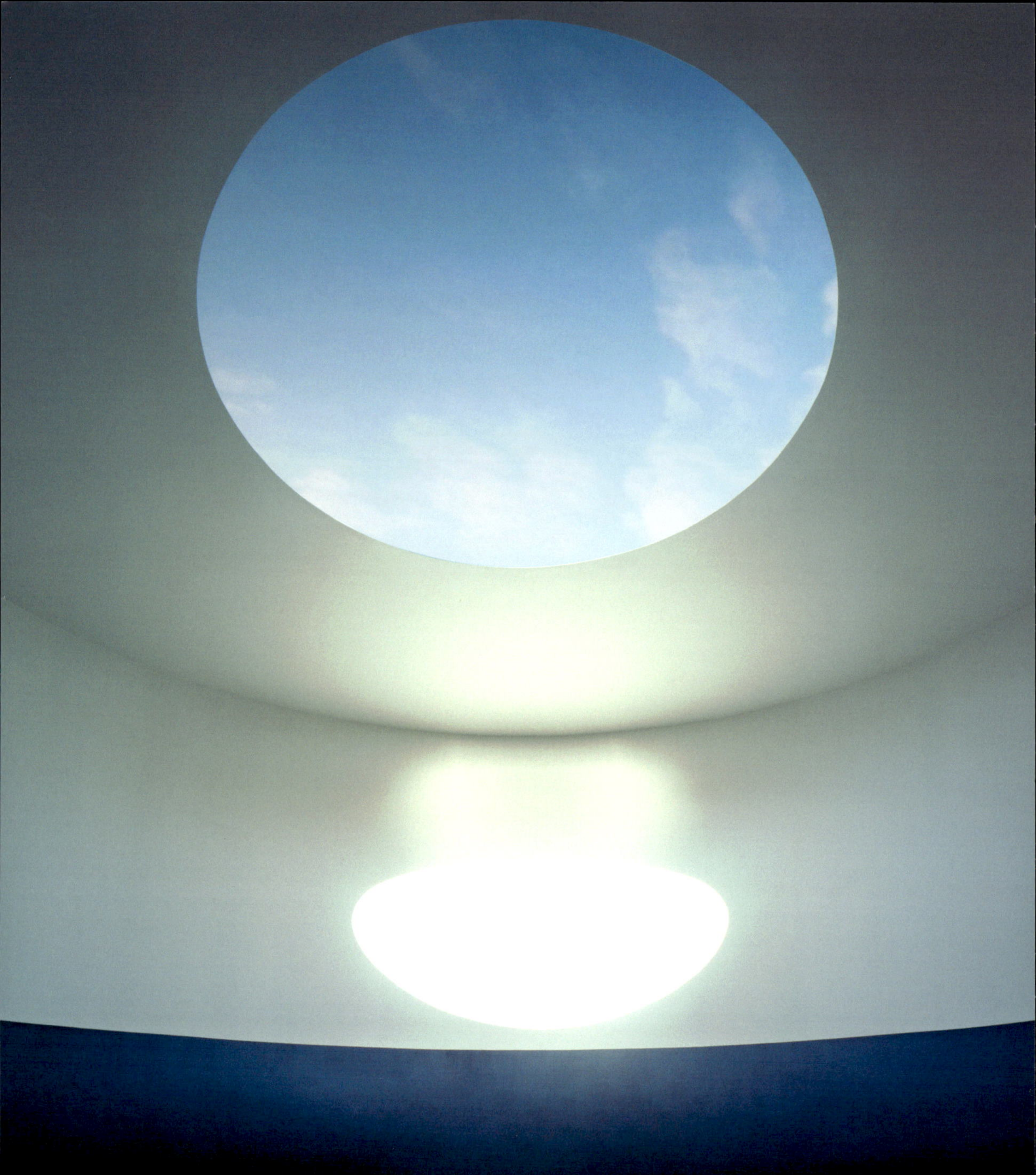

CONTENTS

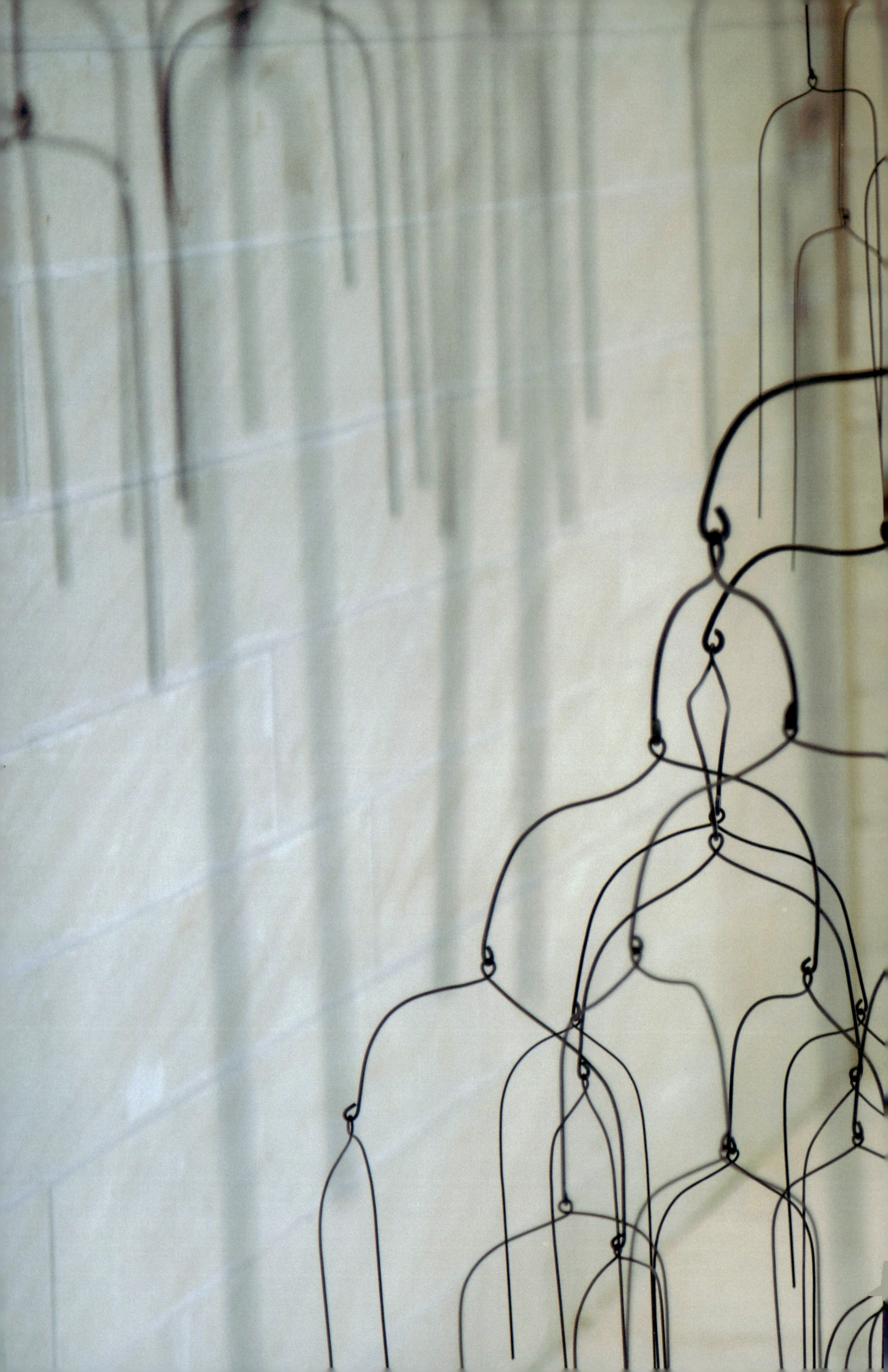

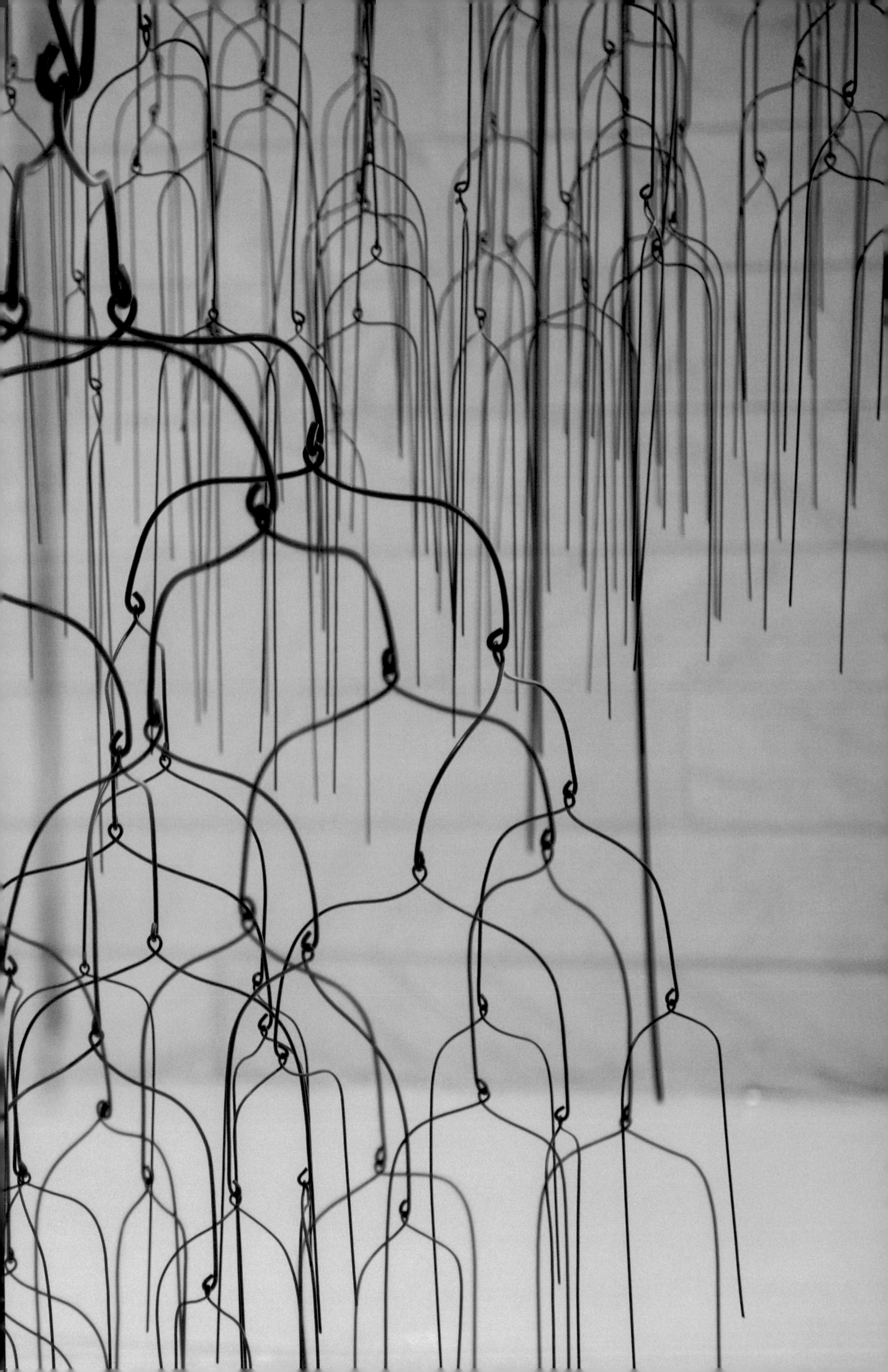

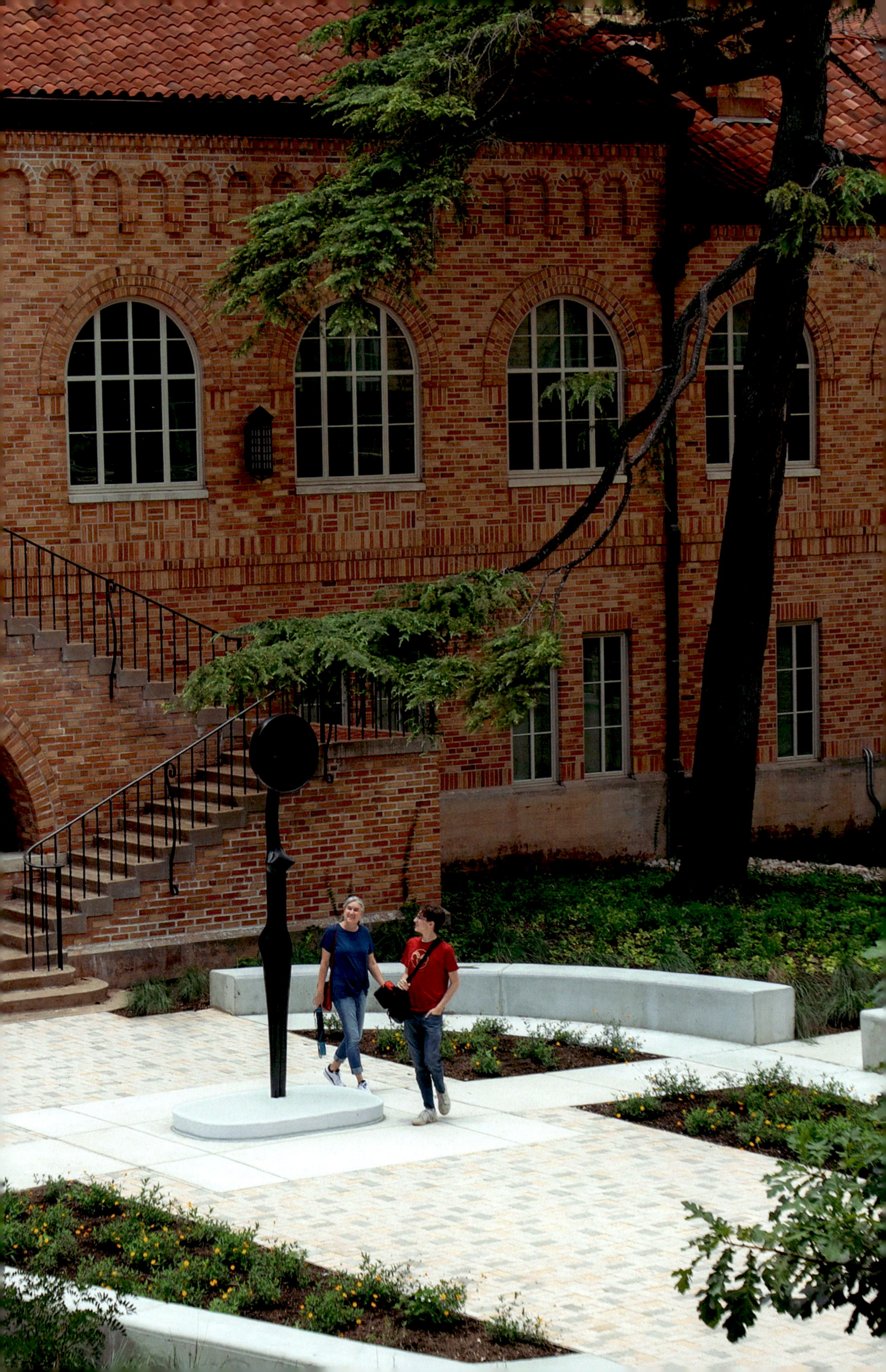

WELCOME

Public art has the profound ability to stimulate curiosity and inspire the imagination in surprising ways. By integrating art into the very fabric of campus, Landmarks creates immersive experiences that are changing how we learn. Its growing collection of fifty works blends seamlessly into our daily lives and prompts us to recognize both our creative potential and shared humanity.

The University of Texas at Austin has long shown its dedication to academic and cultural excellence through efforts to enhance its physical environment. The idea of introducing public art to the campus landscape emerged some twenty years ago as a way to further learning through cultural enrichment. That notion steadily evolved into a defining vision, and Landmarks launched in 2008 with a significant group of sculptures on long-term loan from the Metropolitan Museum of Art. Our partnership offered an auspicious beginning that continues to resonate.

Since its inauguration, Landmarks has built a public art collection that represents an array of styles and conceptual frameworks. It includes notable works by Michael Ray Charles, Mark di Suvero, Ann Hamilton, Sol LeWitt, José Parlá, Marc Quinn, Nancy Rubins, and James Turrell. More recent projects have been launched with Monika Bravo, Beth Campbell, Simone Leigh, Sarah Oppenheimer, Eamon Ore-Giron, and Jennifer Steinkamp. And Landmarks Video continues to present works by some of the most promising and admired artists of our time, with more than 150 screenings to date.

Landmarks transcends the traditional confines of museums and galleries by placing these works in spaces that include plazas, thoroughfares, gardens, and atria. Such familiar locations enable thousands of us to enjoy public art throughout the course of a typical day: between classes and meetings, from windows in neighboring buildings, and as meet-up spots for friends and colleagues. By virtue of being a fixed presence, the art patiently allows new meanings to unfold and our interpretations to evolve. Ultimately, these works of art awaken our curiosity and inspire us to learn and grow.

As students move through the grounds and inhabit academic spaces, public art becomes an integral part of their educational journey. Routine engagement with the collection sparks conversations, challenges students to forge new connections, and fosters a deeper understanding of themselves and one another. In these ways, Landmarks supports the university's commitment to the holistic development of its students, ensuring they become the finest citizens of tomorrow.

In celebrating the transformative impact of Landmarks at The University of Texas at Austin, we extend our heartfelt gratitude to the university's visionary leaders, its steadfast patrons, and our collaborative partners who champion this initiative and propel it forward. And we commend the extraordinary artists whose talents grace our campus with works of art that inspire us and open our minds. Together we cultivate an atmosphere where knowledge and creativity intertwine, empowering generations to explore, discover, and shape a brighter future.

Andrée Bober
Landmarks Founding Director and Curator

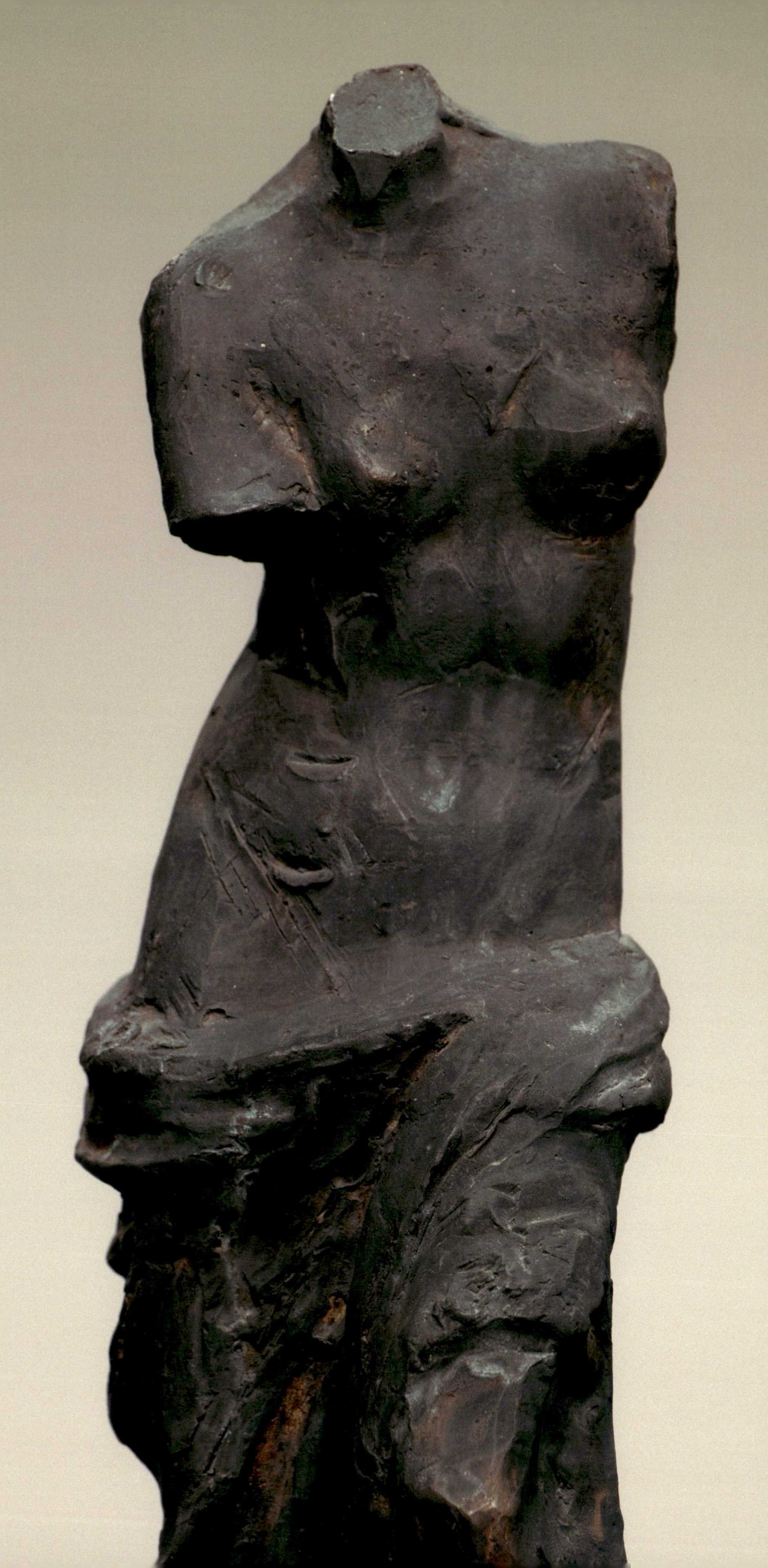

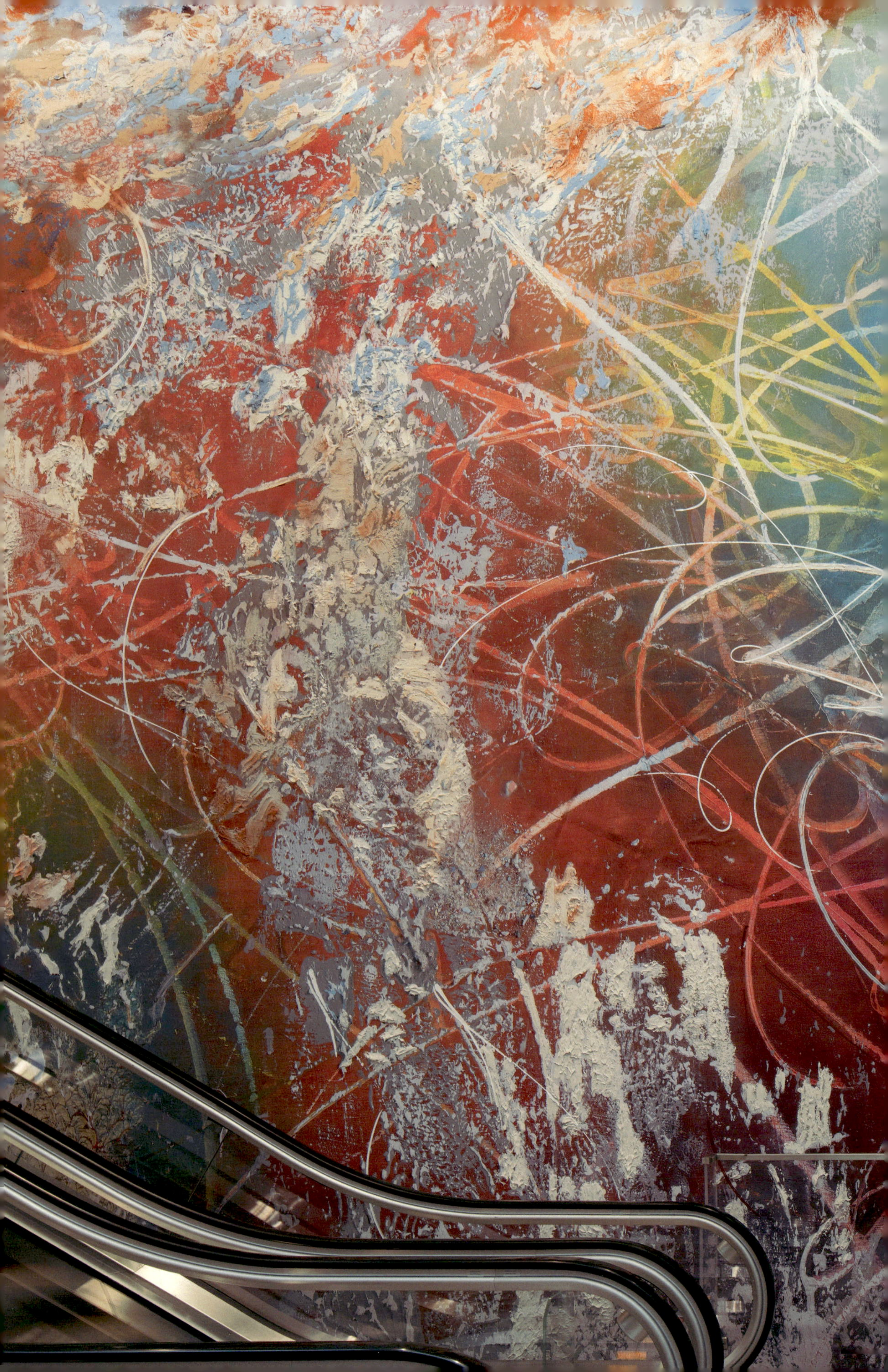

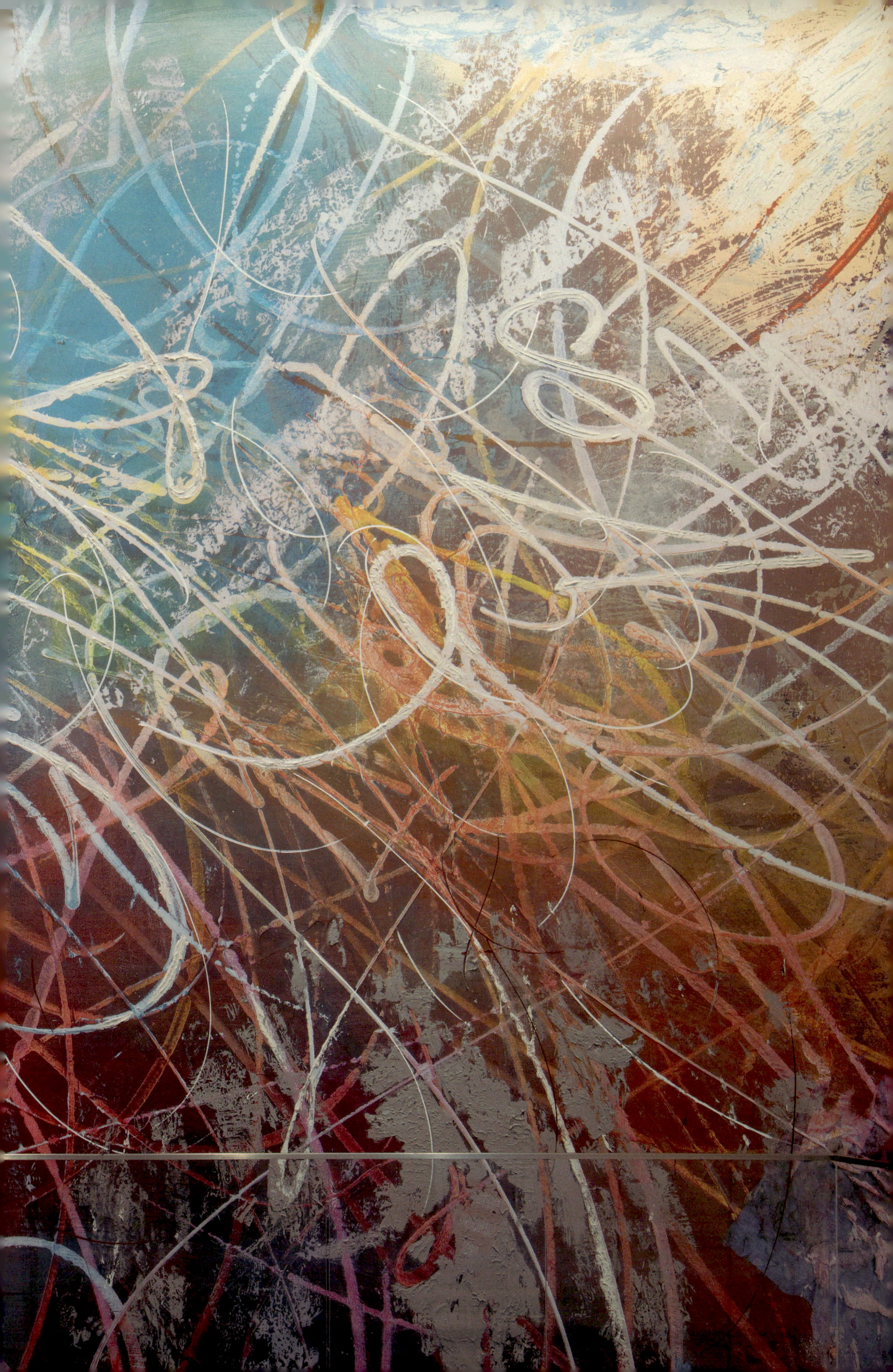

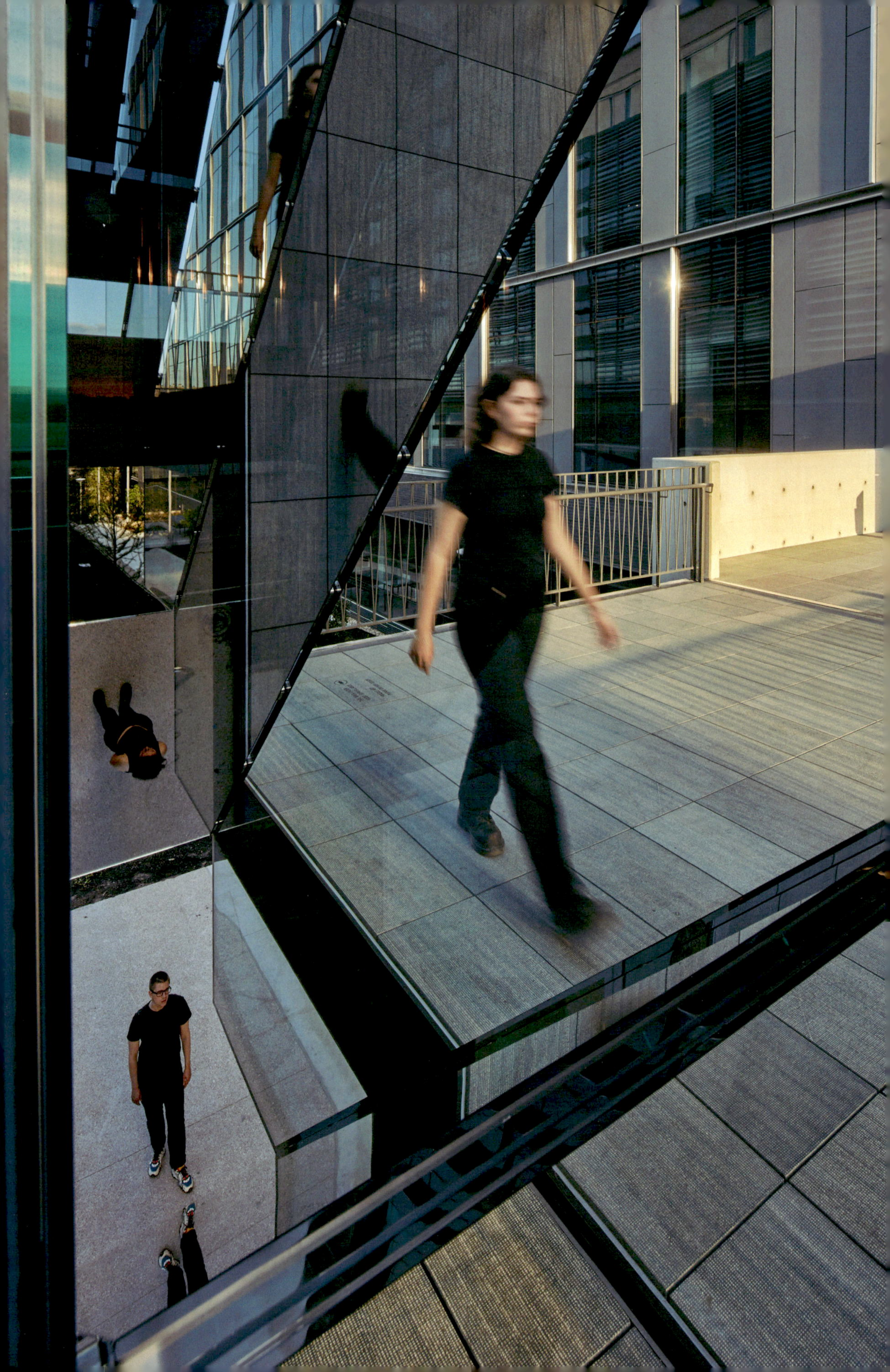

It's being there at all matters a lot. —Adam Gopnik[1]

AS IF BY MAGIC

LANDMARKS AT THE UNIVERSITY OF TEXAS AT AUSTIN

RAINEY KNUDSON

Art matters, and public art might matter most of all. The "public" aspect is key: you do not have to visit a place especially set aside for looking, like a museum or a gallery, to see public art. It is out in the open, there for anybody to experience, a free-for-all for specialists and the uninitiated alike.

But *why* is it there? Why have we, in every culture and era, invariably chosen to place works of art in the midst of our shared spaces?

Art appears in the earliest archaeological record of human beings, long before math, or written language, or even religion. One wonders what is so vital about this activity that, tens of thousands of years ago in what was presumably a hardscrabble existence, our species took the time to paint caves and carve objects.[2] The late graphic designer Milton Glaser answered this question in a 2009 interview titled "What is Art, and What is Not?" arguing, "art is so persistent in all our cultures because it is a means of the culture to survive. And the reason for that . . . is that art, at its fullest capacity, makes us attentive."[3]

The term "attention economy," which emerged with the rise of computer information systems, particularly social media, argues that attention is the great currency that drives contemporary human society.[4] But attentiveness—to nature, food, love, danger, and all the things necessary for our species' survival—has always driven human society. And if art is our most ancient tool for capturing and directing attention, it must at its best make us attentive to that which is truly important—what twenty-first-century people might describe less in terms of survival than as "what makes life worth living." With all due respect to STEM subjects, I imagine few of us on our death beds think about quadratic equations, organic chemistry, or the time value of money. We think about our lives and the people we love. And art—the music, stories, and pictures we love—draws our attention during our life to those things that we think about upon our death. To what makes life worth living.

At its fullest capacity, art wakes us up. It pulls us out of our inner monologues, drawing the focus outside of ourselves and onto some external, shared aspect of our lived experience. This can be true of private art in our homes, be it a postcard tacked to a wall or a precious framed drawing. But this "waking up" quality is especially true of public art.

Imagine you are in a busy public place, your head full of thoughts. Suddenly, a work of art appears in your visual field. If it is a good work of art, it snaps you out of your reverie. It makes you curious. It creates associations, through its materials or form, to recognizable things from the world. A stunning computer-generated video of an aquatic environment reminds you of nature documentaries or maybe a snorkeling trip, but it also mesmerizes with its seductive, repetitive pattern of nature. A series of hazy, poetical portraits invites an expansive understanding of the variety of people in this species of which you are a member.

Although it can be hard to define what public art *is* exactly, it is easy to define what it is not: it is not architecture, although it can have architectural elements. It is not adornment, although it can be beautiful, interesting, and decorative. Crucially for contemporary urban environments, it is not an exhortation to buy something in order to make yourself feel better. Public art is something different. Most of all, it is very hard to do well.

There is no writing about public art that does not acknowledge its tortured place within the larger endeavors of human creativity. Simply put, the world is littered with bad public art. The great examples are exceptions that prove the rule: the "Bean" in Chicago, the Easter Island heads, the Sistine Chapel frescoes, the Statue of Liberty—even Daniel Johnston's *HI, HOW ARE YOU* mural in Austin. The best public art symbolizes its location and captures the imagination of anyone who sees it. It is art *and* icon.

So what makes it so difficult to pull off? The public aspect is a double-edged sword: it is more accessible, true, but people who frequent public spaces often develop a sense of ownership, one that can stoke righteous opinions about how those spaces function and the art that occupies them. It is no wonder that contemporary public art is often described in terms of complications, frustrations, and controversies: the erased histories and the histories being erased, with "the public" sometimes nonplussed or actively hostile to the unexpected art that suddenly appears in their midst.[5] Artists pouring themselves into a work, only to see their idea—or even their final, executed piece—torn down because of vocal naysayers, as was the case with *Tilted Arc*, a work by Richard Serra that was removed from a plaza in New York City in 1989, just eight years after it was installed.[6] Encountering public art is a collective experience, but as the saying goes, you cannot please all the people all the time. Defining what "the average" person wants in the twenty-first century is like nailing Jell-O to a wall. There is no average person, no average "public."[7] The iconic public art of the past, like the Sistine Chapel, was made for a cohesive society. When you embrace complex audiences, how do you reach the public? How can you even define it?

The impossibility of pleasing everybody becomes explicitly urgent on a university campus. It is no coincidence that "university" shares the same etymological root as "universe"—the totality of existence and also the unattainable ideal of universality. It is so hard to make art that comes close to that ideal. With all the obstacles—the divergent opinions, the logistical and political complications, the ever-present scarcity of resources—it is hard to have a good public art program at a university.

Which leads us to the Landmarks collection at The University of Texas at Austin.

Landmarks seems to operate outside all of that public art drama, unobtrusively going about the business of carrying out the school's policy, which stipulates that 1 to 2 percent of capital improvement budgets be spent on art. With a certain lightness and generosity of spirit, Landmarks has quietly transformed the Austin campus over the past seventeen years through the placement of spectacular works of public art, both large and small, inside and out. To the casual viewer, the change has occurred as if by magic.

Indeed, the first works that came through Landmarks—a trove of twenty-eight significant sculptures that arrived on long-term loan from the Metropolitan Museum of Art in 2008—transformed a campus whose public art had previously been restricted almost exclusively to bronze statues of men and wild animals.[8]

Almost overnight, the Met sculptures changed the experience of the campus. Two of the most notable works are Ursula von Rydingsvard's *Untitled (Seven Mountains)* (1986–88), an imposing series of peaks made from rough-cut wood stained dark, and Walter Dusenbery's *Pedogna* (1977), a tower of earth-toned marble situated in the center of the Hall of Noble Words Reading Room, one of the most extraordinary rooms on campus. What is remarkable about these and other works loaned by the Met is that it feels as if they were commissioned by Landmarks directly for their locations, so well are they sited. They seem intentional. Another Met loan, Donald Lipski's pair of giant metal spheres titled *The West* (1987), forms an unmistakable juxtaposition with the iconic Main Tower—a more amusing example of siting, intentional or not.

From the initial Met loan, secured by Andrée Bober, Landmarks' founding director and curator, the collection grew deliberately, piece by piece, so that now one cannot imagine the Forty Acres without it.

The campus of The University of Texas at Austin is a hodge podge. This is a good thing. At a time when places around the globe are becoming visually homogenous and cultural particularities are being sanded down—locales becoming less and less local—the university offers a survey of architectural styles and environments that enliven the campus and keep it from looking like a "theme park for the bookish."[9] Strolling down the newly pedestrian, leafy thoroughfare of Speedway leads you past some varied and beautiful buildings, new and old, on campus.

That stroll is rewarded with a stunning view of one of the most iconic works in the Landmarks collection. Nancy Rubins' explosion of silver canoes that hovers over Speedway at 24th Street, *Monochrome for Austin* (2015), dominates the view from any direction and lodges in your memory perhaps more than any other work on campus. The first time you see it, your foremost question is one of engineering: *Is that thing about to tip over?* No, no . . . whoever made it—with the thin veining of cables holding it together plainly visible—knew what they were doing. Coming closer, you recognize the forms of aluminum canoes silhouetted against the sky. These objects of tranquil, solitary water voyage are bundled up like a bouquet and cinched together so that their gentle curves and pointy ends merge into a monumental form like a deep-sea creature floating over the road. You can walk around it and under it from all sides, as curious and attentive passersby do every few minutes, staring up.

Unlike Rubins' conspicuous tower, Simone Leigh's *Sentinel IV* (2020) is sited in a quieter courtyard that reinforces the implicit, regal dignity of the statue. Enclosed on three sides by the stately architecture of the former women's gymnasium, Leigh's elongated feminine form with an abstracted, disk-like head stands guard, as her name suggests. As with all great art, *Sentinel IV* involves a surprise: a familiar trope (statue of a naked female) with a startling twist (spoon head). She is a beacon, a siren, and a receptacle, too. Like a radio dish, the curved shape of the head suggests both collection and transmission, porously flowing back and forth with whatever signals are out there.

Sentinel IV finds the sweet spot between glib, feel-good trifles (such as a Jeff Koons flower *Puppy*), and abstruse, "difficult" works of art. This is true of most of the works in the Landmarks collection: you do not need to read a novella of supplementary text to understand what the artist is up to. Indeed, Landmarks handles the issue of didactic backup material with tactful simplicity. Each work is given a discreet sign with two or three

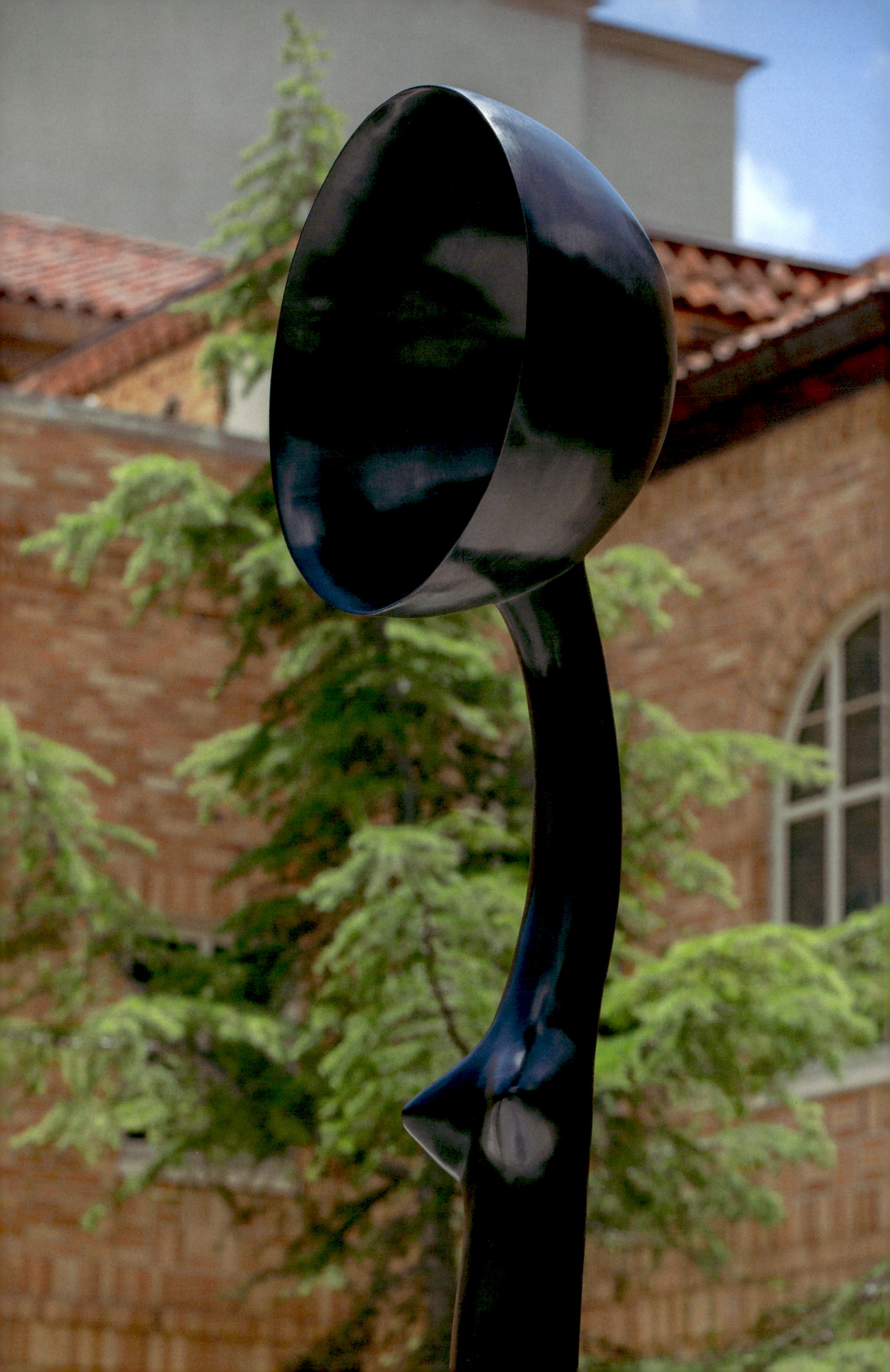

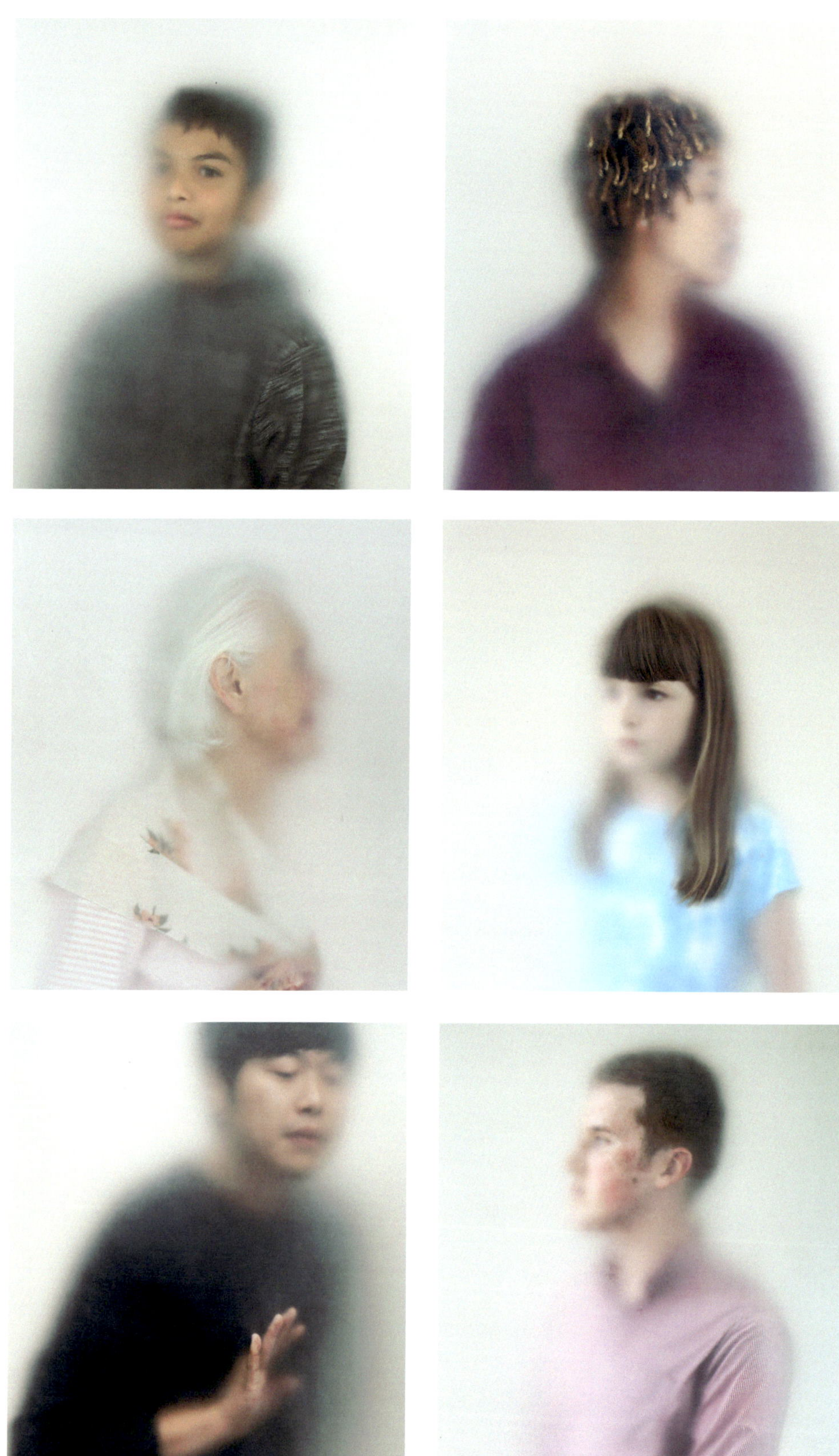

explanatory sentences in English, Spanish, and Simplified Chinese. It is the barest suggestion of what to think—just a nudge, the start of an idea, to help people consider a given work of art more deeply if they are interested. The short texts allow space for viewers to form their own opinions, while also avoiding an austere, "no comment" approach that offers no friendly help to the uninitiated.

This issue of educating the public bedevils all public art. How much is necessary, and what kind is right? Public art, especially in recent decades, has strayed into the arenas of education and social outreach—worthy arenas, but ones to which art is not well-suited. The Landmarks collection may be located in the midst of a great university, but these works are not here to teach us. They are here to draw our attention once again to the world and let us come to our own conclusions.

This is certainly true of Ben Rubin's extraordinary installation *And That's The Way It Is* (2012). Using the grid of the Walter Cronkite communications building façade as his canvas, Rubin projects two streams of text: one taken from *CBS Evening News* broadcasts during the Cronkite era (shown in "typewriter" Courier font); the other a live, closed-caption stream from five news networks (shown in sans serif Verdana font). To sit and watch the piece—to read it—is to marvel at how much the language of the news has changed, and how much the subject matter has not. And the dispassionate presentation of the animation—mere words streaming silently up and down, right and left, along a building façade at night—noiselessly reminds us that so much distressing news, night after night, is just noise that will be forgotten a few decades hence.

Some pieces connect the viewer to our species itself, with a satisfying "aha" of recognition. Ann Hamilton's exquisite series of photographic portraits explicitly argues for a shared humanity. The title, *ONEEVERYONE*, is an elegant invitation to the idea that we are all in this together, however imperfectly and mysteriously. The individual figures in all their variety are lined up along a wall, ghostlike behind a scrim with flashes of clear focus: a face, a hand, a flowered shirt, the rest of which can never be fully known. There is a serenity and even a familiarity in the unknowability of Hamilton's subjects. Quietly contemplated in the waiting area at the Dell Medical School, *ONEEVERYONE* reminds us of the better angels of our nature.

Likewise, commissions by Beth Campbell and Michael Ray Charles suggest a connection to a shared humanity through works that use puzzle and pattern to draw maps of relationships. Charles' *(Forever Free) Ideas, Languages and Conversations* (2015)—a spectacular, elongated comet—combines starburst patterns made from individually joined wooden crutches into a spiky, vigorous whole that formally echoes Rubins' bristling canoes. Sited in the atrium of the Gordon-White Building, home to the centers for study on underrepresented cultures, *(Forever Free) Ideas, Languages and Conversations* implicitly acknowledges histories of inequalities in a space dedicated to exploring those painful histories, as well as new ways of thinking and being.

Campbell's *Spontaneous future(s), Possible past* (2019) is located in the Health Transformation Building, the Dell Medical School's outpatient wing. In two related works—a delicate wire mobile sculpture suspended from the ceiling and a framed drawing nearby—Campbell uses a decision-tree to map out imagined futures and parallel universes. The drawing incorporates gently funny, mundane text in its branches: "I am overwhelmed by all of the stuff I have" leads to two options: "Try to get rid of stuff, but it's so hard," and "Launches me into a full-fledged cleaning spree." Alongside the spark of recognition—we can all relate to this problem—the viewer is invited, by following the paths of Campbell's decisions that fork like a Choose Your Own Adventure book, to imagine her own potential futures.

Two of my favorite works in the Landmarks collection are recent additions. Sarah Oppenheimer's sleek *C-010106* (2022) is an arresting, inscrutable pair of reflective enclosures atop a pedestrian bridge leading to a glossy new engineering building. You cannot help but stop and study *C-010106* as it reorients you within space: up, down, self, sky, and buildings are all inverted into multiple perspectives that question the nature of gravity and of physical matter itself. The piece does not spell anything out for the viewer. It invites curiosity and attentiveness through an austere beauty rooted in scientific inquiry.

Finally, surely one of the most stunning crowd-pleasers among the Landmarks collection is Jennifer Steinkamp's *EON* (2020), a monumental, thirty-foot-long video loop of a dense, mesmerizing underwater environment full of colorful plants and aquatic organisms that are entirely computer animated. Located in the lobby of Welch Hall, the main science building, and situated next to a large seating area with comfortable couches and chairs, *EON* creates a social situation, intentionally or not.[10] Even though its run length is relatively short for video art (2:07 minutes), it is so dense and hypnotic that you can watch it ten times in a row and not identify, exactly, where its pattern recurs.

How has Landmarks done what it has done? Let us not peer behind the curtain; the mystery of how public art occurs is best left behind closed doors. Let us enjoy the Landmarks magic like a Broadway audience that does not have to sit through all the rehearsals. Whatever Landmarks is doing, it is working. The stakeholders who have been involved with its commissions have embraced the unexpected idea and the chancy risk. For no successful public art is without risk: great ideas always seem obvious after the fact, but they are anything but obvious when they are first presented. As with anything worth doing, it is very hard to do well.

NOTES

1. Adam Gopnik, "Introduction: Art in the City," in *City Art: New York's Percent for Art Program* (New York: Merrell Publishers, 2005), 9.

2. According to research published in 2015, this may have occurred hundreds of thousands of years ago. Josephine C. A. Joordens et al., "*Homo erectus* at Trinil on Java Used Shells for Tool Production and Engraving," *Nature* 518 (2015): 228–31, https://www.nature.com/articles/nature13962.

3. "Art, at its fullest capacity, makes us attentive. If you look at a work of art, you can re-engage reality once again, and you'll see the distinction between what you thought things were and what they actually are." From the interview with graphic designer Milton Glaser, "What is Art, and What is Not?" video, 6 min., August 27, 2009, Big Think, https://bigthink.com/videos/what-is-art-and-what-is-not/. Glaser is probably most famous for designing the "I [heart] NY" logo.

4. Wikipedia, s.v. Attention economy, last modified February 18, 2024, https://en.wikipedia.org/wiki/Attention_economy.

5. The brouhaha that greeted *The Embrace* (2023), the Martin Luther King Jr. memorial in Boston by sculptor Hank Willis Thomas is but one recent example of hostility to public art. Wilfred Chan, "It's a Strange Moment We Live in: MLK Sculptor on Backlash to Monument," *The Guardian*, January 19, 2023, https://www.theguardian.com/us-news/2023/jan/19/martin-luther-king-sculptor-boston-hank-willis-thomas.

6. For an excellent discussion of the *Tilted Arc* debacle, see Harriet Senie, *Contemporary Public Sculpture: Tradition, Transformation, and Controversy* (Oxford University Press, 1992). As Senie notes, "Controversy is loud and appreciation often silent and unmeasurable," 230.

7. Katy Siegel makes this point in her brilliant essay "Puppy Love," in *Plop: Recent Projects of the Public Art Fund* (New York: Merrell Publishers, 2004). "[D]iscussions of public art have centered around the question of what 'the public' wants. . . . The most obvious problem with the question is that modern definitions of 'the public' tend to be abstract, ignoring social particularities. . . . When critics, artists, and even politicians talk about 'the public,' they are usually trying to guess what the 'average' person thinks about art, how to appeal to them, or what attitude to strike in relation to them, without asking what an average person might be," 30.

8. As well as one sexy young woman, Anna Hyatt Huntington's *Diana the Huntress* (1927), which was apocryphally modeled after an eighteen-year-old Bette Davis.

9. "Rather than an ivory tower establishment, the University of California San Diego, is a horizontal collage of wood, cement, steel, and glass. Rather than a period theme park for the bookish, it is a well-laid-out subdivision for the adventurously brainy." Robert Storr, "The Fine Art of Not Quite Fitting In," in *Landmarks: Sculptural Commissions for the Stuart Collection at the University of California San Diego* (University of California Press, 2020), 23.

10. In a conversation with Tom Eccles about public art, Tom Finkelpearl argues for looking from an artwork back toward the audience, rather than from the audience toward the artwork, and asking, "What is the social situation or environment created by that artwork?" "Thinking About the Art in Public Art" in *Creative Time: The Book* (Princeton Architectural Press, 2007), 89.

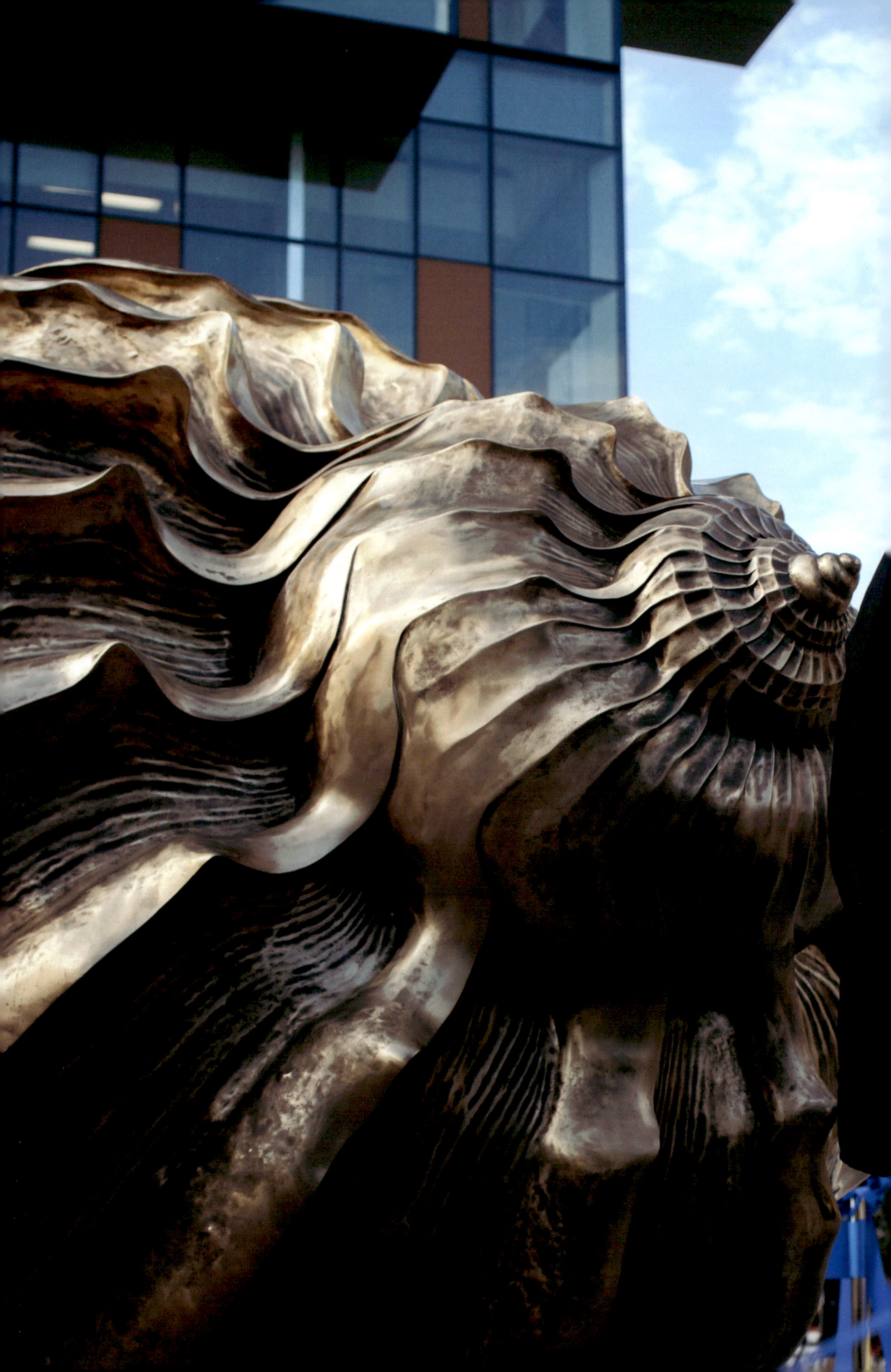

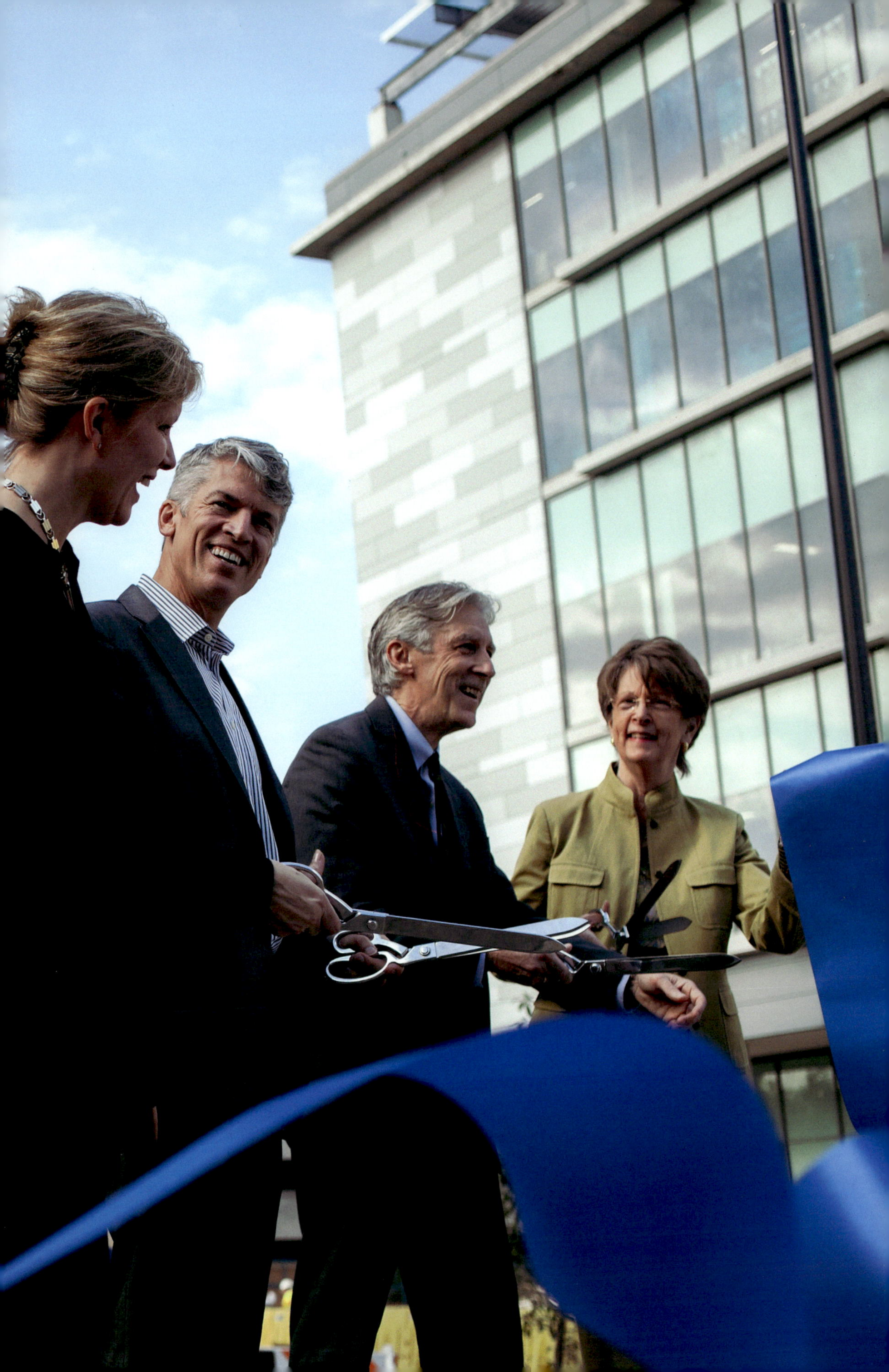

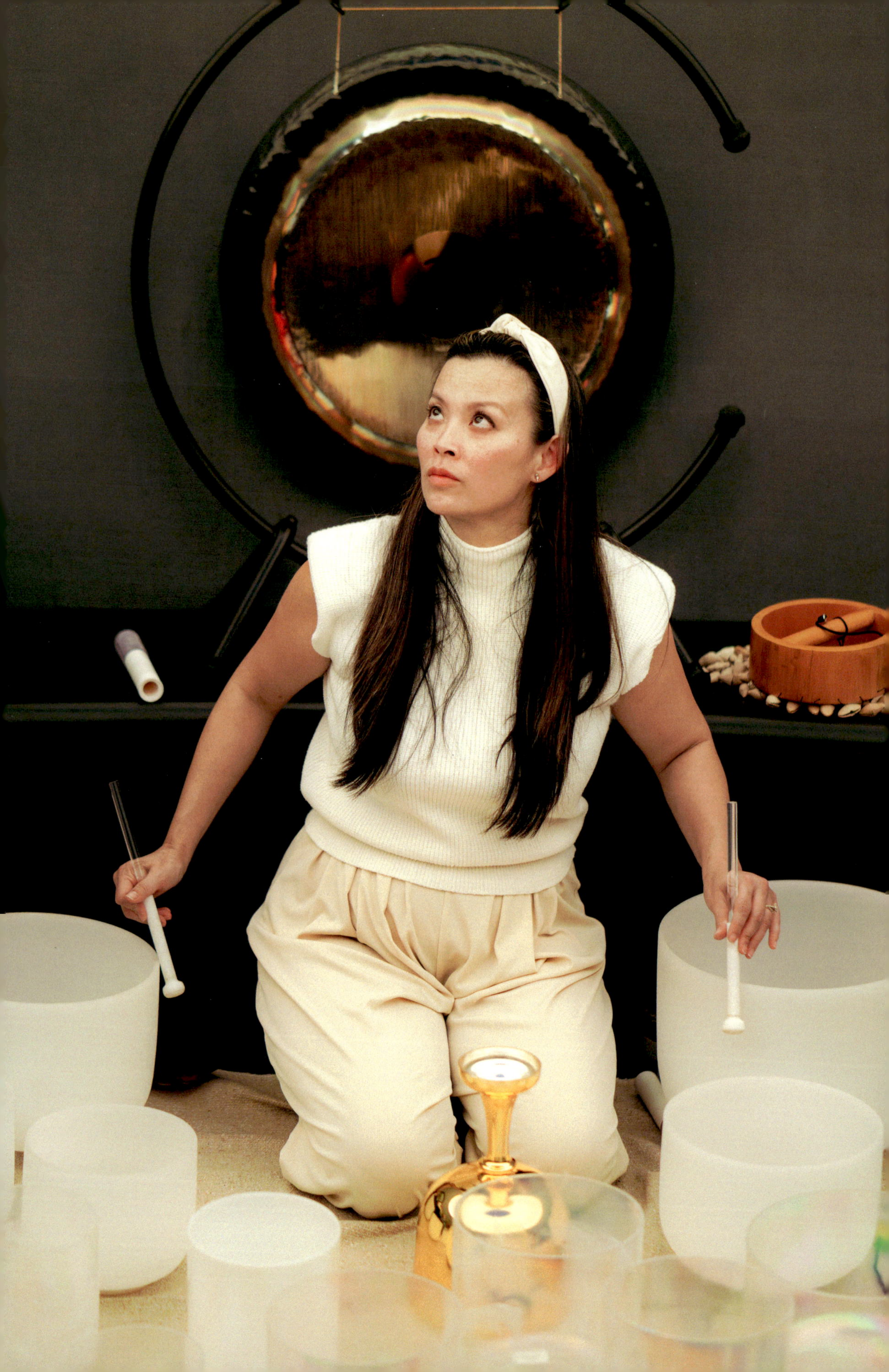

THE HEALING POWER OF ART

KATHLEEN BRADY STIMPERT
LANDMARKS DEPUTY DIRECTOR

Mental health issues among children, teens, and young adults have surged over the past fifteen years. While various theories attempt to explain this rise, most researchers agree that the global pandemic exacerbated an already struggling youth. Consider these statistics: in 2010, 11 percent of students at The University of Texas at Austin were diagnosed with anxiety, and 8 percent with depression. By 2019, those numbers climbed to 14 and 11 percent, respectively. Four years later, in 2023, the rate of college students in Texas who reported heightened symptoms of serious psychological distress soared to 60 percent.

While these figures are troubling, the university offers a wide range of support services to promote student well-being. One unexpected, yet valuable, resource for students is Landmarks. As emerging science increasingly demonstrates, art is not just a visual expression of the human condition; it has the potential to literally change us, benefiting our health in ways that we are only beginning to understand.

Historically, research has focused on the psychological benefits of engaging with the arts, with the rise of art therapy in the 1940s providing early support for this idea. More recent data, however, points to an even broader impact, revealing both psychological and physiological benefits. A 2019 report from the World Health Organization underscored the role of art-based interventions in treating a wide range of conditions. Drawing from more than 3,000 studies, it detailed how art can alleviate pain, lower stress hormones, boost the immune system, and more. A recent survey conducted by the Institute for Learning Innovation yielded similar results. After a two-hour museum visit, 1,900 participants were asked about the intellectual, social, and physical aspects of their experience. More than 95 percent reported feeling "relaxed," "peaceful," "healthier," and "physically and mentally restored," with a renewed "appreciation for the best of human and natural creation."

From enhancing cognition and reducing anxiety, to lowering blood pressure, art has proven to be an effective tool for treating a wide range of mental and physical conditions. As a result, physicians worldwide are reimagining traditional care protocols. Hospitals, retirement homes, schools, and prisons are incorporating art and other creative practices into rehabilitation efforts. Esteemed institutions like Johns Hopkins and The Aspen Institute are administering "cultural prescriptions" alongside conventional medicine. The National Gallery of Scotland is even using arts engagement to help combat addiction. While more long-term studies are needed, the success of these initiatives underscores the strong connection between art and health, even as our understanding of its mechanisms continues to evolve.

Advances in biomedical technology have transformed the current paradigm and catalyzed an exciting new field—neuroaesthetics. This growing branch of neuroscience explores how our minds and bodies respond to aesthetic experiences such as viewing art, listening to music, or engaging in other forms of creative expression. Using MRIs to study brain activity in those creating or observing art, scientists are finding increased activation in the frontal cortex, the region associated with emotions, memory, creativity, and sensory integration. Even more remarkable, they are seeing the co-activation of areas of the brain that typically do not work together. Systems governing pleasure and reward are stimulated alongside those managing perception, motor circuits, and knowledge. In other studies, wearable "smart" devices are detecting shifts in body temperature, heart rate, and other biomarkers. Research also reveals that neurotransmitters like dopamine and serotonin are released during aesthetic experiences, offering mood support and pain relief, among other benefits. These groundbreaking findings demonstrate how art activates multiple neurological and physiological systems, impacting our biology down to the cellular level.

Notably, much of the progress in neuroaesthetics has been driven by universities and other institutions of higher learning. At Drexel University, researchers discovered that just forty-five minutes of artmaking significantly reduces levels of the stress hormone cortisol. Scientists at UC Berkeley found that engaging with the arts leads to lower levels of inflammatory cytokines and improved immune function. Closer to home, a collaboration between UT's College of Fine Arts and the Livestrong Cancer Institute showed enhanced empathy among students and patients who participated in art and storytelling programs.

Landmarks recognizes the importance of these findings and, in recent years, has developed several programs focused on mental and physical health. At the start of the pandemic, a virtual meditation was launched inside James Turrell's Skyspace, *The Color Inside*, allowing students to engage with the calming light sequence online, anytime and from anywhere. A wellness series was introduced, featuring breathwork sessions and sound bath meditations with singing bowls, gongs, and chimes. In collaboration with the Fitness Institute of Texas, Landmarks designed a tour that combines physical exercises with select works from the collection. Partnerships with professors at Dell Medical School have yielded slow-looking exercises that enhance empathy, improve observation skills, and help pre-med students manage stress.

In 2023, Landmarks introduced our most popular wellness program to date: Paws for Public Art. Developed in partnership with the Longhorn Wellness Center, the annual event features art and animals—both proven to reduce stress. Timed to coincide with midterm exams, the program offers mental health breaks when students need them most. Each spring, miniature goats, hedgehogs, rabbits, chicks, and piglets are placed near iconic works from the Landmarks collection. As students eagerly await interaction with the animals, Landmarks shares insights about the art through staff conversations and digital resources, while representatives from the Longhorn Wellness Center offer sleep kits and information on sleep hygiene, social connection, and self-care. These distinctive programs, along with our award-winning collection, make Landmarks a vital resource for student health and an essential part of the Longhorn experience.

Depression, anxiety, and other psychological challenges are often complex and require a multi-faceted approach. While arts engagement alone cannot resolve these issues, the role that Landmarks plays is not insignificant. Students frequently share that a visit to the Turrell Skyspace provided relief after a stressful day, and that a particular sculpture inspired self-reflection or a moment of shared connection. These accounts highlight the value that Landmarks brings to our campus and community, and reaffirm our belief in the power of art to both heal and transform. As Stone Tejada, a recent UT graduate, explained: "The Landmarks collection replenishes me. It reminds me to slow down and appreciate the beauty around me. As a student, having the collection on campus gives me the ability to take a deep breath and remember that we are all capable of creating beautiful things. That peace has been the lifeblood of my years at UT."

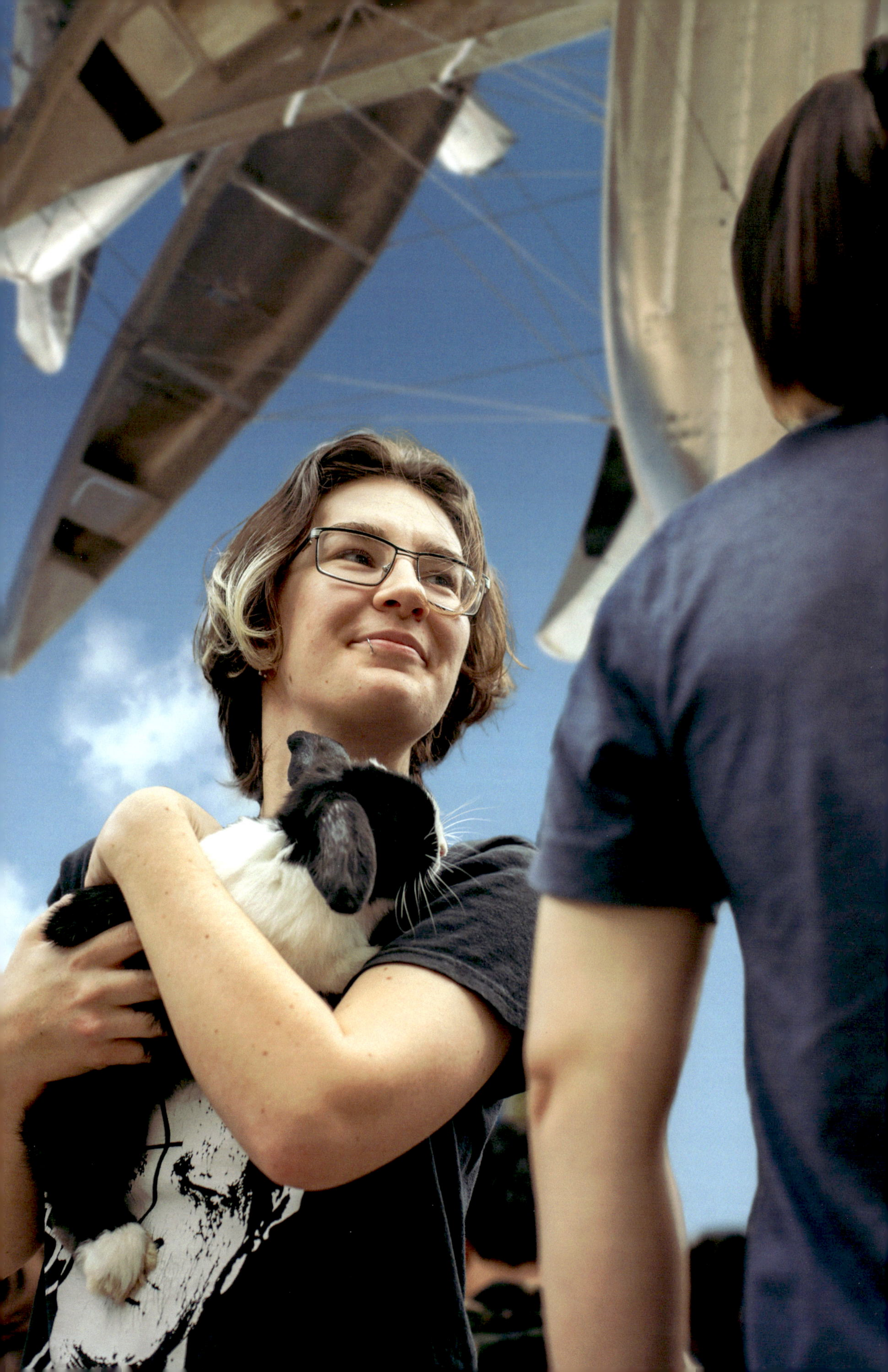

PROGRAMS

Beyond visiting the main campus and spending time with the Landmarks collection, there are many ways curious minds can learn more about the works of public art and their creators. Visit landmarksut.org for information about the collection, special events, and ways to support public art on campus.

EXPERIENCE

VISIT

See Landmarks' collection on the university's main campus. Outdoor works are always accessible, while indoor works may be viewed when buildings are open. James Turrell's Skyspace, *The Color Inside*, is open to all during the day and requires advance booking at sunset. Visit turrellut.org to make a free reservation.

IN-PERSON TOURS

Experience public art on campus with a free docent-led walking, bike, or dog tour. Visitors may join scheduled monthly tours or request a private group tour.

MOBILE TOURS

Take geographic and thematic tours of the collection by using the Landmarks mobile app. Accessible on smartphones and other web-enabled devices, the app features self-guided tours, artist videos, images, and essays in English, Spanish, and Simplified Chinese.

PUBLIC ART CAMPUS MAPS

Take a self-guided tour using a public art campus map or a mobile device. Maps are located at the university's visitor center and at many cultural institutions and libraries on campus.

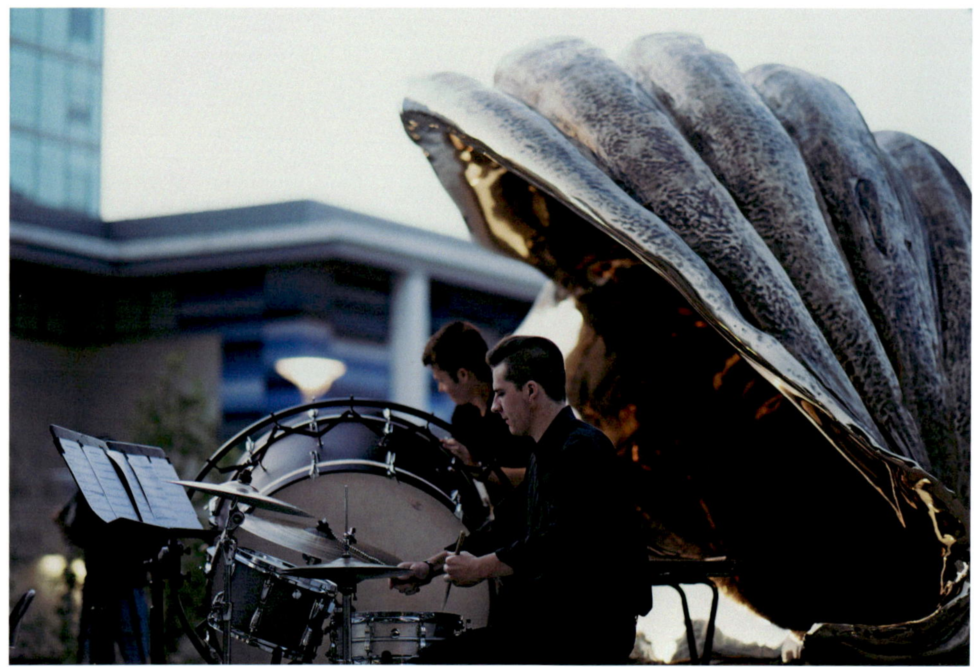

LEARN

EXPERT PERSPECTIVES

Discover insights from leading curators and art historians by reading essays and listening to audio tours. Contributions can be found on the Landmarks website and mobile app.

ARTIST VIDEOS

Explore the collection through short videos that delve into the practices and inspirations of Landmarks' artists. Videos are viewable on the Landmarks website and mobile app.

AUDIO GUIDES

Stream free audio guides featuring works in the collection on the Landmarks website and mobile app. Use your smartphone to listen to the guides while viewing the works of art exhibited on campus.

ACTIVITY GUIDES

Engage younger audiences with activity guides designed for three developmental stages: younger children, older children, and adolescents. Available on Landmarks' website, the guides offer overviews of each work of art, questions for consideration, and activities. Printed guides are available during performances at the Bass Concert Hall.

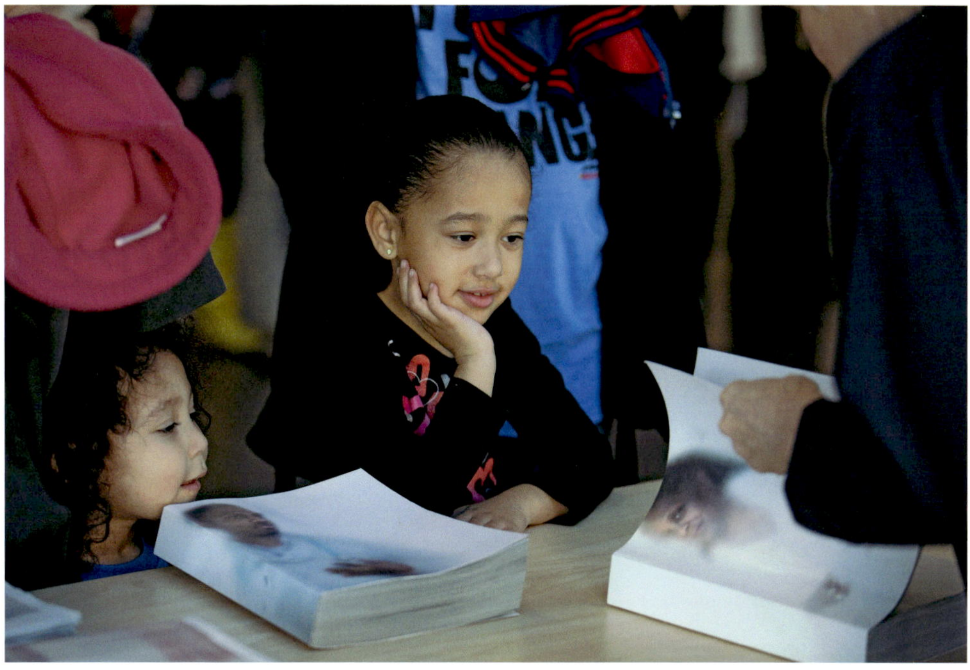

PARTICIPATE

SPECIAL EVENTS

Attend opening receptions, artist talks, performances, and lectures. Join Landmarks' mailing list for updates and follow on social media.

LISTENING WITH LANDMARKS

Stream playlists by Austin musicians inspired by works in the Landmarks collection. Find them on the Landmarks website, mobile app, social media, and Spotify.

SONGS IN THE SKYSPACE

Experience music in James Turrell's Skyspace, *The Color Inside*. This series highlights diverse voices and instruments that enhance the sunset light sequence.

SOUND IN SCULPTURE

Enjoy original compositions by student musicians inspired by the Landmarks collection. In partnership with Texas Performing Arts and the Butler School of Music.

PAWS FOR PUBLIC ART

Take a mental health break with art and animals. Hosted with the Longhorn Wellness Center, this event helps students unwind during midterms.

COLLABORATIONS

Partner with Landmarks on public programs by emailing info@landmarksut.org. Current collaborations include Explore UT, Girl Day, Austin Museum Day, and more.

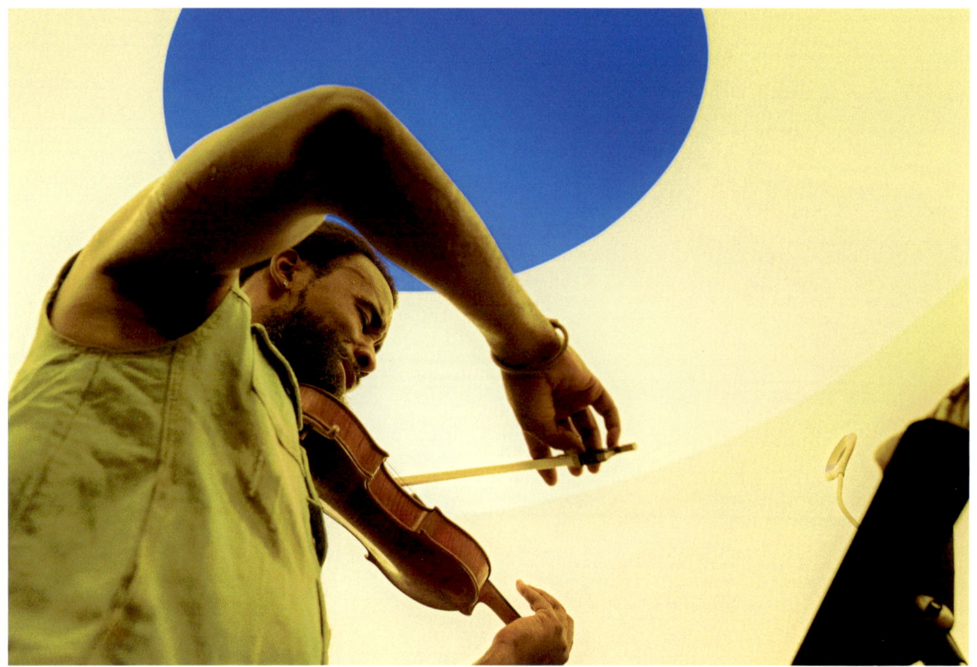

DISCOVER

LEARNING RESOURCES

Explore artist essays and search bibliographic highlights for each work of art on the Landmarks website. Many primary sources are available at the university's Fine Arts Library.

NEWSLETTERS

Receive a monthly email newsletter that highlights programs, upcoming events, and other updates from Landmarks. Sign up on the Landmarks website.

SOCIAL MEDIA

Follow Landmarks for the latest news and updates:
Instagram @landmarksut
Facebook @landmarksut
Vimeo @landmarks
YouTube @landmarksUT

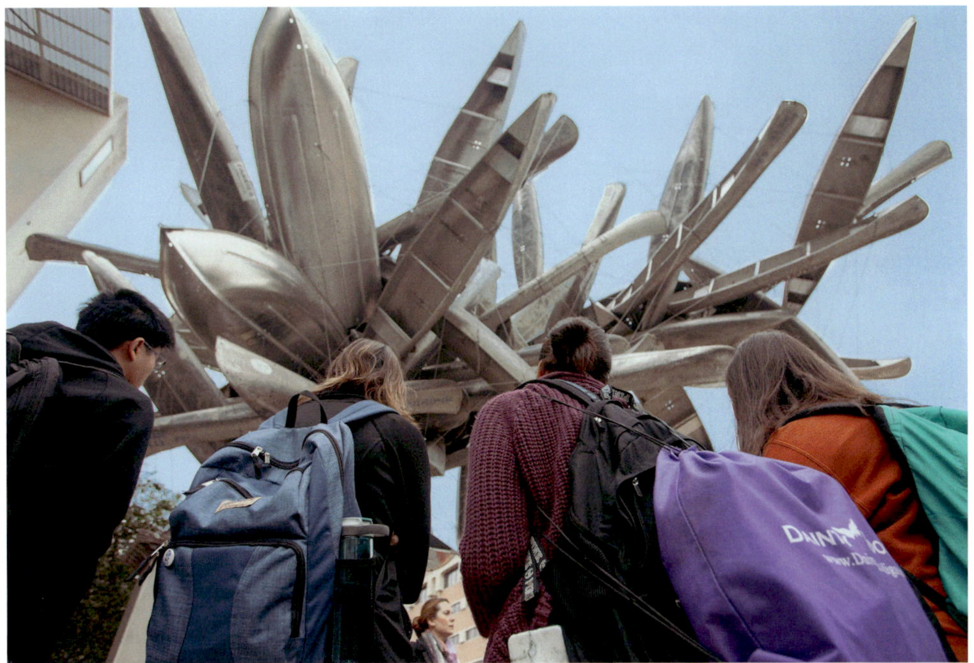

GROW

LANDMARKS PRESERVATION GUILD

Care for the public art collection through the Landmarks Preservation Guild. Volunteers learn basic conservation skills and dedicate time to preserve works of public art for future generations.

LANDMARKS DOCENTS

Introduce the campus community and visitors to the public art collection as a Landmarks Docent. Volunteers offer insights into the artists and their work, foster awareness about modern and contemporary art, and create enriching experiences for participants.

STUDENT INTERNSHIPS

Apply for paid student internships that provide valuable training, networking opportunities, and hands-on experience for success after graduation.

VOLUNTEER

Show your support by volunteering your time and expertise. Simply email info@landmarksut.org to share your interest.

DONATE

If you believe that great art should be free and accessible to all, then please support Landmarks' conservation and education initiatives. Visit landmarksut.org, or call 512.495.4315.

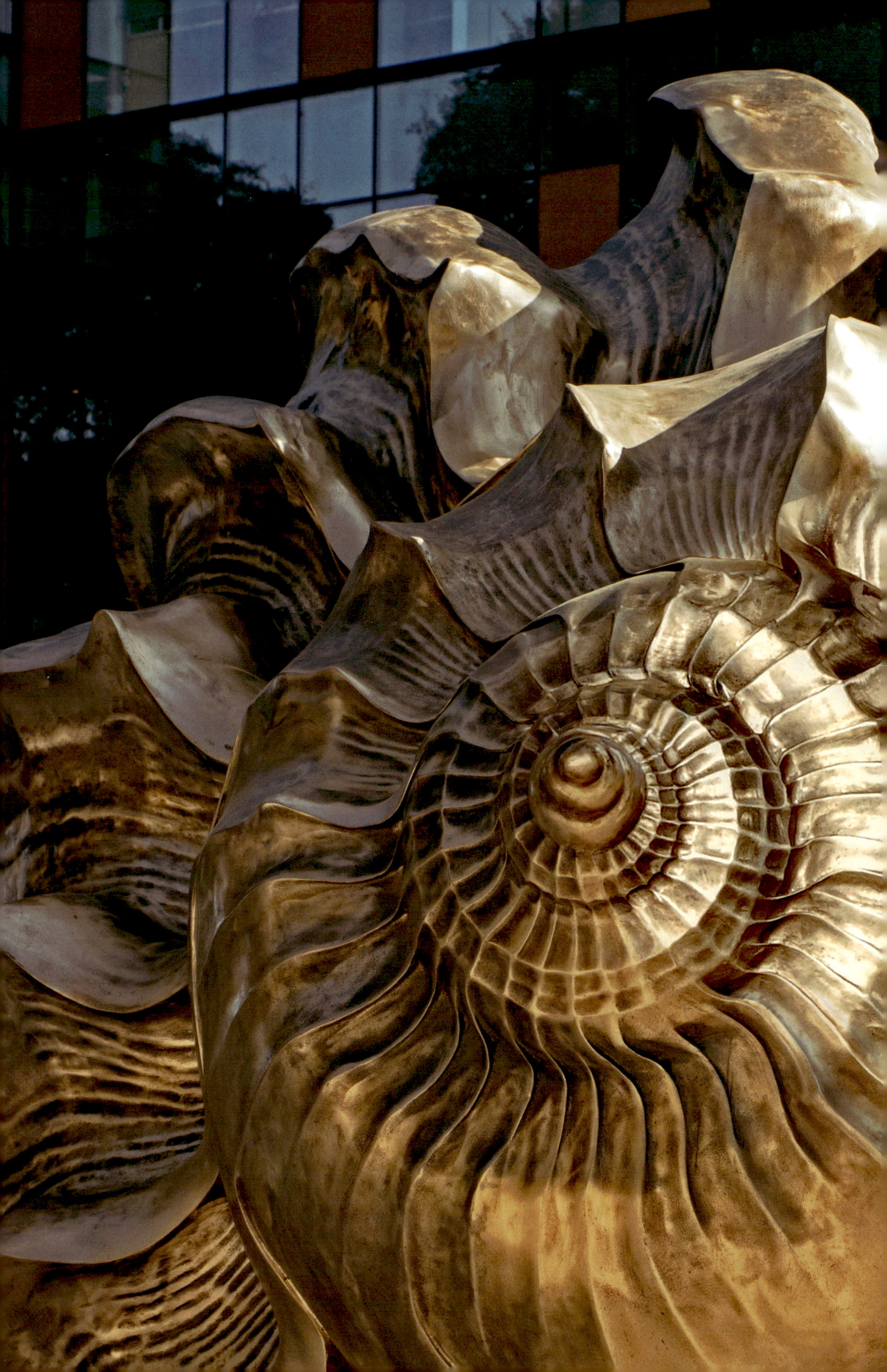

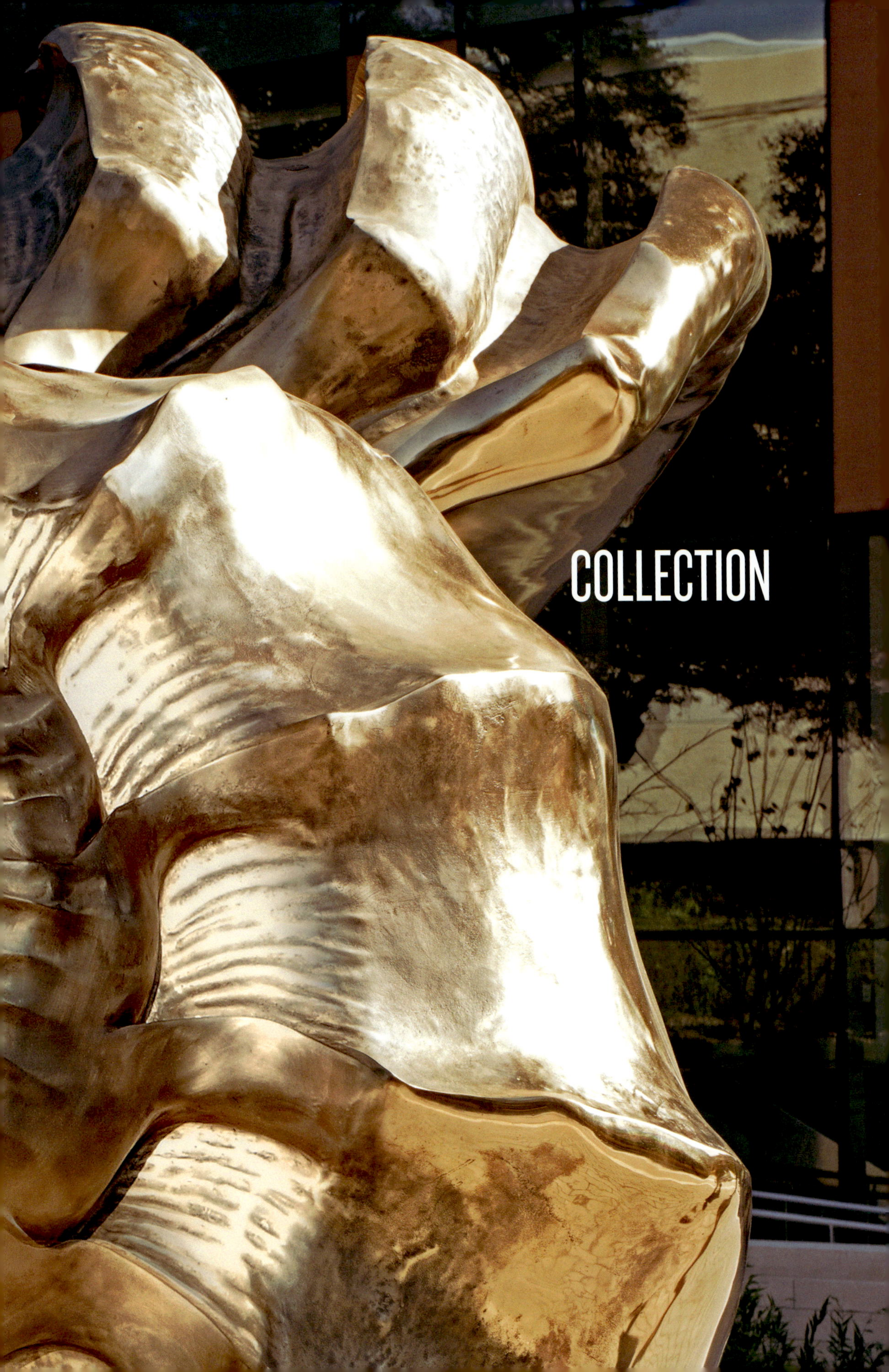

COLLECTION

MAGDALENA ABAKANOWICZ

POLISH, 1930–2017

Profoundly affected by both her solitary childhood and the devastation of World War II, Magdalena Abakanowicz learned to escape loneliness and cruelty by taking refuge in her imagination. When she studied at the Academy of Fine Arts in Warsaw, Poland, in the 1950s, the state-sanctioned artistic style was Socialist Realism. Abakanowicz's decision to paint plants and natural forms amounted to a radical protest, as cultural production was strictly controlled under the country's Communist regime.

In the 1960s, she began working with natural fibers, creating weavings of flax, hemp, horsehair, sisal, and wool. Unlike many women weavers of the time, Abakanowicz rejected utilitarian concerns to create large reliefs and freestanding figures she called *Abakans*: bulbous, flowing, and organic forms suspended from walls or ceilings. These works, with their densely textured surfaces, have a haunting and ominous presence.

As other Polish artists turned from Socialist Realism to abstraction, Abakanowicz became interested in the evocative power of human imagery. Her *Garments* series, for example, suggests standing figures by means of empty clothing. From the 1970s through the 1990s, she glued burlap sacking and other rough fabrics over metal frames and plaster casts of nude bodies to create figural sculptures that are meditations on aspects of collective life and conformity.

As demand for her work increased, Abakanowicz began casting her burlap pieces in bronze editions. Historical context and sculptural form intersect throughout these works, which consist of identical figures. Ranging in groups from four to more than ninety, repetition evokes the dehumanization of totalitarian societies. Whether alone or multiplied in crowds, the larger-than-life figures are stripped of individual features.

Figure on a Trunk offers a solitary human form, headless and hollow—completely anonymous. Nevertheless, this depersonalized identity belies the handmade texture of the sculpture, which shows the workings of the artist's hand throughout. A powerful expression of the human condition, Abakanowicz's sculpture is at once personal and universal—an effigy waiting passively for change and completion.

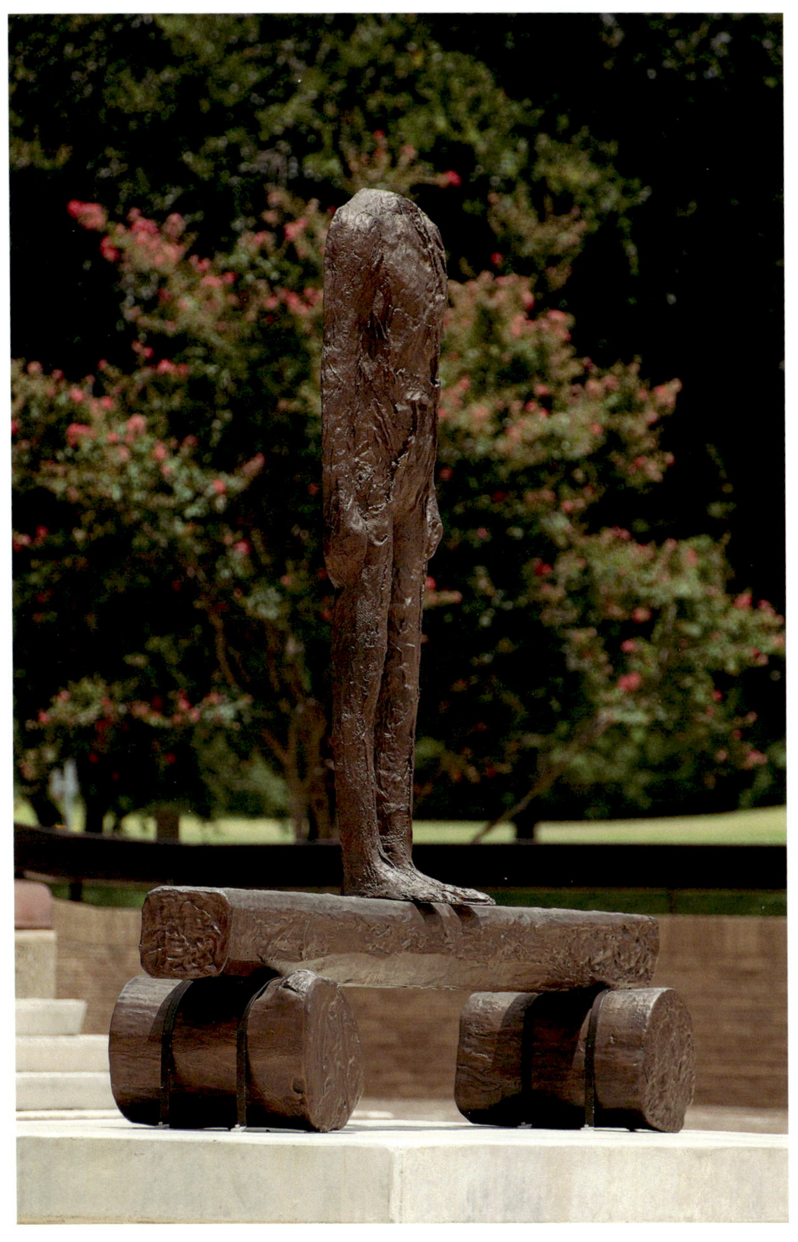

Figure on a Trunk, 2000
Bronze
96 × 103 × 24 inches

Lent by The Metropolitan Museum of Art
Joseph H. Hazen Foundation Purchase Fund, 2000
2000.348a,b

WILLARD BOEPPLE

AMERICAN, BORN 1945

In the 1960s, Willard Boepple's birthplace, Bennington, Vermont, became nationally renowned for the art department at its eponymous college. The school attracted theorists and practitioners of abstract art, including the leading critic Clement Greenberg (1909–1994) and British sculptor Anthony Caro (1924–2013). In 1969, after studying painting on both the East and West Coasts, Boepple returned to Bennington and took a position in the college's sculpture department. He later served as a technical assistant for Caro and other faculty artists working in three dimensions.

Boepple created works using Corten steel, a strong yet malleable material that can be cut, bent, and formed to fabricate works with an extraordinary amount of energy and movement. Although he often begins with a concept, Boepple works intuitively, stating: "Only rarely does the plan survive the making; more often the sculpture takes over, establishing its own rules, its own reality."

Eleanor at 7:15 dates from a dynamic moment in the history of American abstract sculpture. The 1978 exhibition *15 Sculptors in Steel Around Bennington* featured Boepple's work in a survey of the adventurous new art from the region since Caro's arrival in 1963. Just as Boepple had worked as the elder artist's studio assistant, younger artists like Nicholas Pearson (born 1953) later assisted in Boepple's studio. "A tradition was set up," curator Andrew Hudson wrote, like "the apprenticeships of the Renaissance, whereby much learning was passed down in the course of *doing*."

Eleanor at 7:15 is comprised of highly articulated, swirling masses of lively lines with intersecting curves and flat planes. Like many of Boepple's sculptures, this piece is modest in scale and smaller than the average person. The artist feels that proximity allows for a more intimate, immediate exchange. Though the title suggests a narrative, *Eleanor at 7:15* resists a figurative interpretation. Boepple's titles are not meant to be descriptions; they are inspired by places or poetry that evoke a feeling or gesture.

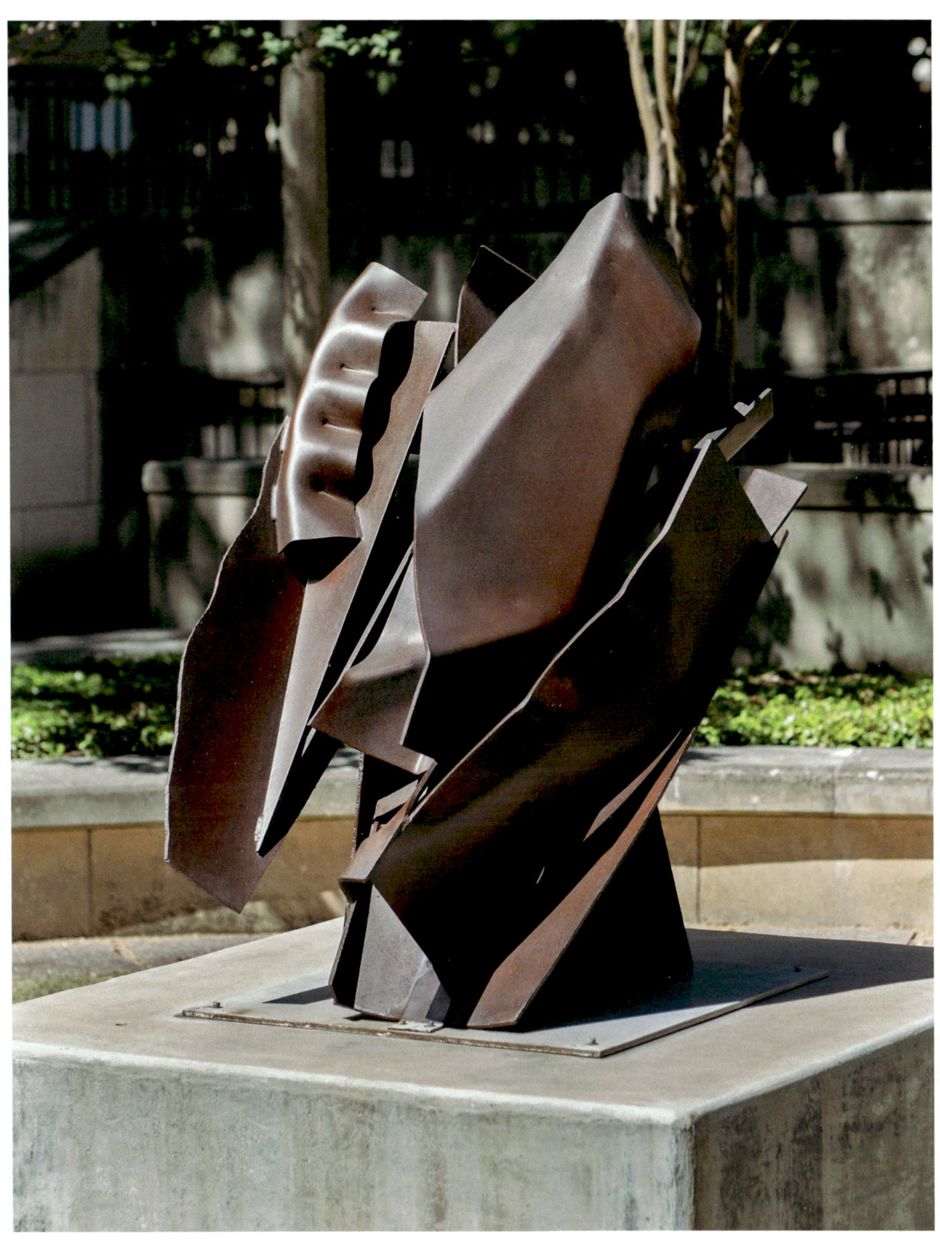

Eleanor at 7:15, 1977
Corten steel
49 × 35 × 45 inches

Lent by The Metropolitan Museum of Art
Anonymous Gift, 1978
1978.567.5

MONIKA BRAVO

COLOMBIAN, BORN 1964

Monika Bravo is a Miami-based multidisciplinary artist whose practice spans still and moving images, sculptural installations, and interactive digital animations. Her work explores the perception of reality through our relationship to space and time. Bravo notes that her works "decipher the laws of the universe," drawing from spiritual traditions such as Taoism, Buddhism, the Vedas, and evolutionary astrology. She creates environments that reference familiar landscapes while challenging conventional linear narratives.

An Interval of Time highlights the evolution of Bravo's artistic practice over the past decade, underscoring her deepening exploration of metaphysical, spiritual, and scientific intersections. A non-linear concept of time shapes her approach, weaving together images, text, and codes to construct multi-layered animations. Inspired by the elemental forces of earth, water, fire, and air, Bravo prompts viewers to consider how they integrate knowledge of the natural world into their lives.

The animation incorporates geological data layered with visuals captured in locales such as Iceland, New Mexico, Colorado, and Bravo's native Colombia. These scenes are juxtaposed with elements such as numerical data, satellite imagery, weather graphs, and poetry. *An Interval of Time* connects empirical science with indigenous weaving practices, emphasizing the universal nature of storytelling—whether expressed through mathematics, visual art, spoken word, or other forms of communication.

Lodged in the space between knowing and not knowing, between nature and fabrication, Bravo's work possesses a liminal quality. By decontextualizing data and separating it from its scientific purpose, she generates a new symbolic language that invites viewers to reconsider their own relationship with time and the planet.

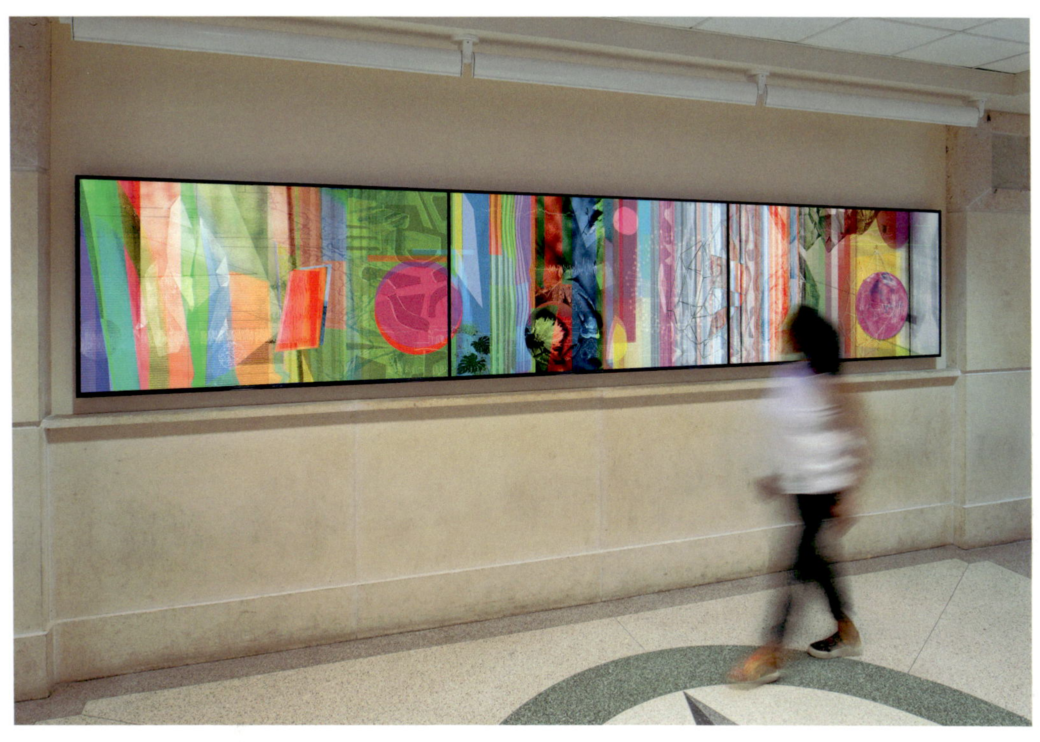

An Interval of Time, 2020
Three-channel digital animation
34 × 186 inches

Commission, Landmarks, The University of Texas at Austin, 2020

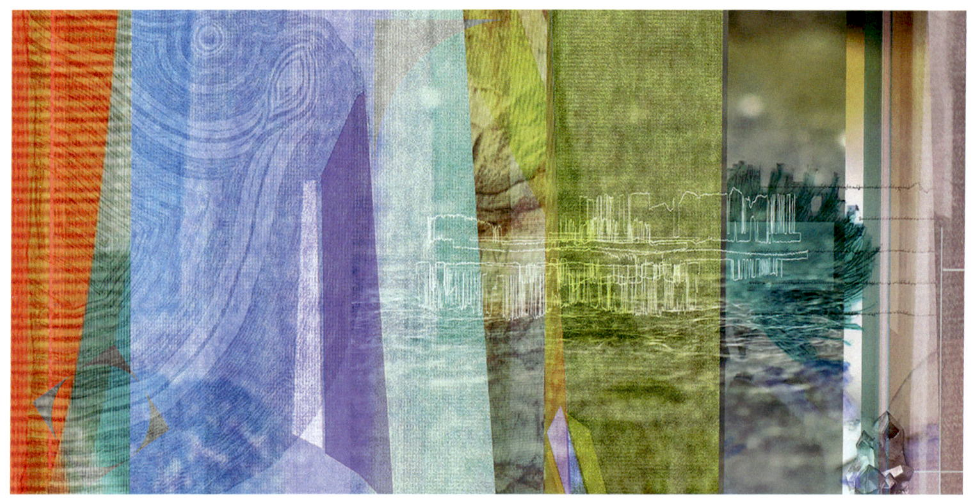

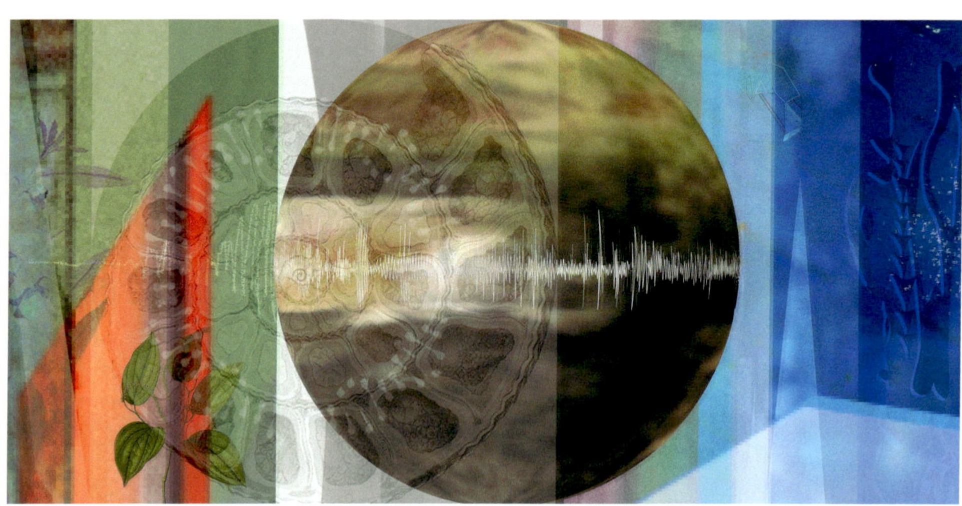

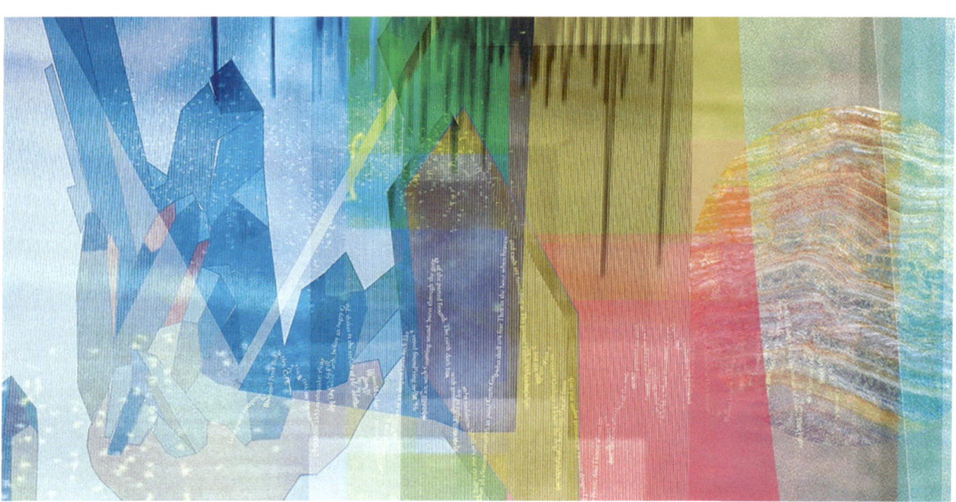

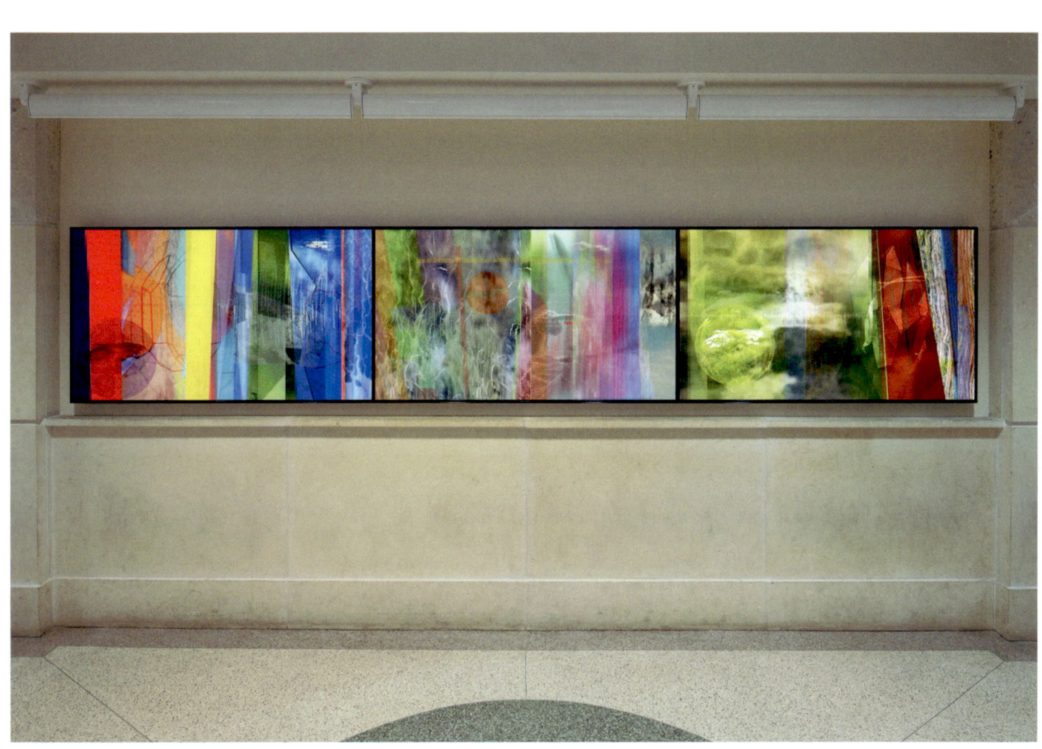

DEBORAH BUTTERFIELD

AMERICAN, BORN 1949

Art and equestrian pursuits have preoccupied Deborah Butterfield since her childhood in Southern California, where she made drawings of the horses she rode. Though she originally intended to study veterinary medicine, she shifted her focus to the arts, studying ceramics in the early 1970s at the University of California, Davis. But after renting a small horse farm, she began making life-sized sculptures of animals—first reindeer, then horses.

Throughout art history, depictions of horses have appeared primarily in scenes of conflict and sport. Statues of military and political leaders on horseback first appeared in ancient Greece as early as the sixth century BCE. They were especially common during the European Renaissance, with monumental statues erected in public squares across France and Italy during the fifteenth and sixteenth centuries.

Since moving to a ranch in Montana in the mid-1970s, Butterfield's primary sculptural subject has been the horse. Unlike earlier triumphalist renderings, she asserts the grace and poise of the equestrian form. Her sculptures diverge from traditional depictions of horses racing or rearing, which often symbolize aggression and competition. Instead, Butterfield's works evoke a sense of tranquility, showing horses in peaceful and natural poses as they stand, graze, contemplate, and rest. Though she initially sculpted in a realist style, Butterfield switched to using natural materials like mud, sticks, and straw.

In 1980, she experimented with scrap metal: cutting, tearing, bending, denting, hammering, and welding the material. This approach allowed her to render the intricate anatomical details of living horses with remarkable accuracy. Despite a high degree of abstraction, the sheets of painted, rusted, and welded steel that comprise *Vermillion* capture the mass and musculature of the animal.

Through her decades of training in dressage, Butterfield is attuned not only to the bodies and motions of her horses but also to the materials she uses to represent them. "Different kinds of metal are like different breeds of horses," she says. "Steel reminds me of Thoroughbreds, for example. Each type has its own tensile strength and its own properties."

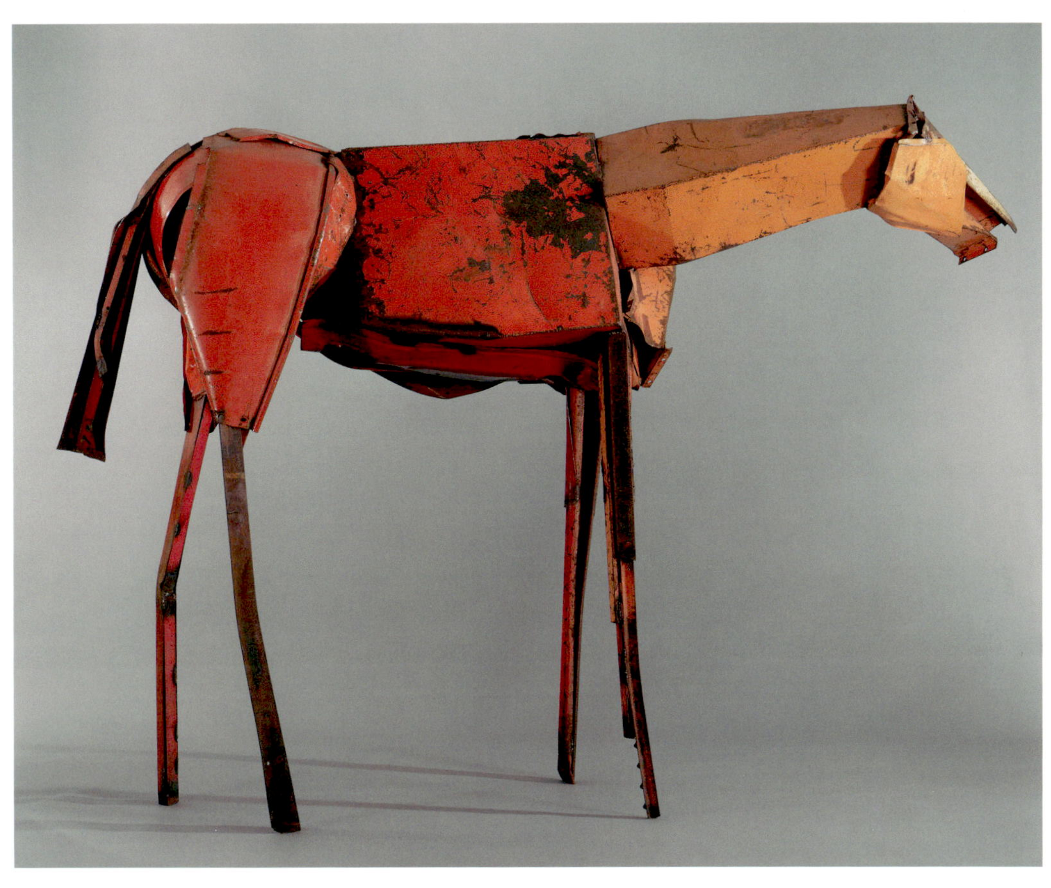

Vermillion, 1989
Painted and welded steel
75 × 108 × 25 inches

Lent by The Metropolitan Museum of Art
Gift of Agnes Bourne, 1991
1991.424

BETH CAMPBELL

AMERICAN, BORN 1971

Delicately charting the human condition with the gravity and humor of real life, Beth Campbell's drawing and mobile for the Dell Medical School reveal the interconnectedness of shared experience. The site-specific commission *Spontaneous future(s), Possible past* is rooted in Campbell's ongoing drawing series she began in 1999—*My Potential Future Based on Present Circumstances*. The series draws upon the artist's interest in rhizomatic structures, circuit boards, and early virtual worlds in order to map imagined futures or parallel lives.

Her text-based drawing for Landmarks, *Spontaneous future(s), Possible past: My Potential Future Based on Present Circumstances (1/13/19)*, is the first in this series that Campbell made in a decade. It draws parallels to spontaneous future cognition, a burgeoning branch of cognitive psychology that explores the random and involuntary thoughts that individuals have about their future.

Campbell begins each work by considering a seemingly mundane or relatable moment from her everyday life—for example, "I just sat on my brand-new glasses while getting into the car," or "I need to buy a new pillow." Using gestural lines, she diagrams a flowchart of possible outcomes unfolding from the event, ranging from fantastical to tragic. Like neural networks, the drawings branch out linearly, accumulating narrative tentacular strands that chronicle various outcomes from choice or chance. The result simultaneously exposes parallel states of mind while questioning our relationship to the future.

Complementing the drawing and also on view at Dell Medical School, Campbell's mobile extends this framework into three dimensions. Referred to by the artist as a "drawing in space," the mobile is crafted by hand-forging steel wires. It mimics the twists and turns of complex structures such as the human nervous system, arboreal roots, and social networks.

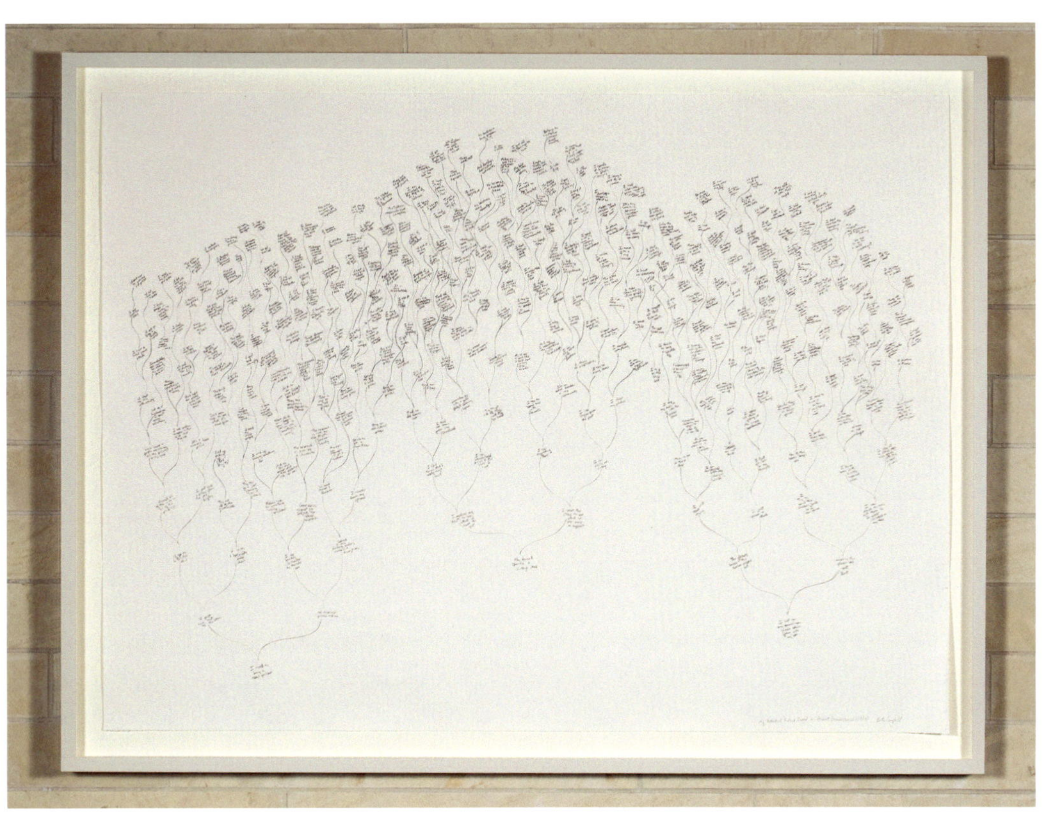

Spontaneous future(s), Possible past,
2019
Pencil on paper
55 3/16 × 75 1/2 inches

Powder-coated steel wire
82 × 156 × 36 inches

Commission, Landmarks, The University of Texas at Austin, 2019

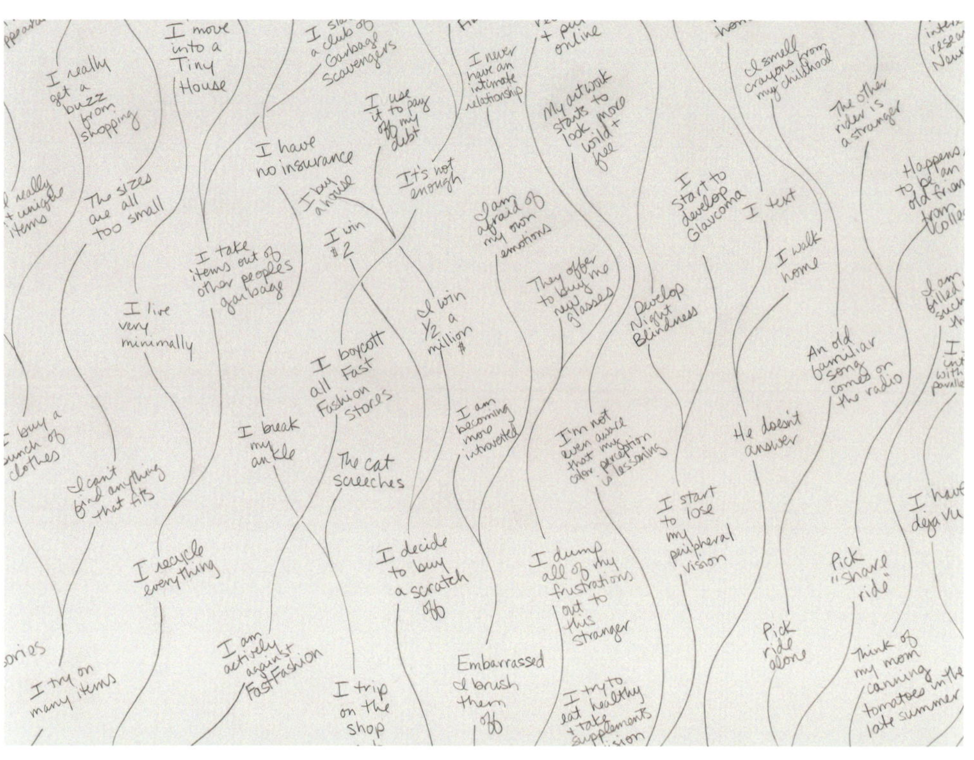
I really get a buzz from shopping
The sizes are all too small
I buy a bunch of clothes
I can't find anything that fits
I try on many items
I move into a Tiny House
I live very minimally
I recycle everything
I take items out of other peoples garbage
I start a club of Garbage Scavengers
I have no insurance
I break my ankle
I am actively against FastFashion
I buy a house
I win $2
I use it to pay off my debt
It's not enough
I boycott all Fast Fashion stores
The cat screeches
I trip on the shop
I win 1/2 a million $
I am becoming more introverted
I decide to buy a scratch off
I never have an intimate relationship
I am afraid of my own emotions
Embarrassed I brush them off
+ put online
My artwork starts to look more wild + free
They offer to buy me new glasses
I'm not even aware that my color perception is lessening
I dump all of my frustrations out to this stranger
I try to eat healthy + take supplements
I start to develop Glaucoma
Develop Night Blindness
I start to lose my peripheral vision
I smell crayons from my childhood
I text
I walk home
He doesn't answer
Pick ride alone
The other rider is a stranger
An old familiar song comes on the radio
Pick "share ride"
Think of my mom canning tomatoes in the late summer
I have deja vu

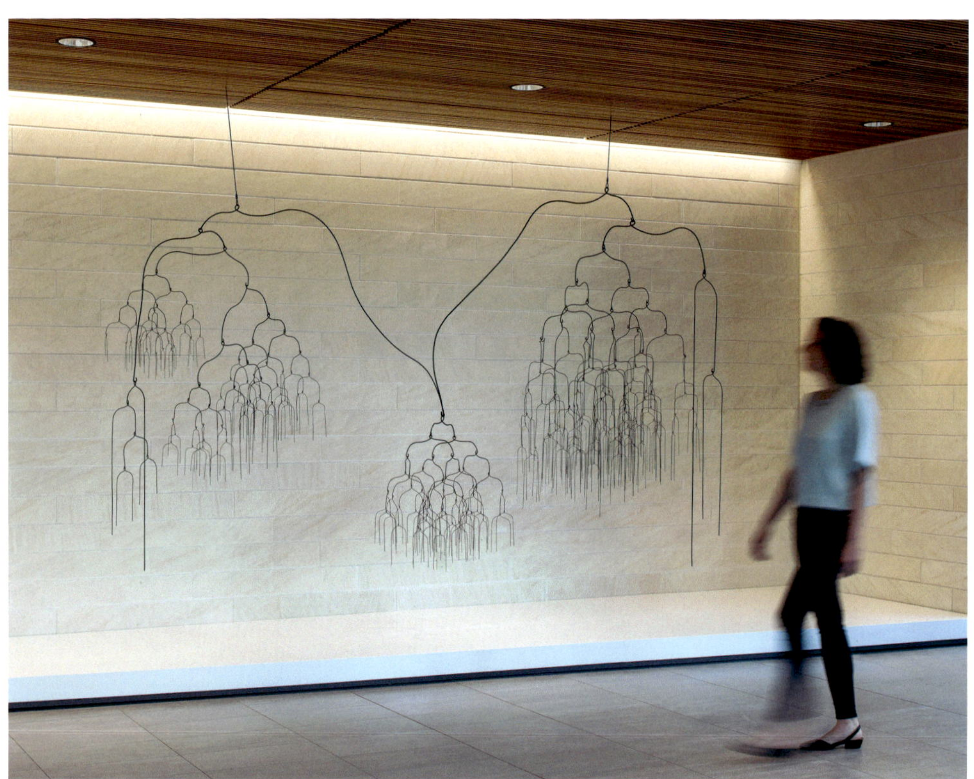

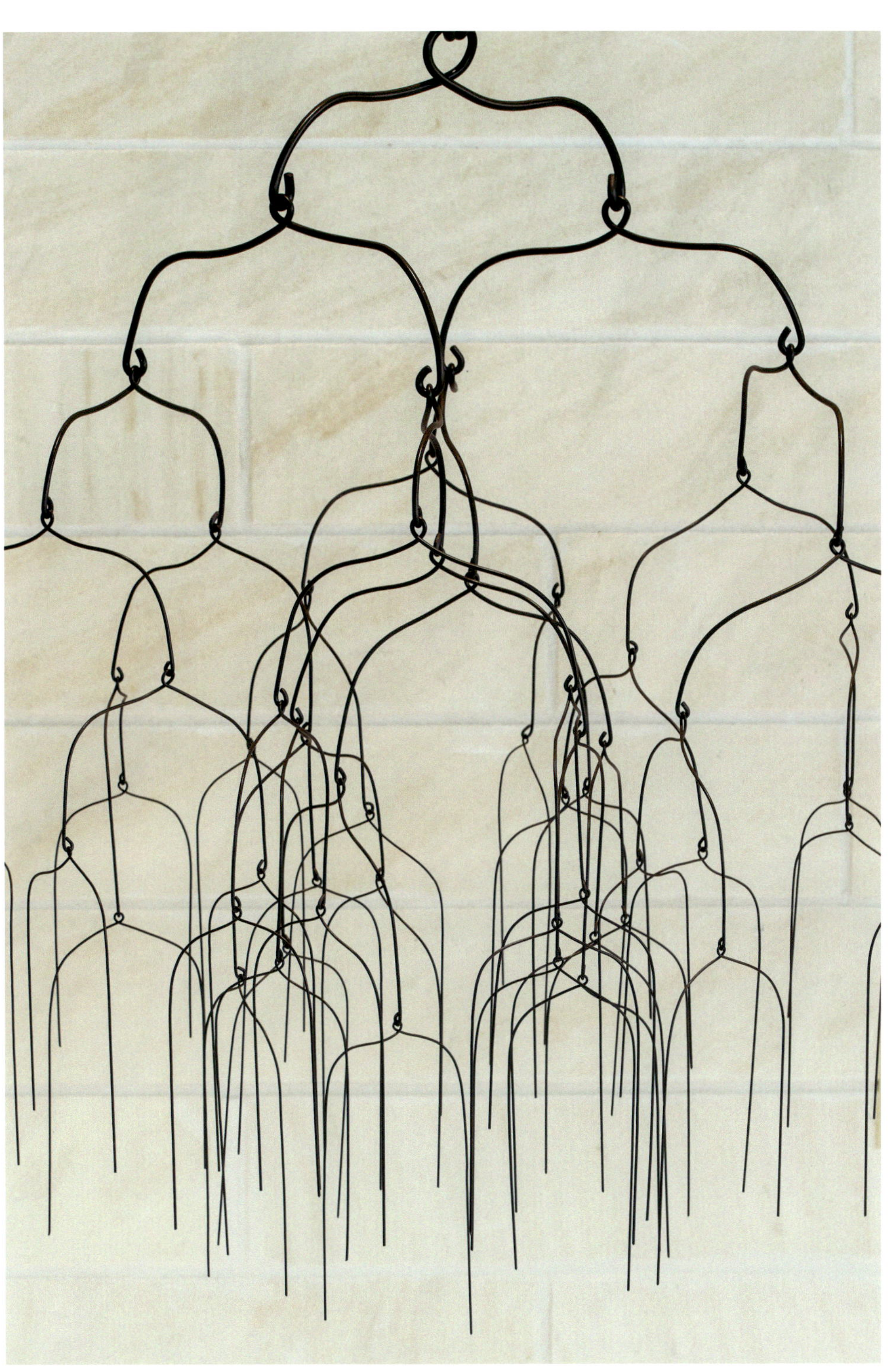

ANTHONY CARO

BRITISH, 1924–2013

Before being drafted into the British Navy during World War II, Anthony Caro studied engineering at Cambridge University. After the war, he enrolled at the Royal Academy in London to train in sculpture. Caro went on to work as a studio assistant to Henry Moore (1898–1986), who was widely regarded as the most important and renowned sculptor in Great Britain at the time. During this period of apprenticeship, Caro made works that, like Moore's, abstracted the human figure.

Caro's first extended visit to the United States in 1959 prompted a radical new direction in his work. He met the modernist art critic Clement Greenberg (1909–1994) and several notable abstract artists, most notably the sculptor David Smith (1906–1965). Upon his return to London, Caro created his first abstract sculptures, developing a new three-dimensional language in works of welded steel that spread laterally, low to the ground. He composed his works intuitively, without preliminary drawings or models, and unified the varying sizes and shapes of the metal pieces by painting the finished sculptures a single color.

During the 1970s, however, Caro felt he had grown "too comfortable" with color. He stopped using paint to focus on the composition of forms in space, and began using wood and clay in addition to steel. In November 1972, and again in May and November 1973, he worked at the Rigamonte factory in Veduggio, Italy. There he experienced a burst of creative activity, assembling fourteen sculptures in ten days. The steel remnants he found in the factory's scrapyard were unlike anything he had previously used. "They all had this sort of soft edge," he explained, "all curved ends and all sorts of rust." Though resolutely abstract, *Veduggio Glimpse* alludes to a landscape tableau. With its arcing silhouette, and rusty, weathered surface, it is among the most painterly of Caro's Italian sculptures.

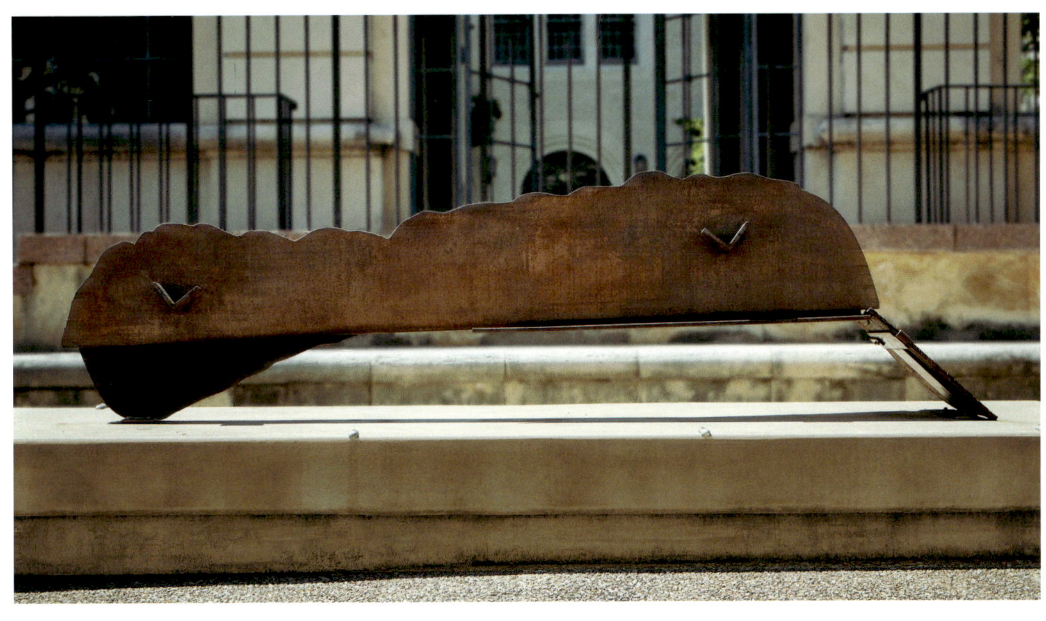

Veduggio Glimpse, 1972–73
Steel
30 × 113 ½ × 18 inches

Lent by The Metropolitan Museum of Art
Anonymous Gift, 1986
1986.440

MICHAEL RAY CHARLES

AMERICAN, BORN 1967

Michael Ray Charles was born in Lafayette, Louisiana, when the non-violent Civil Rights Movement was giving way to riotous social and cultural upheaval. Like artists Kara Walker (born 1969) and Fred Wilson (born 1954), Charles explores African and African American oppression and prejudice. He is best known for work that appropriates derogatory images in order to disparage racist stereotypes. For *(Forever Free) Ideas, Languages and Conversations*, Charles departs from this mode and takes a more metaphorical approach, explaining, "Conceptual and representational applications of power throughout visual cultures past and present have been among my most significant triggers of creative inspiration."

(Forever Free) Ideas, Languages and Conversations is suspended in the atrium of the Gordon-White Building, home to centers that study the history and experience of minority cultures. Charles selected the location because it joins a classic 1952 university building to a newly constructed addition used by students and scholars of the historically marginalized. In designing the atrium's interior, the artist preserved architectural ornaments from the original building and kept rough, exposed surfaces to create a meaningful segue into the polished departmental offices. The result is both sculpture and site—a symbolic transition between the inherited establishment and a future that explores new ways of thinking and being.

Charles' sculpture is made from wooden crutches assembled in groups to create star-shaped wheels. The individual parts maintain their own trajectory yet form a common mass in an energetic composition. When imagining the project, Charles was partly inspired by the activity of scholars who study minority cultures and the challenges they face in academic institutions. Now the centerpiece of a thriving enterprise that champions multiculturalism, *(Forever Free) Ideas, Languages and Conversations* is emblematic of institutional progress and transformation. By claiming the wounds of the past and acknowledging the support needed to heal, it recognizes all who have suffered inequality and carries the promise of hope and growth.

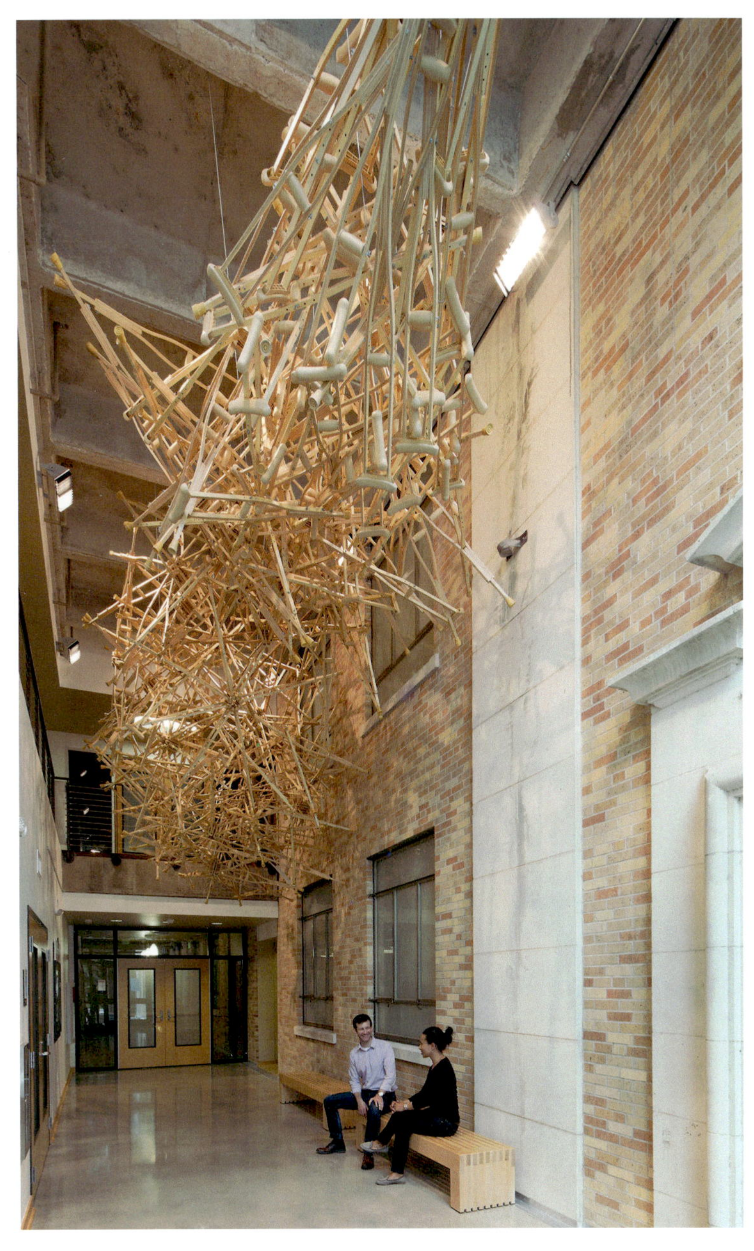

(Forever Free) Ideas, Languages and Conversations, 2015
Wooden crutches, steel armatures, and steel cables
155 × 412 × 125 inches

Commission, Landmarks, The University of Texas at Austin, 2015

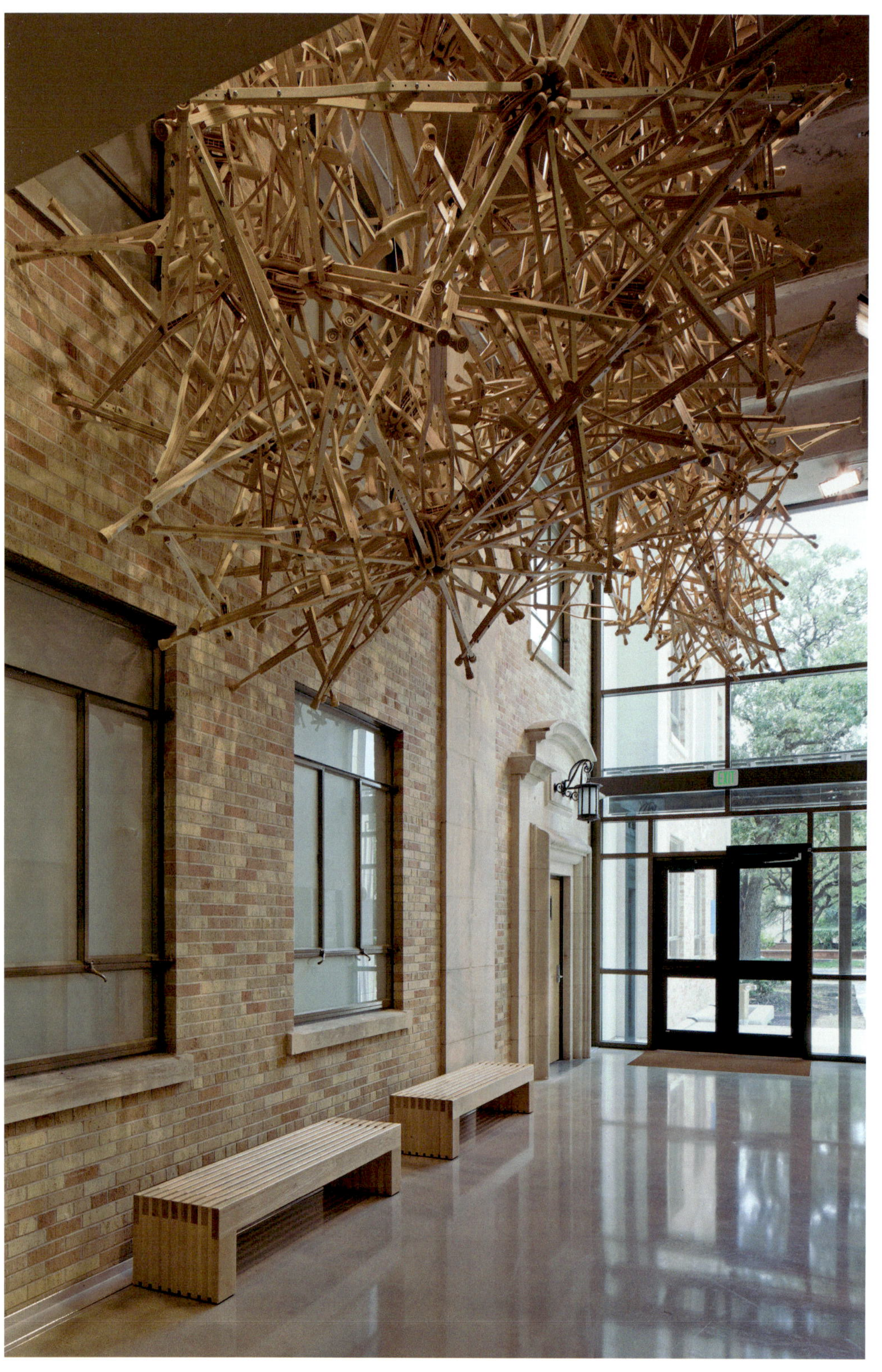
EXIT

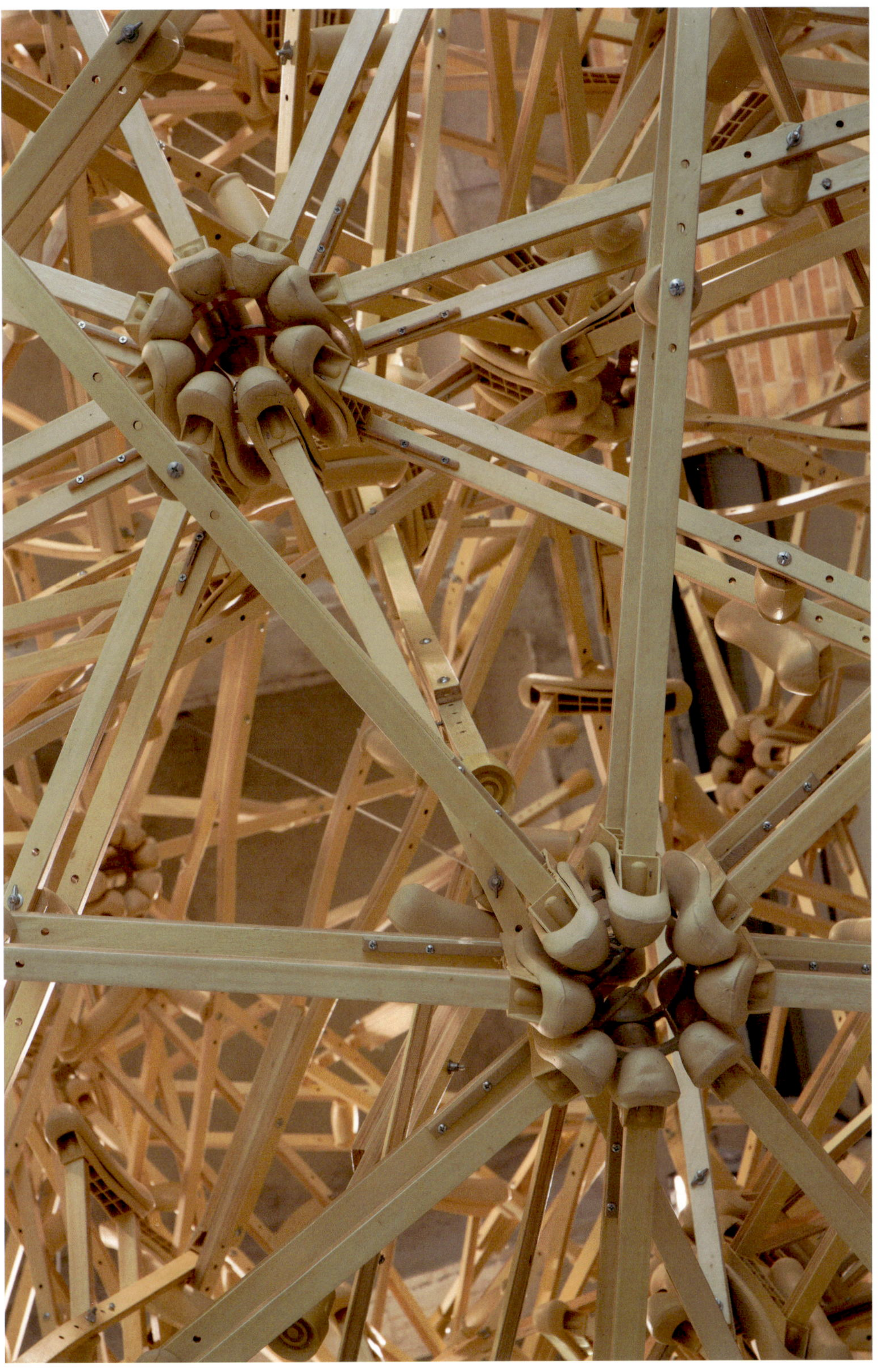

KOREN DER HAROOTIAN

AMERICAN, BORN IN ARMENIA, 1909–1992

In 1915, at age six, Koren Der Harootian fled with his family from their native Armenia to escape the persecution and genocide of the ruling Ottoman Turks. They ultimately settled in Worcester, Massachusetts, where Der Harootian studied art. Initially achieving recognition as a watercolorist, he held solo exhibitions in Provincetown and New York City in the late 1920s, and moved to Jamaica in 1930 to continue his practice. There, Der Harootian befriended sculptor Edna Manley (1900–1987), whose primitive, eroticizing style had a profound impact on his work. Carving in wood and stone using handmade tools, Manley and Der Harootian offered an alternative to sedate artistic traditions and fostered a new genre steeped in Jamaican culture.

Like many artists who straddled the line between figuration and abstraction, Der Harootian also drew inspiration from mythology, which provided more interpretive freedom than historical subjects and offered metaphors for the fear, violence, and conflict of World War II and its aftermath. *Prometheus and Vulture* illustrates the Greek myth of Prometheus, punished by Zeus for stealing fire and giving it to humanity in the form of civilizing knowledge. Angered, Zeus chained him to a mountain where each day a vulture would tear his flesh and eat his liver. At night, his body would heal so the punishment could begin the next day. Finally, after thirteen human generations, the half-divine hero Hercules liberated Prometheus.

The story of Prometheus carried particular resonance during this time. In *Prometheus and Vulture*, the hero strains against his chains, reeling in pain, as the vulture plunges for his daily attack. With the foresight that he would eventually be released, Prometheus endured hundreds of years of torment to bring knowledge to humans. Similarly, many people in Europe, Asia, and America suffered bitterly during the war. But, like Prometheus, they believed their struggle was critical to advancing humanity and that eventually they would be free from oppression.

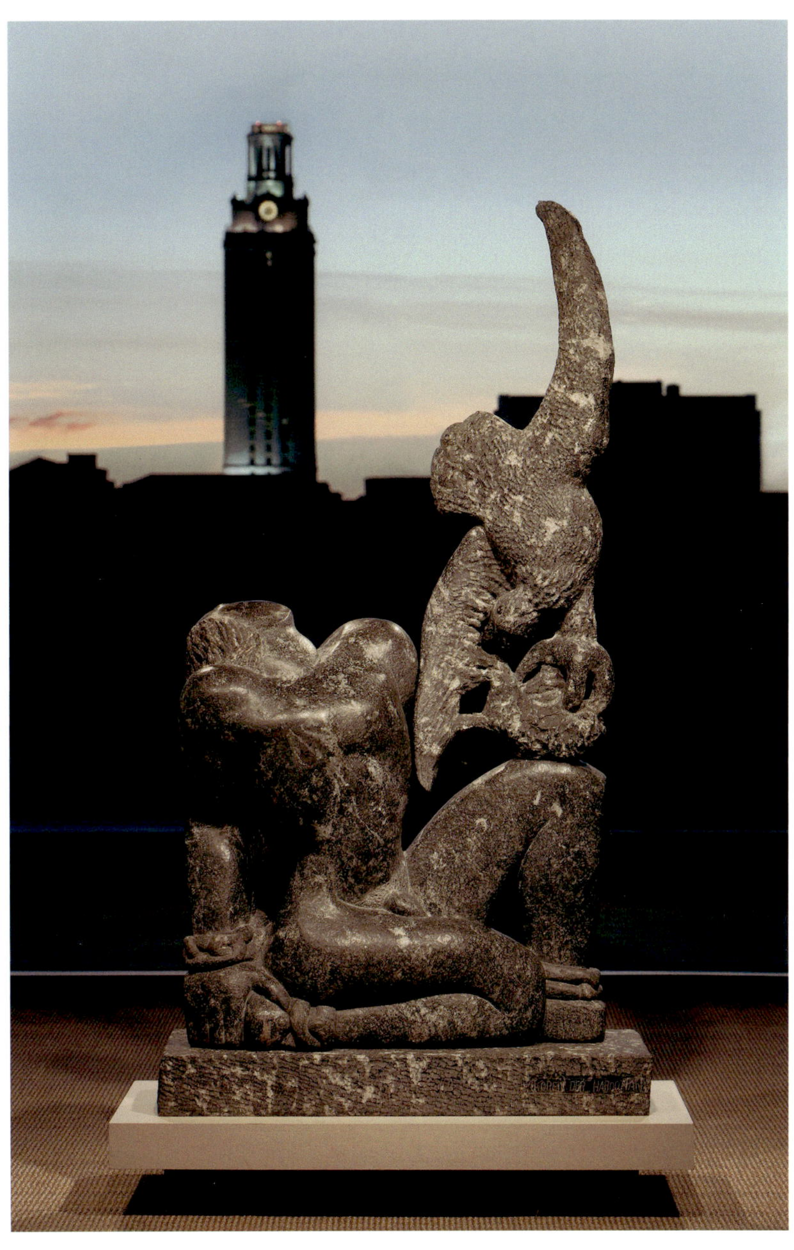

Prometheus and Vulture, 1948
Marble
62 ½ × 33 ¾ × 15 ½ inches

Lent by The Metropolitan Museum of Art
Gift of Haik Kavookjian, 1948
48.142a–c

JIM DINE

AMERICAN, BORN 1935

Born and raised in Ohio, Jim Dine moved to New York in 1958 and established himself in the art world with theatrical Happenings performed in chaotic, artist-built environments. In the early 1960s, he joined a growing number of young artists working with commercial imagery and everyday objects. In contrast to the prevailing trend toward abstraction, Dine and other Pop artists sought to bridge the gap between fine art and life. Pop artists chose ordinary objects as their subjects, presenting them with detachment and irony. For example, Dine painted images of bathrobes, neckties, hearts, and tools, sometimes incorporating actual objects into his compositions—a practice that marked the beginning of his interest in sculpture.

By the late 1960s, Dine turned his attention from ordinary objects to those with personal significance. His composition of objects on a table may pay homage to Alberto Giacometti (1901–1966), whose Surrealist *Table* (1933) features objects referencing the artist's other sculptures. In *History of Black Bronze I*, Dine updated this concept to the 1980s taste for art-historical appropriation. He produced truncated versions of famous monuments from antiquity, like the Greek sculpture *Venus de Milo* and the face of the Great Sphinx of Giza. These are placed alongside casts of household tools that became symbolic subjects for the artist, an association that stems from Dine's time working in his family's hardware store.

The near uniform size and surface quality of the objects on the table elevate the mundane hammer to the level of appreciation warranted by the classical *Venus de Milo*. Dine described his approach in works like *History of Black Bronze I* as "metaphorical realism," where meaning is not rooted in words but in objects. Seen through this lens, the array of items can be understood as a portrait of the artist, his influences, and his techniques.

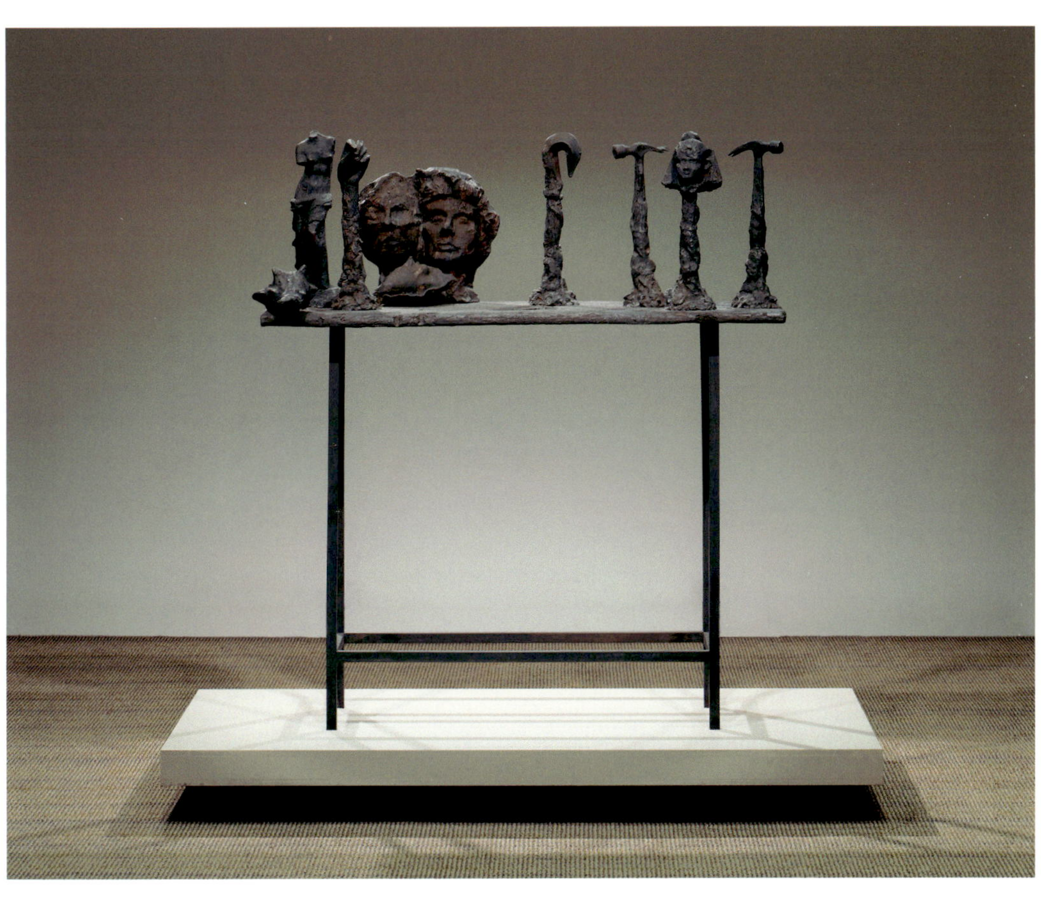

History of Black Bronze I, 1983
Bronze
53 ¼ × 48 × 20 inches

Lent by The Metropolitan Museum of Art
Gift of Industrial Petro-Chemicals, Inc., 1987
1987.363

MARK DI SUVERO

AMERICAN, BORN IN CHINA, 1933

Mark di Suvero is widely regarded as one of the most important sculptors of his generation. As a student, he was deeply engaged in studying and writing poetry, and listening to music ranging from Bach to jazz. Once he began to pursue sculpture, di Suvero found outlets for his interests in other fields that intrigued him, including architecture, mathematics, science, engineering, poetry, and languages.

Grounded in Abstract Expressionism—which emphasizes the direct expression of emotion through line and color—di Suvero was energized by the spaces of New York City, especially those being demolished for "urban renewal." Salvaging the refuse, he pioneered a new form of sculpture in which wooden beams chained together in outward-leaning constructions declared the physical forces that held them in balance. The works engage space in unprecedented ways, and this focus has remained central throughout di Suvero's career. In 1967, he began to build large-scale sculptures with a crane, using steel I-beams and other industrial materials. Learning to operate cranes offered di Suvero a new mode of working, but the process of composing the sculpture remained at the core of his artistic practice.

The heroic sculpture *Clock Knot* exemplifies the power of art to transform public locations. Walking around the work produces constantly changing views that offer surprising spatial experiences of the sculpture. The crossed I-beams and circular "knotted" center of *Clock Knot* suggest a giant clock face with a horizontal "hand" extending to the side. But as one moves around the sculpture, what initially appears as a vertical beam reveals itself to be one arm of an inverted V-form. Is it a clock or not/knot? *Clock Knot* is a work of poetry and power. As visitors move through its spaces, gazing at the sky and experiencing the sculpture's exuberant lift, their imaginations engage with its intricate interplay of visual form and verbal suggestions.

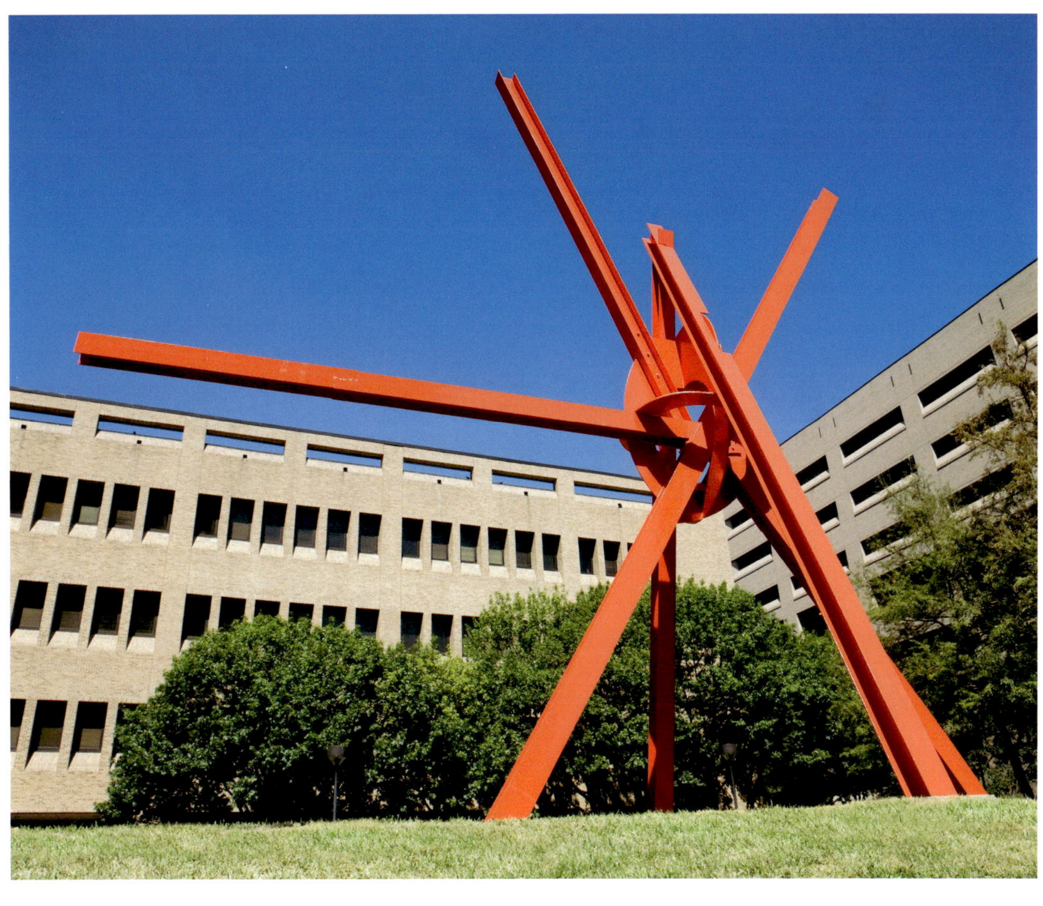

Clock Knot, 2007
Painted steel
498 × 260 × 420 inches

Purchase, Landmarks, The University of Texas at Austin, 2013

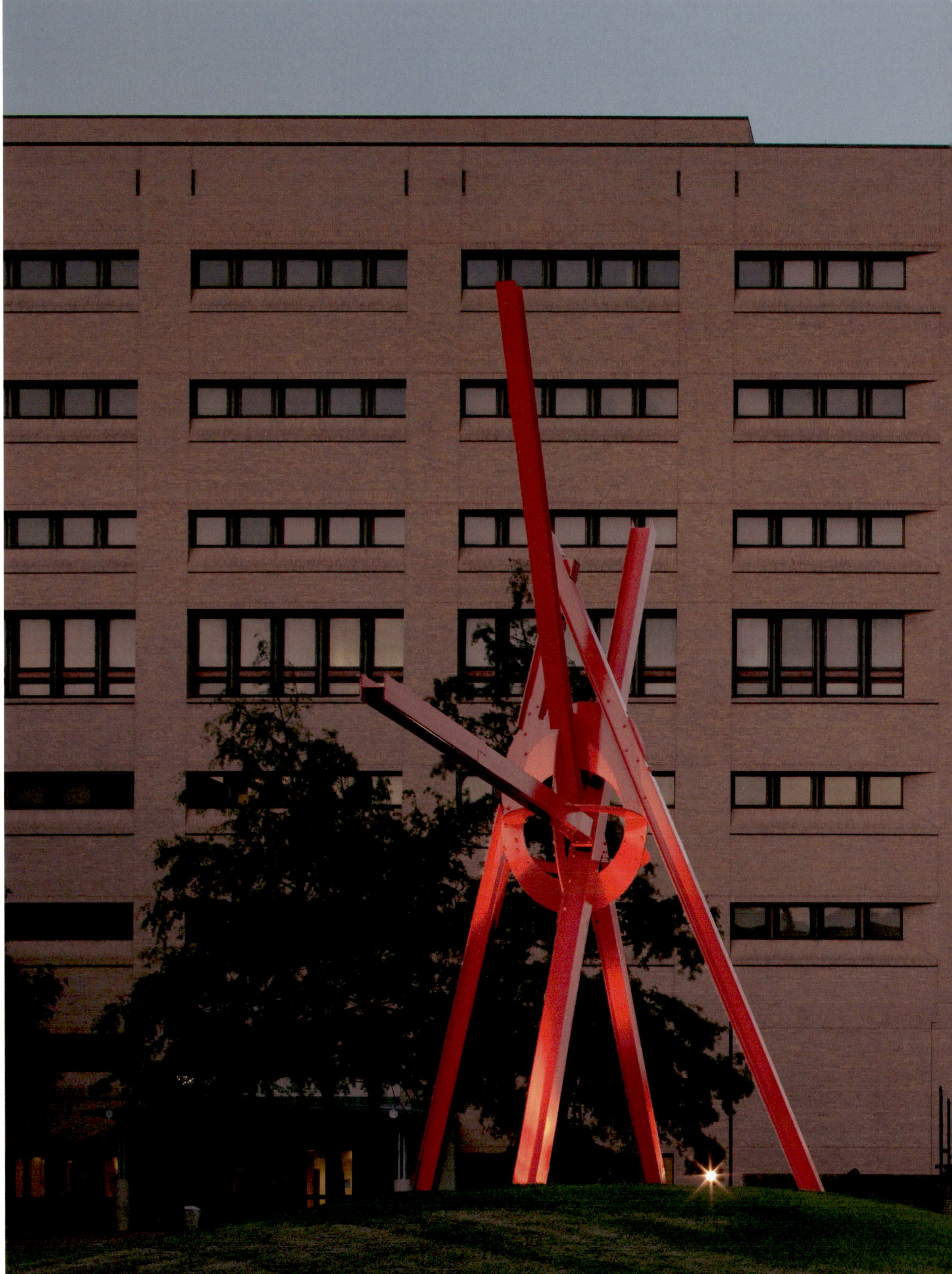

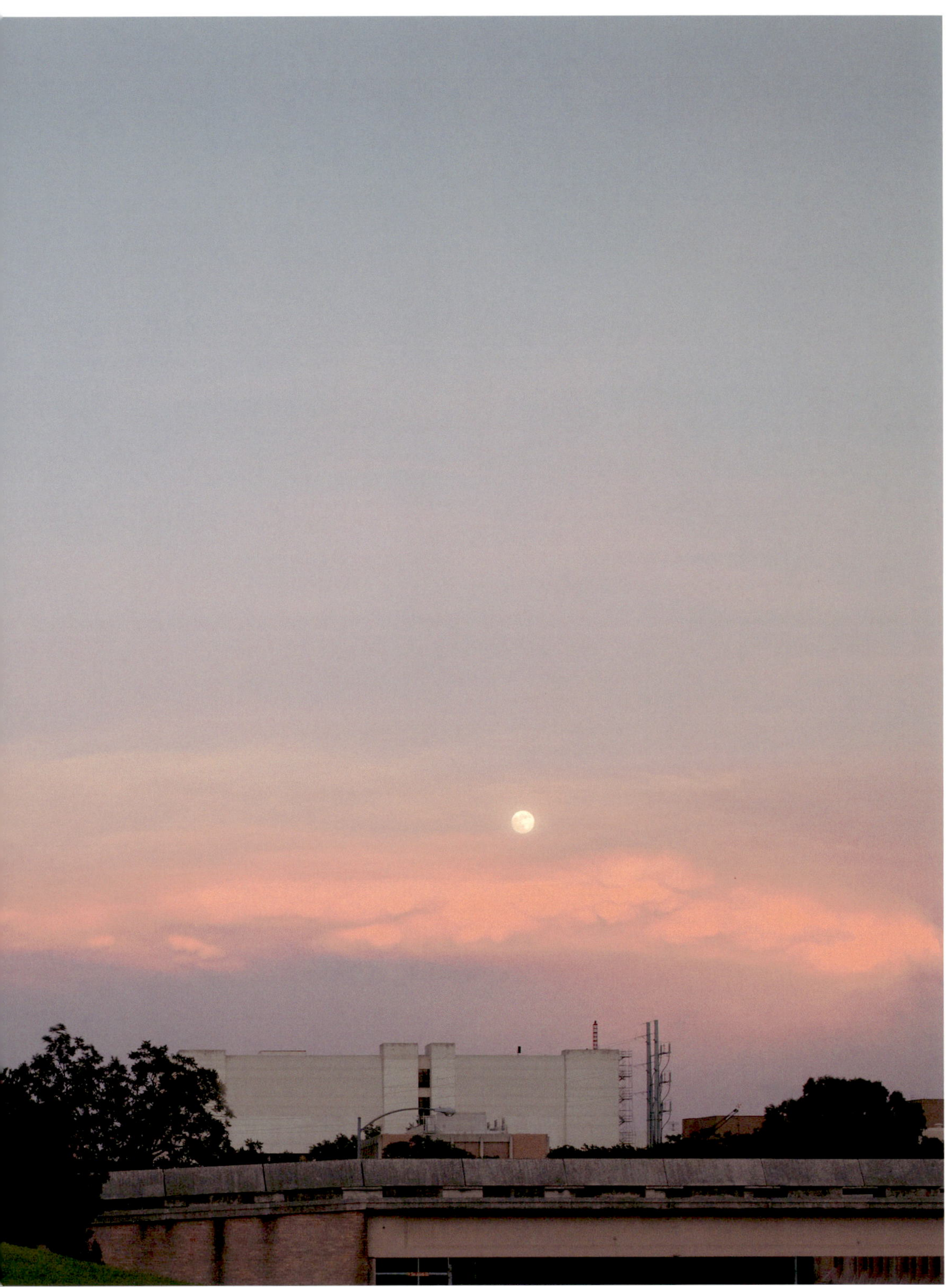

WALTER DUSENBERY

AMERICAN, BORN 1939

Born in Alameda, California, Walter Dusenbery has an artistic lineage that follows an impressive line of masters. After studying at San Francisco Art Institute and the California College of Arts and Crafts, Dusenbery assisted Japanese-American sculptor Isamu Noguchi (1904-1988)—a student of modernist master Constantin Brancusi (1876-1957), who, in turn, had worked in the Parisian workshop of Auguste Rodin (1840-1917).

As a young artist, Dusenbery preferred the tradition of direct carving over the popular method of welding metal sculpture that was prevalent during the 1950s and '60s. Many direct-carve sculptors feel a strong physical and psychic connection to the natural materials they use, a sensitivity that Dusenbery shared with Noguchi. While Noguchi worked in fine marbles and rough basalt, Dusenbery favored travertine, a porous carbonate stone that is easily cut. In its pure state, travertine is white, but mineral or biologic impurities can infuse the stone with color, such as the reddish hue of *Pedogna*.

A large form like *Pedogna* requires considerable geometric calculation and planning. The artist first created a smaller-scale preparatory version of the sculpture from a single piece of red Verona marble. With a footprint shaped like a horseshoe, the sculpture features two contrasting silhouettes—a smoothly rounded edge that arcs upward from the base, and a coarsely chiseled surface that emphasizes the intrinsic qualities of the finely grained stone. The juxtaposition between these two textures reflects Dusenbery's evolution as an artist; though trained in direct carving, he has since become a pioneer in three-dimensional scanning and computer-controlled fabrication.

The title of the sculpture refers to the secluded Pedogna Valley in the Tuscan region of Northern Italy, located about an hour west of Dusenbery's studio in Pietrasanta. *Pedogna* conveys a geological history much older than that of ancient Rome. With striations formed over hundreds of millions of years, the sculpture evokes an ancient aura, referencing sources like the mysterious dolmens of Stonehenge and the lingams of Shiva in India.

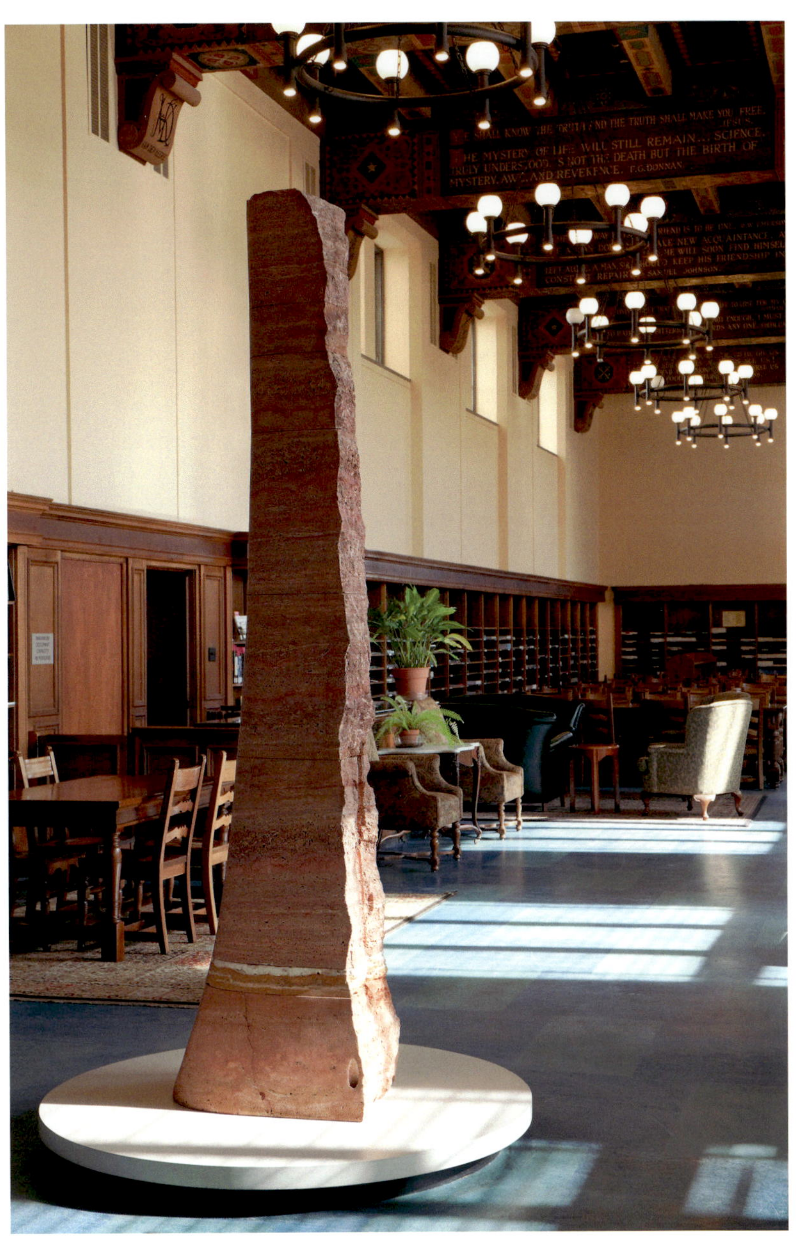

Pedogna, 1977
Travertine marble
102 ½ × 25 ½ × 21 ½ inches

Lent by The Metropolitan Museum of Art
Gift of Doris and Jack Weintraub, 1979
1979.300a–h

DAVID ELLIS

AMERICAN, BORN 1971

Multimedia artist David Ellis grew up immersed in diverse musical influences, from classical jazz to hip-hop. Although he never formally learned to read or play music, his work employs various elements of music-making. Ellis explores movement, change, and rhythm, effectively combining his talent for visual representation with his passion for musical expression.

The collaborative and improvisational nature of music influenced a series of painting sessions that Ellis undertook with the Barnstormers, a group of artists who made large-scale paintings in the early 2000s. Captured with time-lapse video, their work evolved into a style that Ellis called "motion paintings." For *Animal*, he positioned a time-lapse camera overhead to photograph his painting process every few seconds, compiling the images into a stop-motion video. Similar to a hip-hop track, Ellis' motion paintings are an assortment of samples, breaks, and disparate moments that combine to create a rhythmic flow of artistic expression.

Animal is the visual record of Ellis' six-week residency at The University of Texas at Austin. Produced in collaboration with cinematographer Chris Keohane and composed of more than 75,000 still images, the video is inspired by personal conversations and the local Austin environment. *Animal* details the delights of the creative forces of nature that often go unnoticed.

The animation features a kaleidoscope of spectacular creatures, landscapes, and abstractions interspersed with dramatic splashes of paint. The soundtrack, composed by longtime collaborator Roberto Lange, combines a range of unexpected elements that complement the fluid nature of Ellis' practice. Shifting between moments of freedom, discovery, and surprise, Ellis represents the universality of art through the rhythms and movement of life.

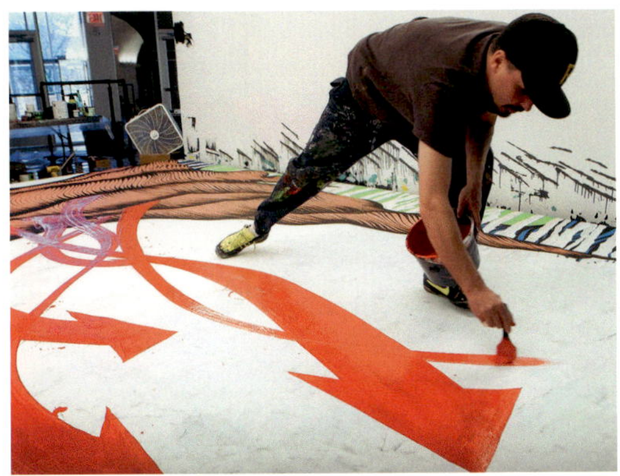

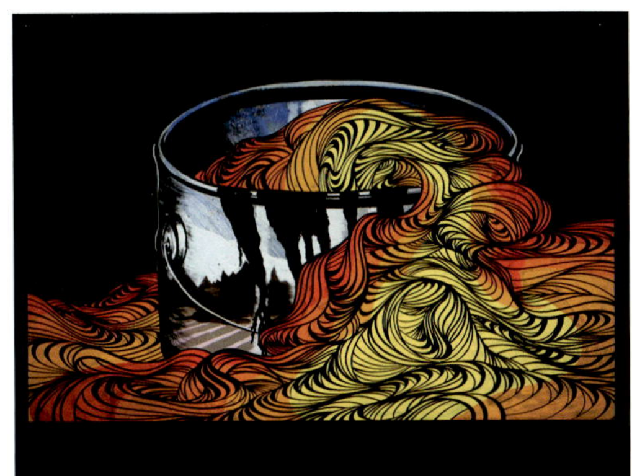

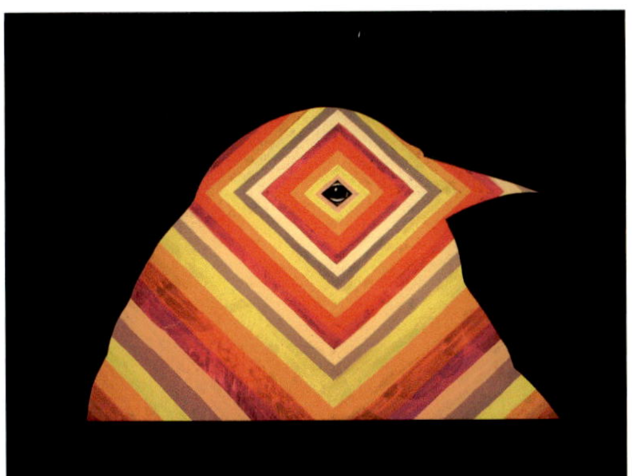

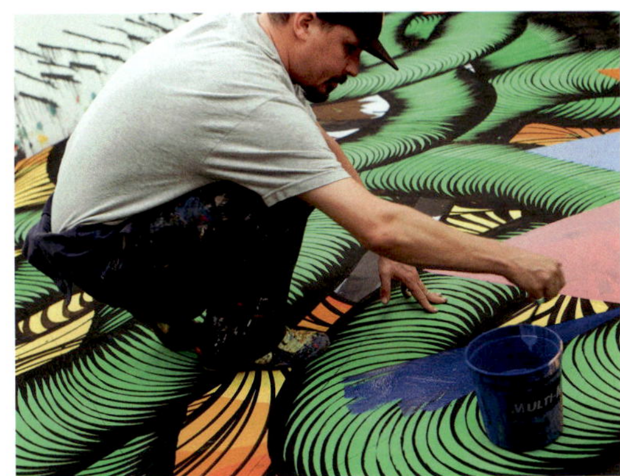

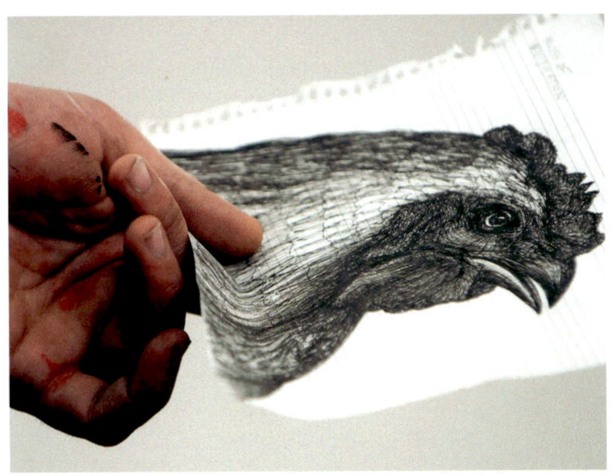

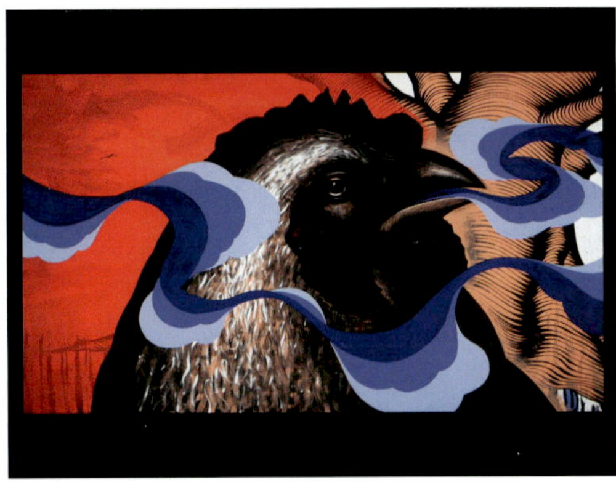

Animal, 2010
Video/Blu-ray disc
9:39 min., color, sound

Commission, Landmarks, The University of Texas at Austin, 2010

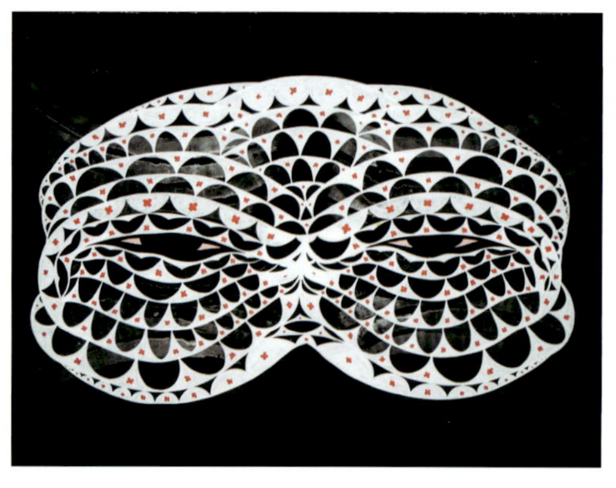
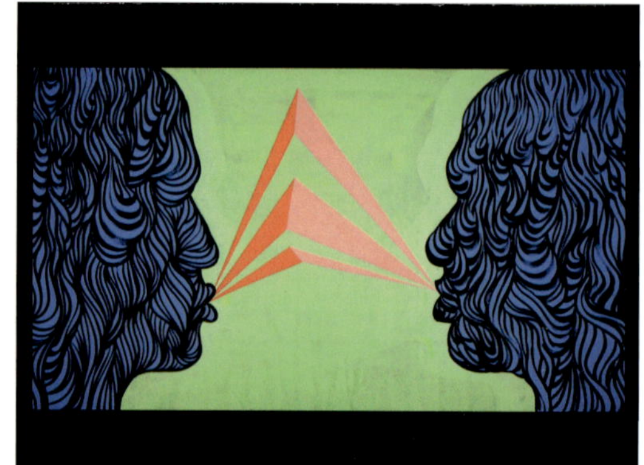
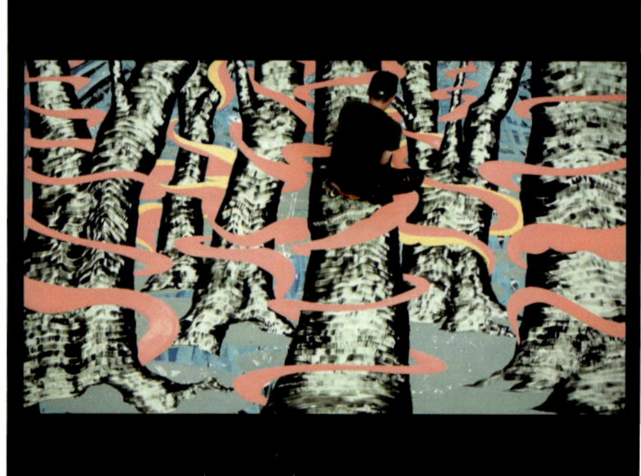
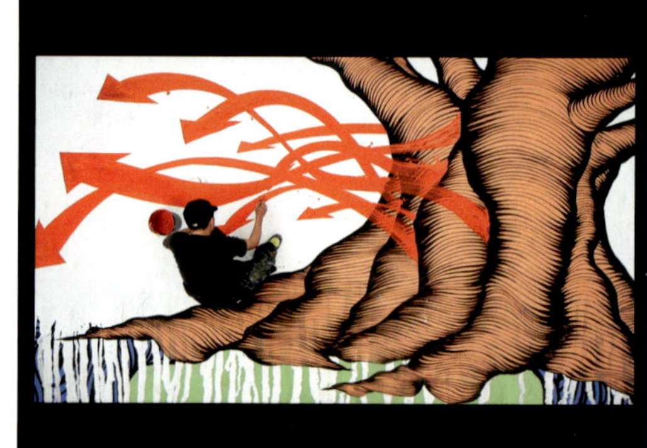
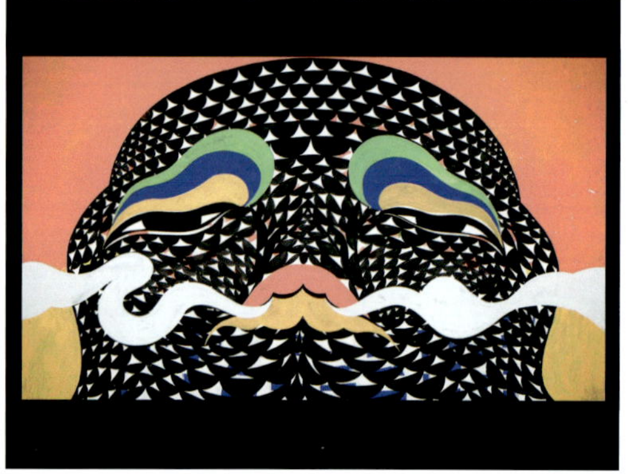
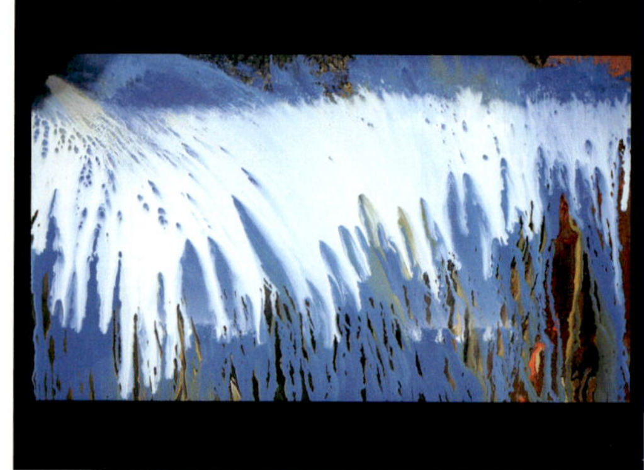

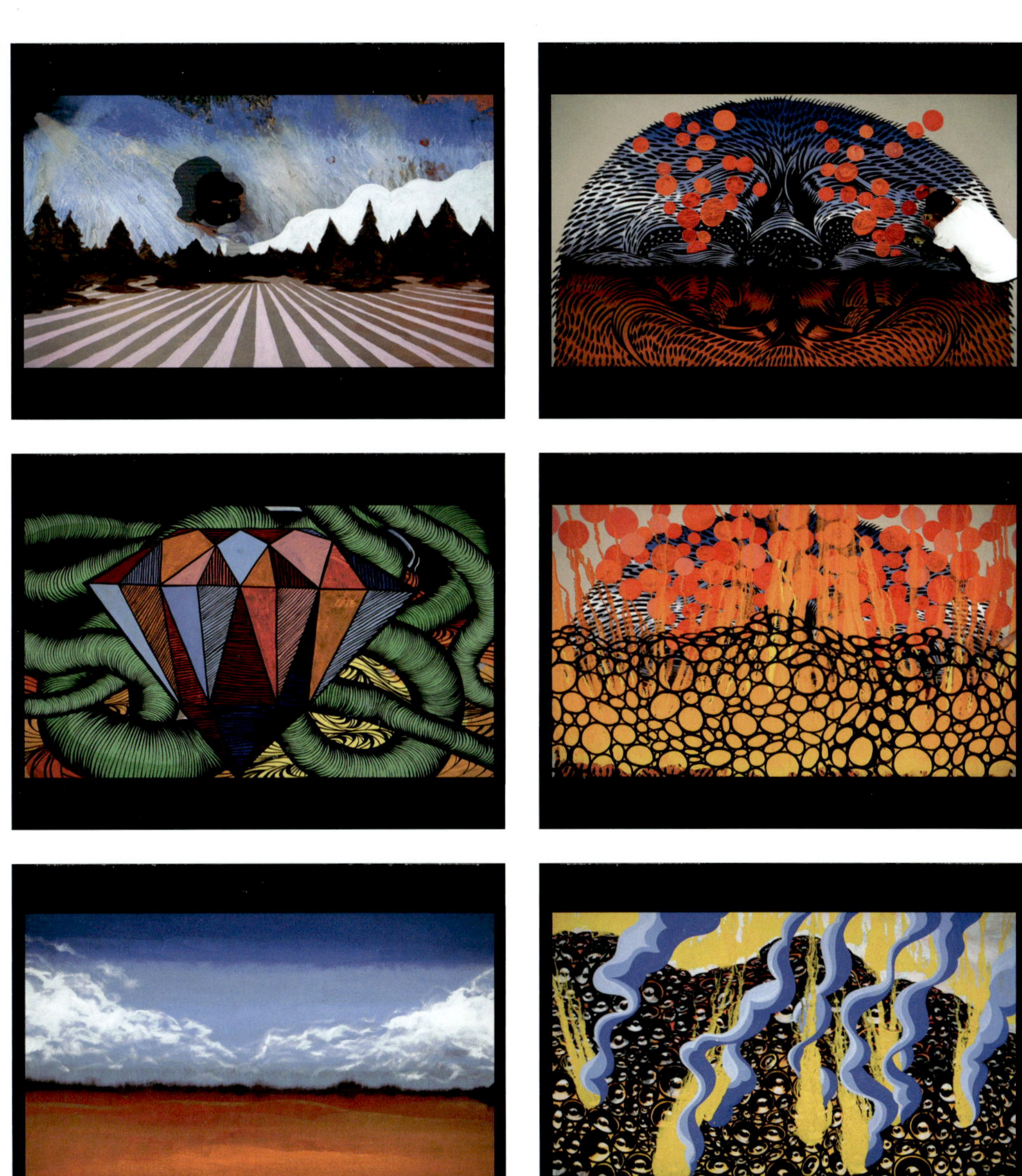

RAOUL HAGUE

AMERICAN, BORN IN TURKEY, 1904–1993

Born Haig Heukelekian to Armenian parents in Turkey, Raoul Hague studied sculpture at New York's Beaux-Arts Institute in the late 1920s before continuing his art education under William Zorach (1887–1966) at the Art Students League. Though Zorach was an early conduit for European modernist styles, his teaching focused on traditional wood- and stone-carving methods, a reassertion of hand crafting and natural materials during an age of mechanization.

Throughout the 1930s, Hague worked with marble and wood in a semi-abstract figurative style similar to that of Abstract Expressionist colleagues Arshile Gorky (1902–1948) and Willem de Kooning (1904–1997). All three artists worked in the Federal Arts Project of the Works Progress Administration (WPA), a Depression-era program that employed artists to create murals and monuments for federal buildings. The community of artists in New York City during this period was strengthened by their shared experience in the WPA.

When Hague was drafted into the U.S. Army in 1941, he needed a place to store his sculptures and rented a building from his friend Hervey White at the Maverick Artist Colony in Woodstock, New York. After his discharge in 1943, he settled permanently in a cabin there. Over the next decade, his work became increasingly abstract, yet his sculptures retained a connection to the natural forms of the trees he carved—large trunks of locally sourced walnut, poplar, sycamore, and locust. This connection is evident in titles like *Vermont Marble* (1946) and *Kaaterskill Butternut* (1953–55).

Big Indian Mountain is named after a peak in the Catskills near Hague's Woodstock studio. While Hague's abstract style aligns with the gestural energy of Abstract Expressionist painting, his forms evoke the rhythms of natural processes. The sculpture's smooth surfaces and flowing curves embody his vision of nature's sensuousness. "I'm affected by the things nature has done, to the rocks, to the trees," Hague explained. "They create a tremendous visual drama. . . . Those sensuous qualities are from there, from the mountains."

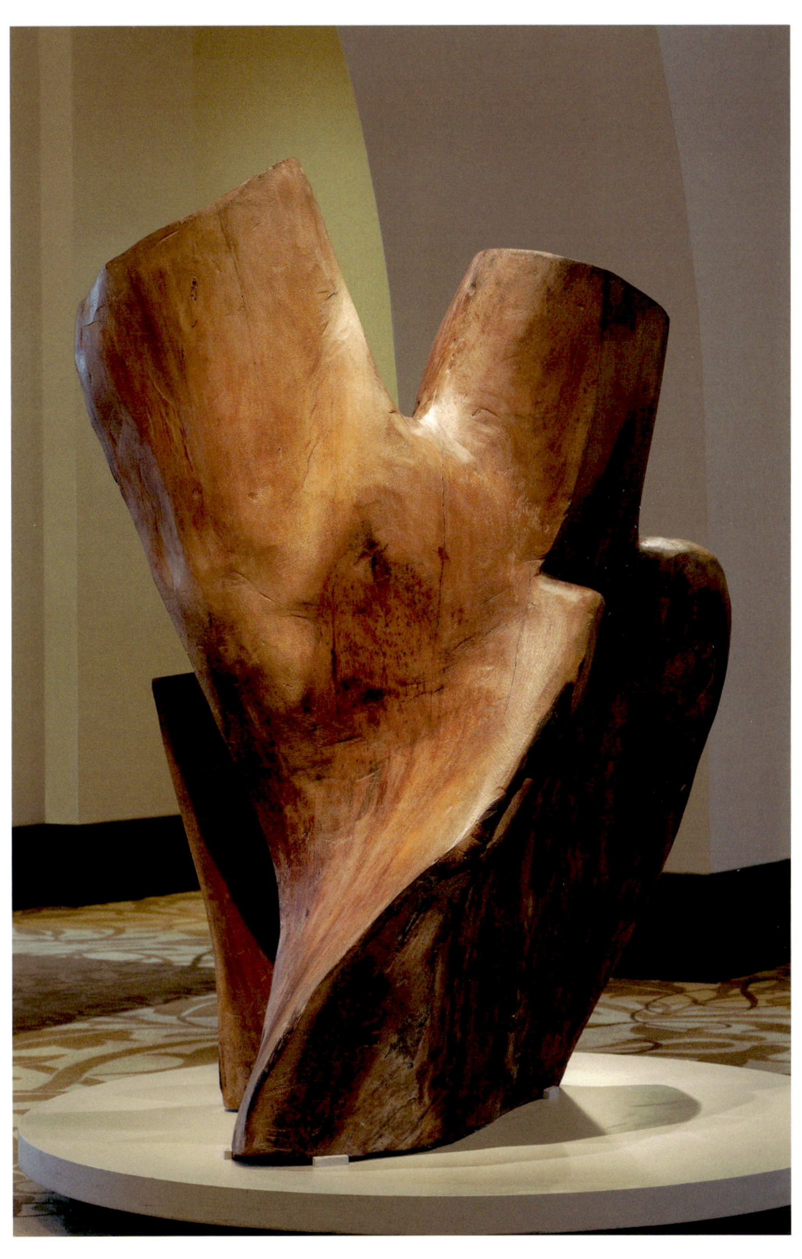

Big Indian Mountain, 1965–66
Black walnut
64 × 45 × 49 inches

Lent by The Metropolitan Museum of Art
Louis V. Bell Fund, 1974
1974.6

ANN HAMILTON

AMERICAN, BORN 1956

ONEEVERYONE is a series of photographic portraits by Ann Hamilton commissioned for the Dell Medical School. The series investigates touch as the fundamental gesture of contact and caring. Hamilton photographed more than 530 participants from the Austin community. They stood behind a frosted, plastic material that puts in sharp focus whatever it touches, while progressively softening receding features. To viewers of the resulting portraits, the cloudy screen becomes the image surface, a translation that binds visual and tactile perception.

Touch has been central to Hamilton's practice from the outset. Among her earliest works was *(suitably positioned)* (1984), in which a man's business suit covered in protruding toothpicks provoked in viewers a heightened experience of tactile sensitivity. Hamilton has merged the tactile and the photographic in many works: *reflection* (1999–2000), a precedent for *ONEEVERYONE*, is a series of photographs shot through multiple layers of slightly wavy glass that produced enigmatic images. Similar portraits were made with the small camera Hamilton placed inside her mouth for *face to face* (2001). Opening her lips exposed the film and transposed her (silenced) mouth into a speaking eye. By the end of the 1980s, Hamilton began to produce the complex, community-engaged, site-related installations that have become her primary focus.

The democracy of art is central to Hamilton's practice, and it is clearly reflected in the openness of *ONEEVERYONE*—from its wide range of participants to the freely available texts and images. This collaborative effort is deepened by Hamilton's commitment to the extended community of the Dell Medical School.

Hamilton references John Berger's *A Fortunate Man: The Story of a Country Doctor*, which thoughtfully examines the relationships between physician John Sassall and his patients. A heightened sense of touch, and an equal ability to see his patients clearly, were central to Sassall's quietly heroic practice. Hamilton's *ONEEVERYONE* represents a similar dedication.

PORTRAITS ON THE FOLLOWING PAGES:

22
Ethan · Porscha
Lael · Ava
Saungeun · Lawrence

79
Kayla · Tory
Ann · George
Rhett · Cirina

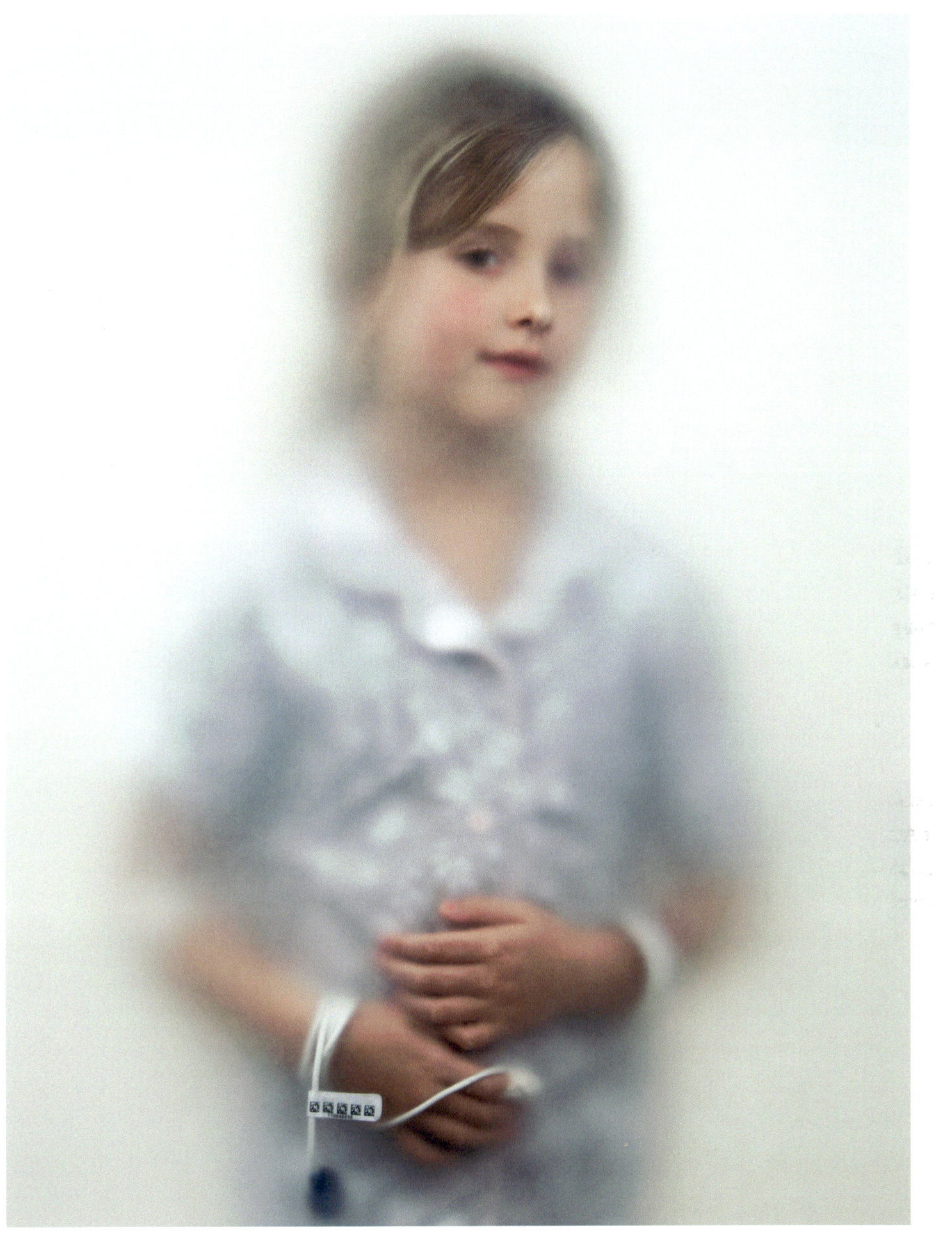

ONEEVERYONE · *Zoë*, 2017
Porcelain enamel
Dimensions variable

Commission, Landmarks, The University of Texas at Austin, 2017

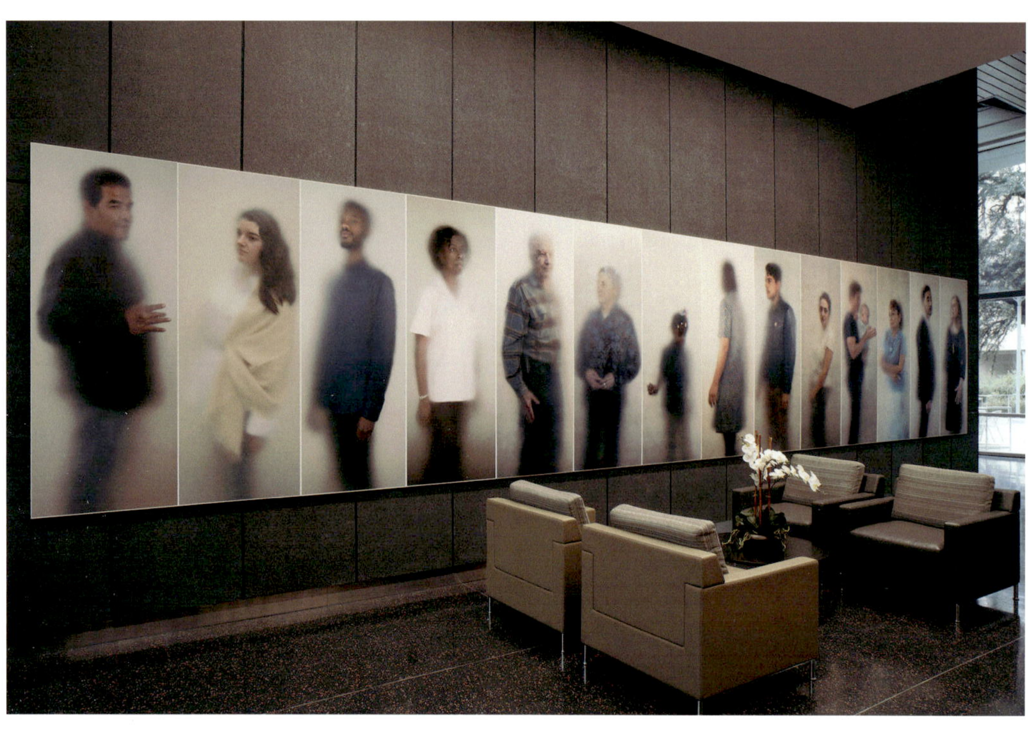

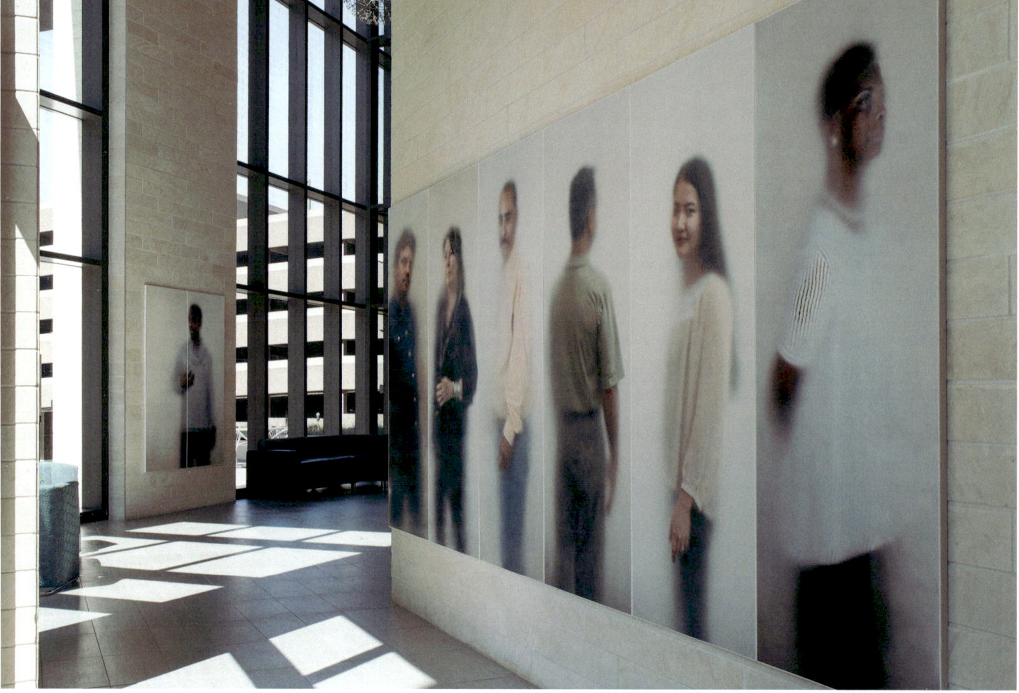

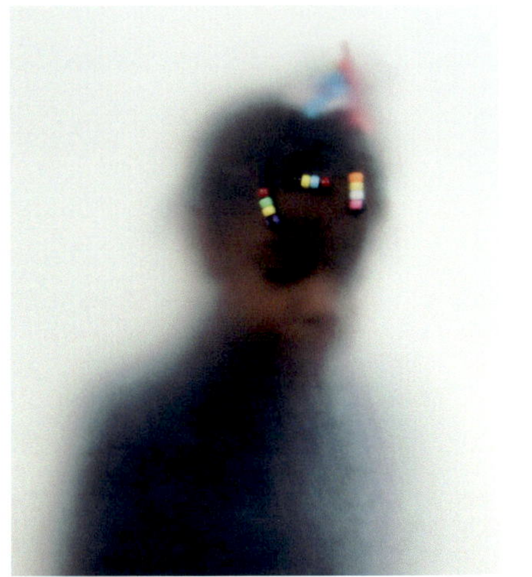
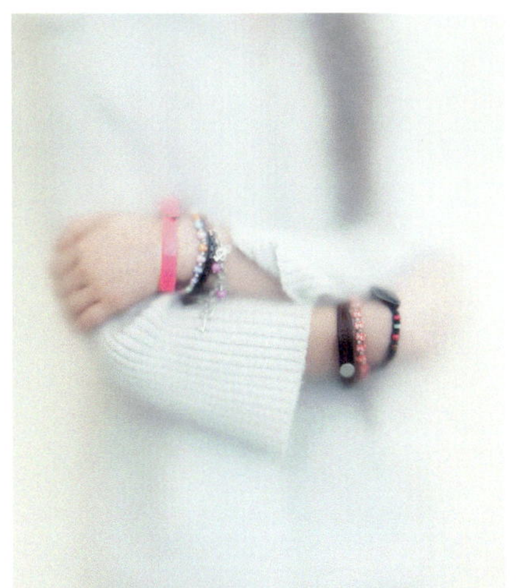
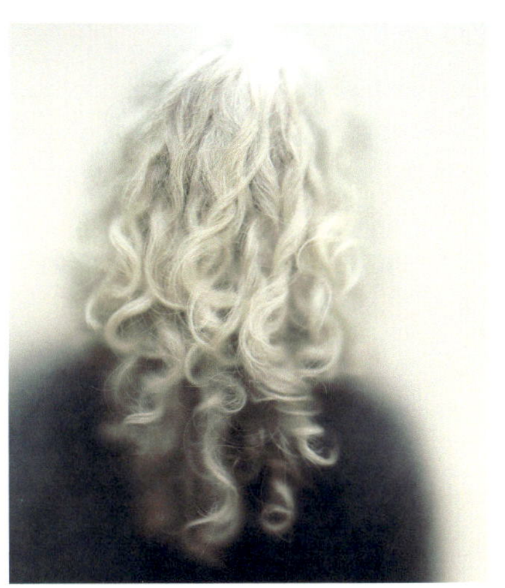
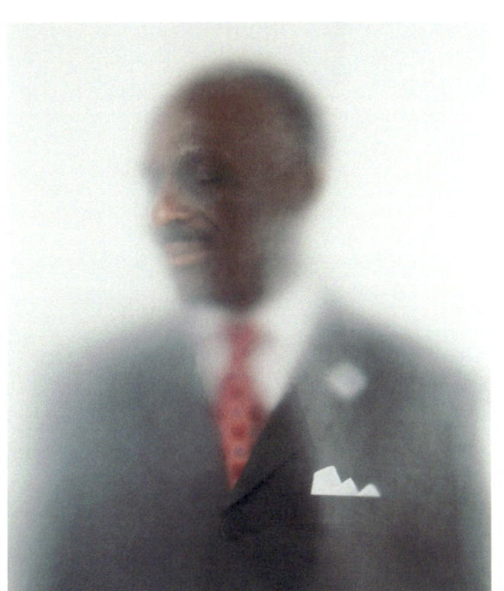
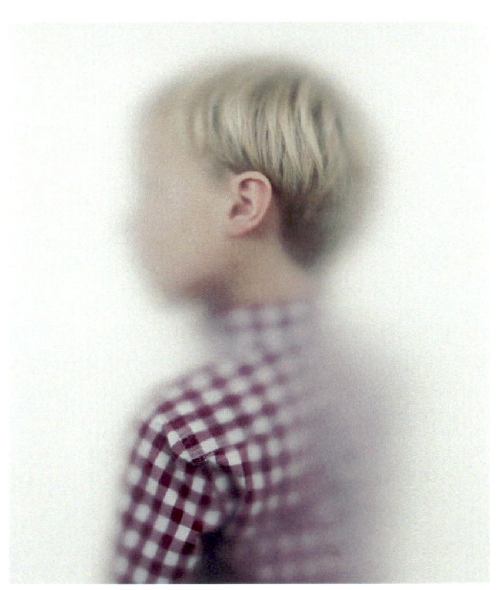
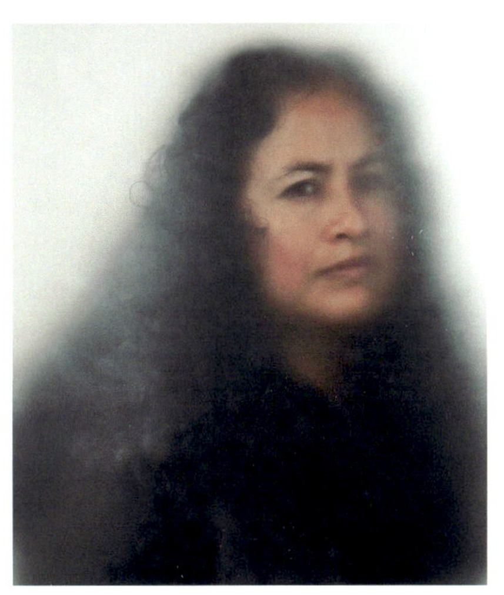

JUAN HAMILTON

AMERICAN, 1945–2025

Juan Hamilton's art emerged from the synthesis of a wide range of influences and sources. The pre-Columbian pottery he saw as a youth in South America inspired his subsequent study of ceramic sculpture at Claremont Graduate University in the late 1960s with artists Henry Takemoto (1930–2015) and Paul Soldner (1921–2011). Takemoto was a pivotal figure in the California Clay Movement, during which ceramicists transitioned from producing functional objects to abstract sculptures, and Soldner developed a process of low-temperature firing inspired by traditional Japanese raku techniques. Hamilton's perspective on life and art underwent a deep transformation following his exposure to Zen Buddhism during a visit to Japan in 1970. Subsequently, this philosophy became a fundamental aspect of his artistic practice.

While his teachers belonged to an earlier generation working in an expressionistic, improvisatory manner, Hamilton's work matured in the context of Minimalism, a style characterized by simple, unitary forms; a monochrome palette; and smooth, highly finished surfaces. While his work reflects these Minimalist qualities, the irregular ovals and teardrop shapes of his clay pieces recall the organic forms of European modernists. Hamilton's connection to earlier modernist art was amplified by the years he spent as a studio assistant and confidant to pioneering artist Georgia O'Keeffe in New Mexico, from 1973 until her death in 1986.

Hamilton conceived of his work as a reflection of his inner state of mind: "They come from inside me," he said. "I feel them three-dimensionally in the center of my chest." Open and dynamic, *Curve and Shadow, No. 2* marks a departure from his traditional use of clay and stone. The sleek, aerodynamic bronze curve appears to rise from the ground like a wave, cresting and receding back into the floor. The importance of the shadow cast by the sculpture, an intangible feature that extends the form, is emphasized in the title. Its transformation in the slowly shifting light affords a meditative experience, making perceptible the passage of time.

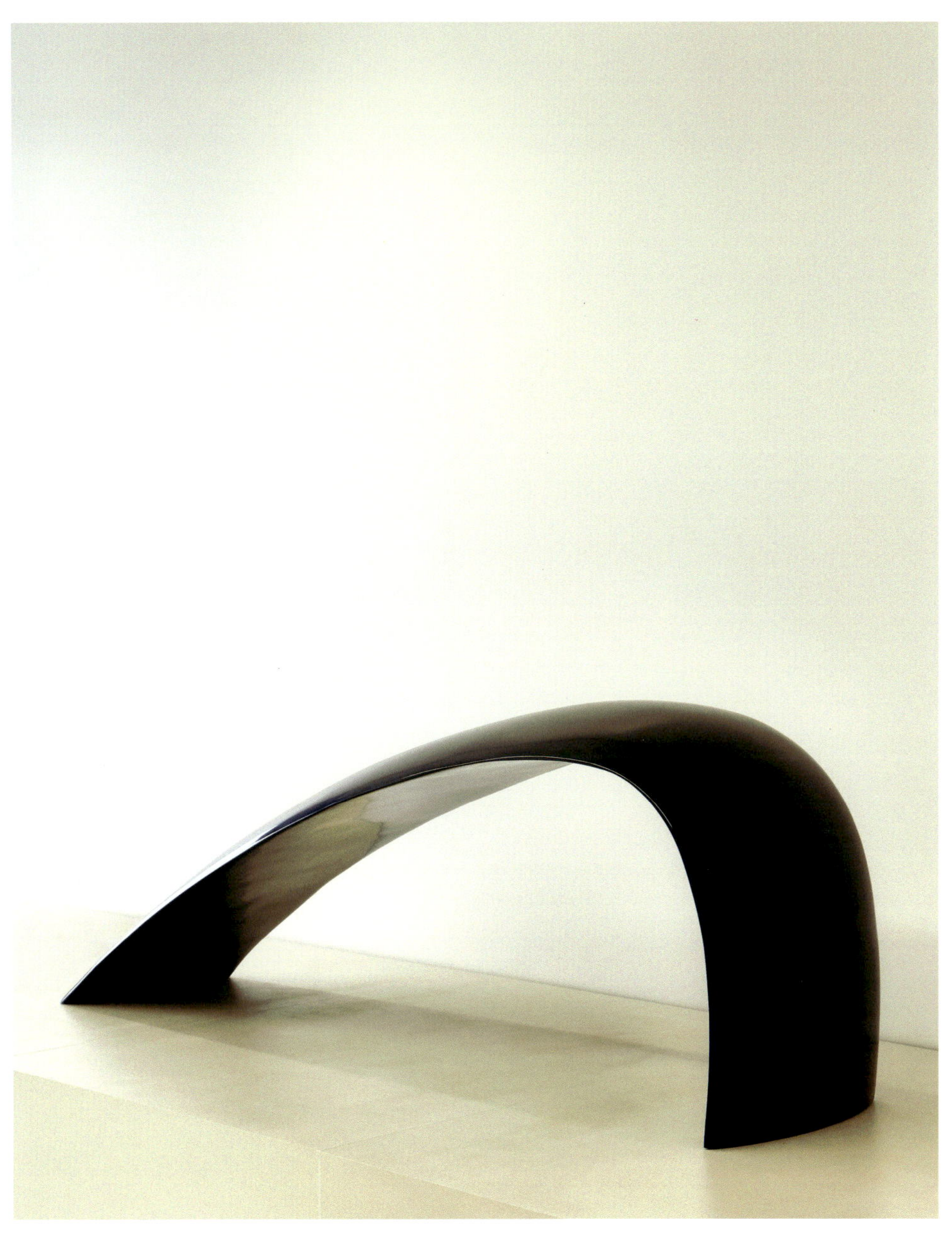

Curve and Shadow, No. 2, 1983
Bronze
32 × 96 × 24 inches

Lent by The Metropolitan Museum of Art
Anonymous Gift, 1983
1983.540.1

DAVID HARE

AMERICAN, 1917–1992

After earning degrees in chemistry and biology, David Hare began experimenting with photography, using his scientific background to explore techniques that manipulate and distort images. As a young man, Hare entered the circle of European émigré artists who arrived in the United States throughout the 1930s, a period of significant cultural exchange. European Surrealist artists who settled in New York City and younger American abstractionists shared an interest in the theories of Sigmund Freud, a pioneer in the field of psychoanalysis. Freud's writing on topics such as trauma, sexuality, and dream states provided a framework for artists to understand the unconscious mind, both as a subject and as a method for artmaking.

As the Surrealist movement faded in the 1950s, Hare adapted his style to a more abstract mode, gravitating toward fragile, slender forms with spindly accents that were supported structurally in bronze. Through abstraction, he extended the Surrealist principle of implying a subject, inviting viewers to draw meaning from the work through their own free associations.

The Swan's Dream of Leda refers to the classical Greek myth in which Zeus desired a beautiful human woman named Leda. In order to seduce her, he tricked her by appearing in the guise of a swan. For an artist steeped in Surrealism and Freudian analysis, the subject offered rich possibilities for sexual innuendo. Yet rather than the literal motifs frequently portrayed by many male Surrealists, Hare's forms, such as the flapping of the swan's wings, evoke more subtle and metaphorical suggestions.

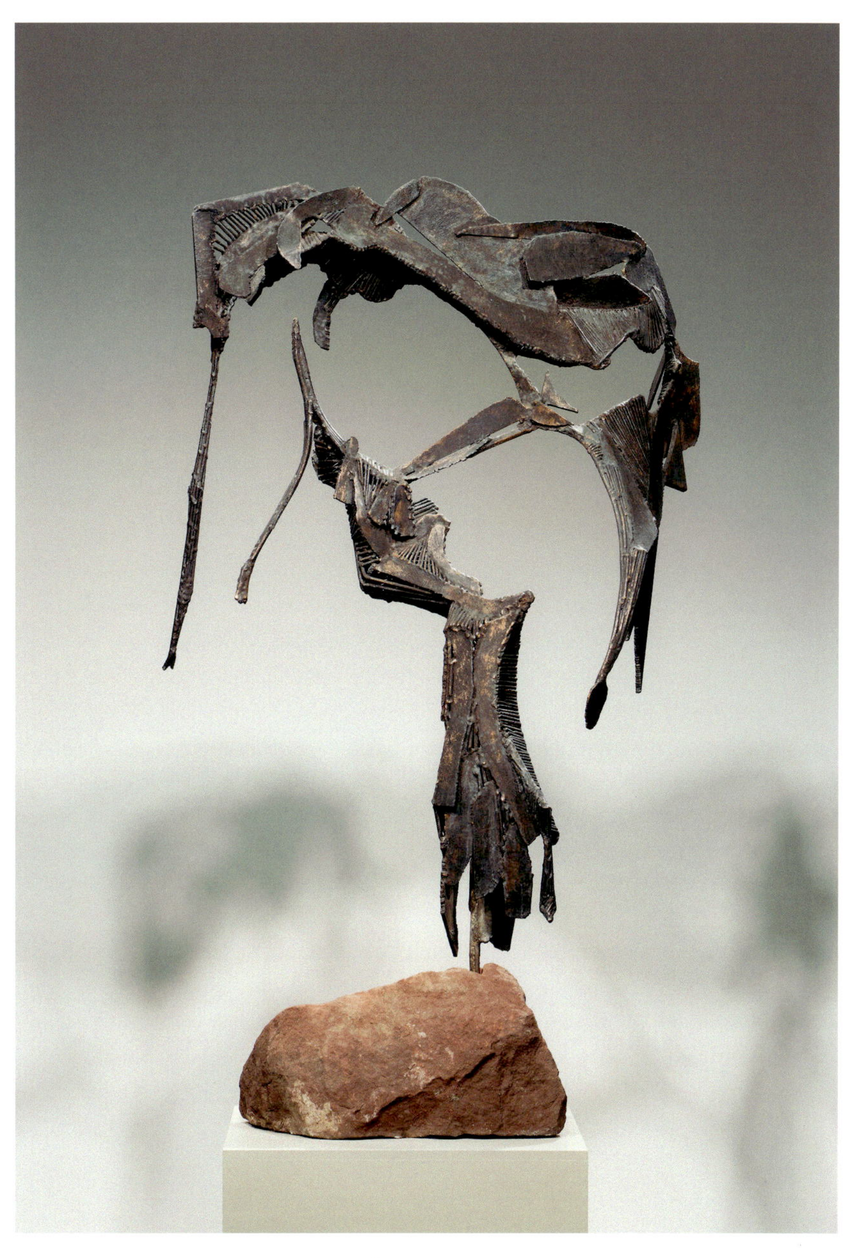

The Swan's Dream of Leda, 1962
Bronze with stone base
53 ¾ × 33 ½ × 9 ¾ inches

Lent by The Metropolitan Museum of Art
Gift of the artist, 1963
63.83a,b

HANS HOKANSON

AMERICAN, BORN IN SWEDEN, 1925–1997

Swedish-born artist Hans Hokanson moved to the United States in 1951 and studied painting in California before relocating to New York City, where he became a master cabinetmaker and furniture designer. After building wooden painting stretchers for the artist Mark Rothko (1903–1970), Hokanson worked as a carpenter for the East Hampton home and studio of painter Willem de Kooning (1904–1997). In 1960, he settled nearby in Northwest Creek, a marshy wetlands area bordered by a forest from which the artist sourced the wood for his sculptures. Throughout the 1960s, Hokanson's forms resembled mill wheels and ship's gears, constructed from separate pieces of carved wood joined together with dowels.

Two important influences shaped Hokanson's later work: the philosophy and aesthetics of Zen Buddhism, and his studies of wooden artifacts from Africa and carvings from Indonesia, which he encountered while working at the Museum of Primitive Art in New York. In the 1970s, Hokanson's work grew in scale as he began carving from single tree trunks, using a chainsaw to wrest forms out of the wood. "The saw takes over," he said in an interview. "It makes me think differently, and my thoughts take shape in the wood." After defining the general, overall form of the sculpture with the chainsaw, Hokanson fine-tuned the details of each piece using hatchets and chisels.

Standing more than eight feet tall, *Source* was carved from a massive cherry tree. The column of wood twists as it rises, with curved edges meeting in ridges that wrap around the tree trunk, offering viewers a variety of perspectives as they move around the work. Hokanson was perpetually inspired by nature and often sculpted outdoors. The chiseled and gouged texture of *Source*, resembling rippling water, enhances its naturalistic qualities. When exhibited at Long Island's Guild Hall in 1980, a reviewer captured the spirit of *Source*, writing that the "forest comes to life again—as sculpture."

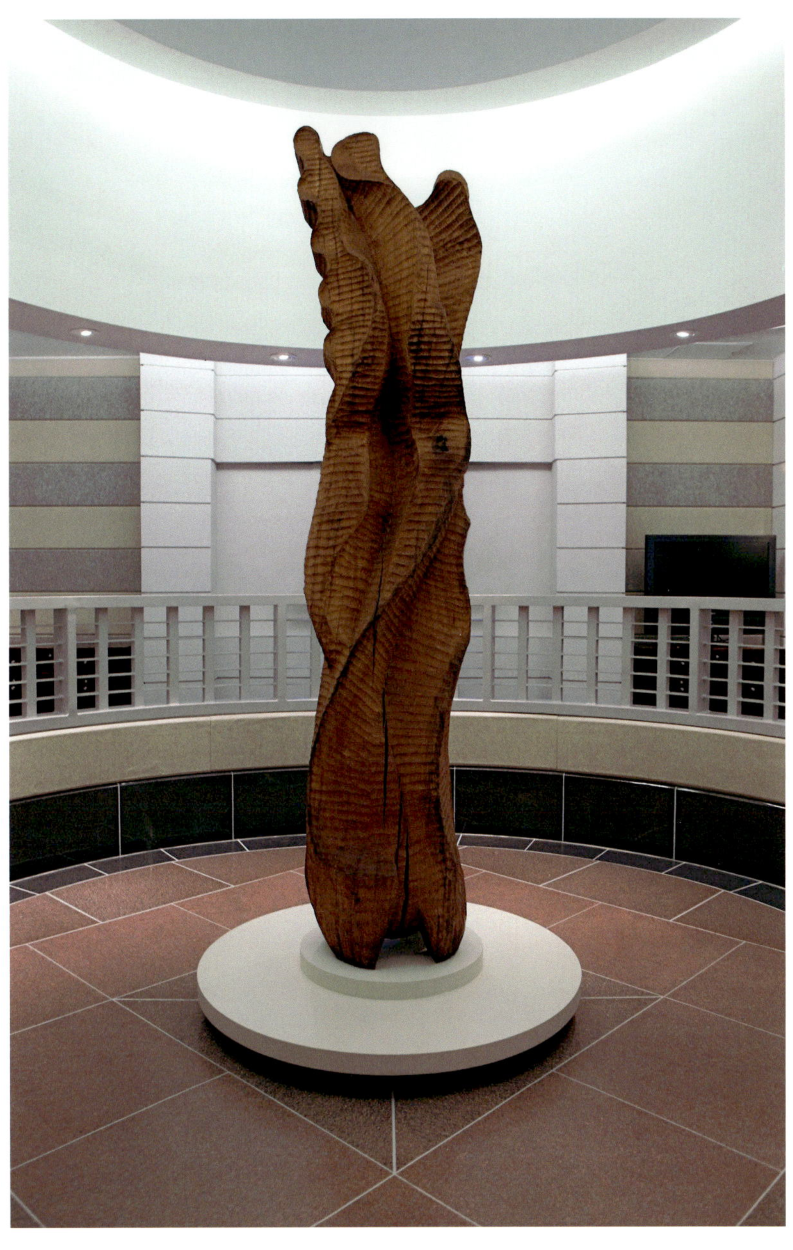

Source, 1977
Cherrywood
98 × 20 × 25 inches

Lent by The Metropolitan Museum of Art
Purchase, Friends of the Artist Gifts, 1978
1978.87

BRYAN HUNT

AMERICAN, BORN 1947

In the late 1960s, just before entering art school, Bryan Hunt worked as a draftsman for NASA's Apollo program. He later attended the University of South Florida intending to become an architect, but was quickly drawn to painting. Hunt moved to Los Angeles to attend the Otis Art Institute, where he earned his BFA in 1971. He explored modern philosophy and literary theory, admiring the purist aesthetics of Barnett Newman (1905–1970) and the Minimalists.

By the 1980s, Hunt began to focus on sources from classical Greek art and culture. His *Maenad* sculptures, although abstract, evoke the swirling draperies of Hellenistic works. *Amphora* engages with both ancient and modern sculptural traditions. A tall, slender, two-handled vessel in ancient Greece, the amphora was usually made of clay and used to store food and drink, especially wine. Instead of a utilitarian container, Hunt's *Amphora* is fluid and visually unstable, with only its two stems obliquely recalling the earlier vessels.

The textured and expressionistic surface of the work reveals the artist's handling and modeling of the clay within the tradition of modernist sculpture. At the same time, Hunt's stylization recalls the black-figure style of Greek vases from the seventh through fifth centuries BCE, which depict silhouetted figures, often with exaggerated features that amplify the drama of the scenes. Drawing from both ancient and contemporary influences, Hunt's *Amphora* demonstrates the vitality of art across centuries.

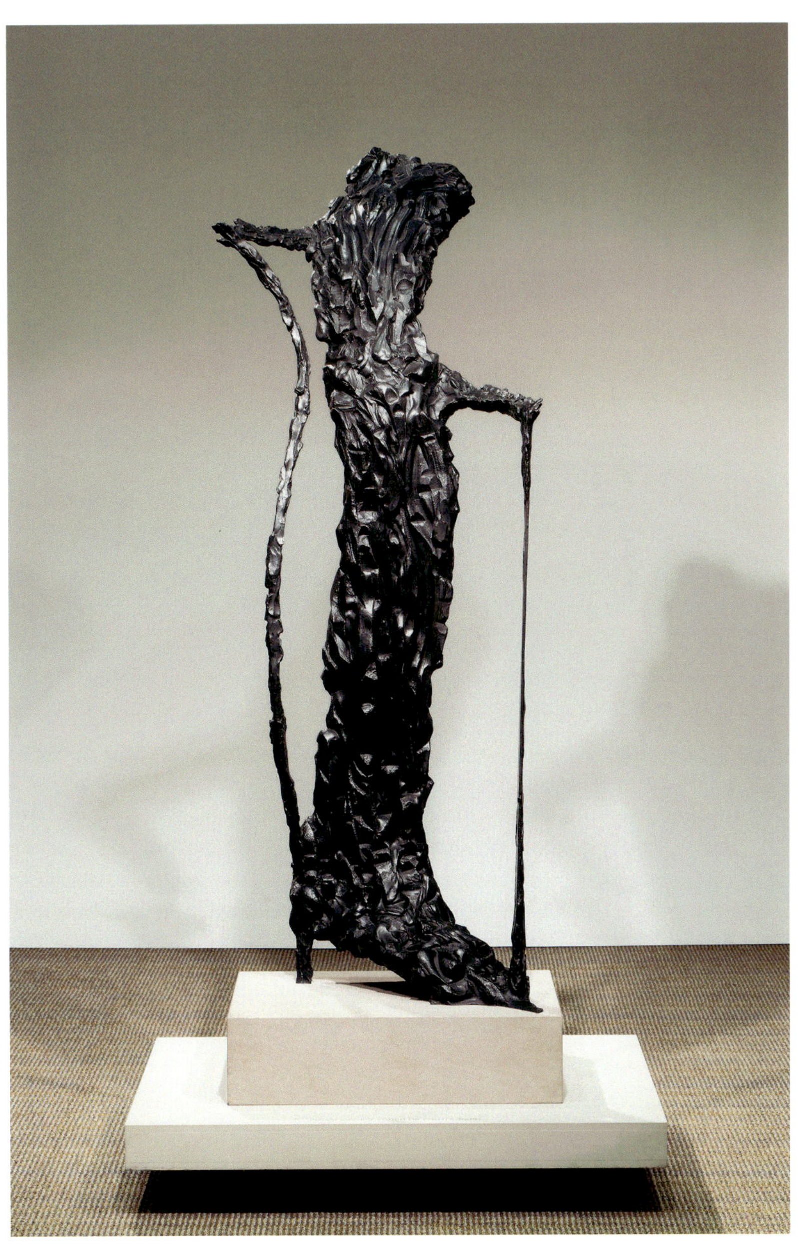

Amphora, 1982
Bronze
97 ¾ × 30 × 25 inches

Lent by The Metropolitan Museum of Art
Purchase, Louis and Bessie Adler Foundation, Inc. Gift (Seymour M. Klein, President), 1983
1983.88a,b

FREDERICK KIESLER

AMERICAN, BORN IN AUSTRIA, 1890–1965

A polymath who made important innovations in the fields of architecture, design, painting, and sculpture, Austrian-born Frederick Kiesler moved to New York in 1926 and quickly found his way into the avant-garde circles of American artists and European expatriates. He originally worked in the International Style, a movement that proposed universal solutions to issues of domestic architecture and commercial design. The straight lines, flat planes, and right angles characteristic of the style embodied the utopian vision that simple geometric forms could foster a more rational and egalitarian society.

Like many European artists, Kiesler's manner of working turned inward during the 1930s, toward the Surrealist project of exploring the subconscious with imaginative and counterintuitive images. *Winged Victory* alludes to the famous ancient Greek statue *Winged Victory of Samothrace* in the Louvre. Created to commemorate a military conquest, the female figure in white marble strides forward with widespread wings. In contrast to the classical beauty of the ancient sculpture, Kiesler's version is fragmentary and abstract: the figure itself has vanished, leaving only its darkened wings collapsing to the ground.

The motif of wings falling to earth evokes other references, such as the Greek myth of Icarus, which resonated with many artists and writers in the years following World War II. With manmade wings of feathers and wax, Icarus became the first human to fly. When he flew too close to the sun, the wax melted, and he plummeted to his death. Similarly, *Winged Victory* offers a poignant visual metaphor for the collapse of the utopian ideals of Kiesler's generation, as well as the destruction often inherent in victory.

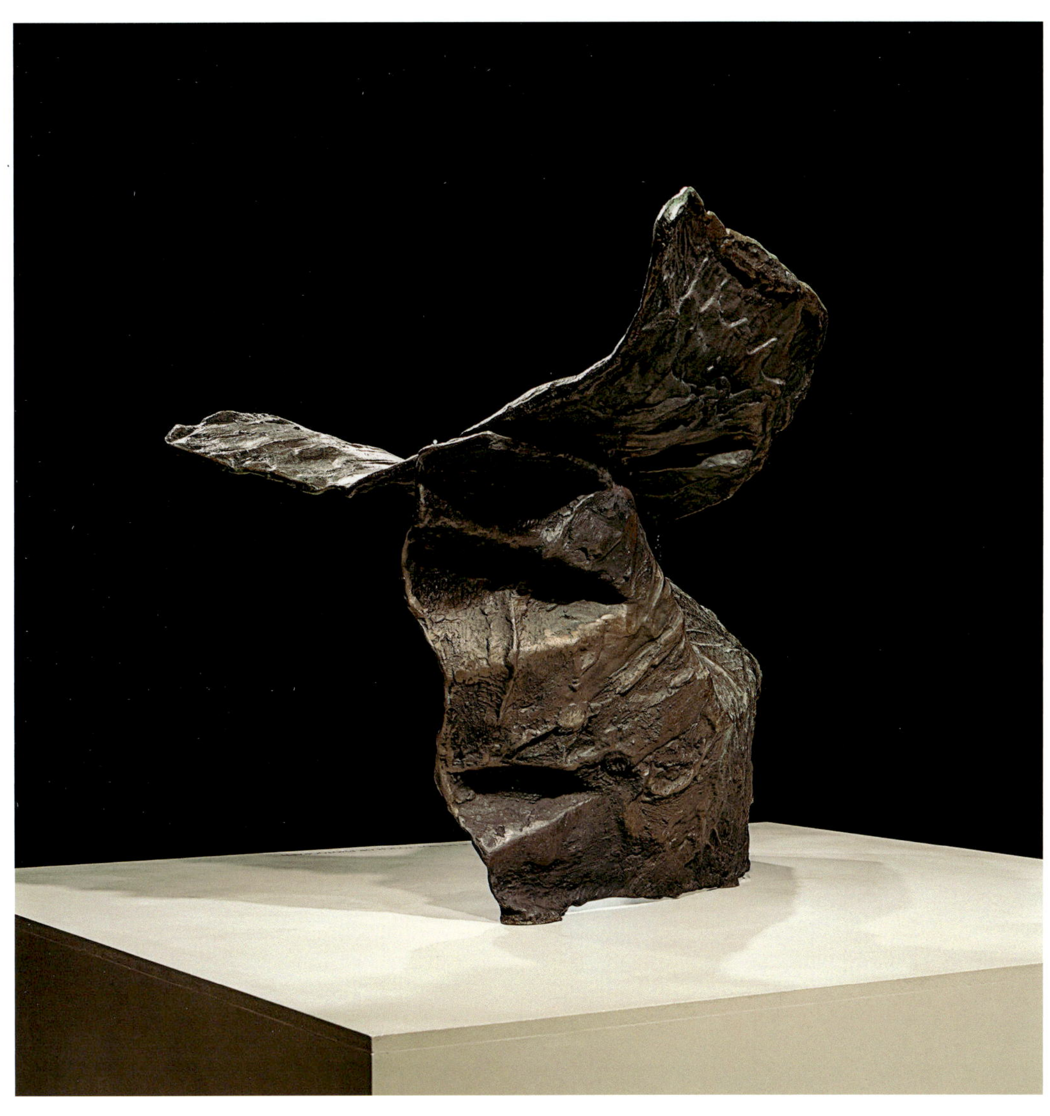

Winged Victory, circa 1951
Bronze
30 × 28 × 24 ½ inches

Lent by The Metropolitan Museum of Art
Gift of Salander-O'Reilly Galleries, Inc., 1983
1983.200

SIMONE LEIGH

AMERICAN, BORN 1967

Simone Leigh uses sculpture, video, installation, and performance art to explore representations of Black feminine forms. Her work draws upon the African diaspora—encompassing cultures and peoples originating from Africa and dispersed across the globe through both forced and voluntary means. Within this framework, Leigh appropriates visual traditions from Africa, the American South, and the Caribbean to create works that reflect the layered histories, identities, and experiences of the diaspora.

Leigh began her artistic career during her college years. While studying philosophy, she took a ceramics class on a whim. She soon developed proficiency in pottery techniques, despite never having attended art school. Her early interest in issues of race and beauty inspired exquisite sculptures of Black women that would later manifest as Leigh's renowned creolization of forms.

Her sculptures are often anthropomorphic, fusing Black female figures with domestic objects or tools, and occasional modern references. *Sentinel IV* is modeled after a Zulu ceremonial spoon, a symbol of status and women's labor within Zulu culture. In taking inspiration from figurative sculpture across the African diaspora, Leigh chooses to represent not a single individual, but rather the collective power of the Black female body more broadly.

Sentinel IV is a slender bronze guardian with elongated proportions and a faceless bowl crown that emanates a mystical presence. In using the term "sentinel"—a watchful guardian—Leigh honors Black femininity while also investigating historical and intersecting ideas of race, beauty, and the association of Black women's bodies with work.

Sited in the central courtyard of the Anna Hiss Gymnasium, *Sentinel IV* stakes radical claim in a moment when Black existence remains under threat. It holds space and holds court—an apt landmark poised to see, hear, and represent—to project Black presence into the future of The University of Texas at Austin, bearing witness to this indelible present.

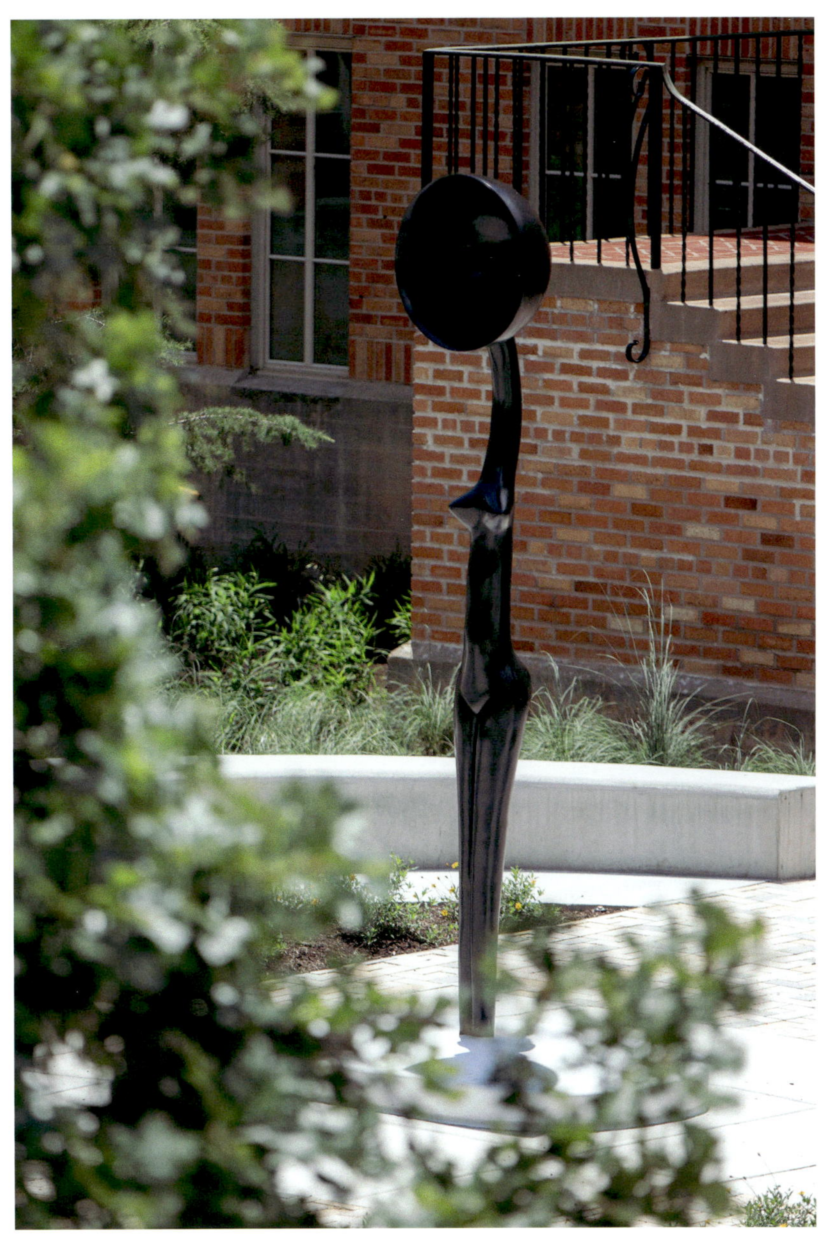

Sentinel IV, 2020
Bronze
128 × 25 × 15 inches

Purchase, Landmarks, The University of Texas at Austin, 2020

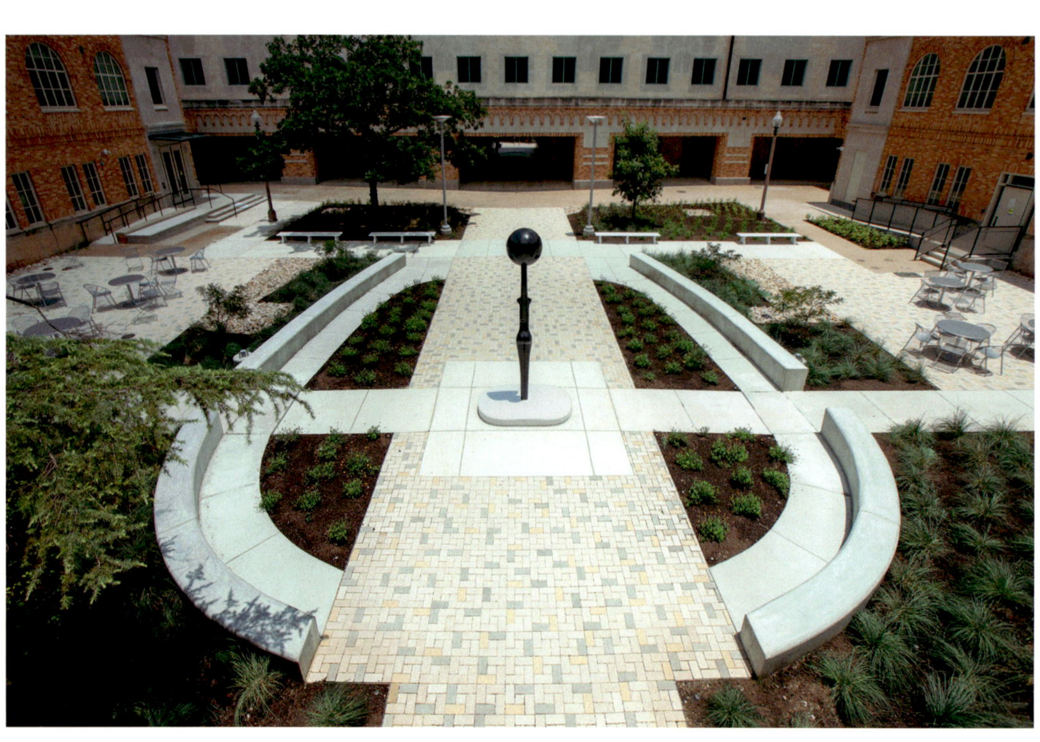

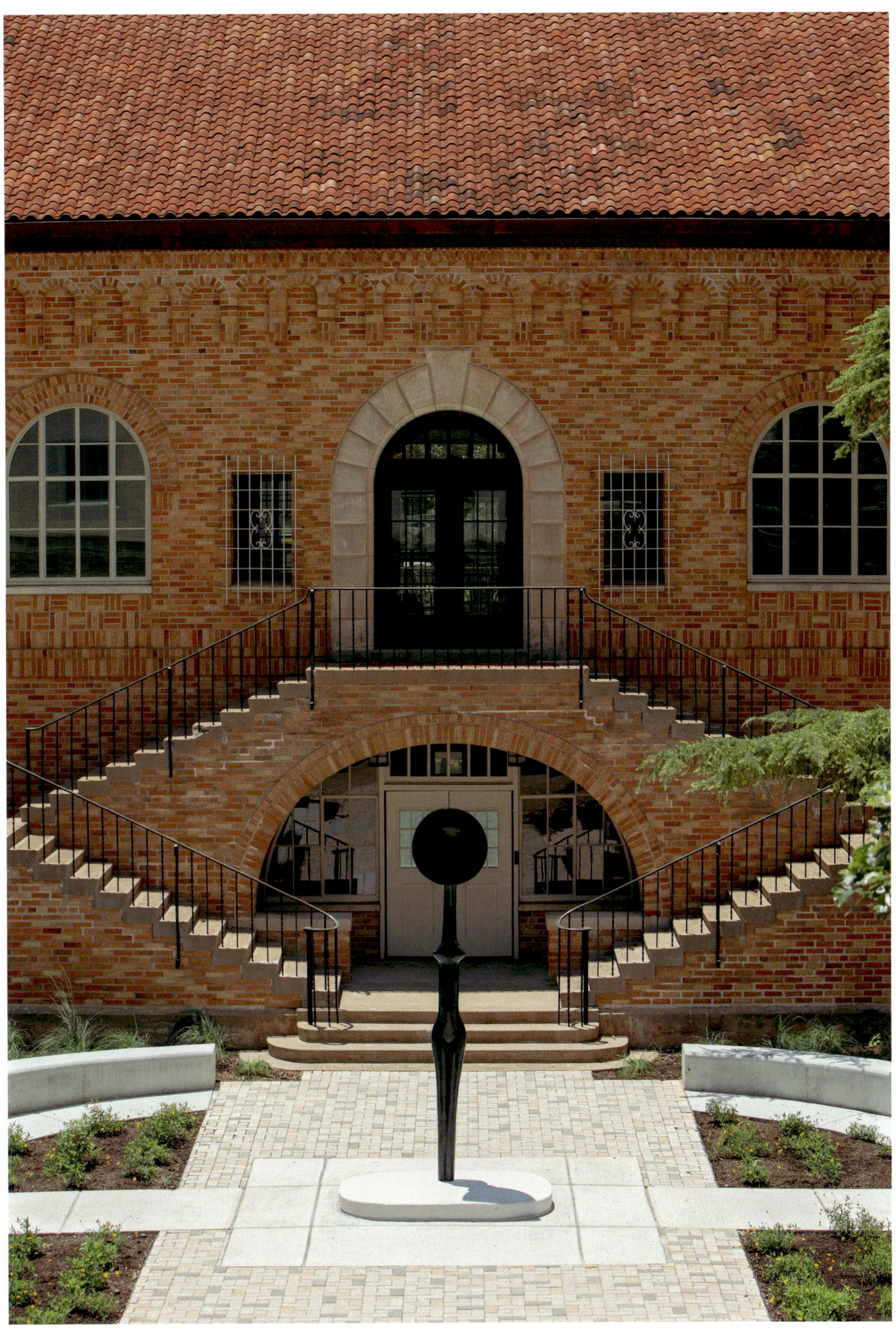

SOL LEWITT

AMERICAN, 1928–2007

During the 1960s, Sol LeWitt helped formulate the tenets of the emerging Conceptual art movement by arguing that the concept behind a work of art was more important than its execution. His instructions-based Conceptual practice proposed a new model of artistic authorship, defined by an artist's ideas rather than the personal touch or mark of the artist's hand. By providing a set of instructions for others to carry out, LeWitt compared his role as an artist to that of an architect or a composer. He drafted compositions that could exist in multiple locations simultaneously and be executed by others, in the same way that many different musicians can play the same Bach sonata.

Although LeWitt is best known for the numerous wall drawings he made during his lifetime, when asked about inventing the medium, the artist quipped: "I think the cavemen came first." Unlike their predecessors, however, LeWitt's wall drawings do not exist as permanent objects but rather as a diagram and a set of instructions.

During the 1980s, LeWitt produced many jewel-toned, ink-wash wall drawings like *Wall Drawing #520*, dramatically expanding his repertoire from the pencil versions that dominated the first decade of his career. In this work—one of the few that the artist conceived for three walls—cubes float across the surface in rich, variegated colors. The palette and slight depth of the geometric figures reflect the artist's interest in Italian Renaissance frescoes spurred by his move to Spoleto, Italy, in 1980.

While these works depart from the more muted palette and systematic logic of LeWitt's early pencil wall drawings, they also reflect his continued interest in the cube as a basic geometric element. Equally significant are the tonal variations achieved in LeWitt's ink-wash wall drawings, which result from layering only primary colors and gray. While the spirit of *Wall Drawing #520* is one of modesty, simplicity, and restraint, the visual impact is lush.

DRAWN BY
Michael Abelman, Rachel Houston, Gabriel Hurier, Eileen Lammers, Clint Reams, Jon Shapley, Patrick Sheehy

FIRST INSTALLATION
Whitney Museum of American Art, New York, April 1987

FIRST DRAWN BY
Catherine Clarke, Douglas Geiger, David Higginbotham, Anthony Sansotta, Patricia Thornley, Jo Watanabe

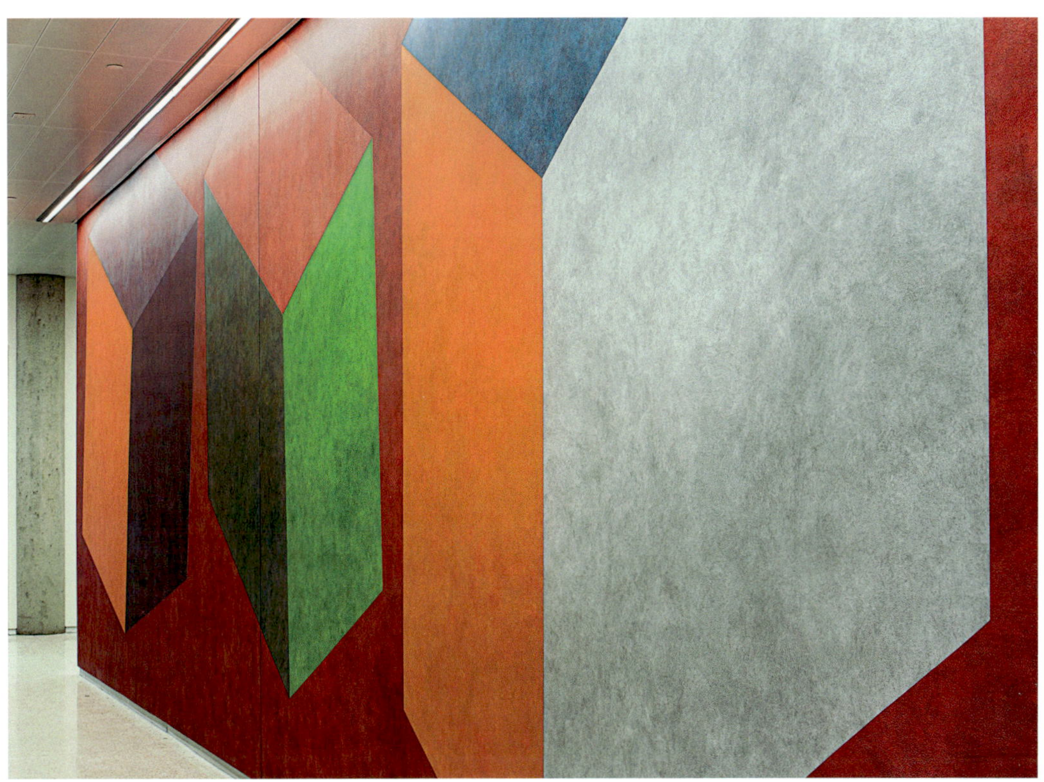

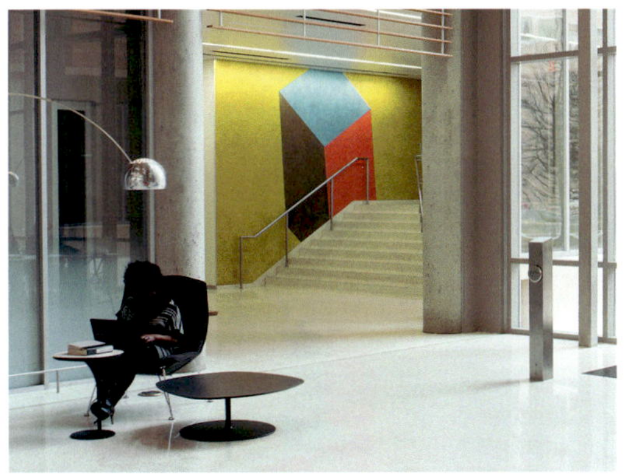

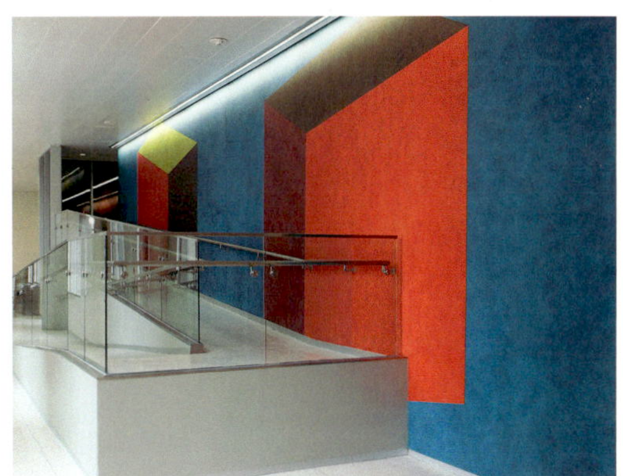

Wall Drawing #520, 1987/2013
Colored ink wash on wall
Three walls: 148 × 450 inches;
148 × 219 inches; 148 × 544 inches

Lent by the Estate of Sol LeWitt

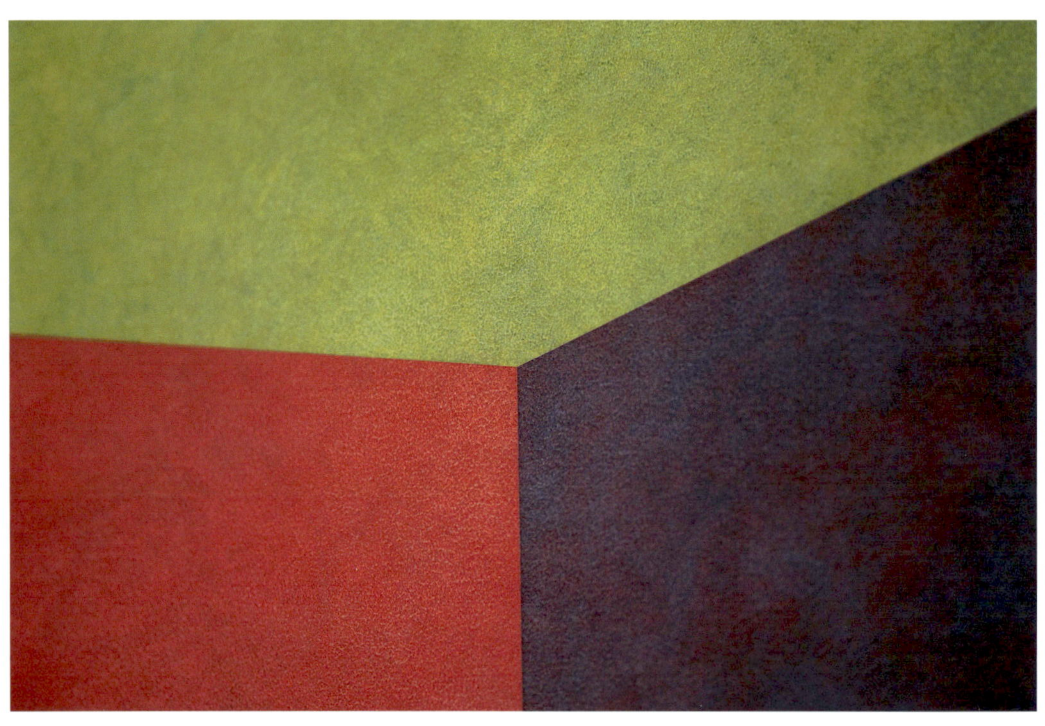

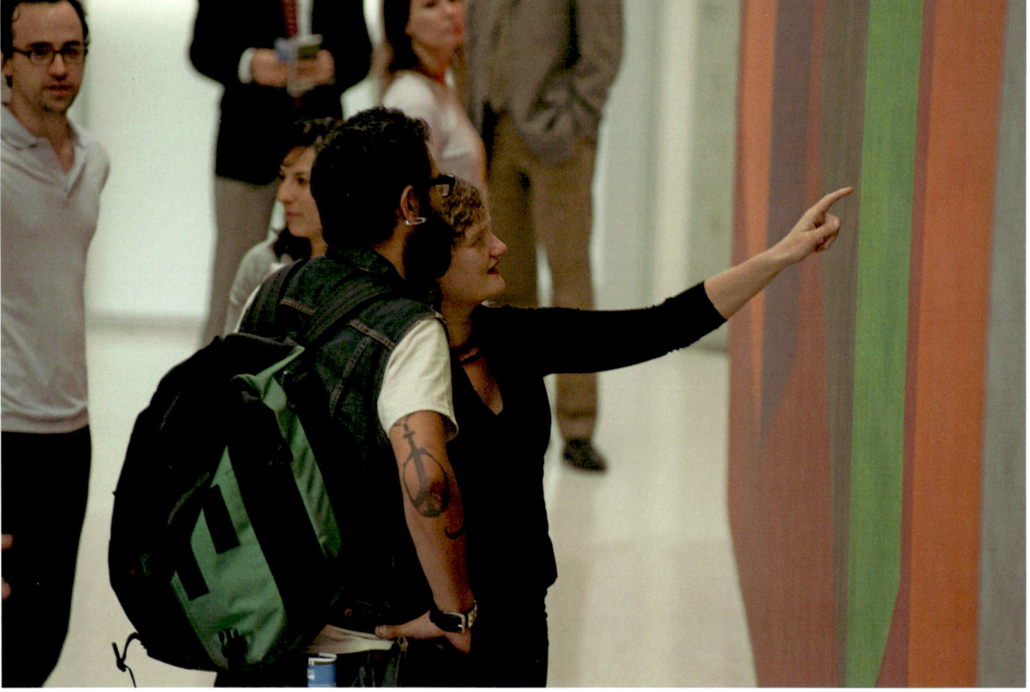

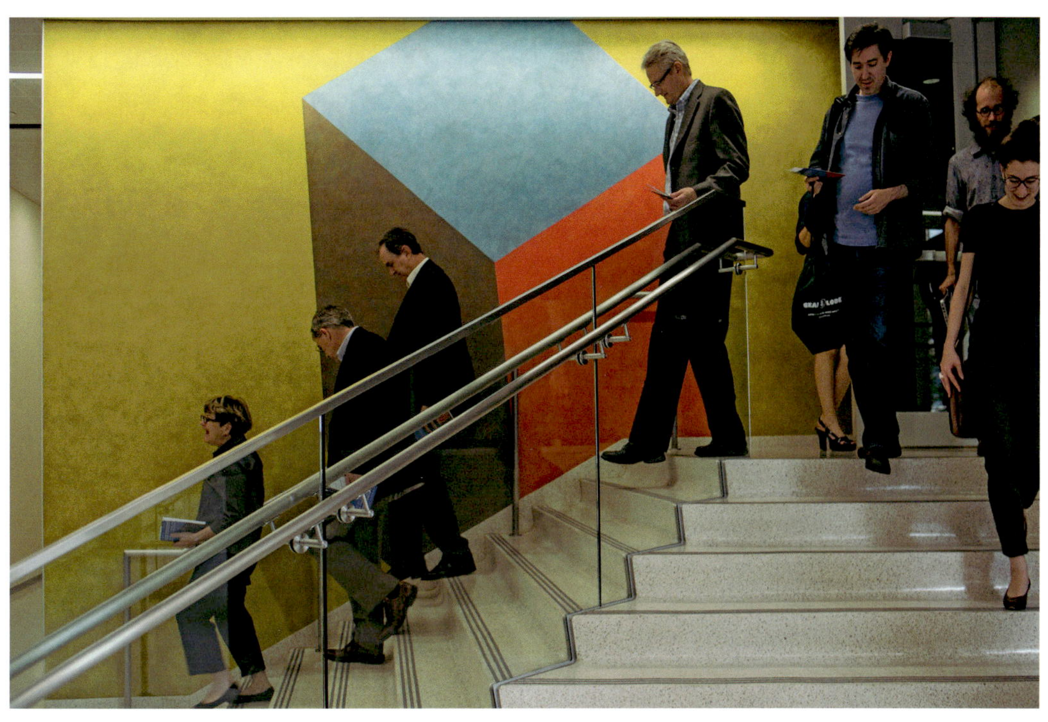

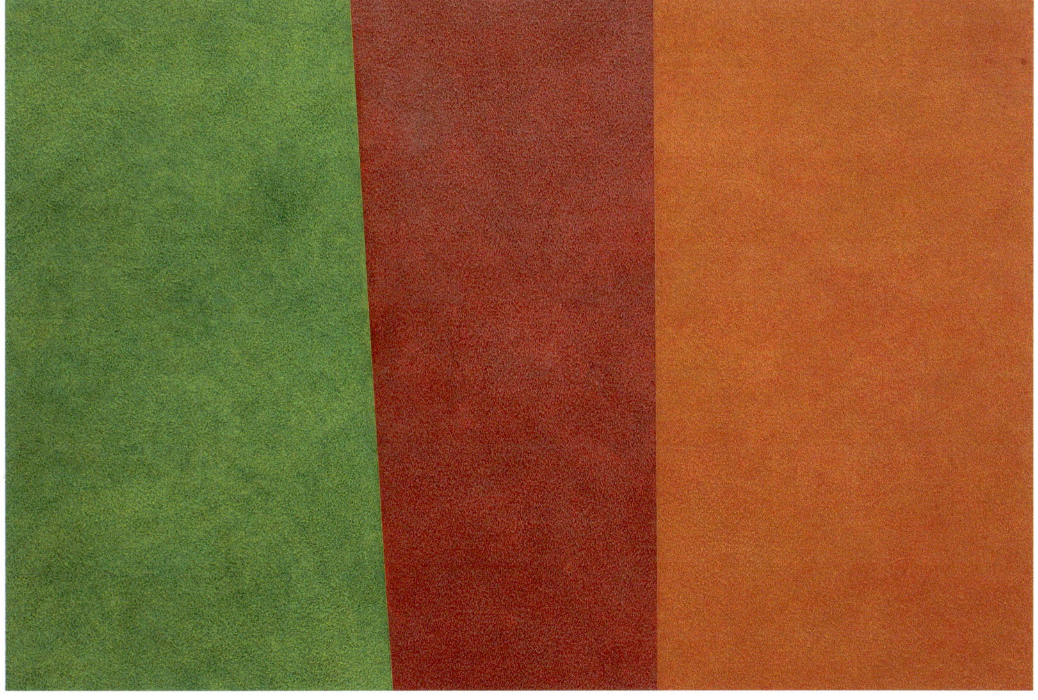

SOL LEWITT

AMERICAN, 1928–2007

Sol LeWitt, a pioneer of Minimal and Conceptual art, exhibited five structures in his first solo exhibition in 1965. With straightforward titles like *Floor Structure* and *Wall Structure*, the rectangular, black wood forms signaled his lifelong commitment to an elemental geometric vocabulary, as well as a sensitive consideration for the architectural context of his work. In LeWitt's art, the wall is never merely a backdrop; it assumes primary importance as a critical component in many of his three-dimensional structures and as the surface upon which his wall drawings are painted or drawn.

Circle with Towers is, in effect, a low circular wall capped at regular intervals by eight rectangular towers made of pale gray concrete blocks. The outdoor structure possesses a discernable logic and rhythm: the towers are four blocks wide while the low walls between them are eight blocks wide—a perfect 1:2 ratio. The forms are laid by hand, one block at a time by local masons. Like many of LeWitt's works, *Circle with Towers* reflects the artist's generosity in welcoming others to interpret his pieces, acknowledging the artists and craftspeople who bring his artistic visions to life as co-creators.

LeWitt introduced concrete block into his work in the 1980s. A humble material, it appealed to his interest in making art that privileged concepts over materials or surfaces. He also appreciated that the rectangular blocks could be stacked, transforming the cube into a repeating motif. While LeWitt's work evolved significantly over his career, the cube appears at each phase and in every medium, from sculpture to photography. Both the square and cube were essential to LeWitt's vocabulary, serving as elemental units and referencing grids made by other artists throughout the twentieth century.

INSTALLED BY

John P. Adame, Christopher J. Alejos, Jesse Carbajal, Rico Aruizo Epifanio, Gustavo L. Gaytan, Isacc Hernandez, Alfredo Martinez, Oscar Martinez, Reymundo Medina, Robert Montalvo, Carl Bermudes Pacheco, Gerardo Sanoteli, Albert A. Suniga, Kenneth O. Tarter Jr., Arthur Trujillo, Francis Munoz Vazquez

The project was carried out by Rudd & Adams Masonry, Inc., under the supervision of Austin Commercial contractors, and Jeremy Ziemann, Principal Oversight, Sol LeWitt Structures.

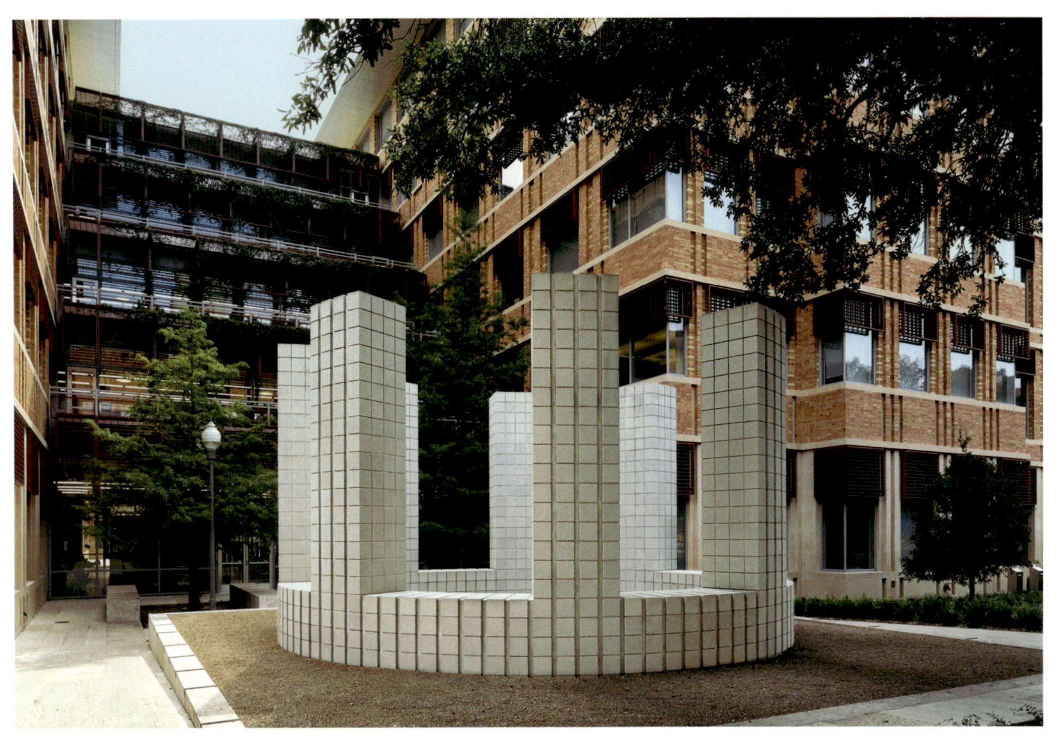

Circle with Towers, 2005/2012
Concrete block
168 × 308 inches diameter

Purchase, Landmarks, The University of Texas at Austin, 2011

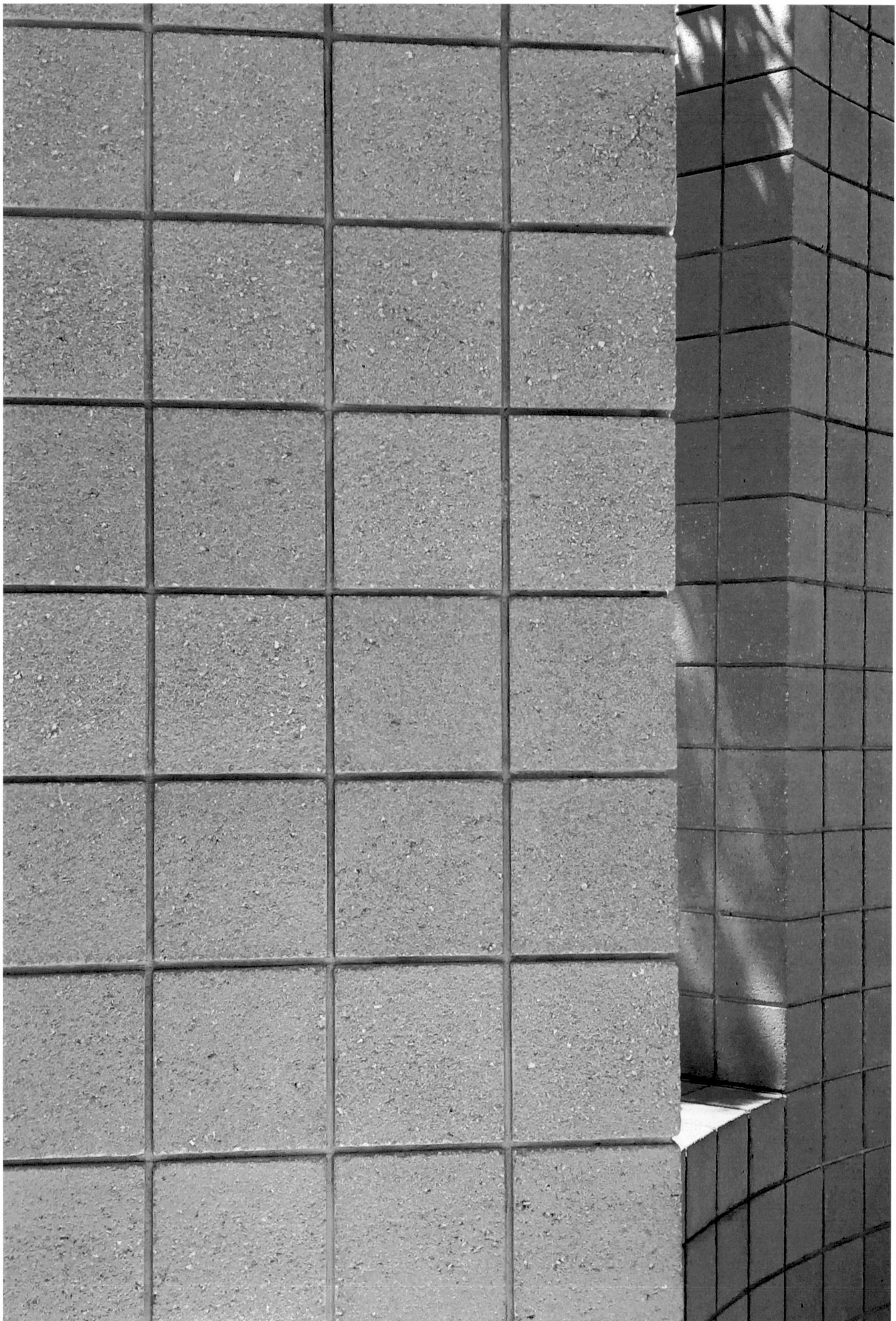

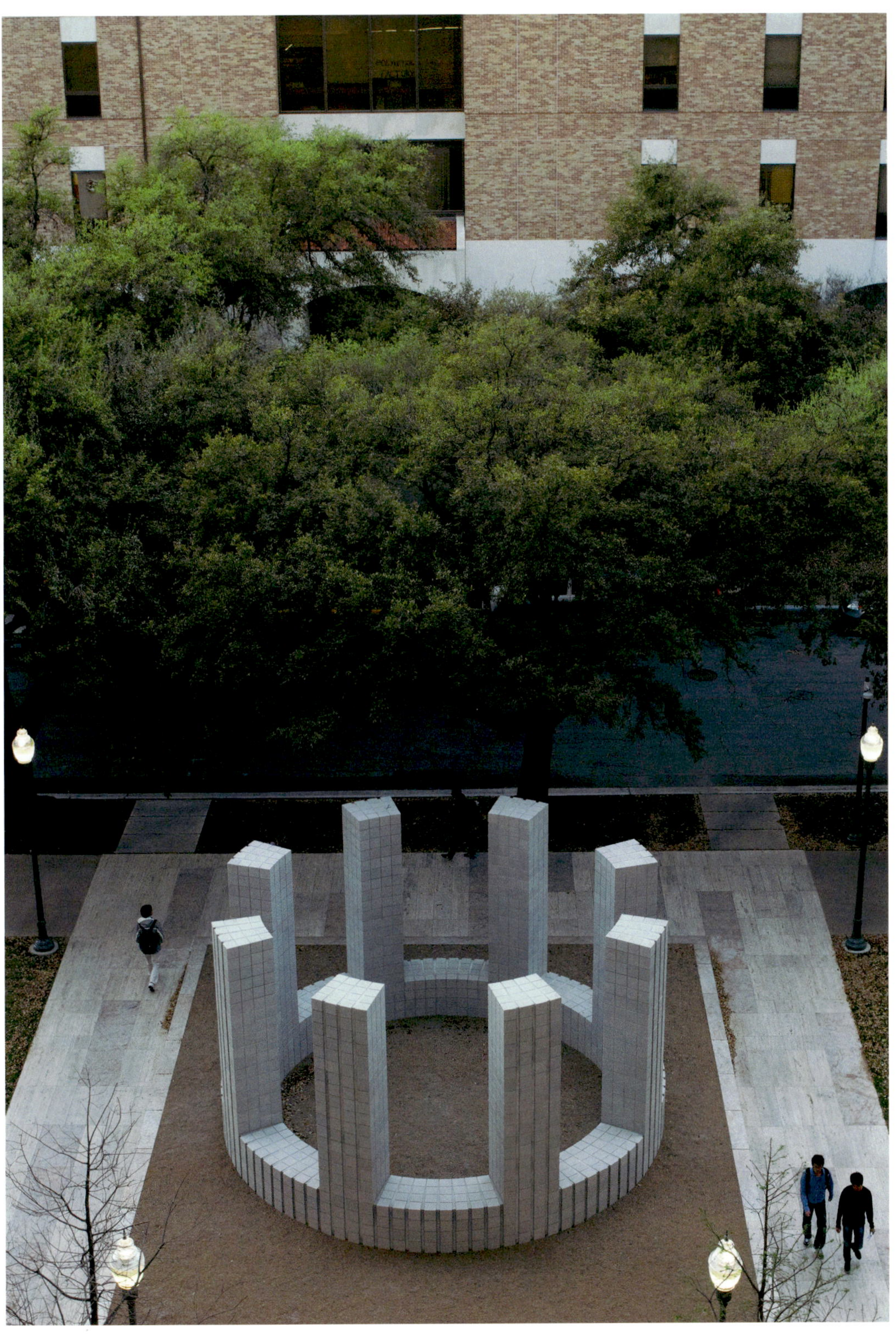

DONALD LIPSKI

AMERICAN, BORN 1947

Like the Dada artists of the 1910s and Pop artists of the 1960s, Donald Lipski uses readymade objects from daily life and assembles them in whimsical and surprising ways. He is best known for creating extensive arrangements of found objects that appear to have little in common, often using humorous and perplexing titles to provoke a range of interpretations. Unlike a formalist artist whose primary goal is visual beauty, Lipski's approach is primarily conceptual. By juxtaposing unrelated objects, he divorces them from their familiar context and creates new situations for contemplation.

The West consists of two spherical buoys, each measuring five feet in diameter. Such buoys mark deep-water shipping channels and are often used to indicate where large commercial and military ships can anchor offshore. The sculpture dates from a period when Lipski was preoccupied with military and transportation technologies. In 1986, he was invited to work at the Grumman Aerospace Corporation in Bethpage, New York. Using discarded components and scrap metal from their salvage yard as well as material acquired from a federal Defense Department surplus warehouse, Lipski made a series of sculptures that suggest wartime manufacture and the obsolescence of outdated equipment.

Instead of providing secure anchorage to ships, the two buoys are shackled uselessly to each other. Lipski glued regular pennies to their surfaces, deliberately patinated to reflect the predominance of capitalism in Western societies and the global reach of the American dollar. A certain conversation starter, *The West* invites the viewer to engage in the mental work of supposing. For some, the title implies uncharted territory, while the suggestive shape of the buoys hints at the brute force and masculine energy needed to conquer the unknown. The pennies attached to its surface—heads on one buoy and tails on the other—evoke odds of a great gamble. As with much of Lipski's sculpture, understanding *The West* is like teasing apart a poem in which multiple meanings can be coaxed and revealed over time.

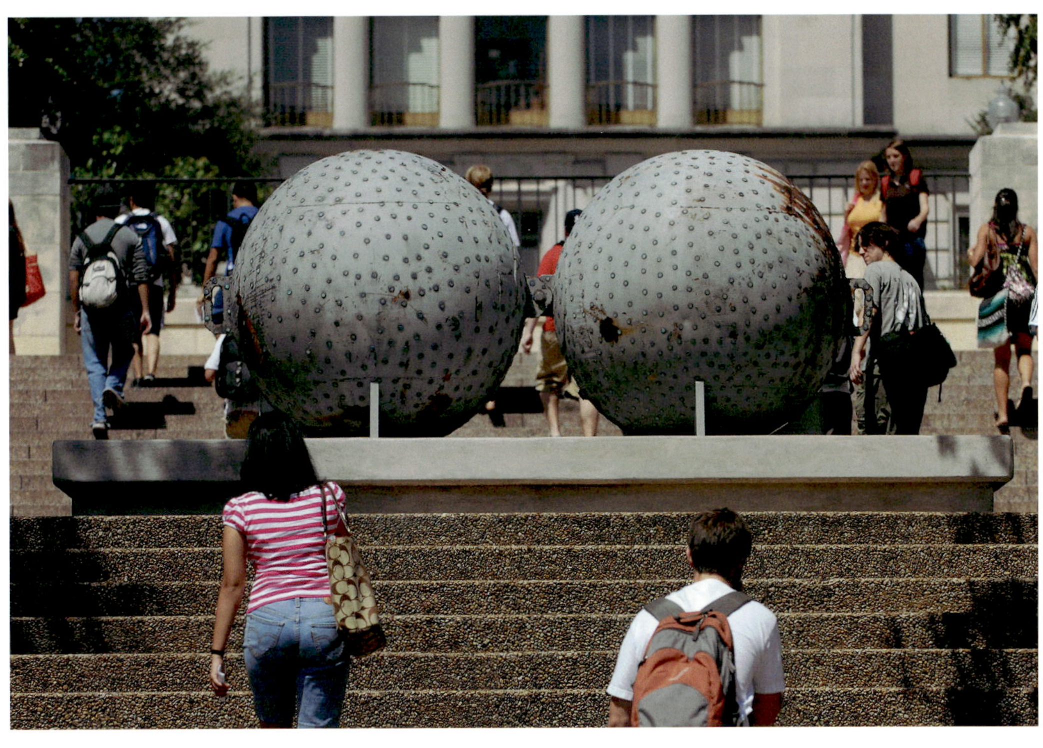

The West, 1987
Painted steel, corroded copper pennies, and silicone adhesive
Each sphere 60 inches in diameter

Lent by The Metropolitan Museum of Art
Purchase, Louis and Bessie Adler Foundation, Inc. Gift (Seymour M. Klein, President), 1988
1988.90a,b

SEYMOUR LIPTON

AMERICAN, 1903–1986

Seymour Lipton graduated from Columbia University in 1927 with a degree in dentistry and briefly ran a successful dental practice. Lacking formal art training, he began carving wood sculptures in the early 1930s. His manual precision as a dentist served him well as a sculptor, and he developed a style that diverged from anatomical realism. Like others of his generation, such as Alexander Calder (1898–1976) and David Smith (1906–1965), Lipton recognized the resonance of metal sculptures in the Machine Age. He began bronze casting in 1940–41; however, after the bombing of Pearl Harbor, the use of metal was restricted to the war effort, leaving Lipton to work intermittently with sheets of scrap metal.

Pioneer is a sculpture from the artist's *Hero* series, a body of work inspired by Joseph Campbell's book *The Hero with a Thousand Faces* (1949), which outlined the archetypes common to mythological heroes across cultures. In a similar manner, Lipton's sculpture, while it evokes a standing person, abstracts the human figure from a specific individual into a universal type. "There is always a pioneering of the human spirit that goes in time," Lipton said of this work. "The hero is the force in man of courage, of the effort to not succumb to the adversaries of life but to struggle and fight them."

Lipton's sculptures of the 1950s addressed themes of regeneration and rebirth. In this context, *Pioneer* can be viewed as representing the cyclical process of life and death. The postwar era of the 1950s was marked by rebuilding, growth, and prosperity, yet it also introduced new anxieties, including the Cold War. Thus, Lipton's sculptures often convey the fragility of life with an underlying threat.

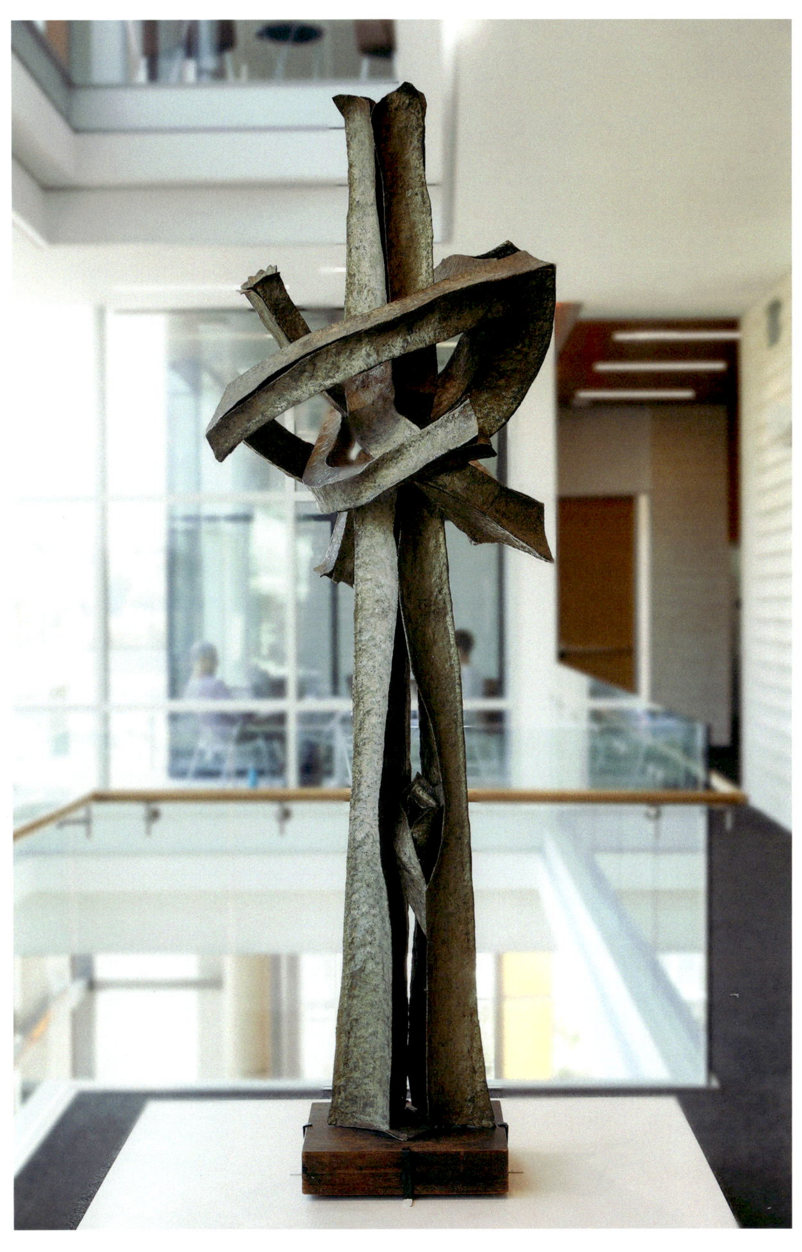

Pioneer, 1957
Nickel-silver on Monel Metal
94 × 32 × 30 inches

Lent by The Metropolitan Museum of Art
Gift of Mrs. Albert A. List, 1958
58.61

SEYMOUR LIPTON

AMERICAN, 1903–1986

In the 1940s, Seymour Lipton created sculptures using the traditional technique of casting bronze. Desiring more direct contact with his materials, he began using sheet metal in the middle of the decade; first lead, then Monel, a nickel-copper industrial alloy known for being resistant to weather and rust. Like the Abstract Expressionist painters who were his contemporaries, Lipton experimented with innovative materials and techniques. He pioneered the use of Monel, which he heated and shaped into armatures of abstract shapes that he soldered or welded together. Using an oxyacetylene torch, Lipton brazed thin rods of nickel, silver, lead, and copper onto the forms, yielding a rugged texture like hand-modeled clay. Once finished, Lipton created a second, "lining" armature that was set inside the initial form to add structural strength.

Compared to *Pioneer*, the sculpture *Catacombs* is more abstract and architectonic. While lacking an explicit narrative, the primary forms consist of hollow, dark inner areas enclosed by sheet metal that gleams in the light. The three main vertical elements resemble totemic figures clustering together and holding up a smaller fourth form, perhaps a child or ceremonial offering. The group suggests a familial or religious ceremony, such as a baptism or burial.

The horror and tragedy of World War II left a lasting impact on Lipton, inspiring somber themes expressed through metaphor. The three concave forms of *Catacombs* recall the work of Polish sculptor Magdalena Abakanowicz (1930–2017), whose similarly hollow figures convey the trauma of war. The term "catacombs" is most often associated with the subterranean burial sites of early Christians who sought refuge from Roman persecution. Viewers might deduce that Lipton meant to represent these physical bodies as temporary shells, a concept widely shared across many religions.

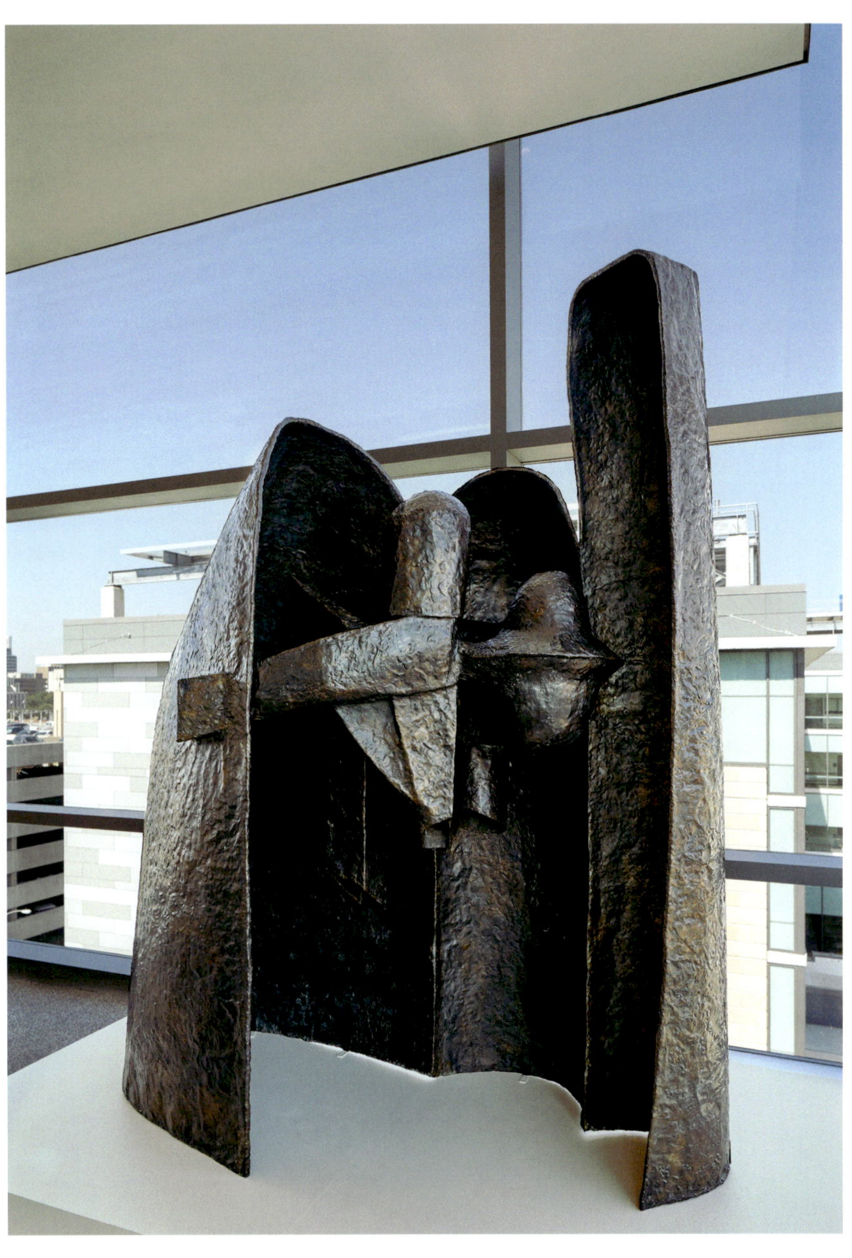

Catacombs, 1968
Nickel-silver on Monel Metal
83 × 68 × 32 inches

Lent by The Metropolitan Museum of Art
Gift of the artist, 1986
1986.276.3

SEYMOUR LIPTON

AMERICAN, 1903–1986

Seymour Lipton, a self-taught artist, found inspiration in nature, machinery, and the human figure. Engaging with the sociological concerns of his time, he wanted to express the emotional, psychological, and spiritual tensions of balancing conflict: "Sculpture is used by me to express the life of man as a struggling interaction between himself and his environment." Lipton developed a style characterized by the tension between curved and straight elements, internal hollows and external shells, and industrial materials and organic forms. He said, "I find 'inner spaces' of man in things outside of himself."

Although *Guardian* presents a totemic figure similar to *Pioneer*, it conveys a more ominous tone. The "body" consists of a solid rectangle below an opening with a hollowed spherical form that suggests a head with a gaping maw, as if roaring an urgent warning. The more intimidating the appearance, the more effective Lipton's pieces are at conveying a sense of protection for the weak against harm, the good against evil. Of his sculptures, the artist said, "Man is still an animal. This was shown to us in the past, but the war showed it up more definitely, more clearly. I used all the means at my disposal … to find images of horror. Subsequently, however, I came to feel that Hell below wasn't the whole story, that man had hope."

Throughout his career, Lipton created a series of monumental, heroic sculptures that express fundamental ideas about human existence—that life is precious but fragile, and that strength is necessary in order to protect it. Despite his dedication to abstraction, Lipton understood his work to be involved in a timeless and universal tradition: "The human figure has always and everywhere been almost synonymous with sculpture. Man has been the exclusive subject for sculptors in every society. He has shaped his gods in his own image."

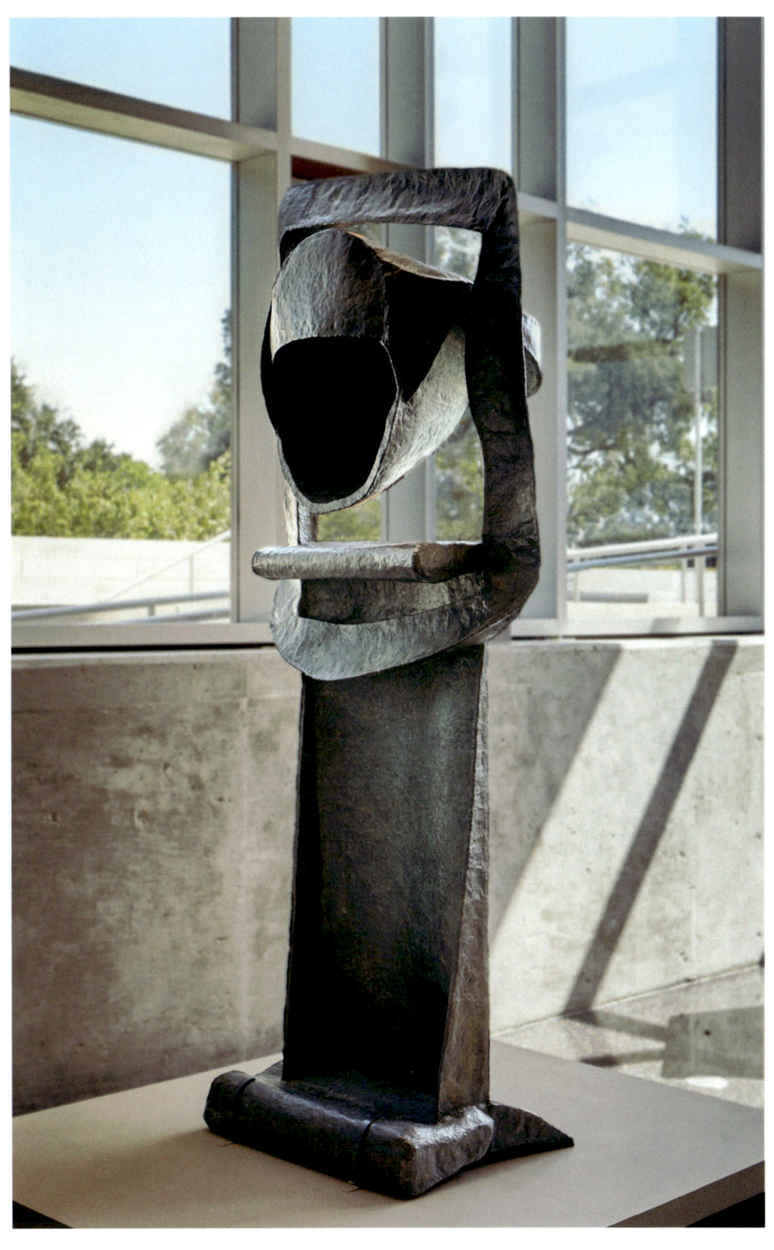

Guardian, 1975
Nickel-silver on Monel Metal
96 ¾ × 39 ¾ × 26 ¼ inches

Lent by The Metropolitan Museum of Art
Gift of the artist, 1986
1986.276.4

BERNARD MEADOWS

BRITISH, 1915–2005

As an undergraduate art student, Bernard Meadows worked in the studio of Britain's preeminent sculptor, Henry Moore (1898–1986), who taught him the value of preliminary drawings and the techniques of direct carving. Many of Meadows' early sculptures reflect Moore's smoothly hewn Surrealist figural style. During World War II, Meadows volunteered for the Royal Air Force, serving in India, Ceylon, and the remote Cocos Islands in the Indian Ocean. The wildlife there became a central inspiration for the sculptures of crabs and birds that preoccupied the artist through the 1950s. These animals served as "human substitutes," he explained, "vehicles [for] expressing my feelings about human beings."

During a trip to Italy in 1960, Meadows studied Renaissance statues of Roman generals and combatants donning heavy armor and weapons. The contrast of outward violence and inner vulnerability seemed to capture the anxious mood of the era when major powers were locked in a cycle of perpetual defense and threat. Inspired, Meadows created a series of twenty armor-clad figures he described as "aggressive, protected, but inside the safety of the shell, they are completely soft and vulnerable."

Augustus refers to the Roman emperor who ushered in the Pax Romana, a period of relative peace from 27 BCE to 14 CE. The sculpture abstracts the human figure with an abbreviated head and arms. The bulk of the figure is a torso wearing a shield of armor that is cracked and broken, indicating the hardships faced during his reign. "I have become interested in the tragedy of damaged figures," Meadows said around the time he created *Augustus*. In contrast to heroic depictions of Roman leaders, the sculpture is transformed into a metaphor for the anxiety of the postwar period.

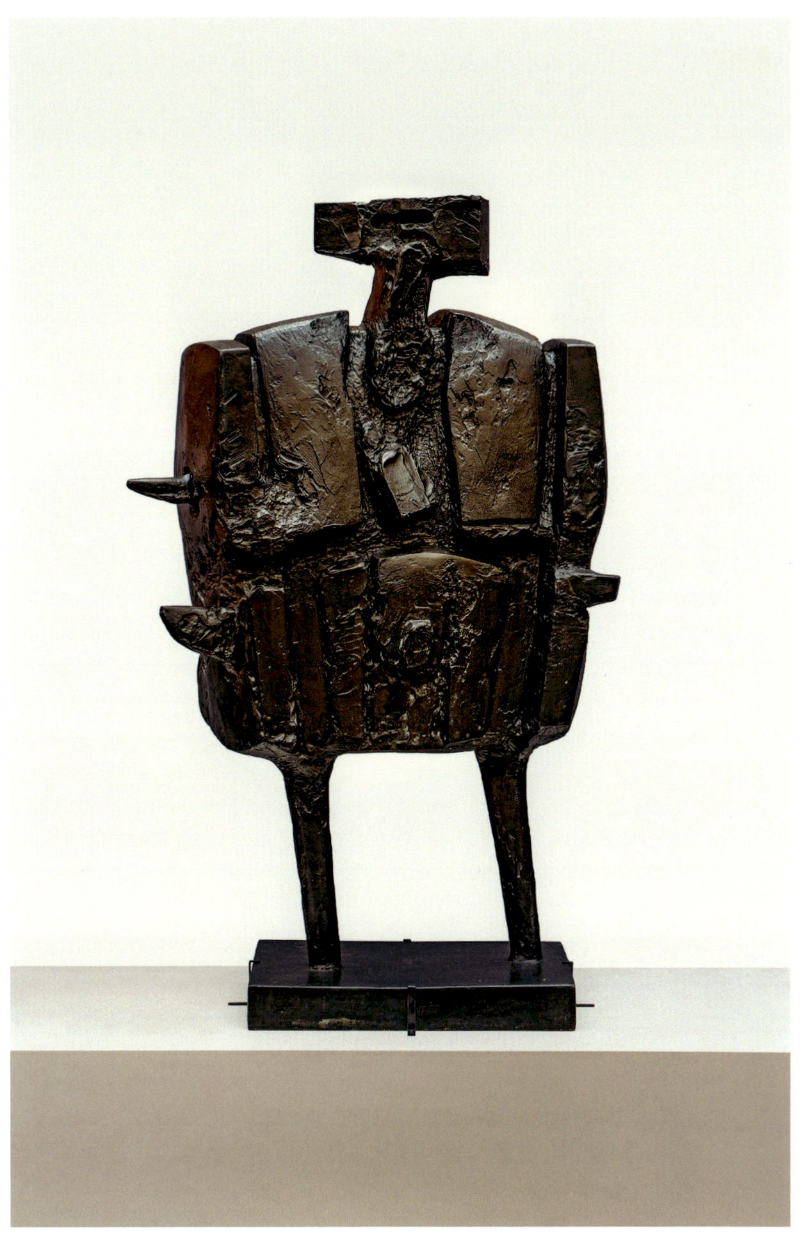

Augustus, circa 1962
Bronze
64 ¾ × 39 ½ × 22 ½ inches

Lent by The Metropolitan Museum of Art
Gift of Genia and Charles Zadok, 1988
1988.120

ROBERT MURRAY

CANADIAN, BORN 1936

A painter and printmaker, Robert Murray made his first sculptures during a formative stay at the Instituto Allende in San Miguel, Mexico, in 1958–59. During the summers of the 1950s and '60s, Murray found himself studying at the Artists' Workshop in Emma Lake, a magnet for abstract artists near his hometown of Saskatoon. At the 1959 session, he met painter Barnett Newman (1905–1970), whose color-field paintings inspired the large, painted steel sculpture Murray made after moving to New York in 1960. "I see them as color configurations," Murray said of his sculpture. "Perhaps because I began as a painter rather than a sculptor, I still tend to think of my sculpture as three-dimensional color." While his works are typically monochromatic, their ridges, folds, and interior spaces interact dynamically with sunlight, producing subtle shifts in hue and luminosity throughout the day.

Murray's creative process begins with small models that he bends, folds, and cuts from cardboard or thin aluminum sheets, which he refers to as three-dimensional drawings. These serve as starting points for full-scale sculptures, which he fabricates in collaboration with the foundry Lippincott Sculpture in North Haven, Connecticut. The final sculptures are not merely enlargements of the maquettes, however, as Murray continues to adjust and refine the work improvisationally during fabrication. His method involves beginning with flat sheets of metal, which he curves and bends using industrial rollers rather than prefabricated shapes. By 1974, Murray's sculptures became more freely formed, with "crunches" and folded edges, almost like paper.

The title *Chilkat* references the northwestern region of the artist's native British Columbia, Canada. The Chilkat River flows fifty-three miles from the Chilkat Glacier to the Chilkat Inlet. The area was named for the indigenous inhabitants, a branch of the Tlingit people, who are renowned for their carvings and weavings.

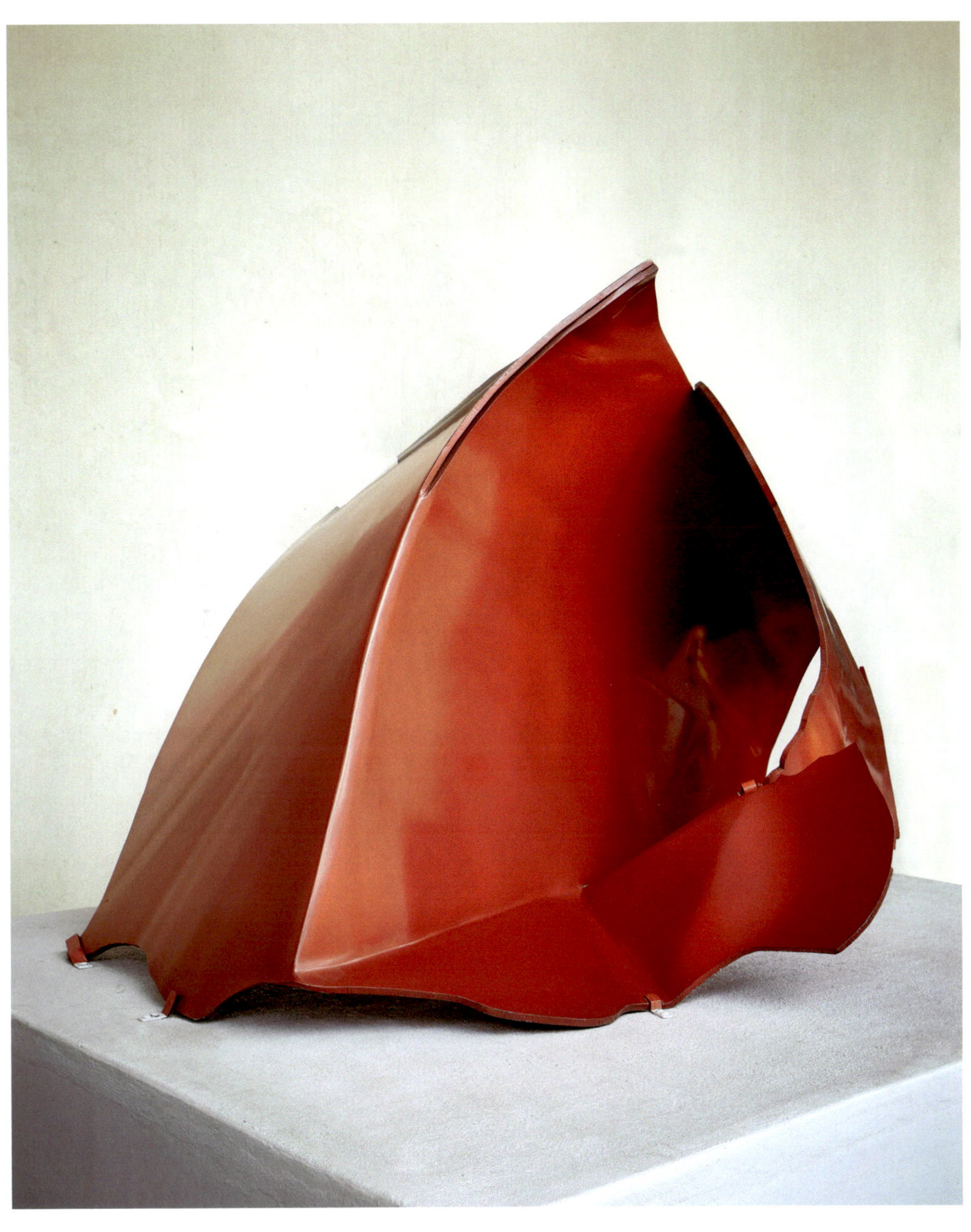

Chilkat, 1977
Painted aluminum
51 × 61 × 81 inches

Lent by The Metropolitan Museum of Art
Purchase, Anonymous Gifts, 1978
1978.83

SARAH OPPENHEIMER

AMERICAN, BORN 1972

New York-based artist Sarah Oppenheimer creates works of art that alter the built environment and shift our frame of spatial reference. Pushing the boundaries between sculpture and architecture, Oppenheimer questions the limits of both mediums, upending our experience of inside and out, and inverting our sense of what is near and far. By reorienting the spaces we inhabit, the artist sets out to reconfigure the way we see and are seen.

With an MFA in painting from Yale University, Oppenheimer operates within the disciplines of mechanical, structural, and behavioral engineering. This interdisciplinary approach makes *C-010106* ideally situated between two buildings at the Cockrell School of Engineering.

At each end of the footbridge, a pair of diagonal reflective glass plates are sandwiched between a pair of clear glass sheets. At the intersection of the four panes, the glass passes through an incision in the bridge. The reflective surfaces within this space create unexpected views, enabling pedestrians on top of the bridge to see the reflections of those underneath, and vice versa.

Bridges typically serve as connectors between spaces and people by making travel more efficient. Oppenheimer disrupts this functionality by installing glass forms aligned with the bridge's north/south and east/west axes, creating a "switch" that interrupts the flow of traffic and the habits of movement. As a result, *C-010106* introduces new relationships between people and heightens awareness of the shifting light, sound, and seasons that surround us.

Oppenheimer names each work of art using a system that describes the relationships between the art and its surroundings. The title *C-010106* begins with *C* as shorthand for cinema, which the artist defines as the way an image is perceived as a projection on a flat surface. The remaining numbers indicate additional characteristics such as position, sight lines, and boundaries.

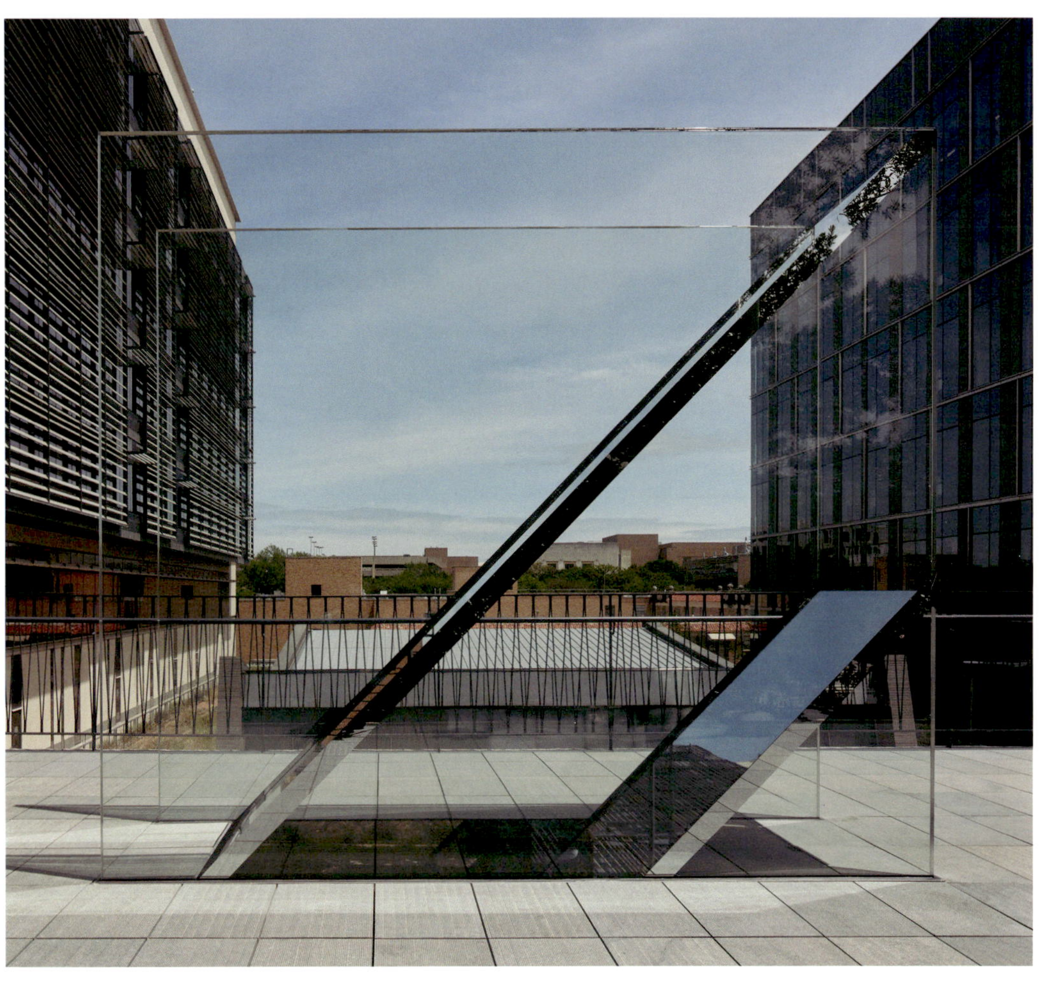

C-010106, 2022
Aluminum, steel, glass, and architecture
Two forms: 191 × 124 × 34 inches and
156 × 124 × 34 inches

Commission, Landmarks, The University of
Texas at Austin, 2022

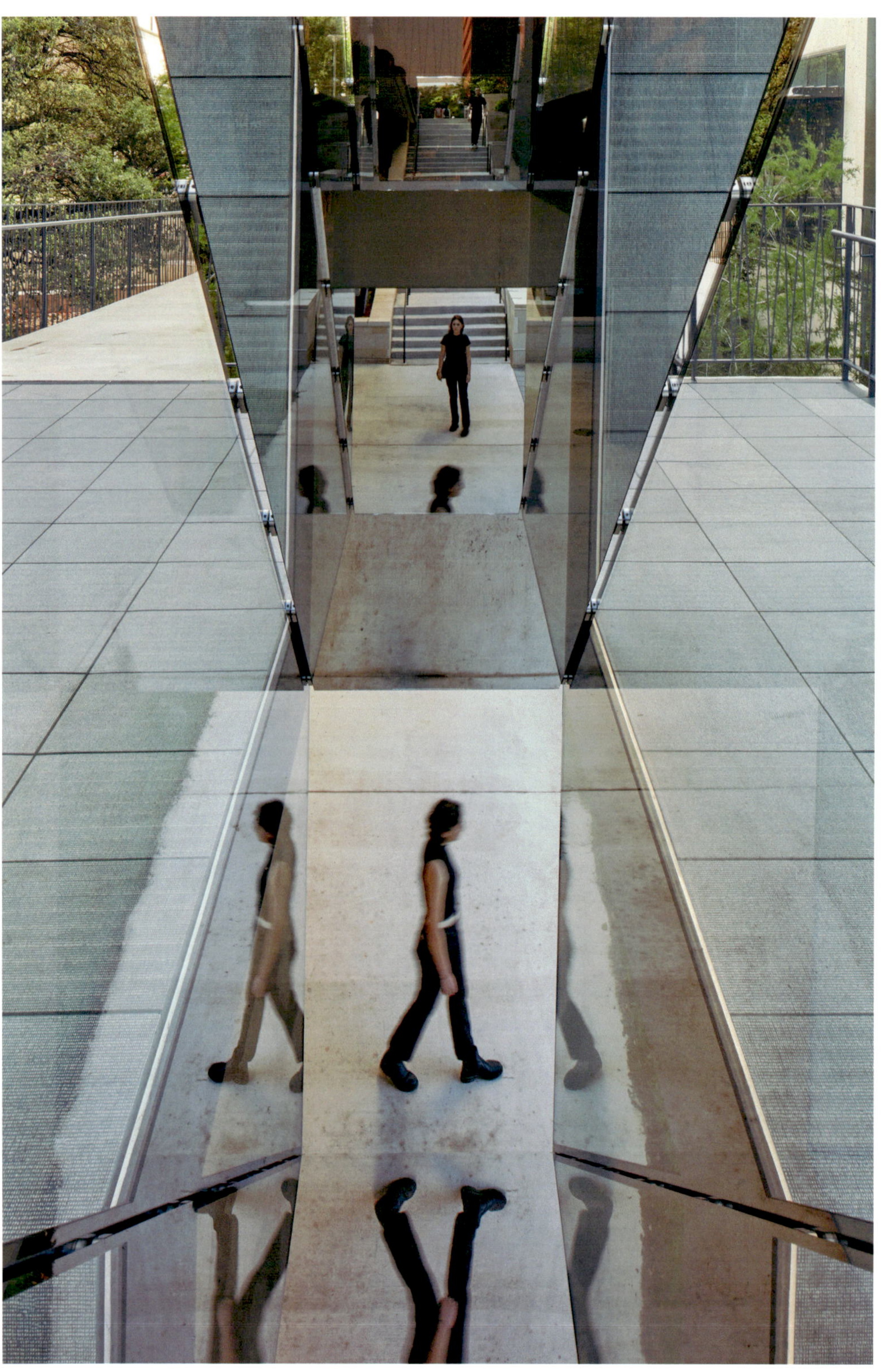

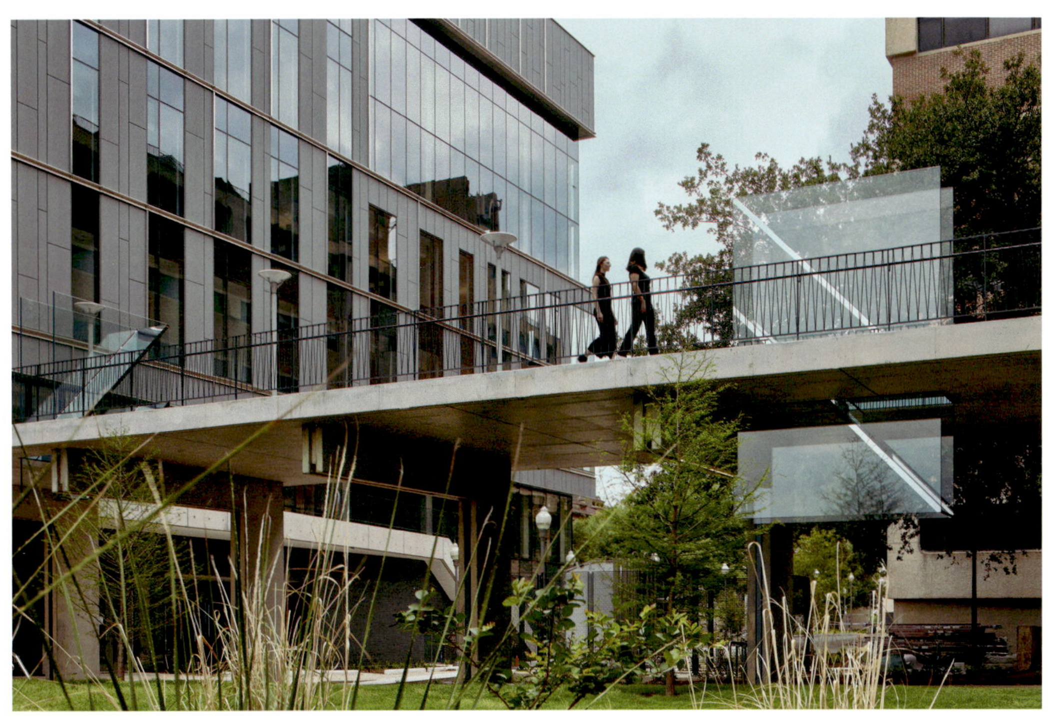

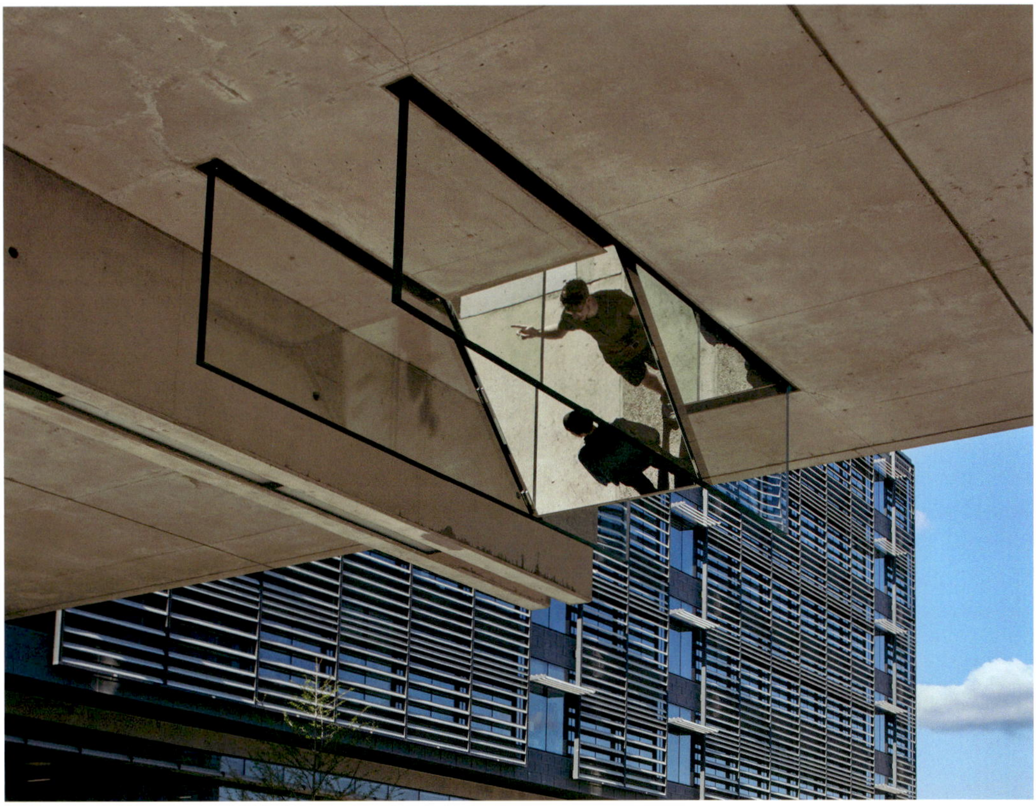

EAMON ORE-GIRON

AMERICAN, BORN 1973

Los Angeles-based artist Eamon Ore-Giron is interested in exploring the intersections of different cultures and identities. He is deeply connected to the Latinx community and challenges the erasure of its stories from art history and the broader North American public sphere. Drawing from a broad range of artistic movements and traditions, he produces a fresh visual language that creates new meanings as well as unexpected connections between European, pre-Columbian, contemporary Indigenous, and popular Latin American influences.

Ore-Giron created *Tras los ojos (Behind the Eyes)* for the university's Department of Psychology. The art began as a small painting later reproduced as a large digital print on canvas. Its design was partly inspired by ophthalmological diagrams illustrating how visual information is processed.

The artist's personal history also influenced his decision to focus on the eye. At age twenty-eight, he noticed a small black spot in his vision. Initially dismissing it as temporary, he later discovered it was a genetic condition shared with his father. This condition played a pivotal role in his family's decision to emigrate to the United States instead of settling in Peru. The experience encouraged Ore-Giron to reflect on the role of anatomy in our perception of reality.

While *Tras los ojos (Behind the Eyes)* employs the vocabulary of hard-edged geometric abstraction, it also references the natural world. The work's palette of rich, solid colors evokes the moments before sunset, with a series of conical shapes and gradient rays in shades of purple, sky blue, and pale pink. Ore-Giron describes the gently curving lines at the top of the work as "the stratosphere of the painting," and "the edge of the atmosphere where things start to bend." The result is a striking metaphor for the flow of information between the external world and the mind.

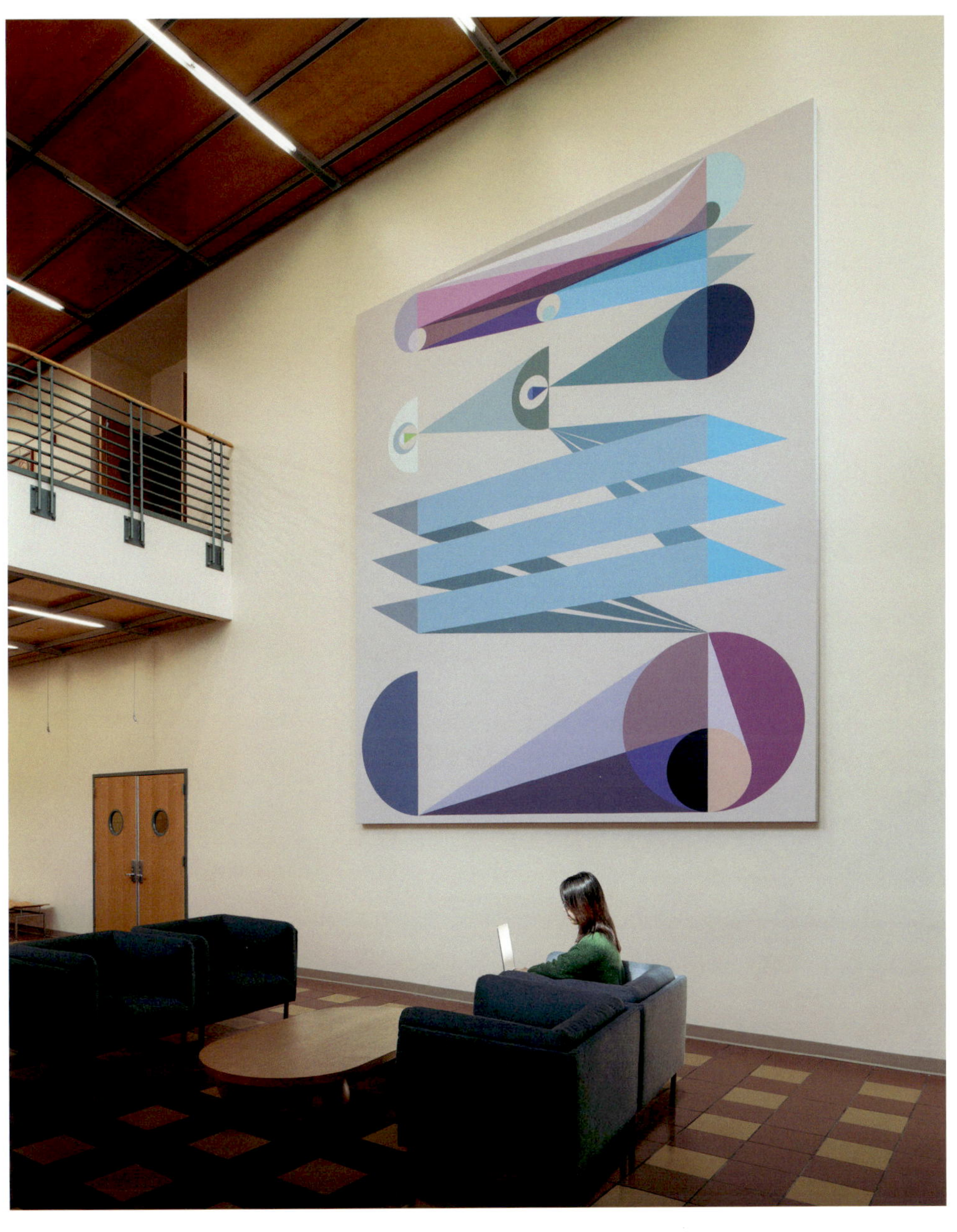

Tras los ojos (Behind the Eyes), 2023
Digital print on canvas
187 × 156 inches

Commission, Landmarks, The University of Texas at Austin, 2023

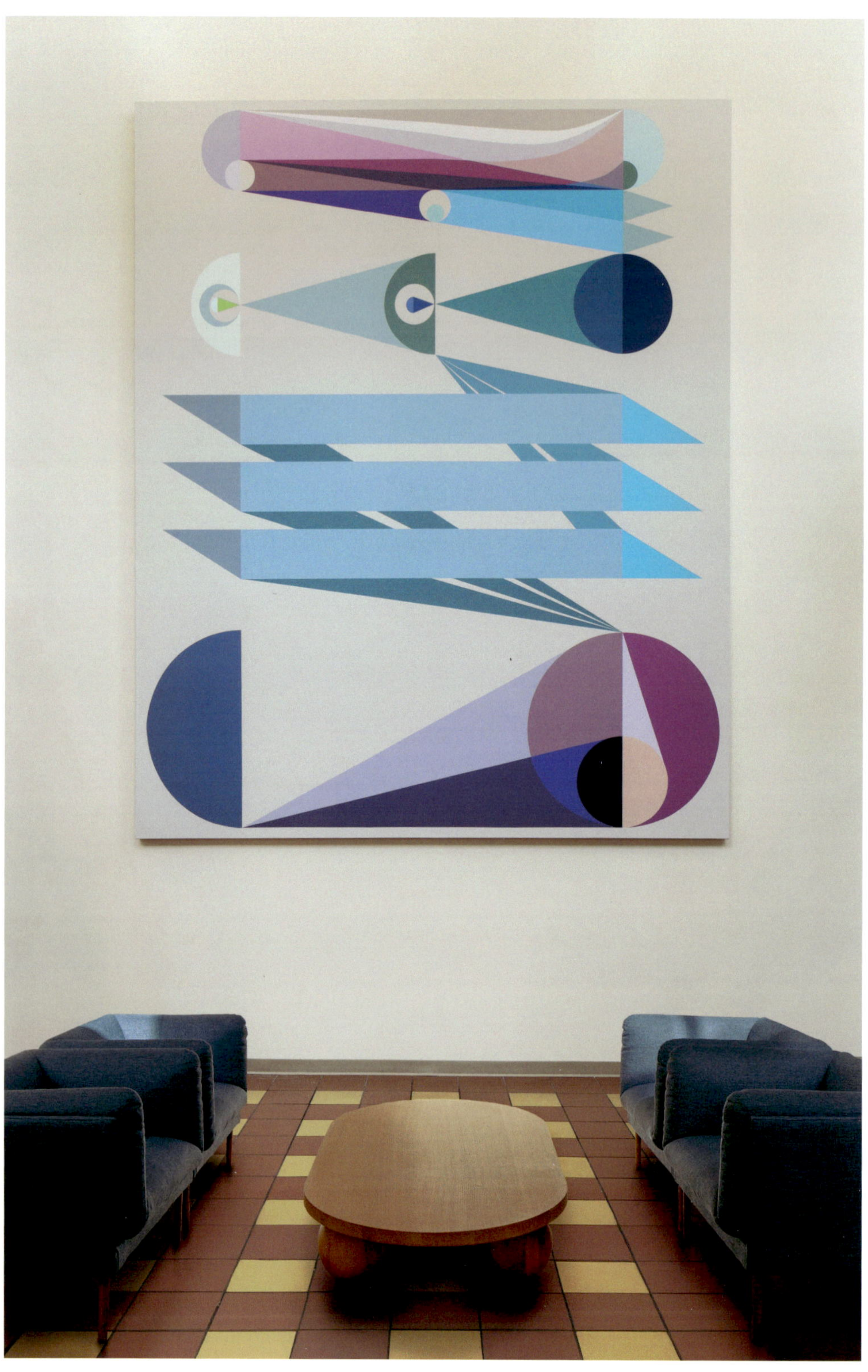

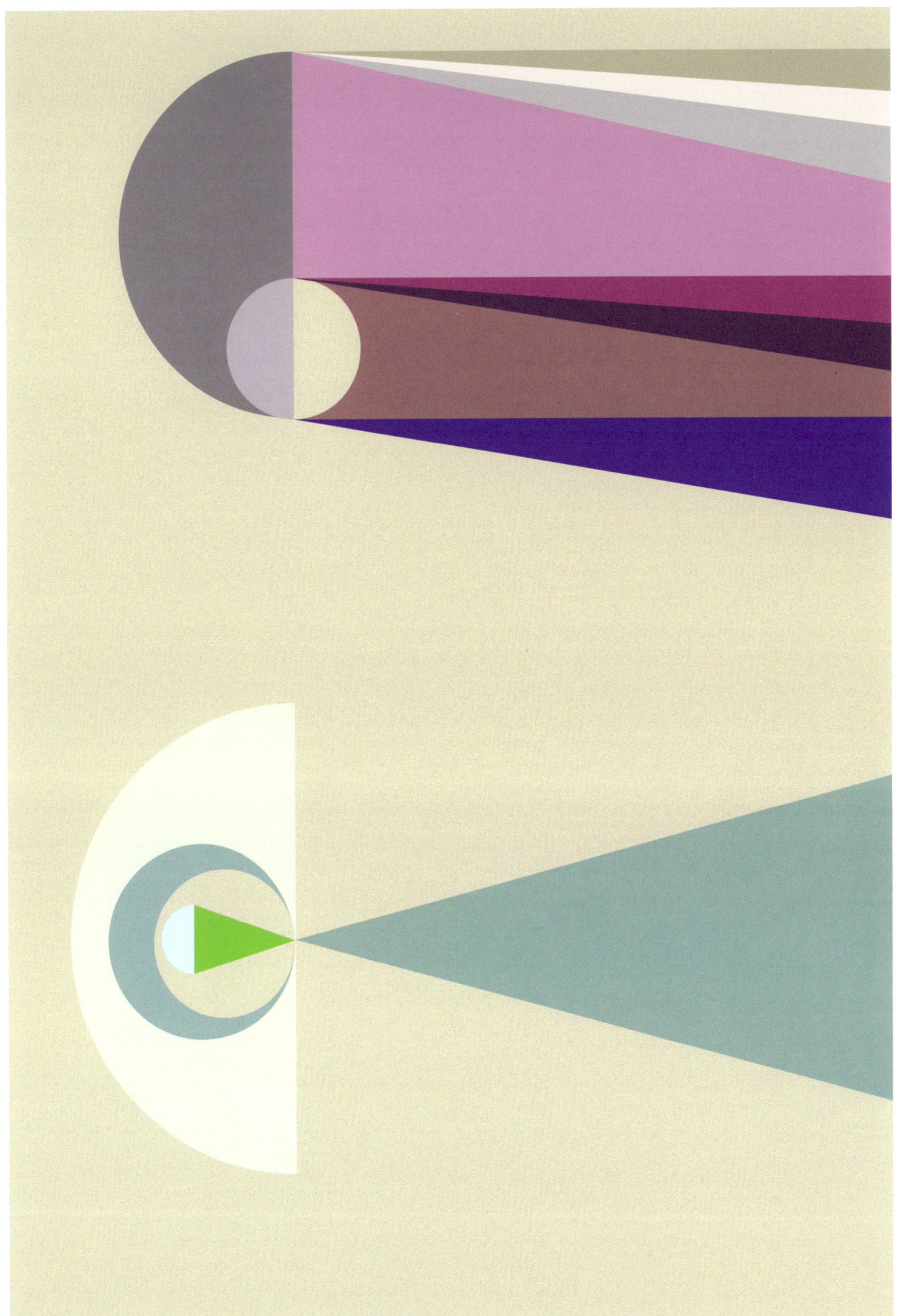

EDUARDO PAOLOZZI

BRITISH, 1924–2005

Like Bernard Meadows (1915–2005), Eduardo Paolozzi was deeply affected by the politics and circumstances of World War II. Before the war, he studied at London's Slade School of Art, where he absorbed the ideas of Surrealist artists and writers. Advances in technology and the mechanization of cultural production preoccupied Paolozzi. He began to express these issues through collage, a technique favored by Dada and Surrealist artists for its ability to provoke both intellectual and psychological responses. Shortly after the war, Paolozzi made a series of collages combining pictures of classical sculptures with images of modern machines. The works are an expression of the turmoil caused by the old European order colliding with the new technological world.

One of Paolozzi's significant innovations was translating the aesthetic of collage into sculpture. In *Figure* and related works from the 1950s, he gathered discarded machine parts and technological components, pressing them into slabs of wax. After casting these in bronze, he stacked the pieces atop one another and welded them together into semiabstract, robot-like figures. With their uncanny, futuristic appearances, Paolozzi's figures seem at once recognizable and unfamiliar.

Paolozzi's sculptures relate to the emergence of cybernetics in the arts, literature, philosophy, and science. The idea of automata (humanlike machines) had appeared in science fiction in tandem with the increasing use of machines during the Industrial Revolution of the nineteenth century. In stories, robots were often viewed as ominous: anthropomorphic yet inhuman; intelligent yet soulless; an uncontrollable threat to human supremacy. After World War II, scientists began publishing accounts of efforts to merge electronics with human capabilities, making the robots of science fiction seem feasible. Combining humanoid appendages and machined parts, Paolozzi's bionic *Figure* appears like a prototype for a future cyborg.

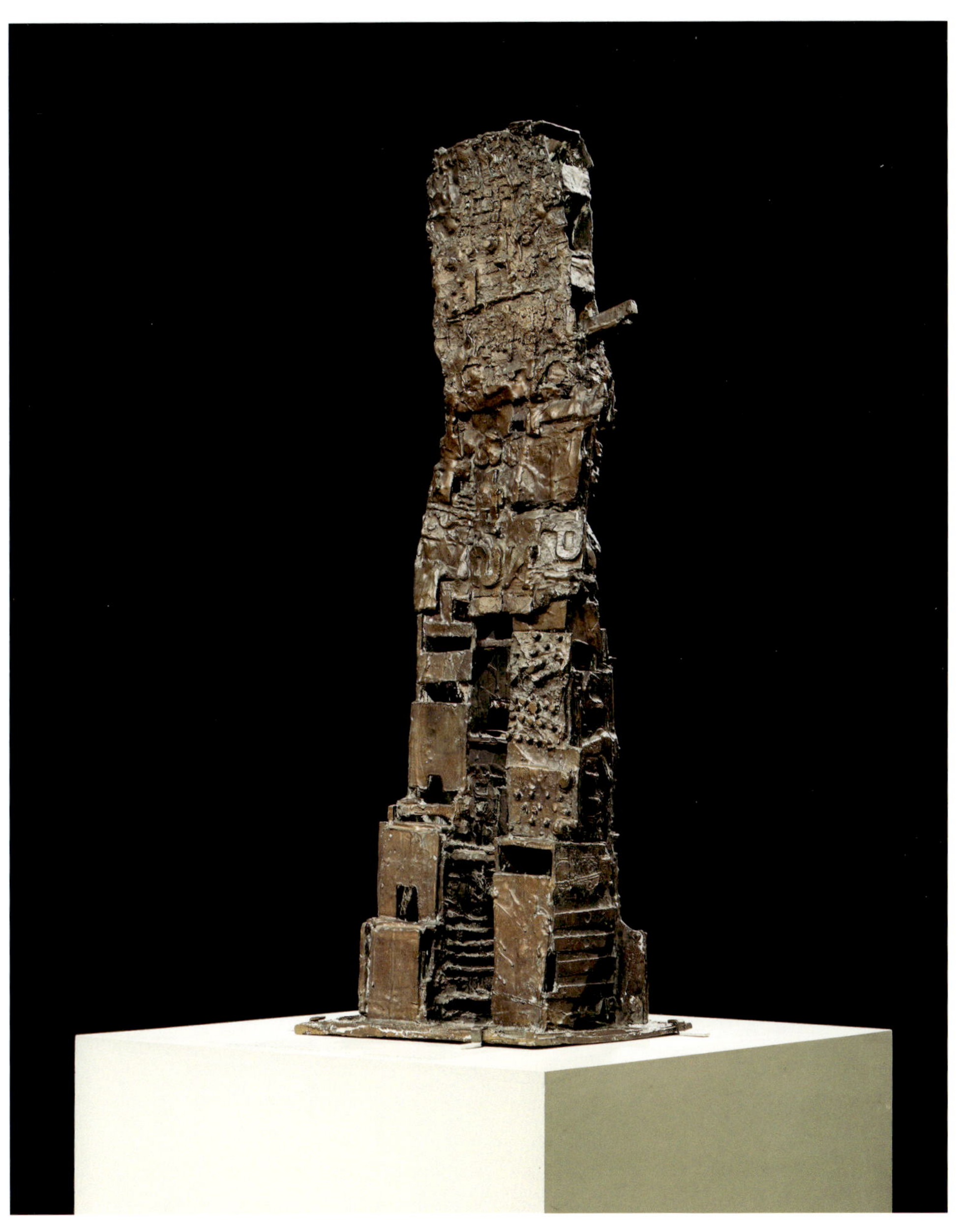

Figure, circa 1957
Bronze
36 ¼ × 12 ⅜ × 10 ½ inches

Lent by The Metropolitan Museum of Art
Gift of Margaret H. Cook, 1996
1996.439

JOSÉ PARLÁ

AMERICAN, BORN 1973

Multimedia artist José Parlá finds inspiration in the history and experience of urban environments. His work is characterized by exuberant compositions featuring multilayered, viscous surfaces with dense pigments and overlapping calligraphic arcs. *Amistad América* is composed of these elements with a scale and metaphoric complexity that is unprecedented.

Parlá began painting as an adolescent, experimenting with graffiti and learning lessons that would inform his mature artistic practice. In addition to mastering the technical agility and sheer speed required for clandestine street painting, Parlá also developed an appreciation for the rigor of physical performance, and an awareness that his body could translate the rhythms of music into visual expressions. Equally significant, he acquired a lifelong affinity for walls: as substrates for painting, as witnesses to history, and as cultural metaphors. In their scarred and decayed surfaces, he perceives humanity's innate drive to make marks, connecting primeval cave paintings to contemporary urban scrawls.

Amistad América renders Austin through Parlá's eyes, with a palette that evokes its vast skies, abundant nature, and pulsing urban core. The painting suggests a continental map that connects Austin to a broader ecology. It also contains obscured fragments of calligraphic letters that form the words *Austin*, *Guadalupe*, and *King*. These not only locate the mural physically at the intersection of Austin's Guadalupe Street and Martin Luther King Jr. Boulevard, but they also symbolically acknowledge the work's position at a place of Latinx and African American history and culture.

The painting offers a sweeping visual landscape that conjures Austin itself while situating the city within the larger geopolitics of the Americas. The title underscores that connection: *La Amistad* was a nineteenth-century Spanish trading ship that plied the Caribbean. Its African slave cargo famously mutinied in 1839 to reclaim their freedom. Parlá chose the title both to commemorate this turbulent history and to celebrate its conciliatory and optimistic resonance: from Spanish, *Amistad América* translates to *Friendship America*.

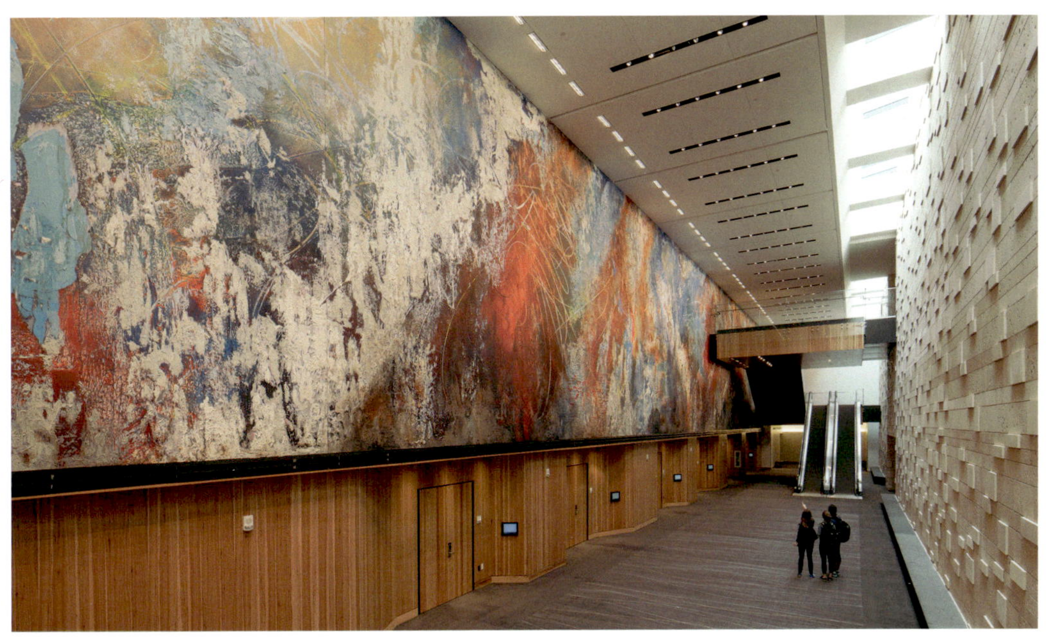

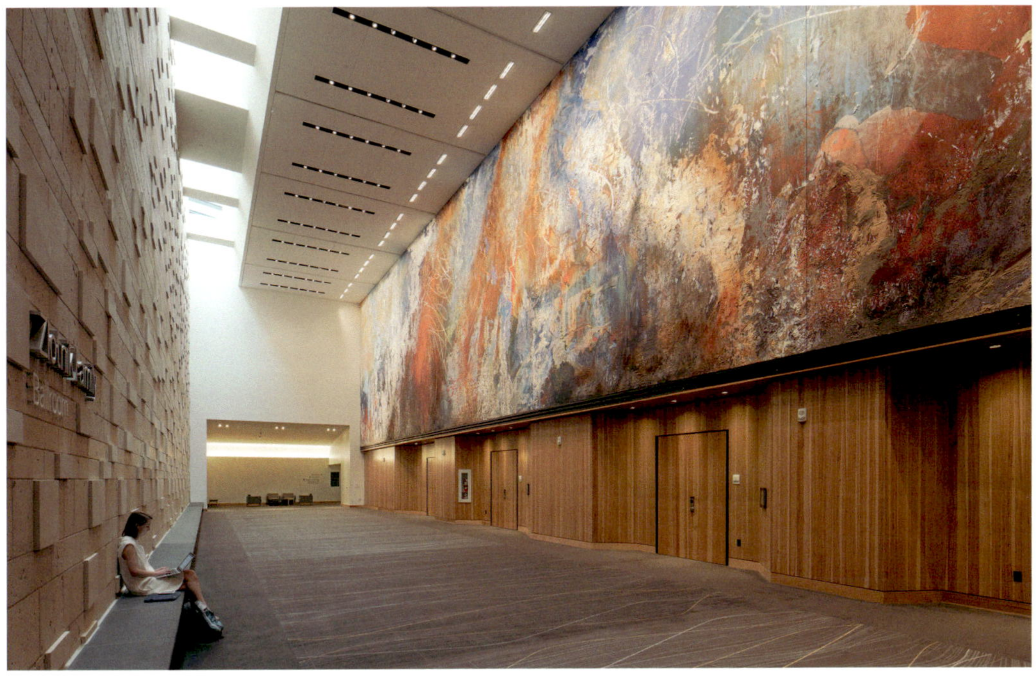

Amistad América, 2018
Acrylic, plaster, and ink on canvas
304 × 1947 ¾ inches

Commission, Landmarks, The University of Texas at Austin, 2018

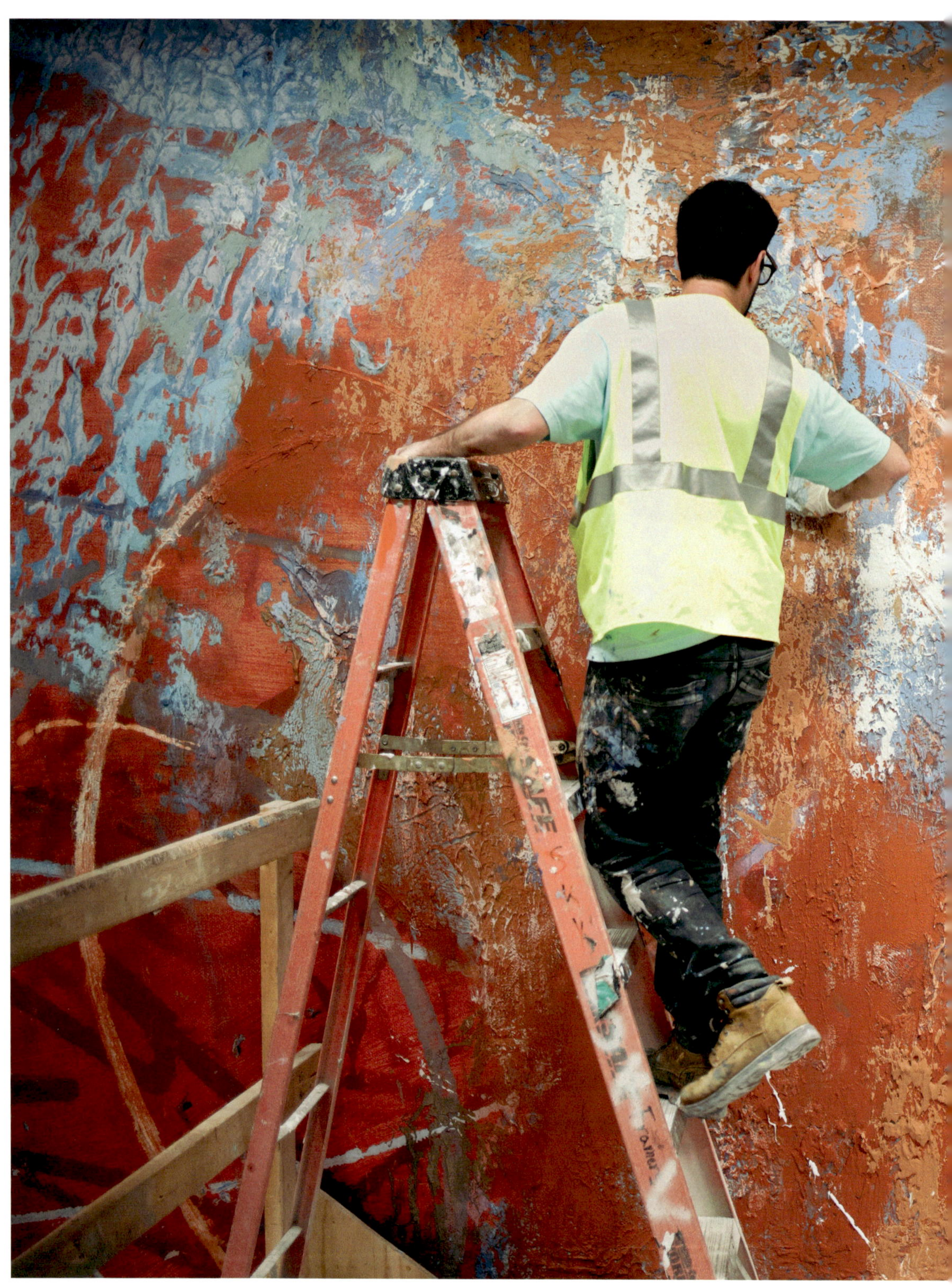

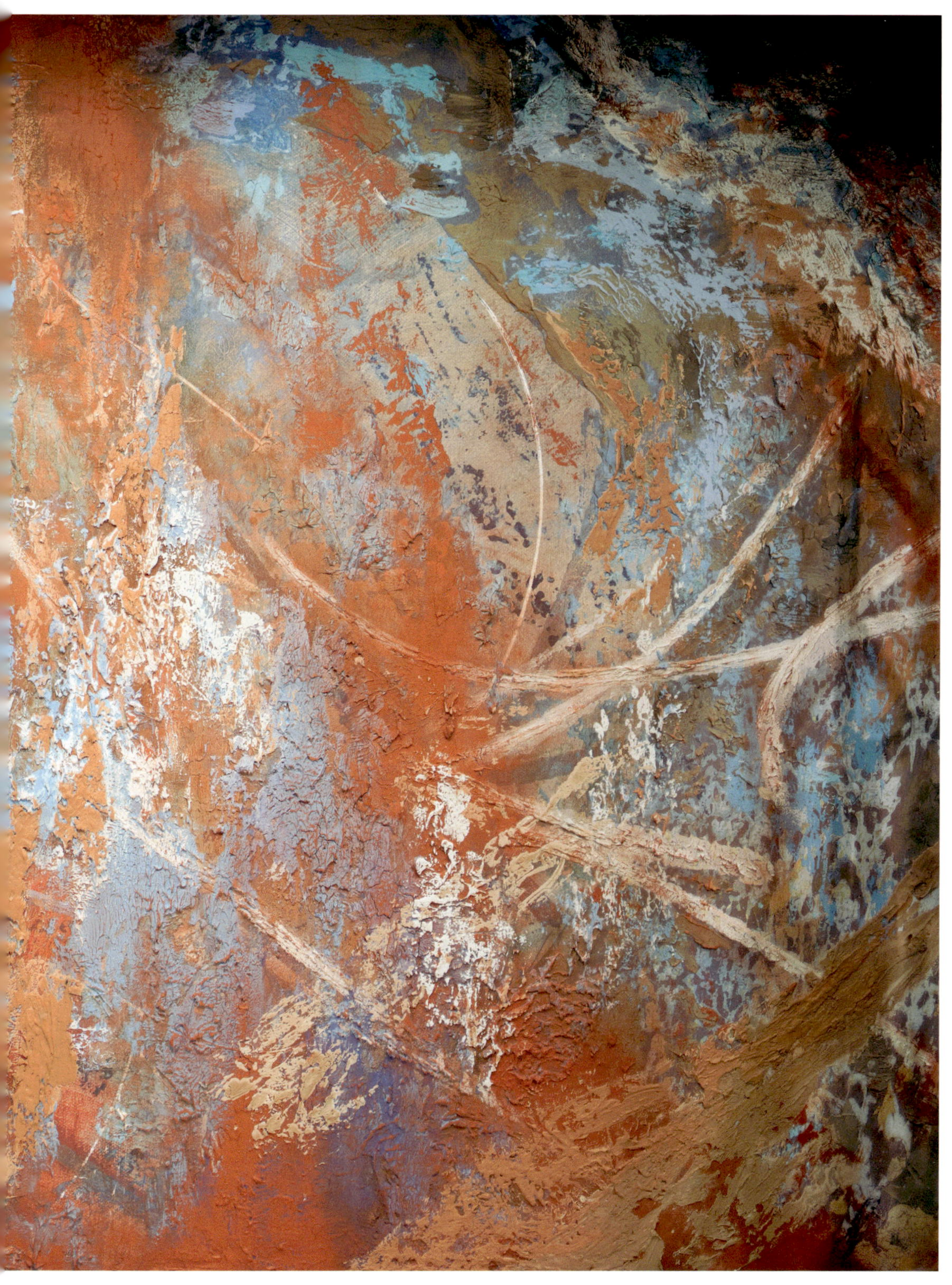

BEVERLY PEPPER

AMERICAN, 1924–2020

Restlessly inventive, Beverly Pepper made significant contributions to postwar sculptural styles and movements. After studying painting and sculpture in Paris following World War II, Pepper settled in Rome in 1950. She worked with clay and wood throughout the 1950s before transitioning to large metal sculptures that feature thin, ribbon-like strands of steel looping and curling through space. By the mid-1960s, she began incorporating geometric forms into her work, such as open, chrome-plated boxes that conveyed a sense of motion, aligning with the emergence of Minimalism.

Pepper was one of ten artists invited to Spoleto, Italy, in 1962 to create sculpture in local steel factories. There, she became friends with pioneering steel sculptor David Smith (1906–1965). Like Smith, Pepper learned to cut and weld large sheets of steel so that she could fabricate her own sculptures.

A leading figure in the Land art movement of the early 1970s, Pepper executed commissions for universities, corporate collections, and public plazas. Her first project, designed for the Northpark Center in Dallas (1971), featured low-lying triangular and pyramidal forms sloping into and out of the ground. Her sensitivity to the environment informed later works, including a group of monumental sculptures constructed in 1979 for the Piazza del Popolo in Todi, Italy. Inspired by Roman landmarks such as the Columns of Trajan and Marcus Aurelius, Pepper constructed four towering steel columns (rising 35 feet tall) that resemble industrial tools. "They're an extension of my hands," she said. "I've always worked with tools. I simply began to transfigure them."

The totemic forms of *Harmonious Triad* developed out of the Todi monuments. Dissatisfied with the color and texture of Corten steel, which was then the most common material used for large-scale sculptures, Pepper experimented with ductile iron at the John Deere Foundry in Illinois. In *Harmonious Triad* and other works from this period, she pioneered its use as a sculptural material. Though its vertical poles may suggest the human figure, Pepper intended them as pure abstraction.

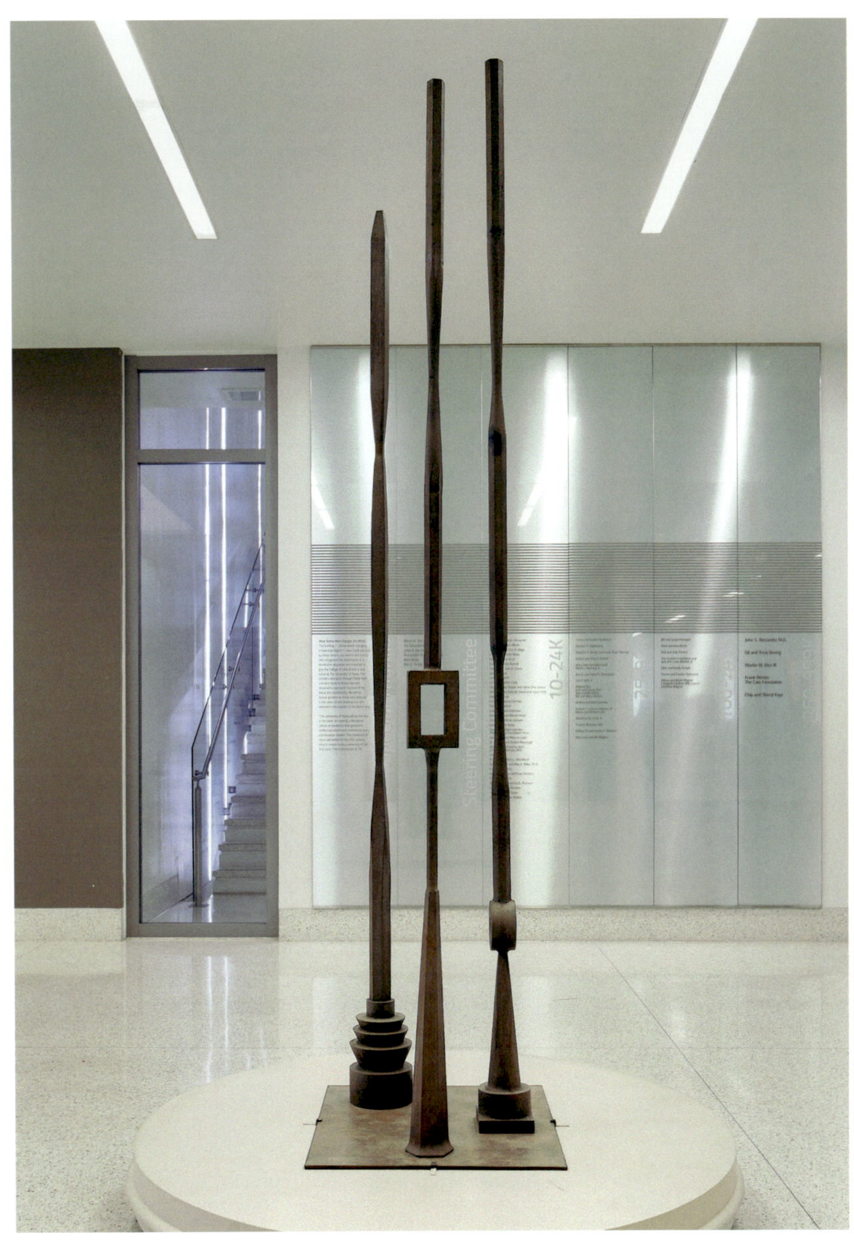

Harmonious Triad, 1982–83
Cast ductile iron
96 × 26 × 24 inches

Lent by The Metropolitan Museum of Art
Gift of Charles Cowles, 1983
1983.521a-d

JOEL PERLMAN

AMERICAN, BORN 1943

Using industrial-grade steel plate to fabricate geometric abstract sculptures, Joel Perlman embraced the purely visual aesthetics championed by critic Clement Greenberg (1909–1994), prioritizing form over subject.

Perlman's works of the 1980s are pictorial, essentially flat arrangements best seen from a frontal viewpoint like a painting. He drew inspiration from the abstract compositions of the vanguard Russian artists Kasimir Malevich (1879–1935) and El Lissitzky (1890–1941). Although created in the 1910s and '20s, their work—characterized by the dynamic energy of geometric forms tilted on a diagonal axis—experienced a resurgence of interest in the 1960s and '70s.

The composition of *Square Tilt* likely draws from the urban architecture of Manhattan, which Perlman could see through his studio windows. While not explicitly representing the soaring cityscape, *Square Tilt* and other works from this period capture the characteristics of the city: powerful, broad, and monumental. Perlman allows the inherent strength and durability of the industrial steel to play a large role in the overall aesthetics.

Square Tilt typifies Perlman's best-known compositions, which employ square or rectangular frames surrounding large openings. The sculpture functions as a window that offers viewers the opportunity to peer through a physical and metaphoric portal. Seen indoors against a blank wall, the work invites appreciation of its abstract vivacity. In other settings, especially outdoors, the large central opening interacts with its environment. *Square Tilt* consequently carries connotations of openness, far horizons, and passage into other domains of perception and thought. Smaller rectangles of steel plates attached to the frame introduce a harmonic interplay of forms. Despite its considerable size, *Square Tilt* conveys an impression of airy weightlessness.

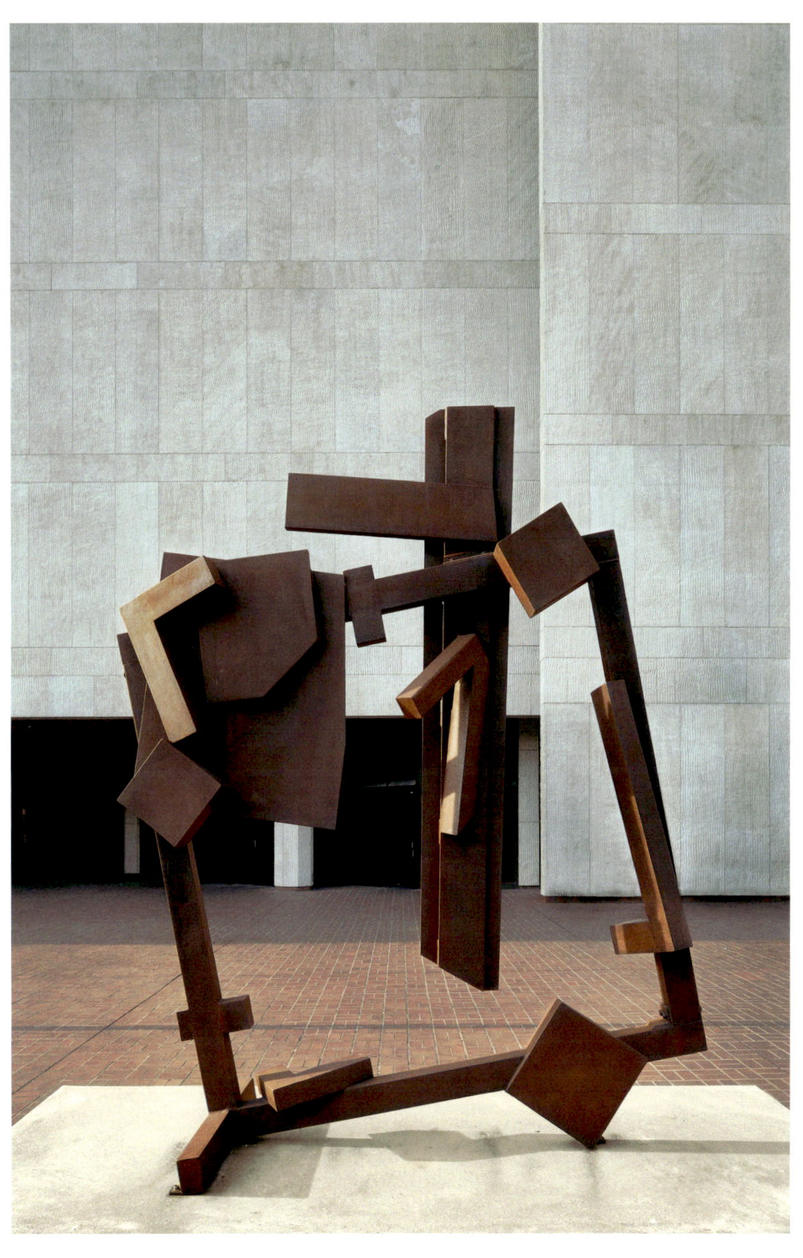

Square Tilt, 1983
Steel
120 × 96 × 36 inches

Lent by The Metropolitan Museum of Art
Gift of Mr. and Mrs. L. William Teweles, 1986
1986.442a-d

ANTOINE PEVSNER

FRENCH, BORN IN RUSSIA, 1886–1962

During a sojourn in Paris from 1911 to 1914, Antoine Pevsner encountered Cubism and Futurism, two radical new approaches to artmaking that favored abstraction over representation. After the Soviet Union withdrew from World War I in 1917 and the threat of conscription had passed, he and his brother, sculptor Naum Gabo (1890–1977), returned to Moscow to participate in the utopian fervor of building a new egalitarian society. Pevsner began sculpting works that could, in theory, be adapted for use in architecture and urban design to serve the public. Influenced by his brother's innovative constructions, Pevsner's sculptures were small in scale due to severe material shortages in the fledgling Soviet Union.

In 1923, Pevsner emigrated permanently to France, where, in the exhilarating art environment of Paris, he joined other artists who embraced the new aesthetics of geometric abstraction. He developed a style based on convex and concave forms, primarily funnel-shaped vortices that seemed to fold into and through one another. He adopted the Futurist emphasis on diagonal linear elements, originally known as "lines of force."

After the devastation and destruction of World War II, Europeans hoped for a lasting peace as they rebuilt their lives and countries. *Column of Peace,* conceived as a maquette for a large memorial that was never completed, consists of intersecting, upwardly rising diagonals. The torsion and projection of these forms create the illusion of elements emerging from and receding into different points in space simultaneously. For viewers familiar with the original utopian meanings underlying abstract art, the sculpture conveys a message of hope for progress.

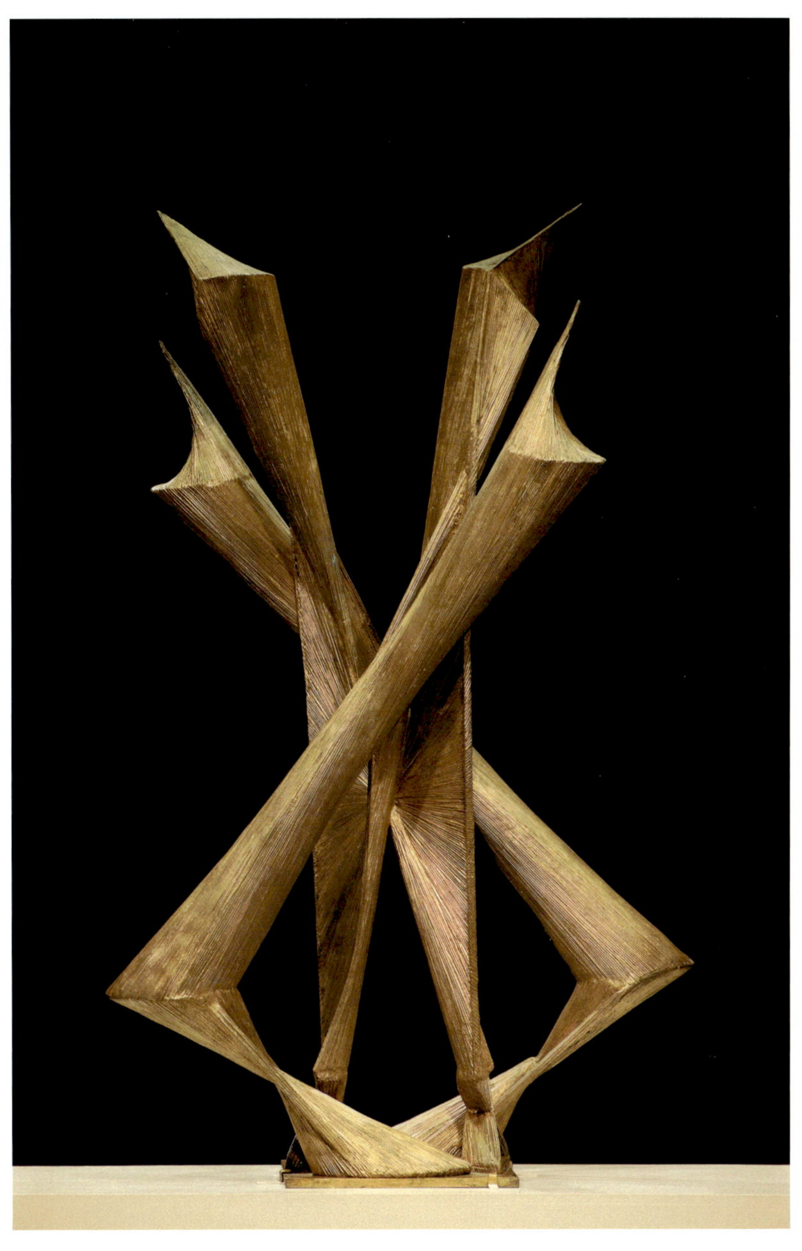

Column of Peace, 1954
Bronze
53 × 35 ½ × 19 ¾ inches

Lent by The Metropolitan Museum of Art
Gift of Alex Hillman Family Foundation,
in memory of Richard Alan Hillman, 1981
1981.326

MARC QUINN

BRITISH, BORN 1964

In his sculptural series *The Archaeology of Art*, Marc Quinn creates monumental forms from seashells. The conch for *Spiral of the Galaxy* is based on a specimen in the British Natural History Museum collection. For Quinn's work, the conch was scanned in three dimensions, then a mold was created and cast into bronze. The resulting figure is familiar in its proportion and surfaces, but strange because it no longer invites intimate handling. Its altered material and scale transform it into a solid, architectural form that occupies public space and interacts with the urban ecosystem.

Quinn first gained public attention in the early 1990s through his affiliation with the Young British Artists (YBAs). Among his earliest and most iconic works is *Self* (1991), a cast of his head made from ten pints of Quinn's frozen blood, an amount equal to the volume in his body. In a 2013 interview, the artist described the YBA movement as focused on "bringing real life into art." In both *Self* and *Spiral of the Galaxy*, Quinn's impulse is holistic and metaphysical, translating the substance of life into image.

Spiral of the Galaxy is easily recognized as a direct descendant of the small shell it models. However, by dramatically altering the material, scale, and surroundings, the shell acquires a mythical quality, quivering between reality and fantasy. Quinn has called seashells "the most perfect pre-existing sculptural 'readymades' in our natural world," referring not only to the graceful intricacy of their forms, but also to the wonder of their natural production.

The sliding scales along which a society measures fragility and strength, ephemerality and endurance, even life and death, are central concerns of Quinn's art. Throughout his career, he has explored the unstable margins of life and the meanings we find in them: the vital interconnectedness of all life forms across time; the desire to still a passing moment or to live forever; and the aspiration to live in harmony with nature and other people.

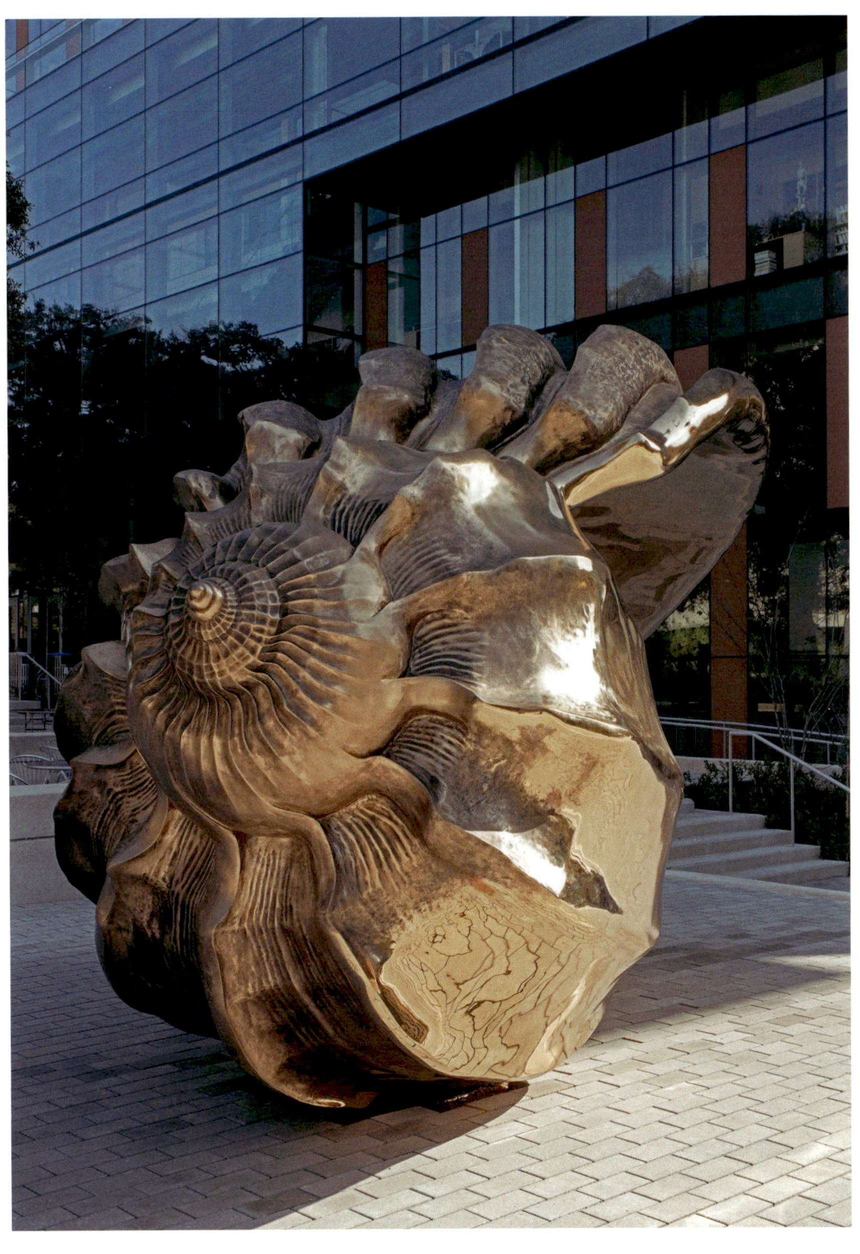

Spiral of the Galaxy, 2013
Bronze
131 × 196 × 100 inches

Purchase, Landmarks, The University of Texas at Austin, 2014

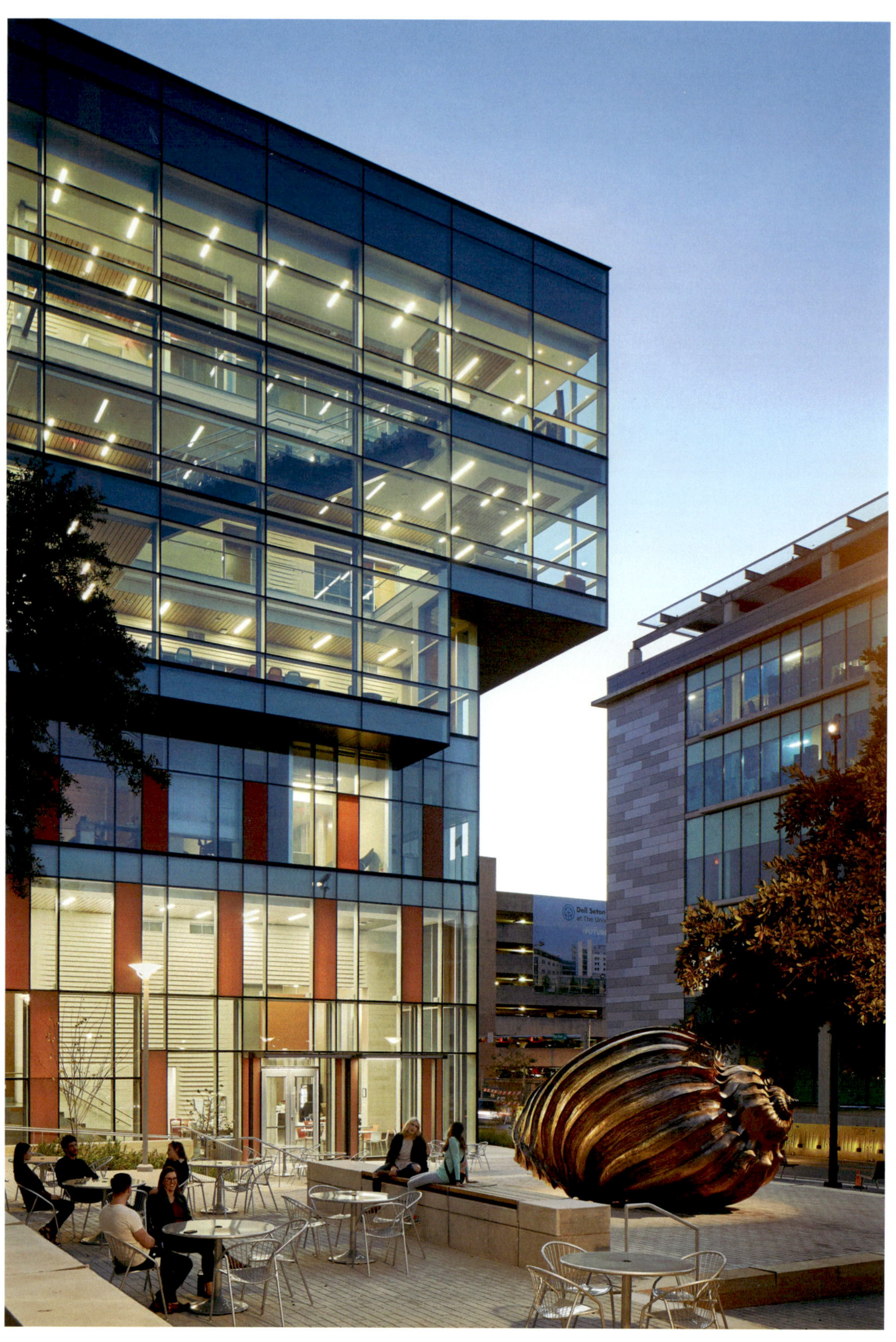
Dell Seton

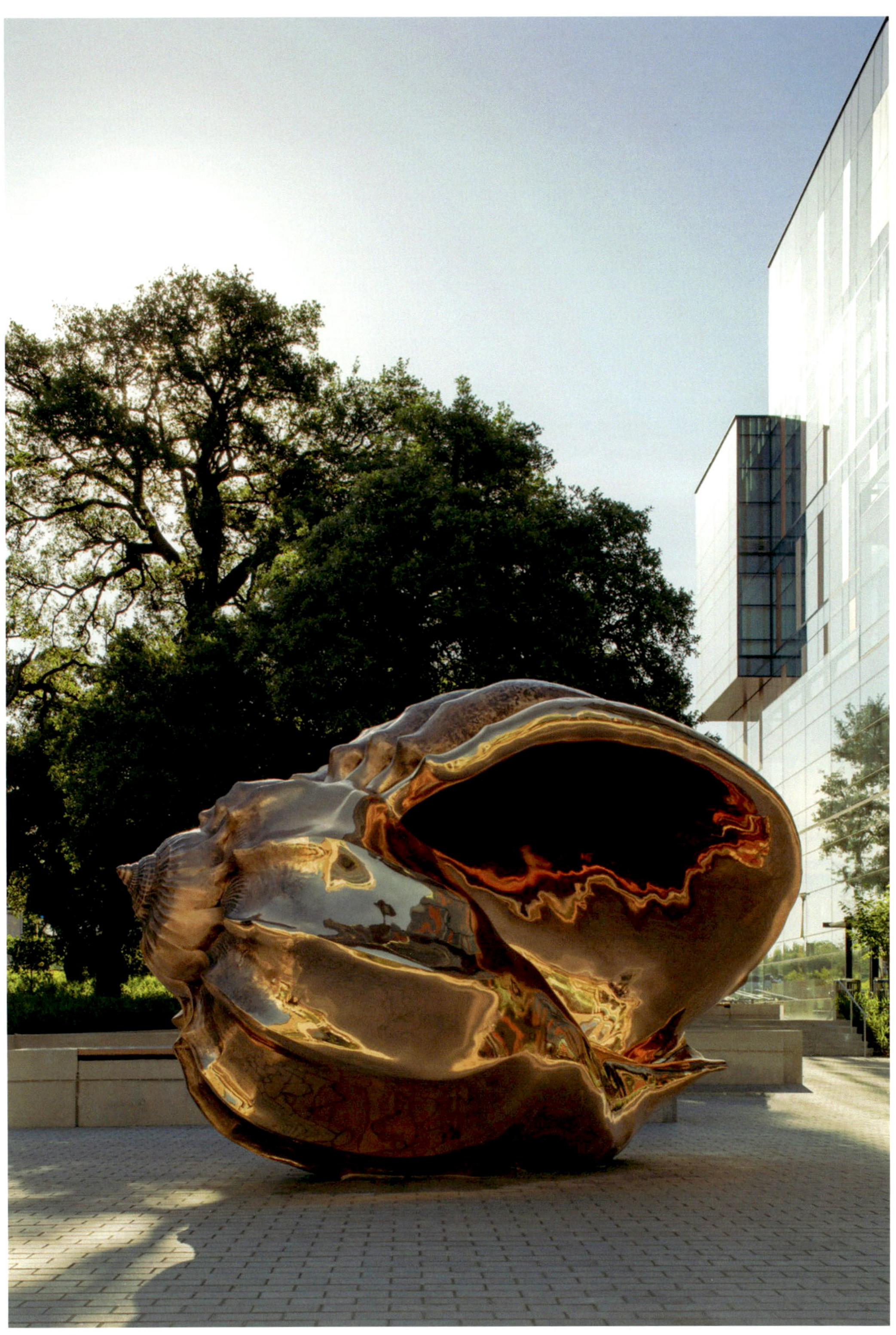

CASEY REAS

AMERICAN, BORN 1972

Casey Reas is a leading artist in the genre of software art, defining both the practice and the theoretical discourse in the field. In 2001, he partnered with fellow MIT student Ben Fry (born 1975) to initiate and create Processing, an open-source programming language and visual environment for coding. Today, artists, designers, and students around the world use Processing for visual prototyping and for programming images, animation, and interactivity.

Reas' software art typically explores systems, specifically their emergence and underlying instructions and conditions. Instructions form the basis of all generative art, in which an autonomous system—such as a machine or computer program—creates a work of art based on rules outlined by the artist. The instruction-based nature of software art points to art-historical roots in Conceptual art. Reas explicitly references the work of Sol LeWitt, who generated works through a set of written instructions for others to interpret.

A Mathematical Theory of Communication blends Conceptual art and information science by merging aspects of both in order to create an experiential data landscape. For this commission, Reas captured television images with an antenna, then processed the images using algorithms—or "instructions"—he designed. The abstracted images were processed again, generating some forty thousand results, from which Reas chose two perspectives with converging energy. The images were inkjet printed to create the mural on two walls.

The title of this piece references a highly influential article (1948) by Claude Shannon, considered one of the founding texts of information theory. Shannon proposed that messages are transformed into a signal by a transmitter, then sent through a channel, decoded by a receiver, and finally delivered to a destination. Reas adopted the title to capture the visual and conceptual theory of communication unfolding in his art, emphasizing that as viewers, we become receivers who decode the imagery. While the title of the work suggests a technologically or scientifically driven exploration, the project itself is highly visual, conceptual, and experiential.

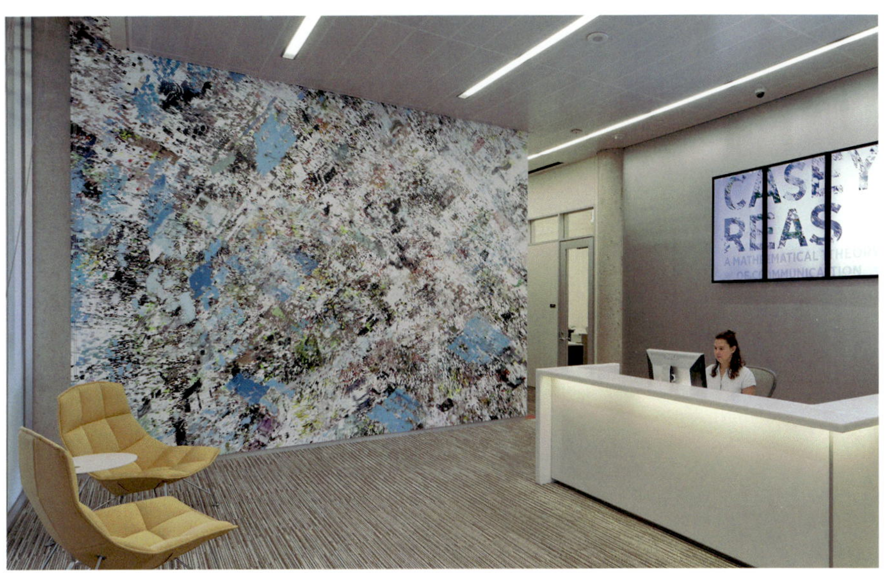

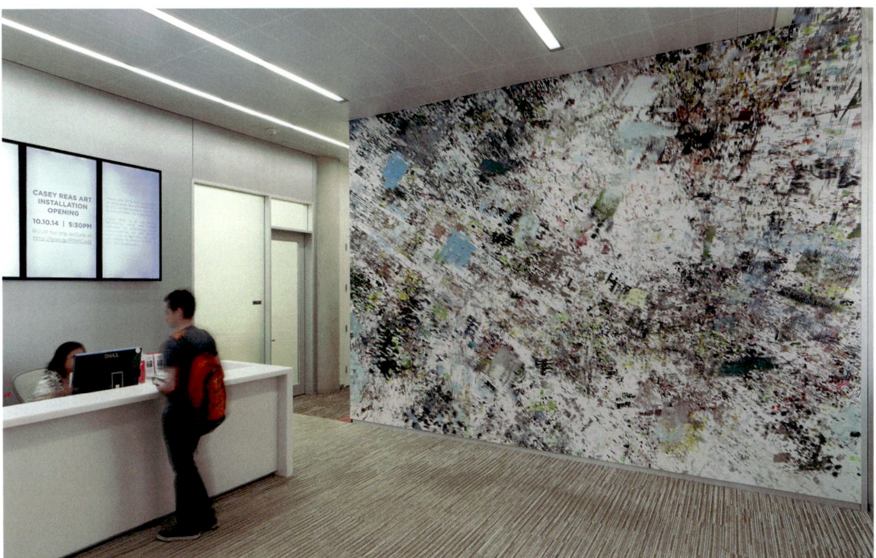

A Mathematical Theory of Communication, 2014
Inkjet print
Two walls: 167 × 198 ¼ inches;
167 ½ × 190 ¾ inches

Commission, Landmarks, The University of Texas at Austin, 2014

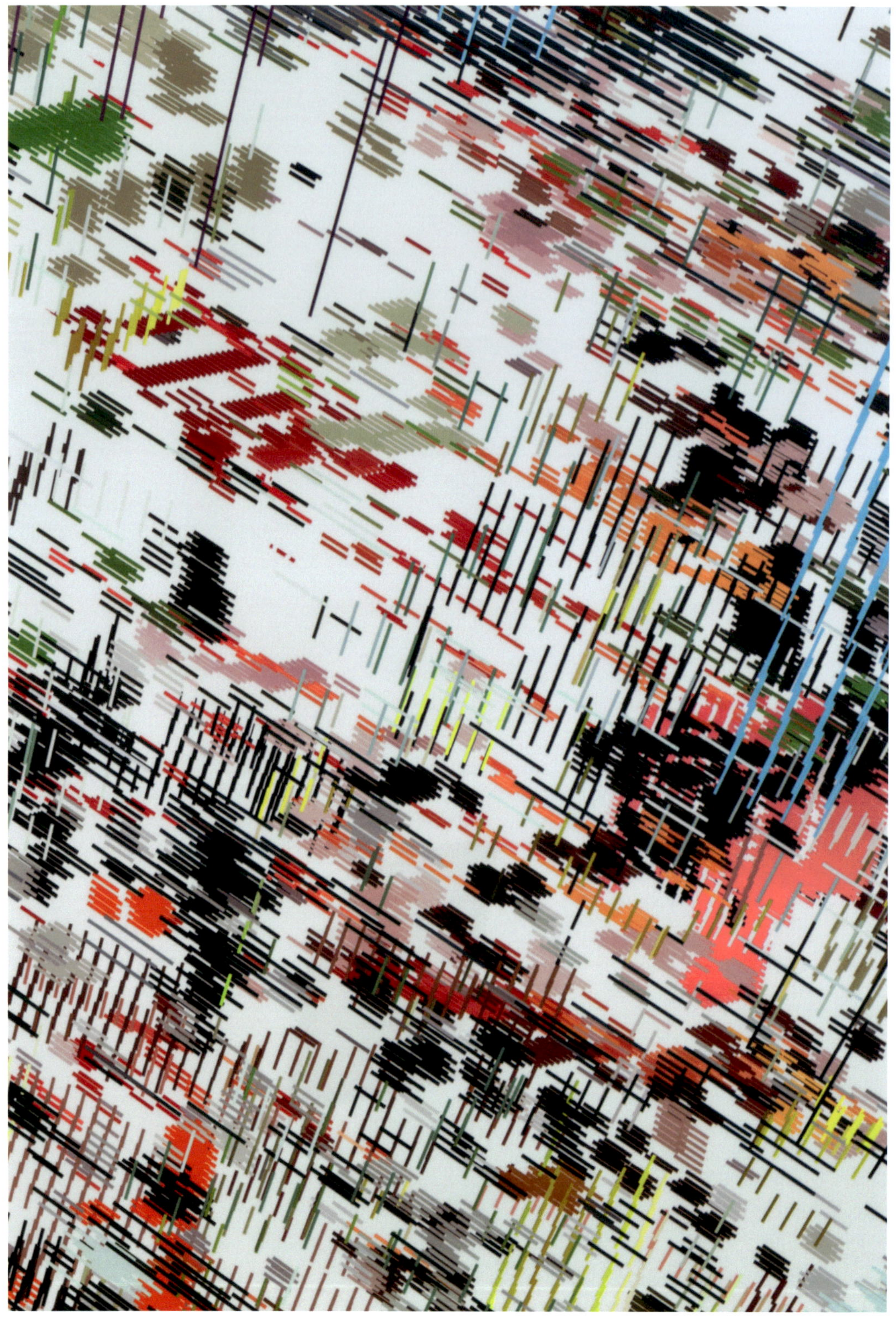

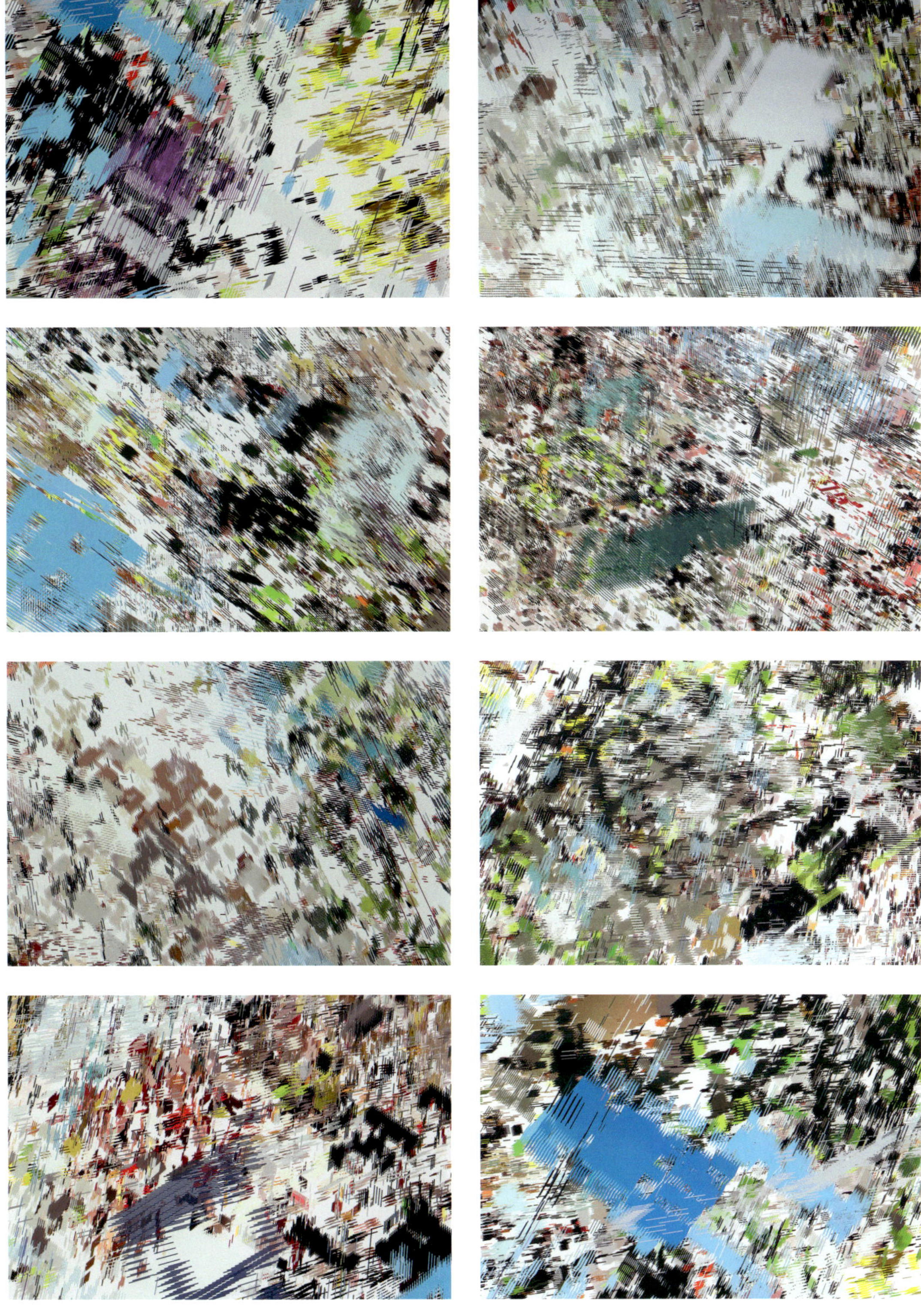

PETER REGINATO

AMERICAN, BORN 1945

In the late 1960s, when the modernist aesthetic of geometric abstraction dominated sculpture, Peter Reginato found such rigid shapes impersonal and lacking individuality. Instead, he embraced the dynamic energy of organic forms, drawing inspiration from artists like Alexander Calder (1898–1976), Julio González (1876–1942), Pablo Picasso (1881–1973), and David Smith (1906–1965). Reginato began by sketching fluid shapes on sheet metal, which he cut with a blowtorch and joined with spot welds. These combined pieces appeared to float in a delicate, rhythmic dance. His goal was to translate the spontaneity of drawing into three dimensions: "I like to think that all my rippling, swelling forms could easily be flying wildly in space." His bold use of color further animated these lively forms.

Lowery Stokes Sims, the curator who acquired Reginato's work for the Metropolitan Museum of Art, noted, "Peter Reginato defied the modernist strictures of truth to materials and form by using color and sensuous, biomorphic shapes, even evoking content." She compared his approach to the work of artists of color who forged art reflecting identity and cultural nuance, and to women who elevated craft and domestic arts in the context of fine art. By distancing himself from both Minimalism and Pop Art, Reginato created works full of vitality with uplifting spirit. As he once remarked, "Essentially, my work is joyous."

The title *Kingfish* pays tribute to Tim Moore, an actor and comedian best known for portraying George "Kingfish" Stevens on the controversial television show *Amos 'n' Andy* (1951–53). Moore, one of the first African American television celebrities, had a long career in vaudeville and radio. However, *Amos 'n' Andy* was criticized for its racist caricatures, leading to its cancellation after protests from the NAACP. In 2019, Reginato added the subtitle *An Homage to Tim Moore* to acknowledge the complexities surrounding Moore's role and the show's legacy. The sculpture invites reflection on America's history of racial representation and the evolving interpretations of cultural artifacts, offering a nuanced lens on these entanglements.

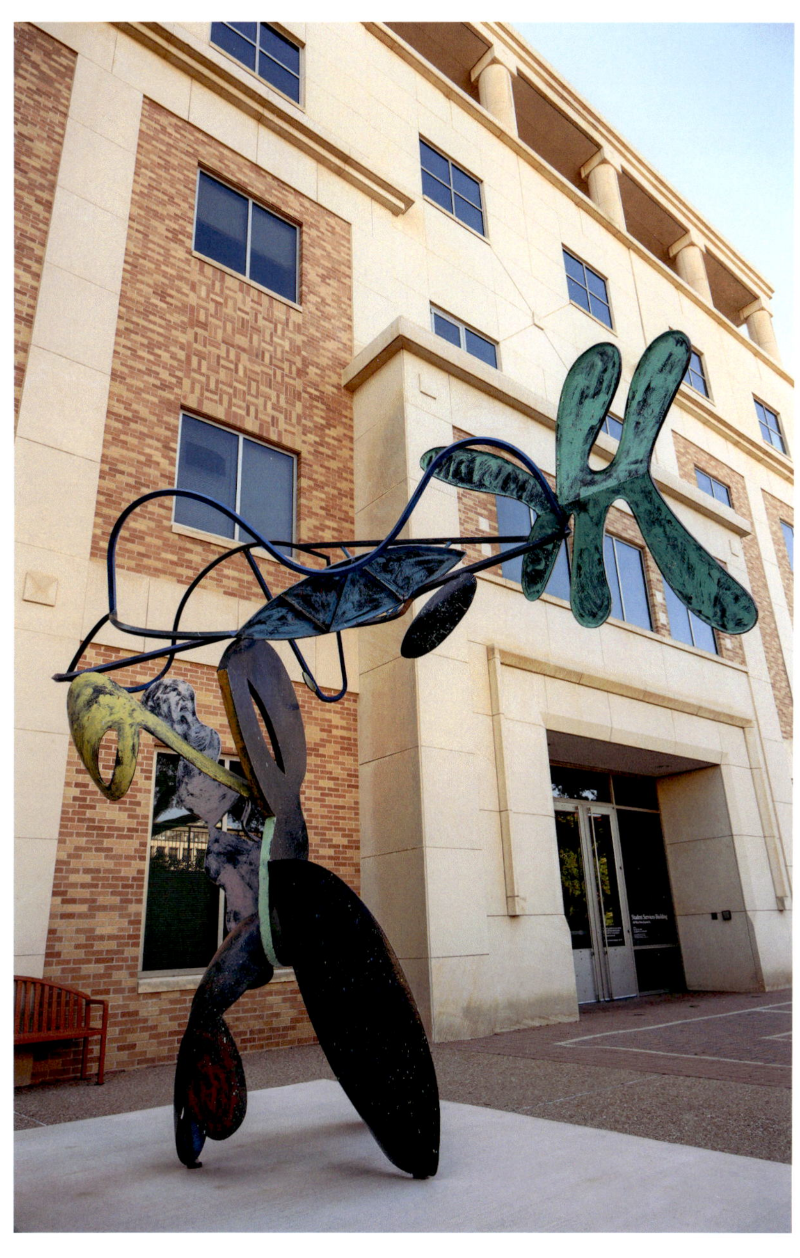

Kingfish: An Homage to Tim Moore, 1986
Painted steel
113 × 121 × 62 inches

Lent by The Metropolitan Museum of Art
Purchase, Lila Acheson Wallace Gift, 1987
1987.226

BEN RUBIN

AMERICAN, BORN 1964

A pioneering figure in contemporary media art, Ben Rubin creates work that communicates patterns of information, thought, and language via electronic media. Whether conceiving a work of intimate or monumental scale, he composes algorithms and computational systems, often relying upon a selected data source to generate nonlinear results. The transformation of the familiar into the unexpected, captured through gracefully simplified forms, results in works that are quietly provocative and engage viewers as participants.

Visible every evening in the Walter Cronkite Plaza, *And That's The Way It Is* projects an interwoven grid of text from two sources: closed caption transcripts of five live network news streams, and archival transcripts of CBS Evening News broadcasts from the Cronkite era (1962–1981) housed at the university's Briscoe Center for American History. Rubin's software scans for various patterns in speech and grammatical constructions, then selects sequences of text. The artist visually distinguishes these sources by using two typefaces that evoke the technologies of their respective eras: Courier represents the Cronkite material, and Verdana is used for the live broadcasts.

And That's The Way It Is translates the spoken language of televised evening news into written fragments. The layering of information—textual and visual, contemporary and historical—engages the viewer cerebrally as a distilled source of information, and viscerally as a purely visual experience of luminescent crescendos and diminuendos. The speed and immediacy of live fragments heightens the viewer's anticipation from one composition to the next, while the insertion of historical phrases activates a dialogue between the past and the present. Projected on an architectural scale, the work offers streams of language that suggest the activities transpiring behind the façade of the communication building.

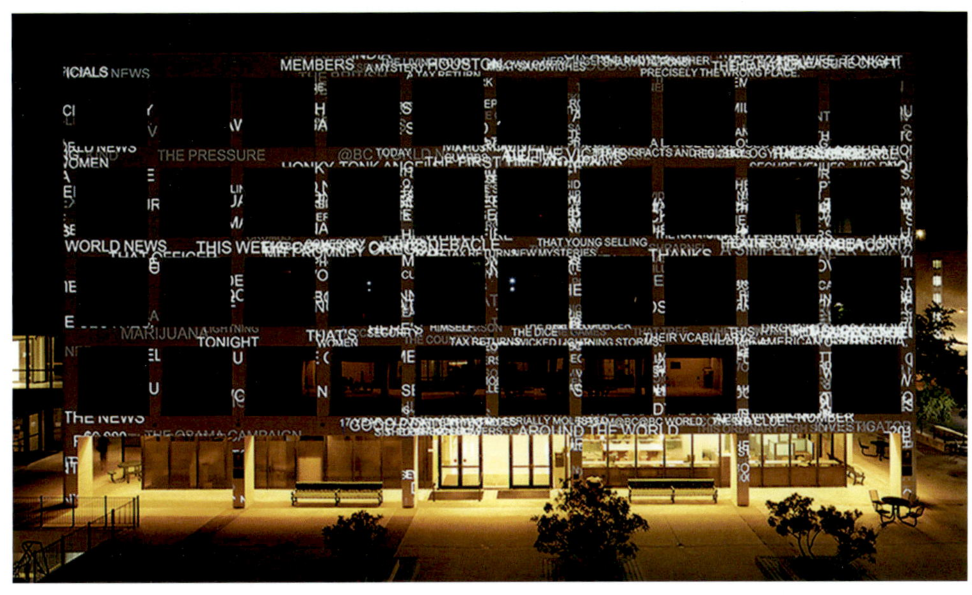

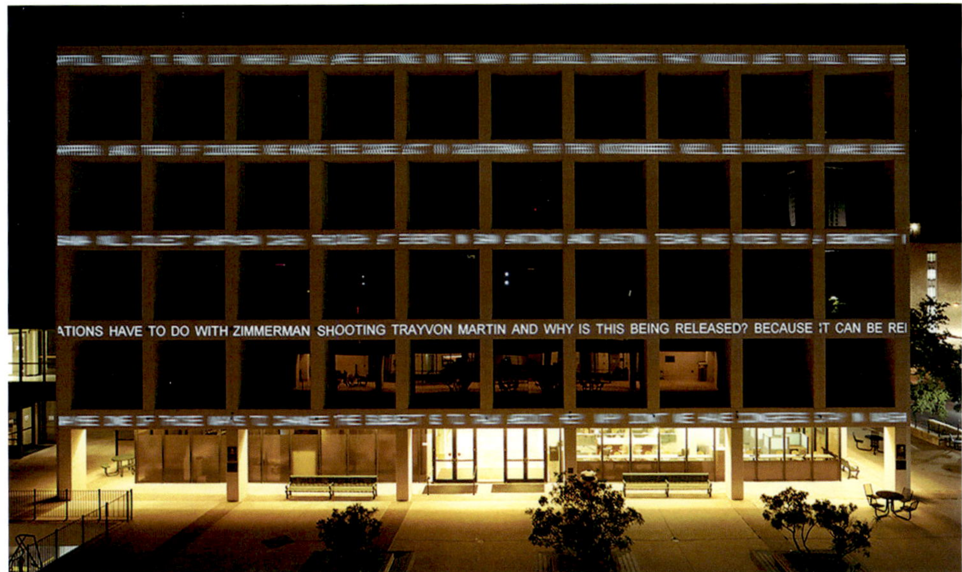

And That's The Way It Is, 2012
Six-channel video projection
Approximately 120 × 42 feet

Commission, Landmarks, The University of Texas at Austin, 2012

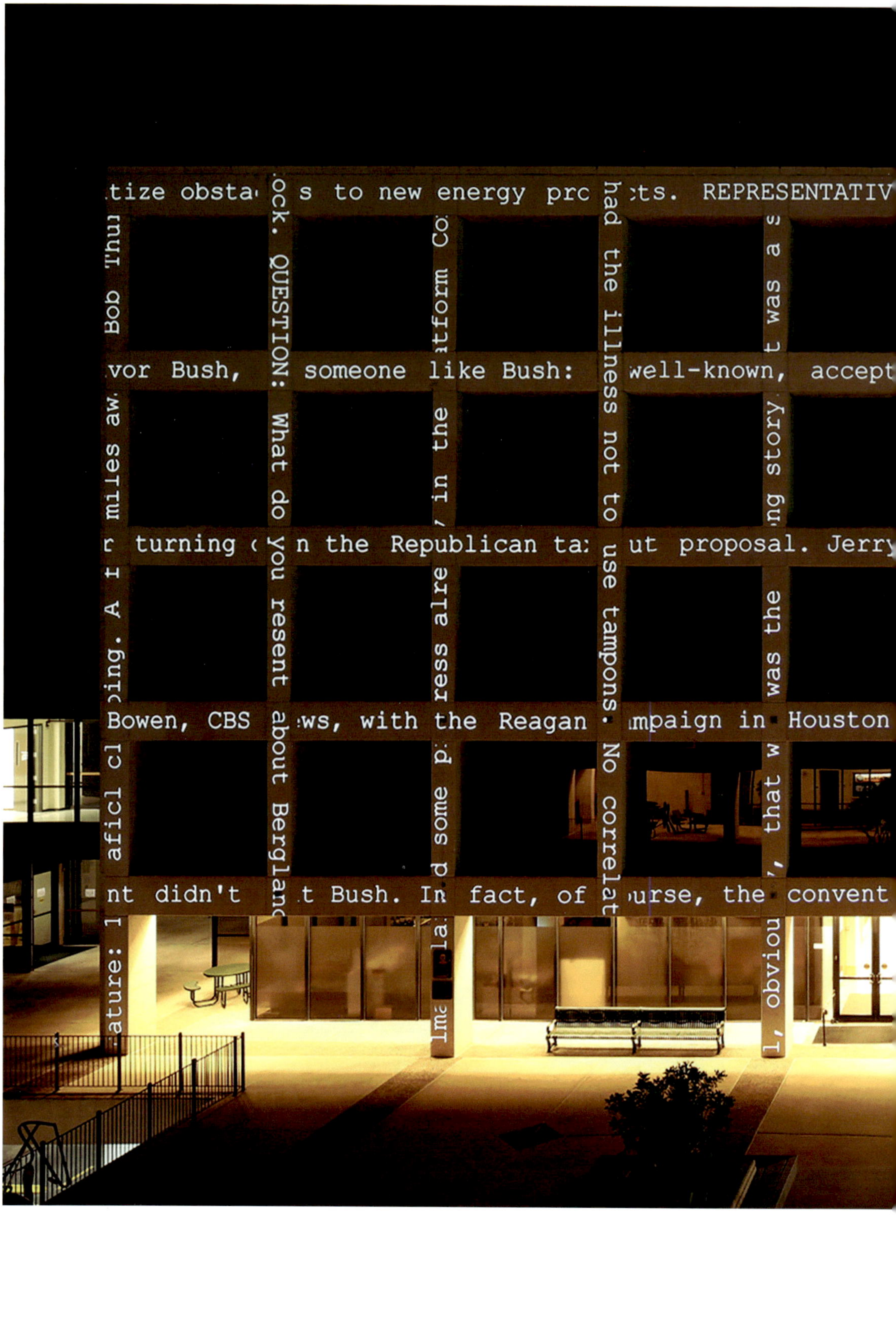

tize obsta s to new energy prc cts. REPRESENTATIV
vor Bush, someone like Bush: well-known, accept
r turning n the Republican ta ut proposal. Jerry
Bowen, CBS ws, with the Reagan mpaign in Houston
nt didn't t Bush. In fact, of urse, the convent

ature: 1 aficl cl ping. A r miles aw Bob Thu
ock. QUESTION: What do you resent about Bergland
Ima ld some p ress alre , in the atform Co
had the illness not to use tampons. No correlat
l, obviou , that w was the ng story t was a s

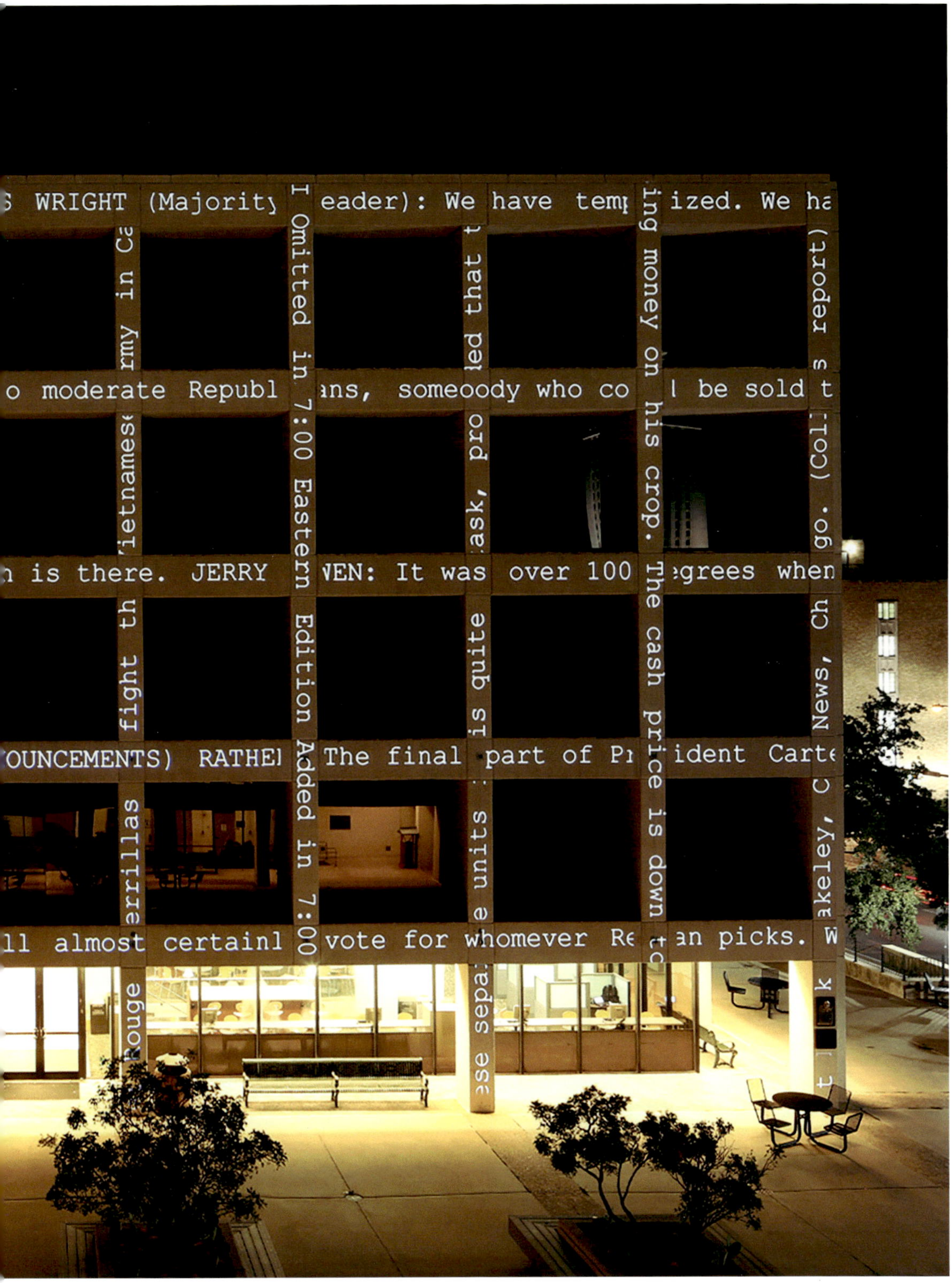

S WRIGHT (Majority eader): We have temp ized. We ha

o moderate Republ ans, someoody who co l be sold t

n is there. JERRY WEN: It was over 100 egrees when

OUNCEMENTS) RATHEI The final part of Pr ident Carte

ll almost certainl vote for whomever Re an picks. W

NANCY RUBINS

AMERICAN, BORN 1952

A sculptor who salvages the unlikeliest of everyday objects, and a draftsman who uses paper and graphite as sculptural materials, Nancy Rubins is well practiced in upending tradition. Her works that are labeled "drawings" share the physical presence and spatial dynamism of sculptures in the round. *Drawing* is lustrous and dark, absorbing and deflecting light in a way that complicates its contours.

Early on, Rubins explored ways of transgressing boundaries between mediums. *Drawing and Sawhorse* (1975) featured a large sheet of paper, thoroughly covered in graphite and draped over a sawhorse to suggest an animated form; two protruding sawhorse legs made it look vaguely bovine, as did a boxy, headlike extension of the graphite-covered paper. In *Drawing* (1974), a penciled sheet of paper was simply slung over a length of heavy rope as if it were laundry on a clothesline.

These and other early hybrids of sculpture and drawing introduced a way of using paper to which Rubins would return. Generally attached directly to the wall—sometimes spanning corners and occasionally also pinned to the ceiling or allowed to spill onto the floor—these fully three-dimensional works are robust survivors of a working process that leaves them battered, gouged, and ripped; pinned and re-pinned; and, above all, covered side to side and top to bottom in furiously drawn strokes of dark, glistening graphite. The resulting rough-edged configurations, gathered into folds, resemble sheets of gleaming lead. Like the early drawings on sawhorses, these later works on paper sometimes assume a vaguely figurative quality. Even more primordial are the associations invoked by the graphite, which lends a mineral glint to the surfaces of the drawings and a sense of seismic collision to the constituent sheets' abutted edges.

Rubins uses pencil to engage light in a way that makes her drawings' surfaces expand; the illusion they create is of exaggerated size, not weight. Nor do they conform to the rectangular shape of a conventional sheet of paper: they are not discrete objects—they cannot be framed; they are not, in any ordinary sense, images.

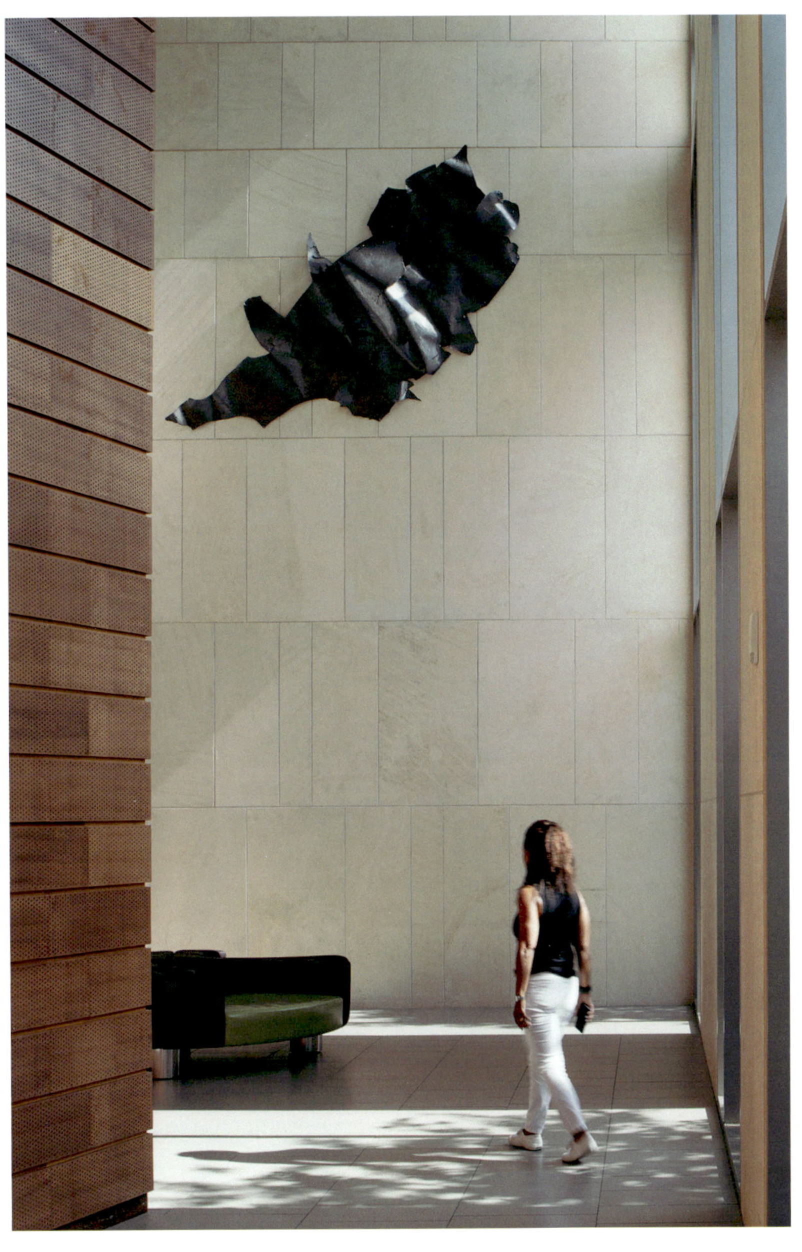

Drawing, 2007
Graphite on rag paper
81 × 132 × 23 inches

Purchase, Landmarks, The University of Texas at Austin, 2016

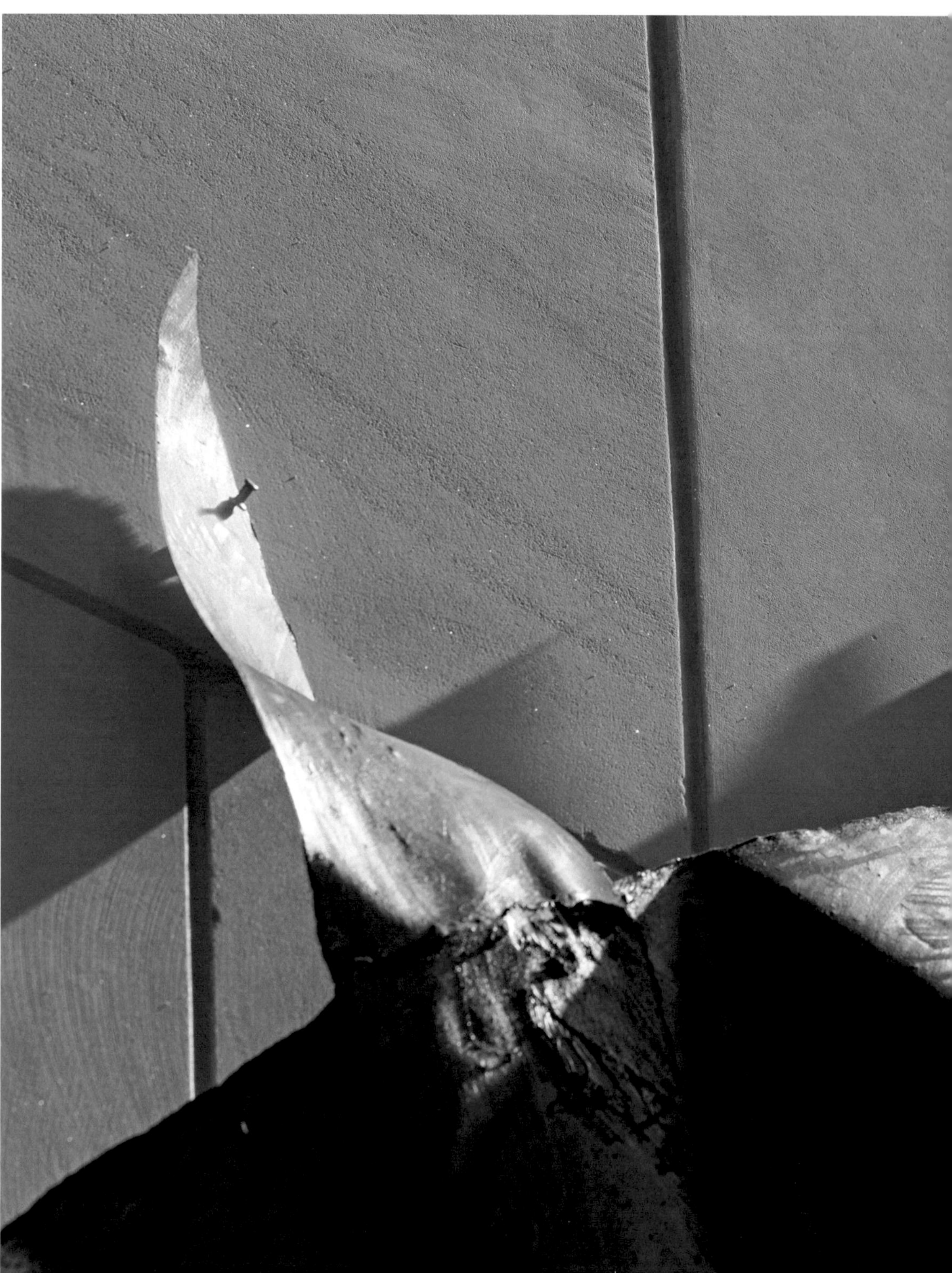

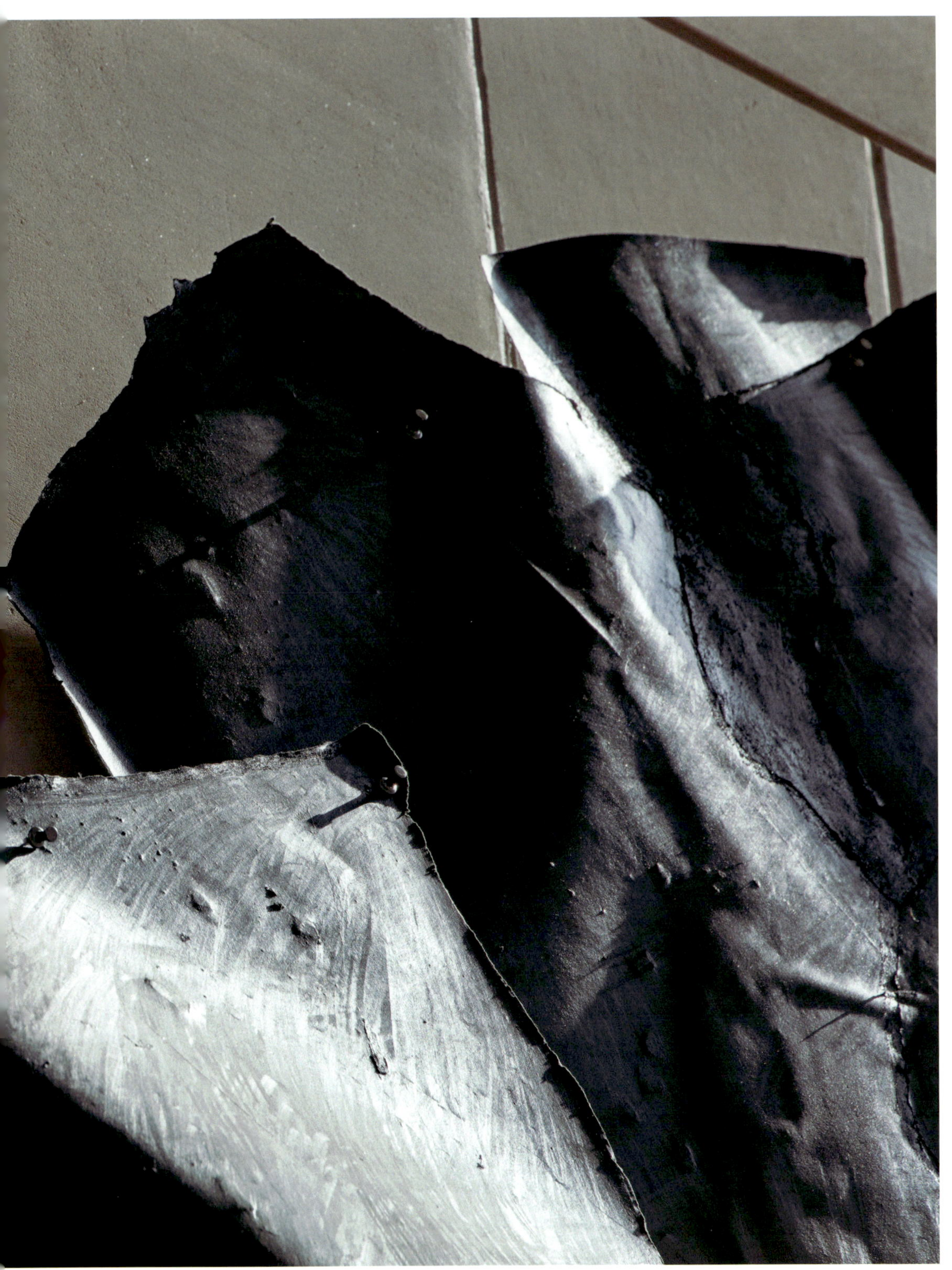

NANCY RUBINS

AMERICAN, BORN 1952

Balancing with improbable grace, *Monochrome for Austin* boasts seventy recycled aluminum canoes and small boats clustered at the end of a listing column. It deploys a sense of mass and scale that can be compared to a performer's perfect timing, a characteristic that is ever-present in the work of artist Nancy Rubins. Her sculptures combine surpassing delicacy and indomitable strength, a polarity that is even more striking when encountered outdoors.

While still a student in the early 1970s, Rubins experimented with sculpture by using wet clay to stick coffee cups to suspended tarps; the cups popped off as the clay dried. In another project, a hybrid of sculpture and drawing, she used a small electric fan to create a work that involved graphite-covered paper spattered with red paint. More recently, an exhibition of sprawling sculptures made from vintage animal-shaped playground equipment was titled *Our Friend Fluid Metal* (2014), referencing the molten phase of the constituent metal. Porous boundaries between disciplines and the fluidity of the mediums themselves are qualities that appeal to Rubins.

By the late 1980s, Rubins' constructions had reached colossal proportions. She added trailer homes, water heaters, and mattresses to the materials tethered together, and, later, fighter-jet wings and fuselages. By the mid-1990s, Rubins had begun to assemble brightly colored fiberglass canoes and kayaks into oversized bouquets that flower overhead with exuberance. The *Monochrome* series, which began in 2010, brings to the fore the grace of the unpainted metal forms. Examples from the series can be found at the Buffalo AKG Art Museum (formerly the Albright-Knox Art Gallery), New York; Gateway Park at the Navy Pier, Chicago, Illinois; and l'Université Paris Diderot, France.

The vessels evoke a different kind of movement and life than Rubins' earlier work. In contrast to the thundering flight of retired military aircraft, canoes glide gently through the water, suggesting a kind of simple solitude. Swirling on currents of air, the canoes in *Monochrome for Austin* are removed from their associated landscape and combined in a visually precarious mass, giving the impression that they are suspended in time and space.

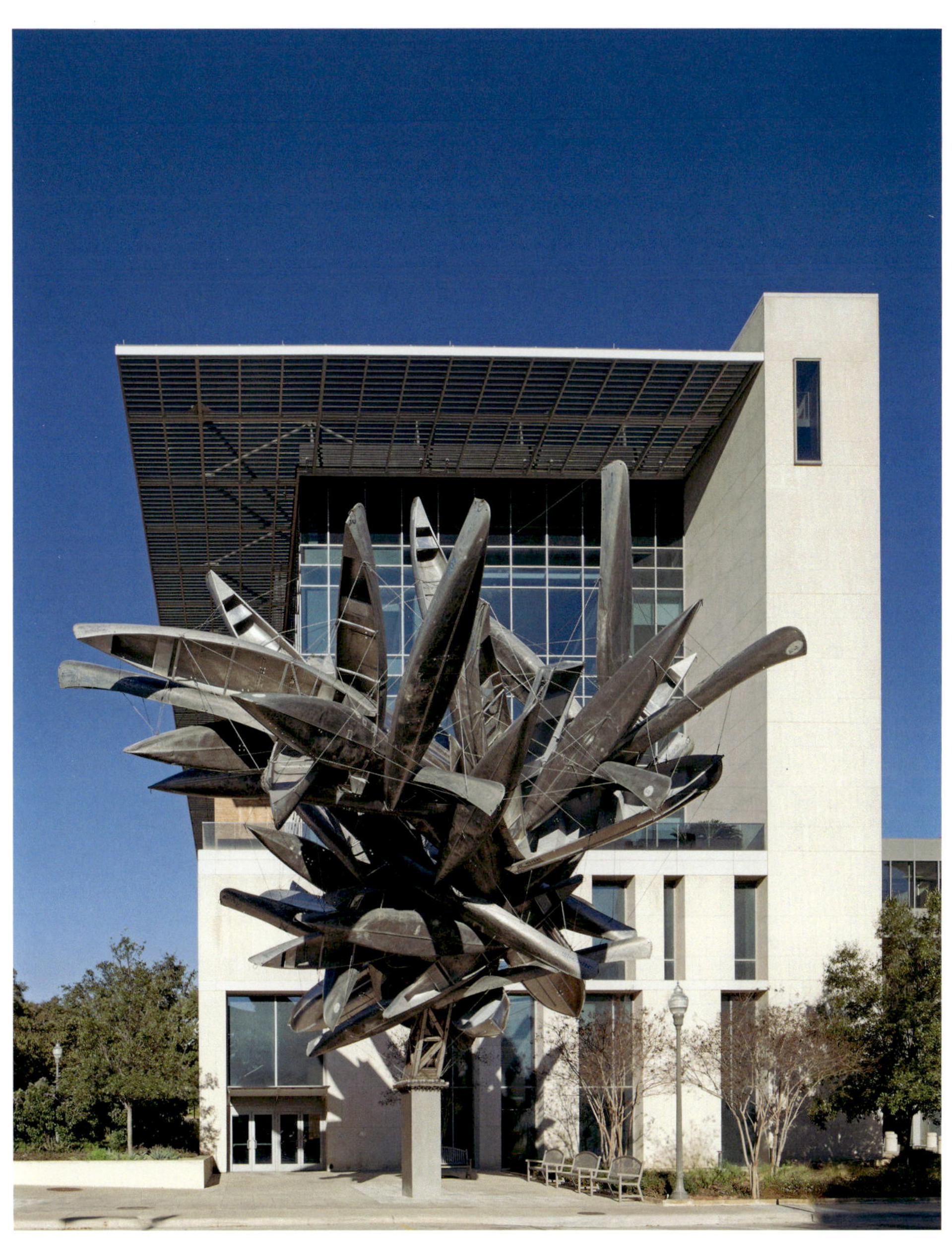

Monochrome for Austin, 2015
Stainless steel and aluminum
600 × 642 × 492 inches

Commission, Landmarks, The University of Texas at Austin, 2015

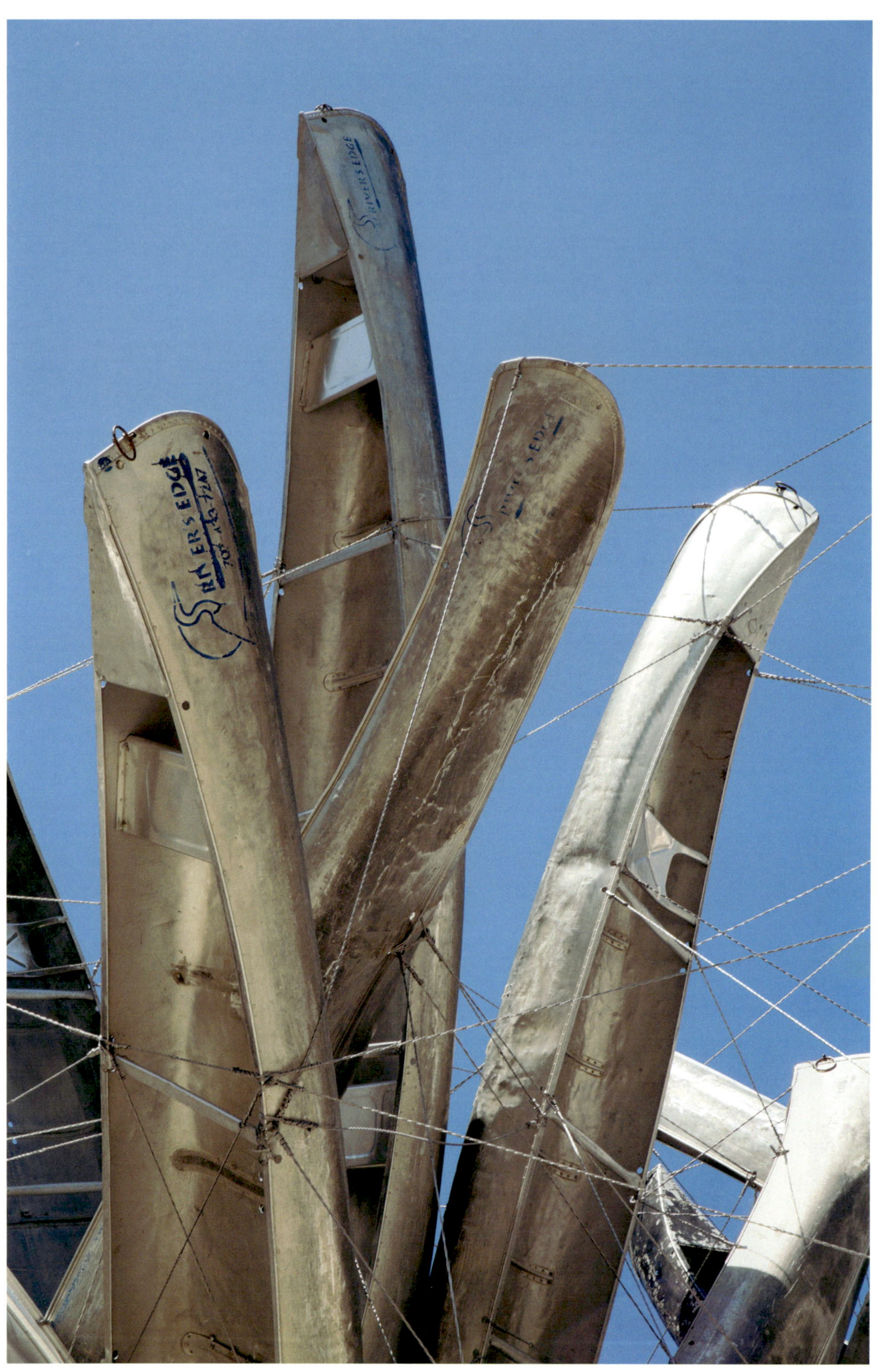
RIVERS EDGE

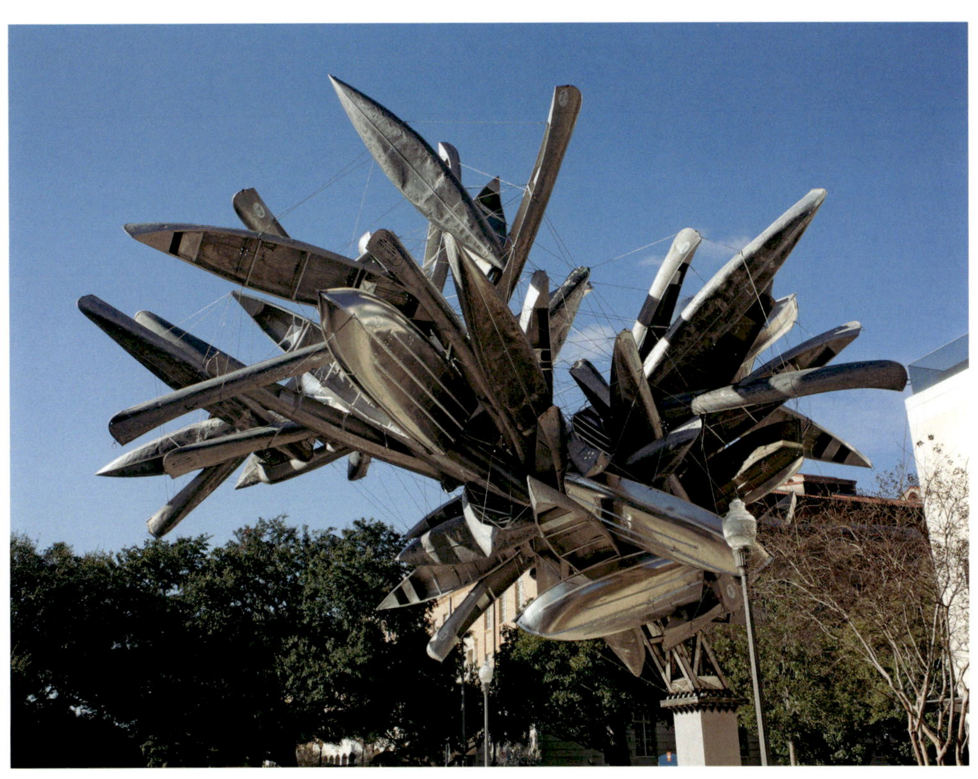

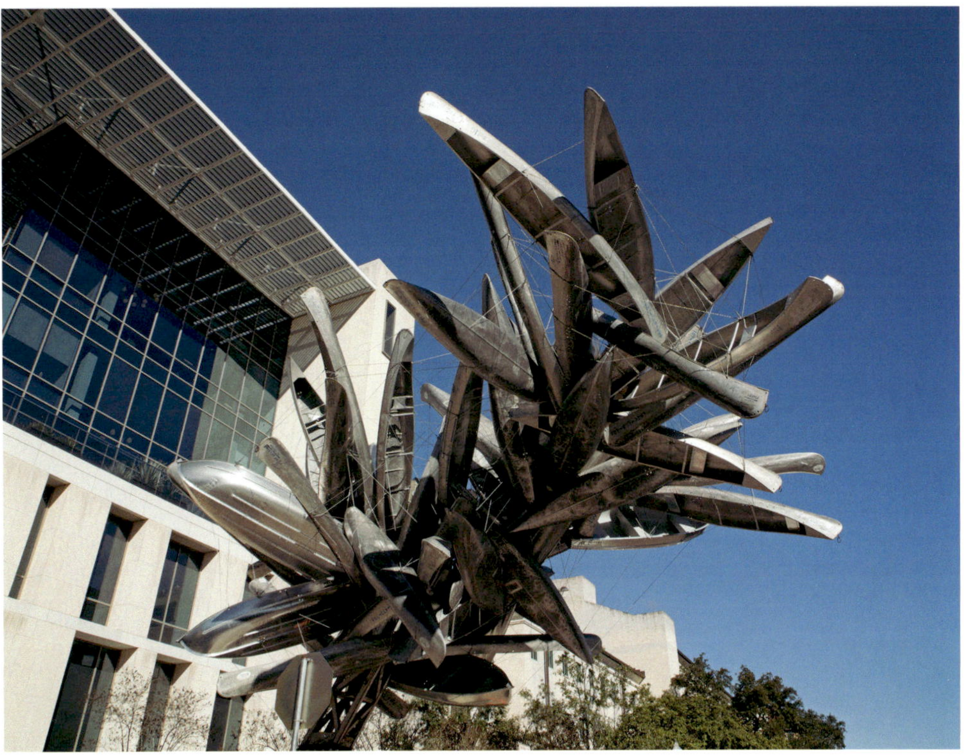

TONY SMITH

AMERICAN, 1912–1980

A polymath with interests as diverse as mathematical biology and modernist architecture, Tony Smith worked as a mechanical draftsman for his family's municipal waterworks company while studying at the Art Students League in New York City. He trained as an architect in the 1930s and worked for Frank Lloyd Wright (1867–1959), whose use of mass-produced, modular homes inspired Smith to open his own architecture firm a few years later.

After moving to New York City, Smith became close friends with Jackson Pollock (1912–1956) and the Abstract Expressionist painters, subsequently designing a home for painter Theodoros Stamos (1922–1997) and exhibition spaces for a number of New York art galleries. During a two-year sojourn to Europe in the mid-1950s, Smith embarked on an ambitious series of abstract paintings, bringing his skills as a draftsman to the linear geometry of his compositions.

Ten years later, at age fifty, Smith began working in the medium for which he is best known: large-scale steel sculpture. The monumental scale and immersive quality of Smith's sculpture was undoubtedly influenced by his architectural background. Indeed, *Amaryllis* began as an attempt to realize his vision of a "cave of light"—an open sculptural volume that would immerse and envelop the viewer. He worked with large sheets of plywood, combining multifaceted geometric elements like the cube and rhomboid arranged in linear configurations, which were later executed in steel by industrial fabricators. As curator Robert Storr observed, the sculpture "is based on compound articulations of two triangulated modules, the tetrahedron and the octahedron."

Though the reductive form and monochrome black surface of *Amaryllis* call to mind the aesthetic of Minimalist art, Smith's use of complex geometry contrasts with the simple mathematical progressions and elementary forms of Minimalist artists Sol LeWitt (1928–2007) and Robert Morris (1931–2018). The twisting angles of *Amaryllis* create a complicated, multivalent mass that changes dramatically as one moves around the work—shifting from flattened to dimensional, or from balanced to asymmetrical.

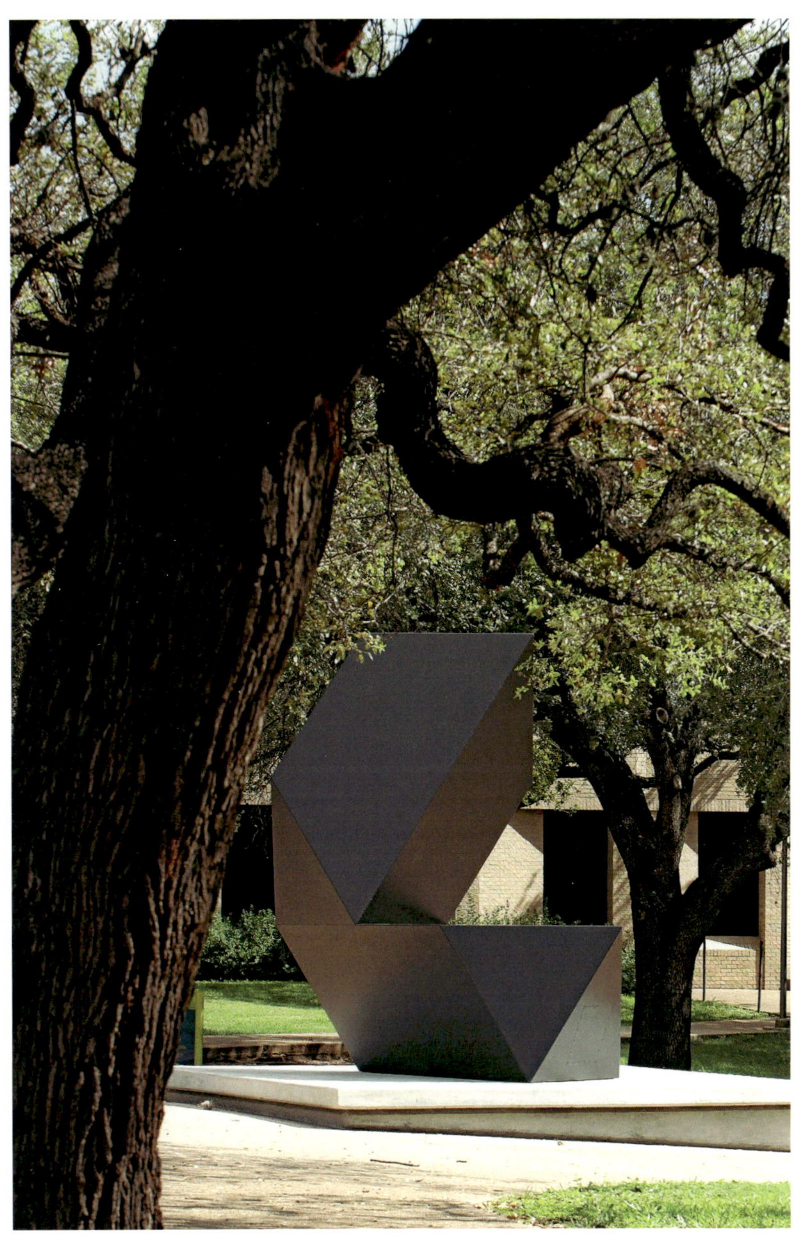

Amaryllis, 1965
Painted steel
135 × 128 × 90 inches

Lent by The Metropolitan Museum of Art
Anonymous Gift, 1986
1986.432ab

JENNIFER STEINKAMP

AMERICAN, BORN 1958

Among the pioneers of digital imaging, Jennifer Steinkamp is one of the medium's most celebrated artists. She draws inspiration from the natural world, using digital technology to create large-scale, hypnotic installations that pulse with recognizable life. Her scenes transform architectural spaces into hyperreal environments that blur the line between the animate and the virtual.

Steinkamp leans heavily on the history of abstraction and perception, suggesting a lineage with the California light movement. However, since her seminal installation *Eye Catching* (2003), her work has moved away from abstraction toward figuration. Steinkamp has steadily refined her craft, creating an enormous vocabulary of digital objects that tend to appear randomly while being carefully composed. *EON* is an extension of this stylistic development and arguably the culmination of an artistic evolution spanning some thirty years.

The panoramic world of *EON* reveals biomorphic shapes that undulate across the screen, punctuating an aqueous background with bursts of pink, yellow, and multicolored fragments. It functions like a frieze or gigantic scroll, impossible to absorb at a single glance. In it, we see bubbles and loose aggregates of matter that resemble a swarm of living organisms and plants. While *EON*'s forms evoke primordial biological life or exotic marine organisms, they are in fact generated through dense layers of digital animation and fictionalized by Steinkamp's imagination.

EON is indebted to the most current thinking in the life sciences. Representing an alternative to natural selection and biological competition, it draws inspiration from the concept of symbiosis, which holds that the mutual cooperation and interdependence of unlike organisms as essential to the evolution of life forms. While Steinkamp considers *EON* a vision of primordial ecology, it also presents an imagined future—an optimistic alternative to the challenges of global pandemics and climate change.

Commissioned for the College of Natural Sciences, *EON* signals the research activity that takes place in Welch Hall. A vision as powerful as it is beautiful, *EON* serves as a reminder that life on Earth began through cooperation, and that our future depends upon it.

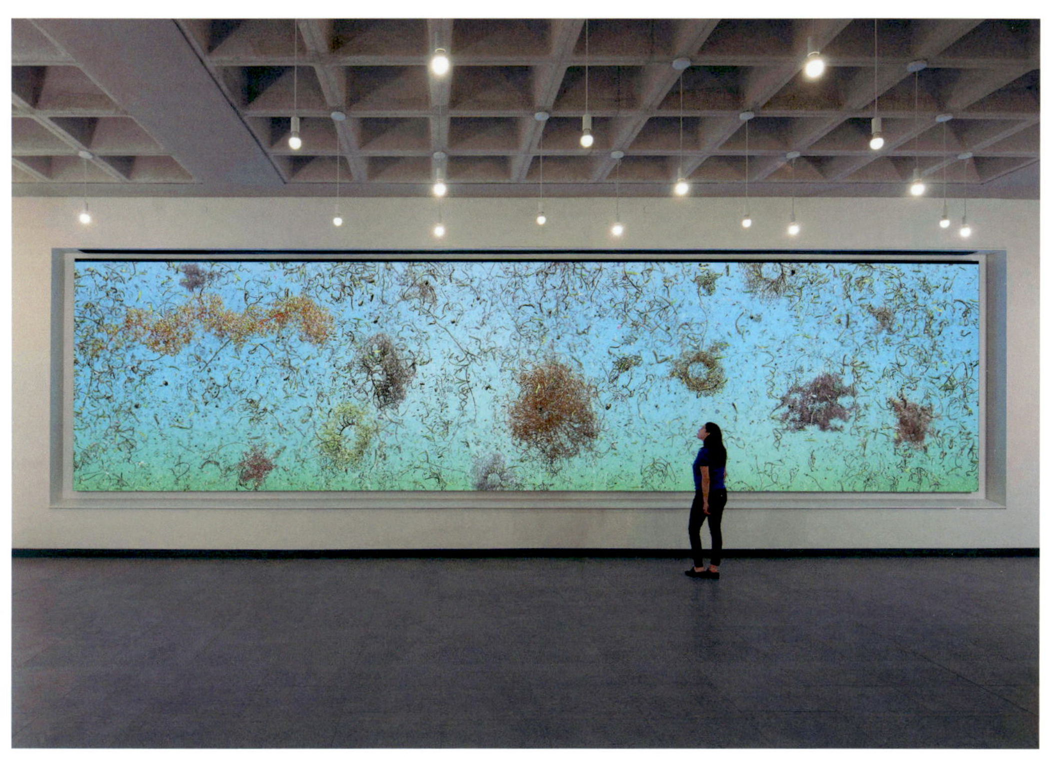

EON, 2020
2:07 min., looped, video installation
360 × 108 inches

Commission, Landmarks, The University of Texas at Austin, 2020

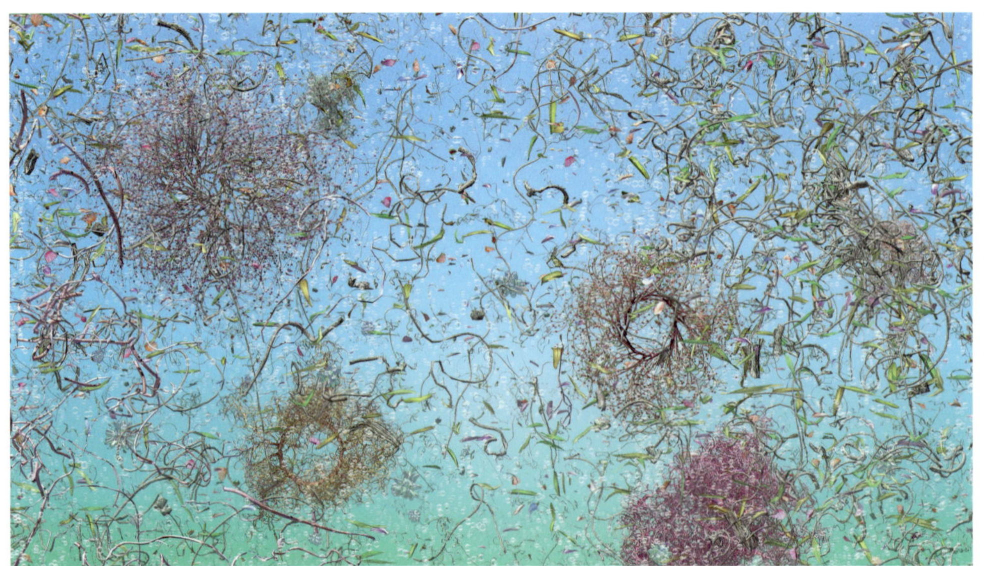

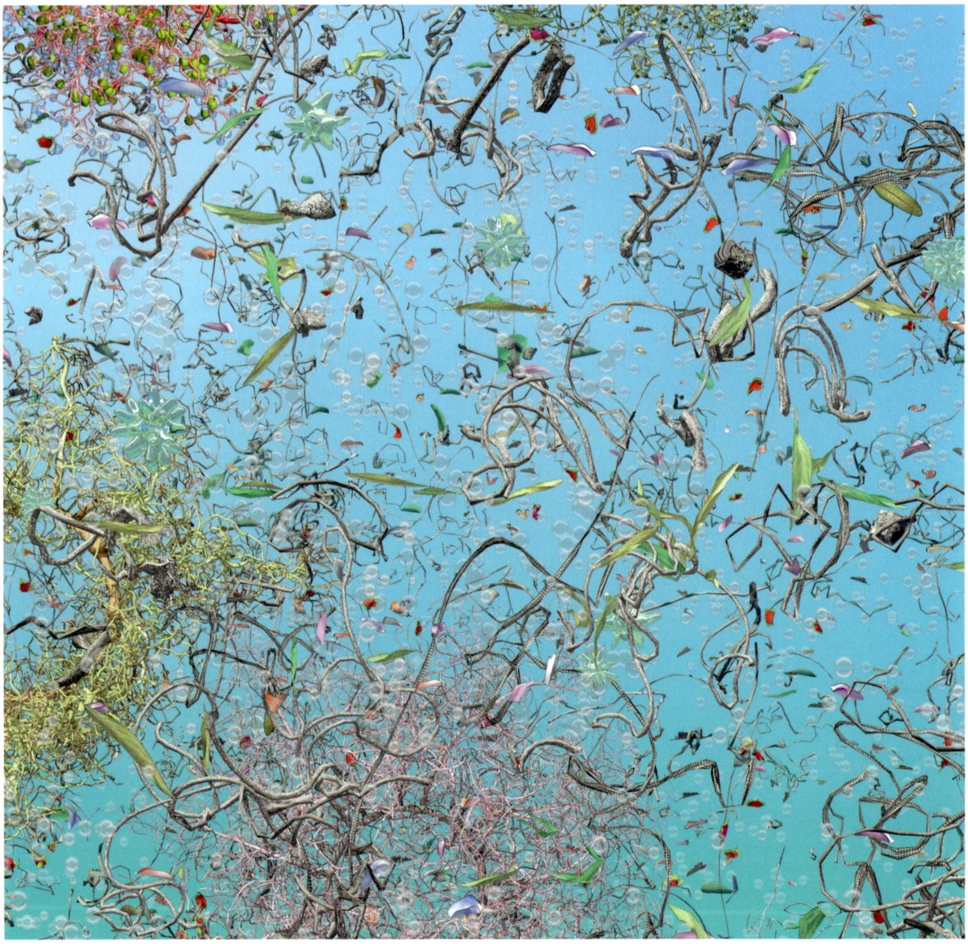

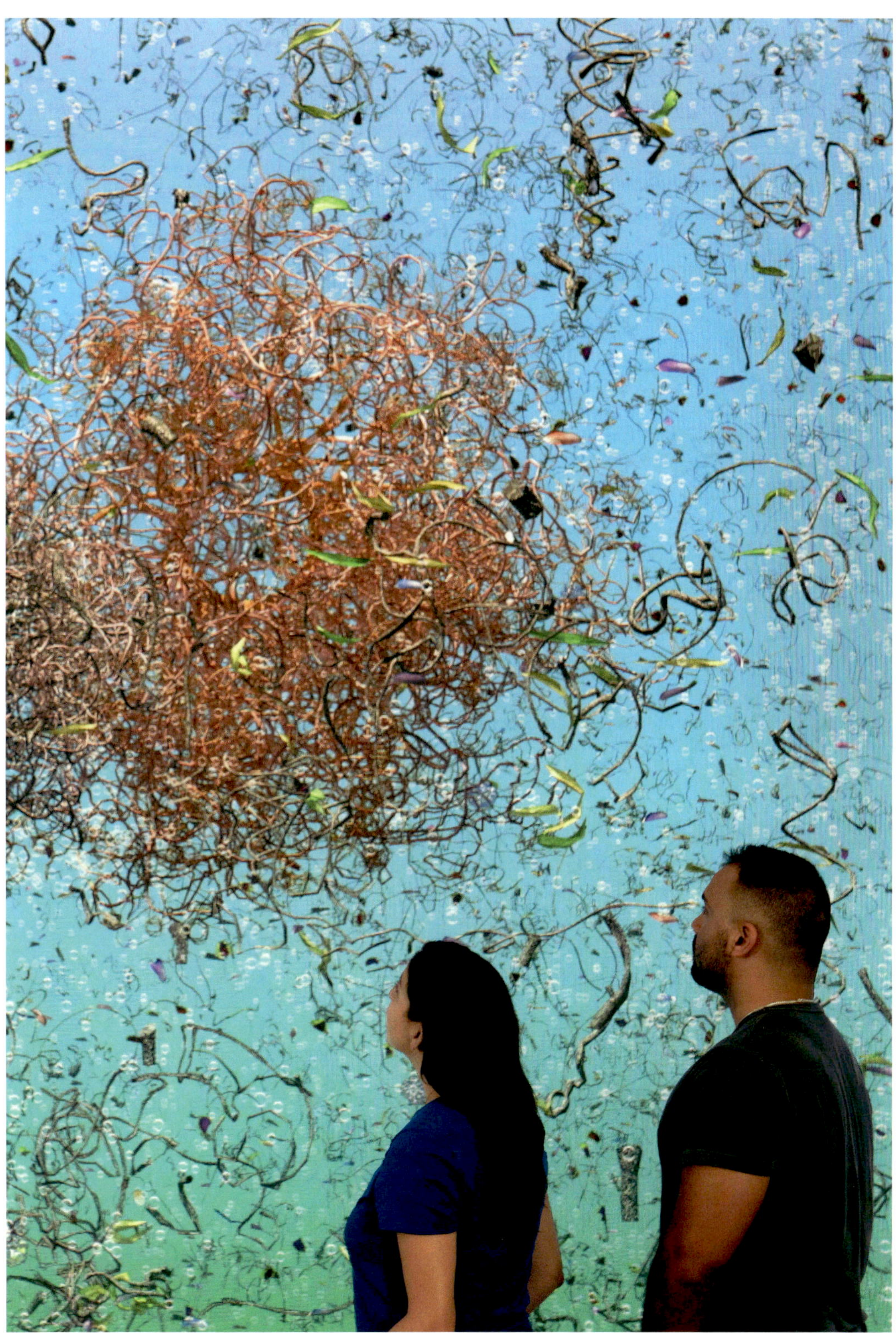

JAMES TURRELL

AMERICAN, BORN 1943

James Turrell's artistic medium is light—not as depicted in paintings or incorporated into sculptures, but light itself. His art invites viewers to engage in intimate, transformative experiences with light, appreciating its transcendent power. Through projections, printmaking, and site-specific installations, Turrell's work is influenced by Quaker simplicity and the practice of going inside to greet the light of revelation.

In the 1960s, Turrell began to experiment with light projections and installations that allowed external light to penetrate interior spaces, enabling viewers to perceive color within darkened environments. In some works, he cut sections of walls to reveal the sky. These cuts evolved into Skyspaces, architectural rooms with sharp-edged apertures in the ceiling that seem to bring the sky down through the opening, almost within reach.

The Color Inside, Turrell's eighty-fourth Skyspace, is located on the rooftop of the William C. Powers, Jr. Student Activity Center. Like many of his works, it is a destination—a serene and contemplative space for the campus community and visitors alike. Defined by its architectural simplicity, the Skyspace stands out for its intimate proportions, refined palette, and lyrical design. Open throughout the day as an oasis for quiet reflection and introspection, it transforms at sunrise and sunset. Programmed light sequences bathe the space in radiant washes of color, causing the sky to appear in unimaginable hues.

When naming *The Color Inside*, Turrell explained, "I was thinking about what you see inside, and inside the sky, and what the sky holds within it that we don't see the possibility of in our regular life." The space he created fosters quiet contemplation, cultivating a heightened awareness of light's capacity to reveal not only the world around us, but also the depths within ourselves.

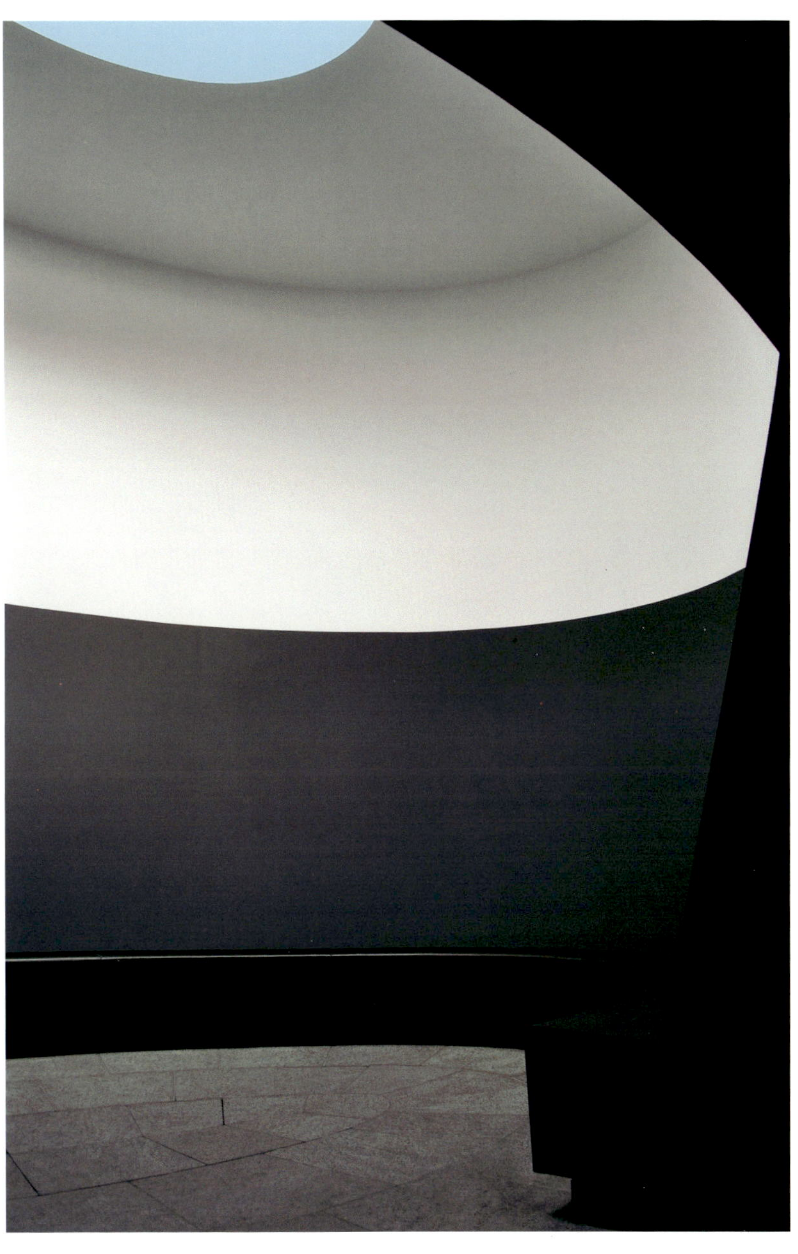

The Color Inside, 2013
Black basalt, plaster, and LED lights
224 × 348 × 276 inches

Commission, Landmarks, The University of Texas at Austin, 2013

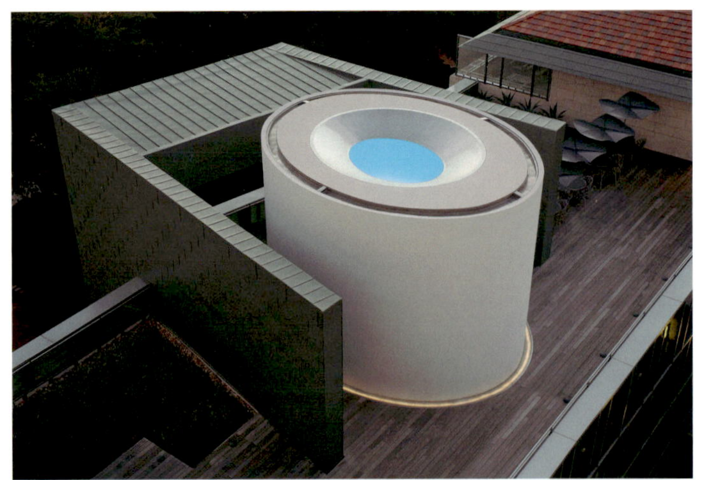

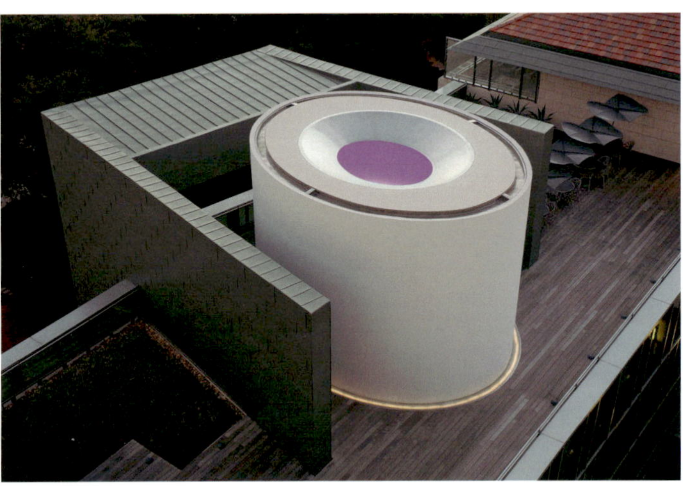

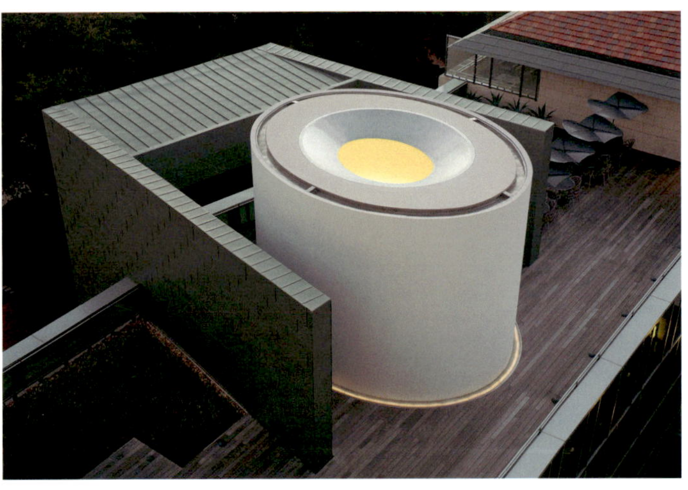

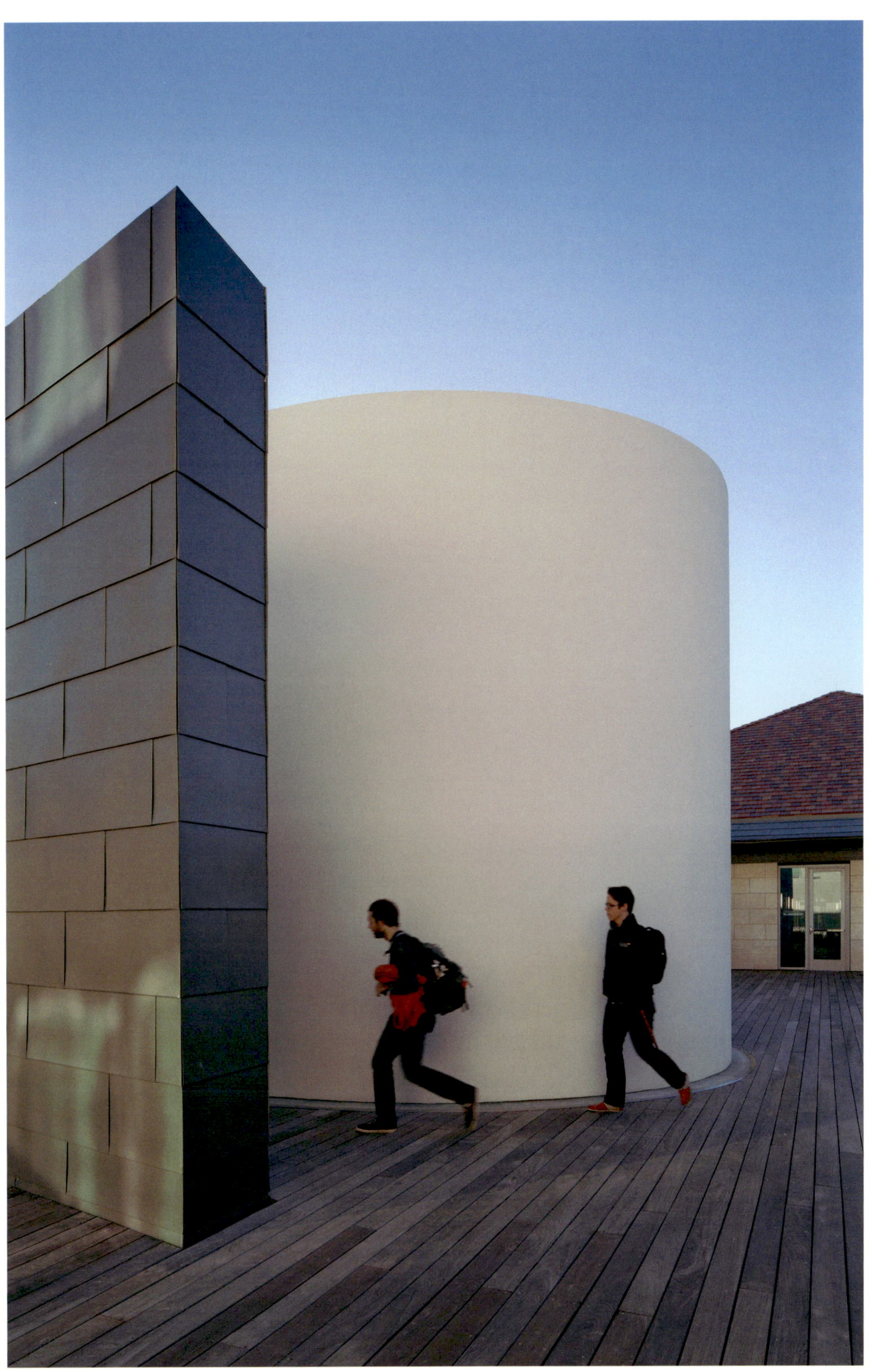

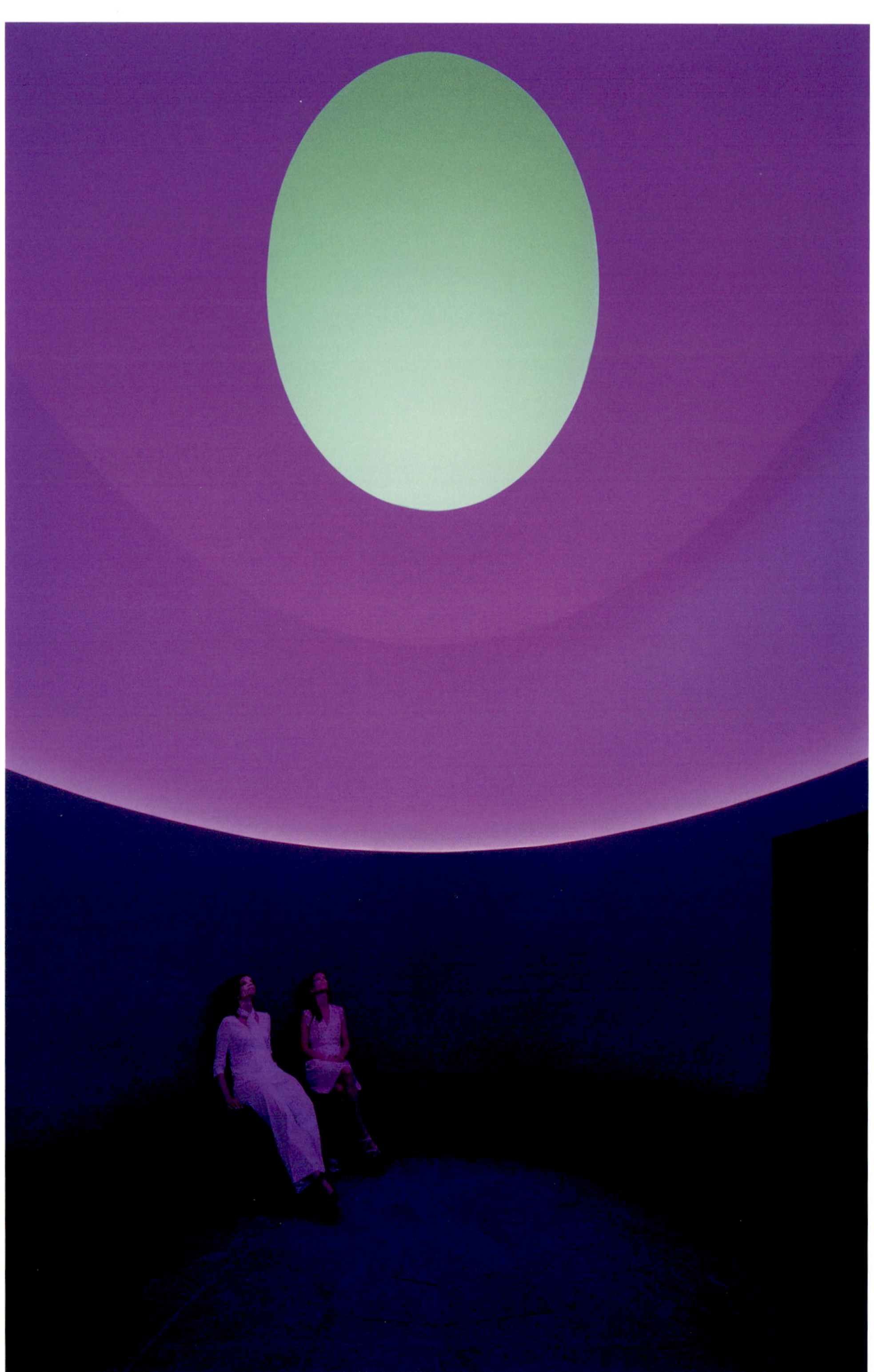

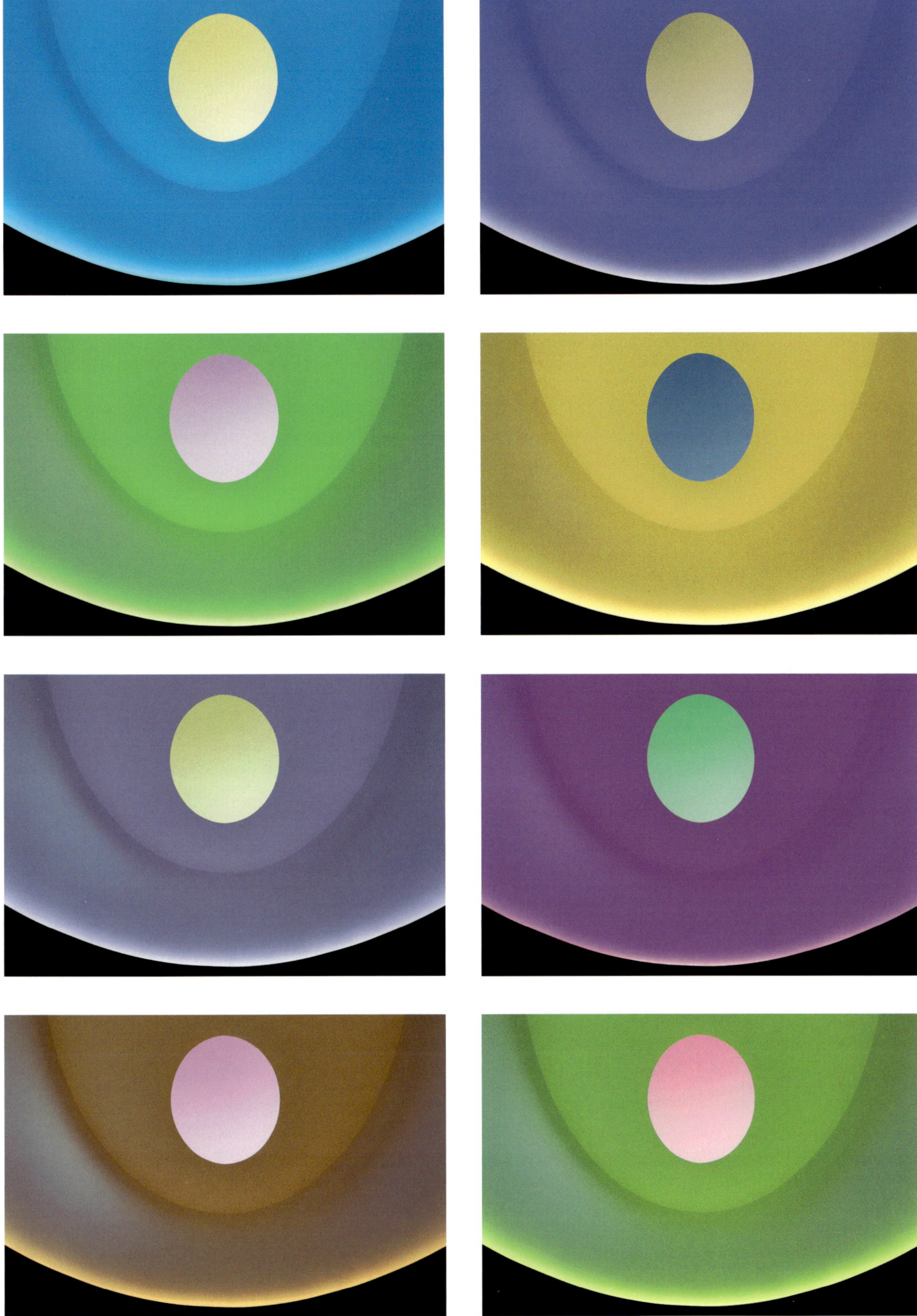

URSULA VON RYDINGSVARD

AMERICAN, BORN IN GERMANY, 1942

The daughter of a Ukrainian peasant woodcutter who fled to Germany in 1938, Ursula von Rydingsvard spent the first eight years of her life in a succession of refugee camps until 1950, when her family settled in Plainville, Connecticut. Determined to become an artist, she studied painting at the University of Miami and the University of California, Berkeley, earning her MFA at Columbia University in 1975.

When she arrived in New York in 1973, Minimalism was at its height. Like the Minimalists, von Rydingsvard shares the use of prefabricated materials, specifically, commercially available 4x4 cedar beams. In contrast to the Minimalists, however, she works against the mass-produced quality of the material. Sculpting in an intuitive and organic way, the artist reengineers the standardized material and returns it to a more natural state. Thus, she joined the new generation of sculptors loosely labeled "Postminimalist."

Von Rydingsvard works primarily in cedar, using chain saws, circular saws, traditional hand chisels, and mallets to carve the wood into monumental, craggy forms. She often enhances these surfaces by rubbing them with powdered graphite, producing a rich interplay between the dark gray of the graphite and the reddish-brown cedar. This nuanced coloration evokes the weathered patina of time.

Von Rydingsvard's connection to wood is deeply personal, rooted in her Polish-Ukrainian heritage and formative years in German refugee camps, where wood was essential for tools and shelter. "It's somewhere in my blood. . . . Working with it and looking at it feels familiar."

In *Untitled (Seven Mountains)*, the layered wood evokes the geological striations of desert canyons or archaeological excavations. The subtitle hints at her being one of seven siblings, adding an autobiographical layer to the work. With every gouge and cut prominently visible, von Rydingsvard's sculptures embody the raw, physical, and expressive act of sculpting, transforming humble materials into forms that feel ancient and enduring.

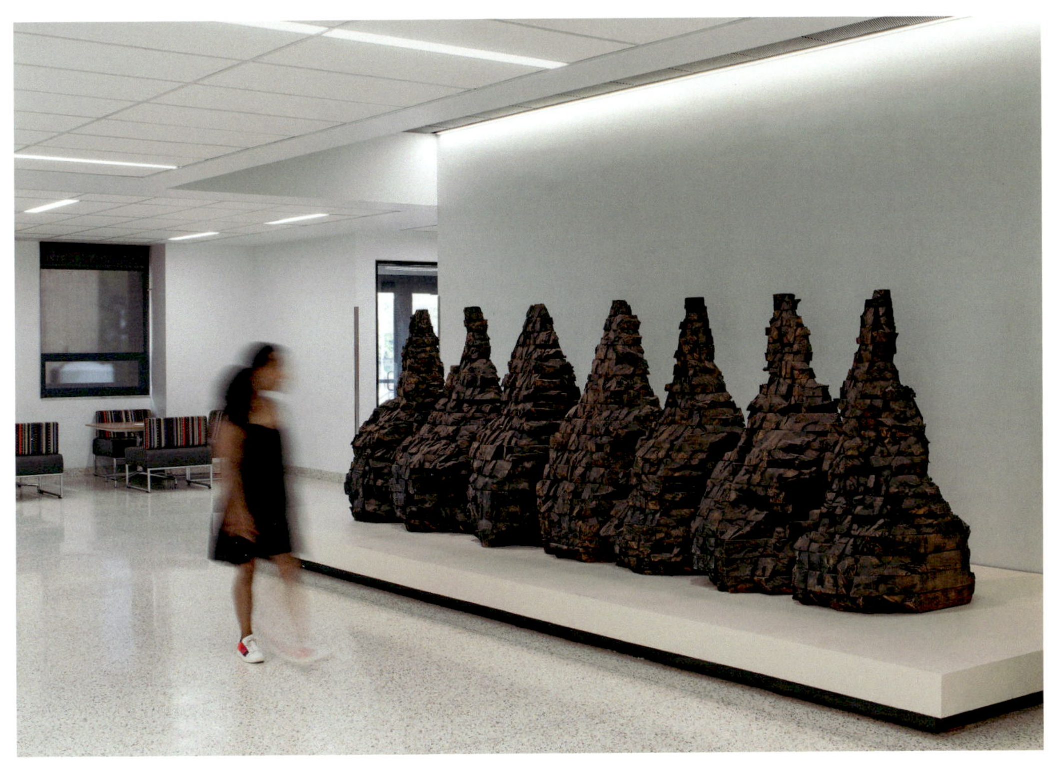

Untitled (Seven Mountains), 1986–88
Cedar and graphite powder
62 × 201 × 42 inches

Lent by The Metropolitan Museum of Art
Purchase, Lila Acheson Wallace Gift, 1988
1988.257a-u

ANITA WESCHLER

AMERICAN, 1914–2001

As a young woman, Anita Weschler studied at three of the leading art schools in the United States—Parsons School of Design, the Art Students League, and the Pennsylvania Academy of Fine Arts—where she learned both traditional and modern styles of painting and sculpture. Her talent was widely recognized early, with her work featured thirteen times in the Whitney Museum's Annual Exhibition of Contemporary Art between 1939 and 1956.

A founding member of the Sculptors Guild, Weschler navigated fluidly between realistic and abstract styles. The cast bronze bust of her teacher William Zorach (1887–1966), housed in the collection of the Smithsonian American Art Museum shows her mastery of representational sculpture. While Weschler preferred casting to direct carving, she was drawn to the natural texture of stone. In her search for an alternative to bronze, she innovated her own method of stone casting, in which aggregate cements and crushed stone are poured into a mold to achieve a natural texture.

During the late 1930s and early 1940s, Weschler made a series of sculptures exploring antiwar themes, employing the simplified forms and strong contours characteristic of primitivism. *Victory Ball* exemplifies this approach, with blocky figures whose postures recall the influence of Paul Gauguin's (1848–1903) post-Impressionist style and faces not unlike Picasso's (1881–1973) early use of African masks. The figures are arranged in an ambiguous relationship, with five of them grouped together, but each looking in different directions. Though one woman, separate from the group, faces them dancing, the overall heaviness of the work and rigidity of the figures' motions seem to counteract the celebration of a victory ball.

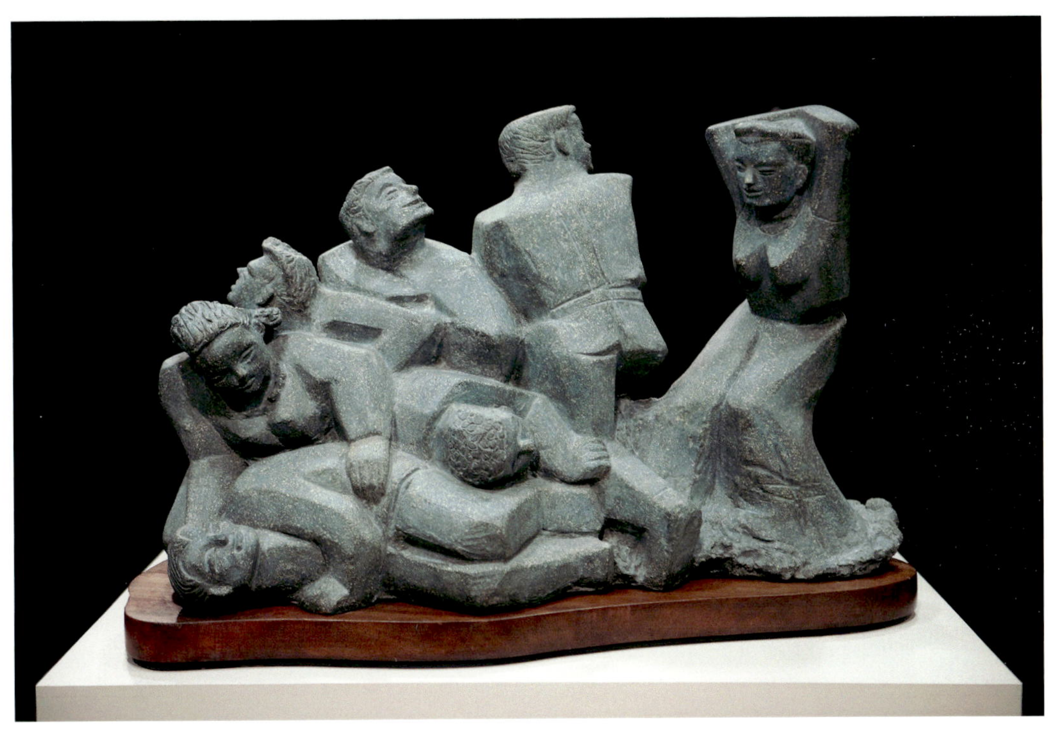

Victory Ball, 1951
Cast stone
24 × 41 × 23 ½ inches

Lent by The Metropolitan Museum of Art
Purchase, Morris and Rose Rochman Gift, 1982
1982.43

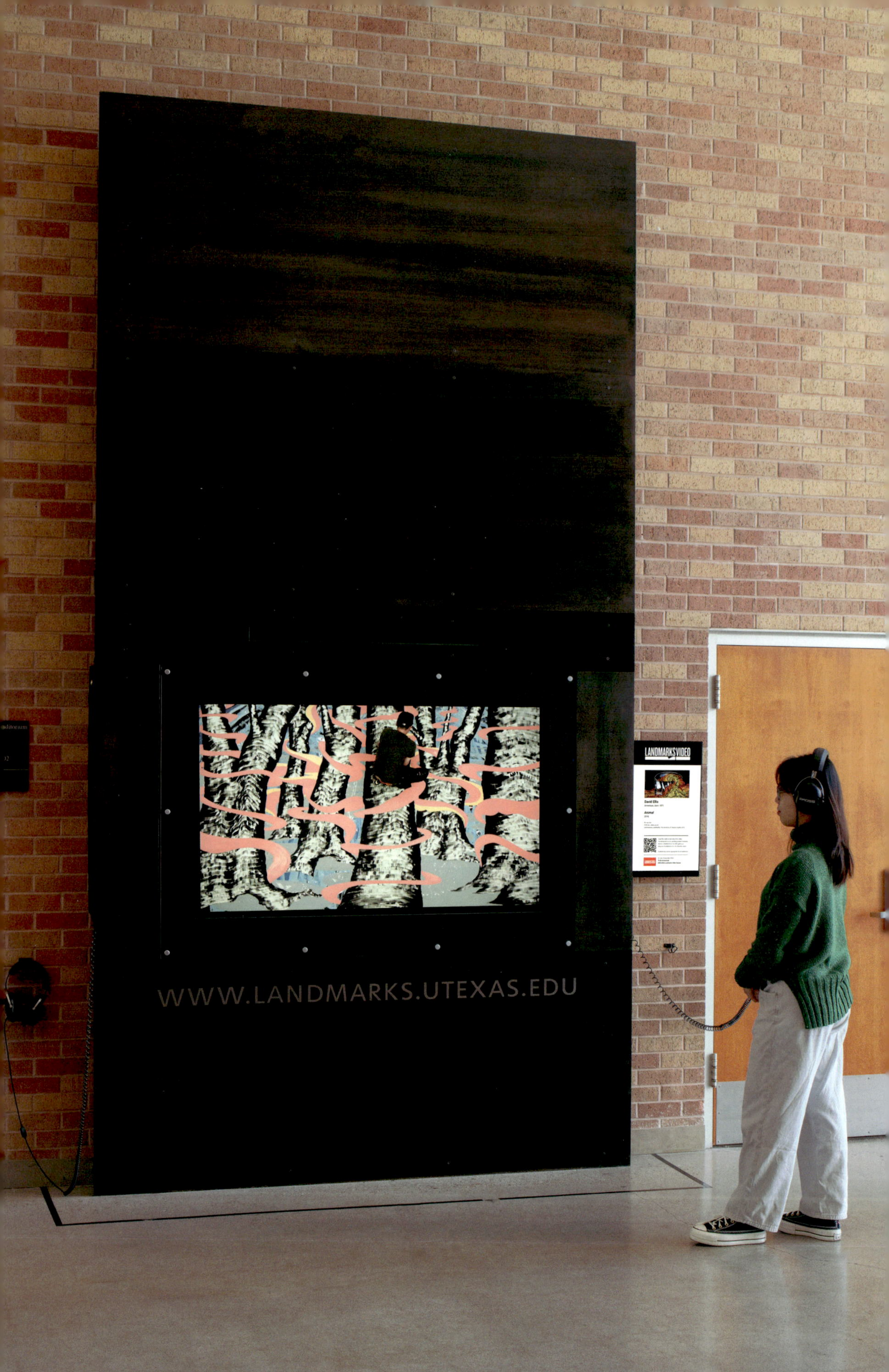
WWW.LANDMARKS.UTEXAS.EDU
LANDMARKSVIDEO

LANDMARKS VIDEO

Landmarks Video presents some of the most promising and admired works of video art from the past six decades. The program familiarizes audiences with significant titles, stimulates conversation and research, and situates the genre of video art alongside the presentation of more traditional media. Featuring a new artist each month, Landmarks Video is displayed on a media station in the atrium of the Fine Arts Building. An original essay about each artist and their work is available at landmarksut.org.

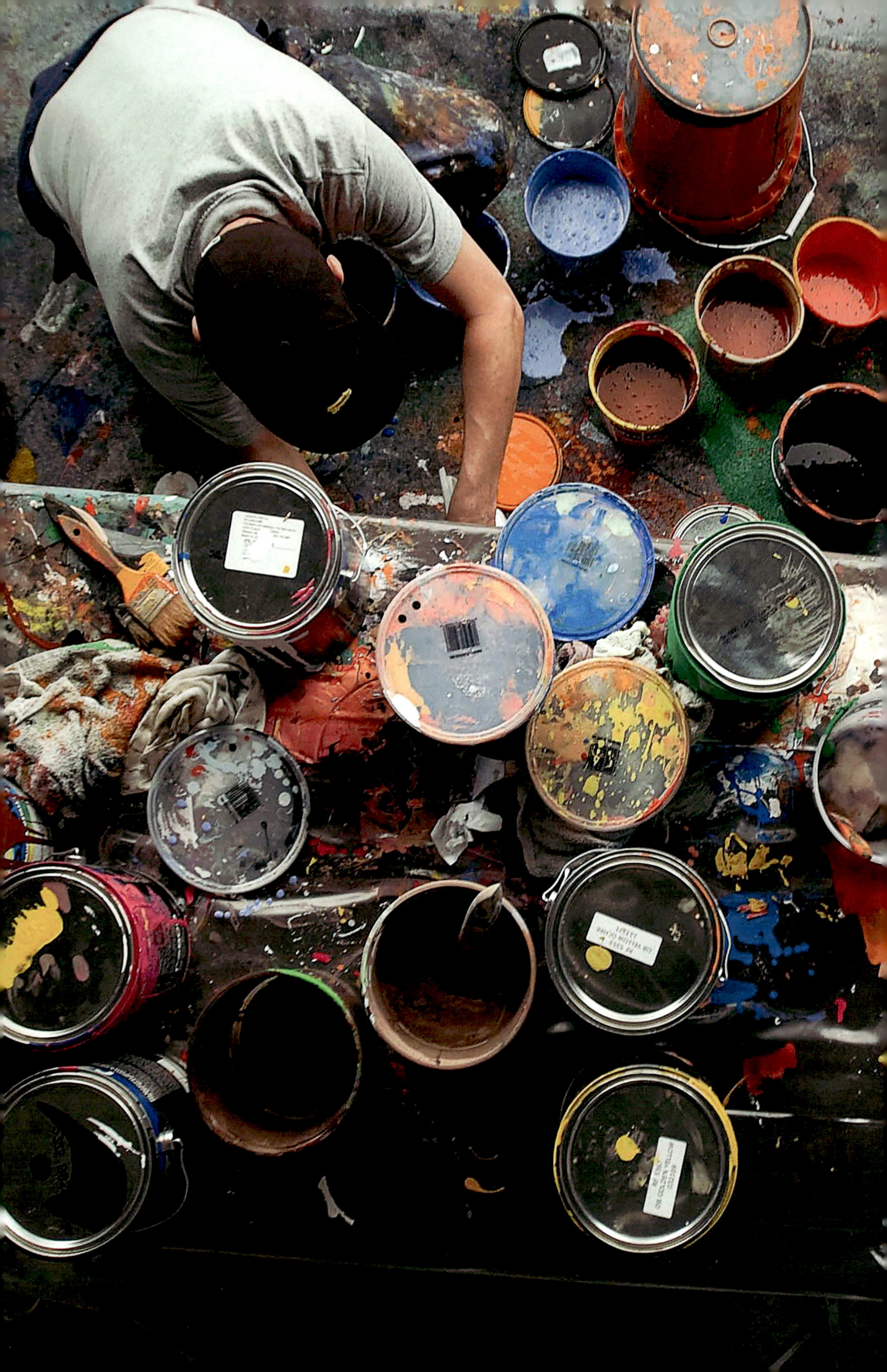

VIDEO ART
A CURATORIAL PERSPECTIVE

KANITRA FLETCHER
LANDMARKS VIDEO CURATOR

In 2008, as a part-time program assistant at Landmarks, I had no idea that I would embark on an eleven-year career as curator of Landmarks Video. The early days, when three of us shared a two-desk office are long gone. As Landmarks grew, so did its vision of the types of media to include in a public art program. While most people expect to see sculpture, Landmarks took an innovative approach by establishing a media station to screen videos in the Fine Arts Building. In doing so, our program has become a vital showcase and resource for video art.

We have featured classics in the field, such as Dara Birnbaum's *Technology/Transformation: Wonder Woman* (1978–79); Howardena Pindell's *Free, White and 21* (1980); and highlighted lesser known, international works, including Adrian Balseca's *Suspensión I* (2019); Ventura Knopová's *Tutorial* (2015); and Athi-Patra Ruga's *Over the Rainbow (Queens in Exile Series)* (2016–17). With works like these we demonstrate the complex ways artists express their ideas through moving images and new forms of technology, often expanding their practices and pushing the boundaries of artistic disciplines and art historical categories since the 1960s.

My passion for discovering new artists and videos, along with my time spent considering the works and my commitment to curating a compelling season each year, has been fulfilling. I am honored to share this program with students, staff, faculty, and other visitors. I am also grateful to the generous artists, galleries, and lenders who have allowed us to showcase their works. And a special thanks goes to the Landmarks staff for their support and patience.

Working with our director, Andrée Bober, to finalize selections each year has been a pleasure, often leading to lively discussions and occasional friendly debates. I appreciate not only the times we are in agreement but also the rare moments of tension as they help us articulate the reasoning behind our selections and ultimately strengthen the program. I look forward to future discussions and viewings, continuing to watch artists develop their practices, and growing Landmarks Video toward another milestone anniversary.

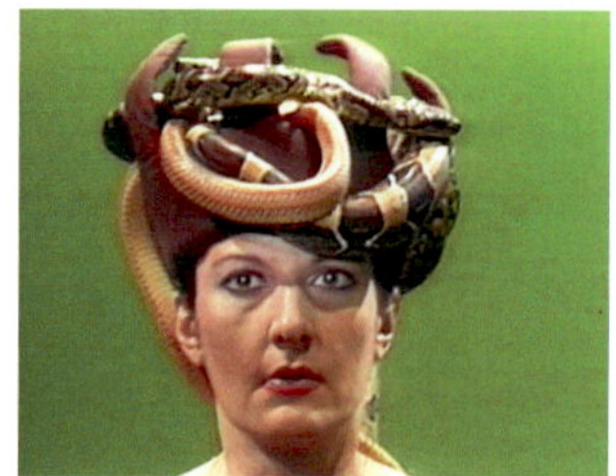

MARINA ABRAMOVIČ and CHARLES ATLAS

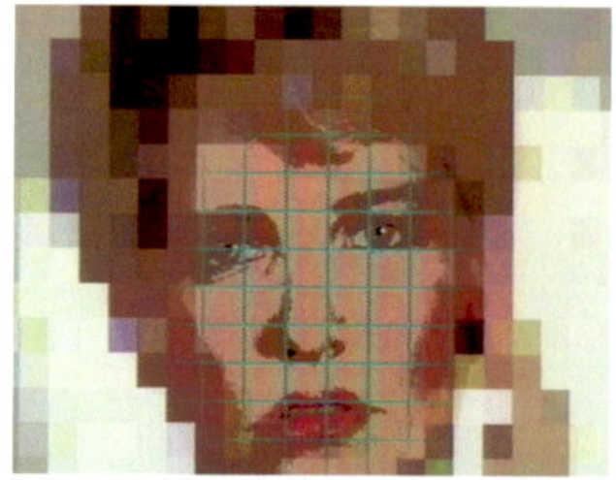

MAX ALMY

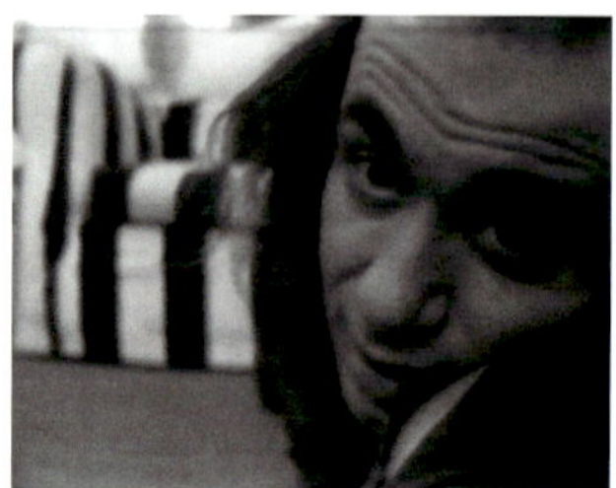

VITO ACCONCI

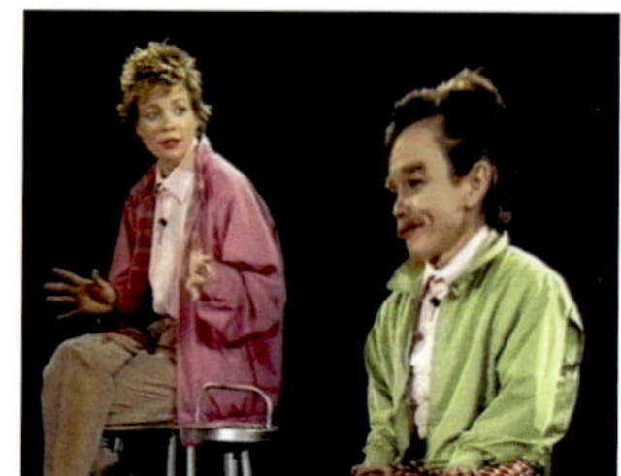

LAURIE ANDERSON

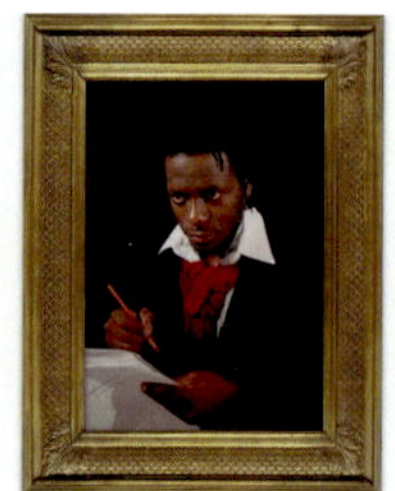

TERRY ADKINS

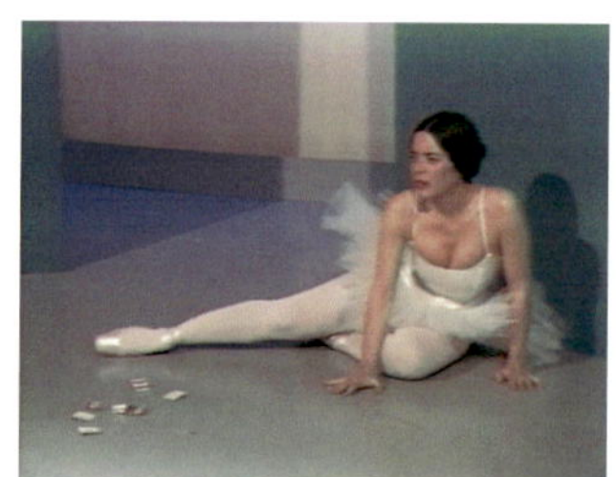

ELEANOR ANTIN

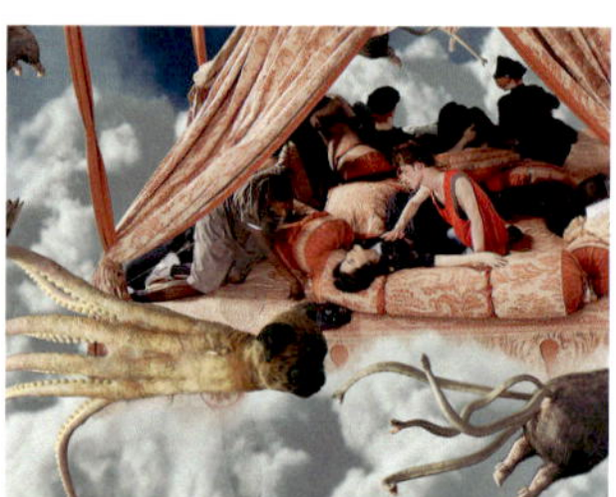

AES+F

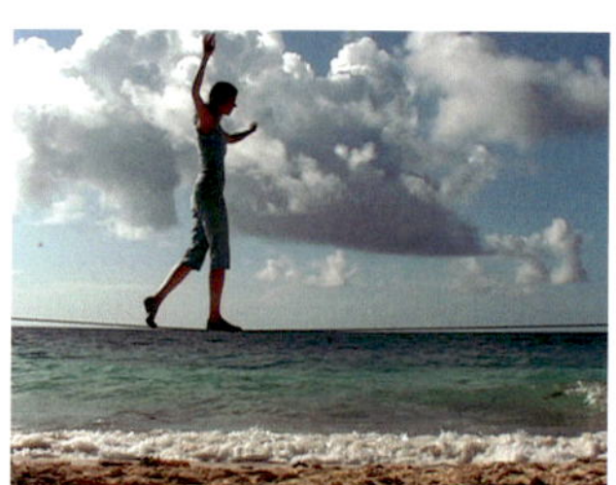

JANINE ANTONI

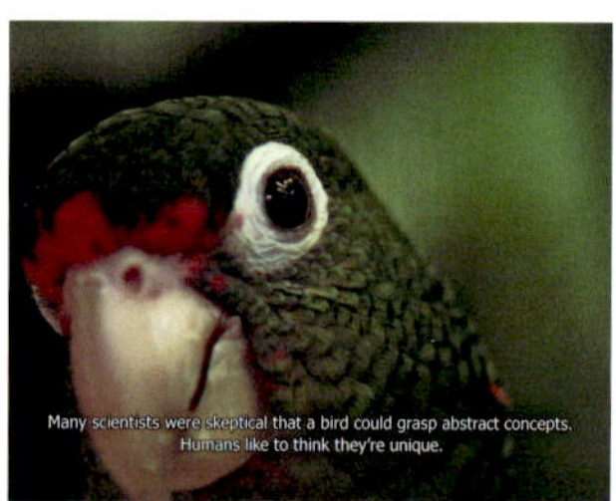

ALLORA & CALZADILLA

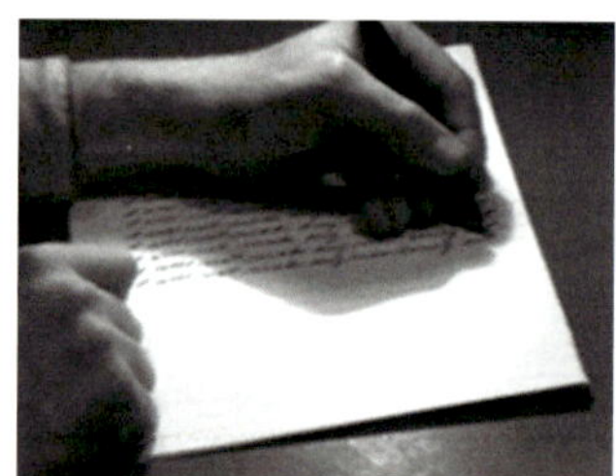

JOHN BALDESSARI

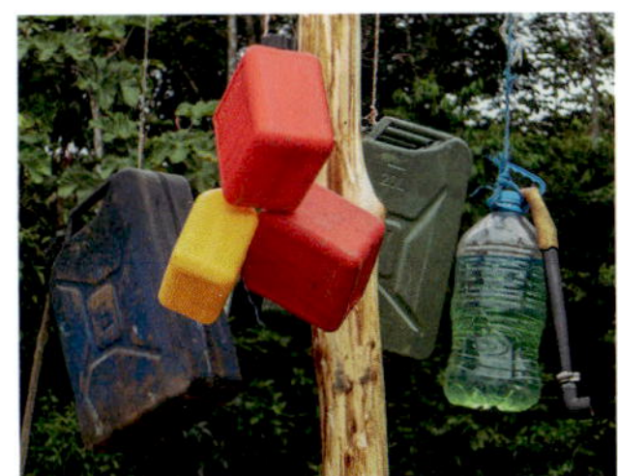
ADRIÁN BALSECA

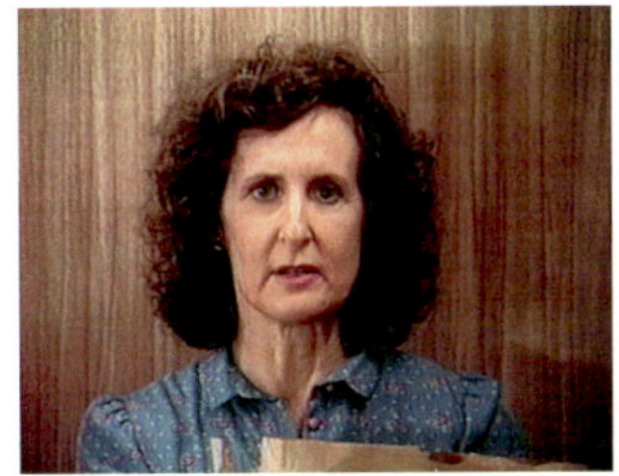
BURT BARR

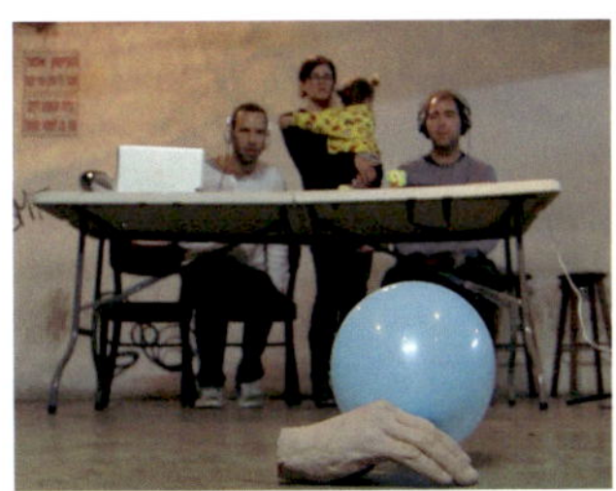
GUY BEN-NER

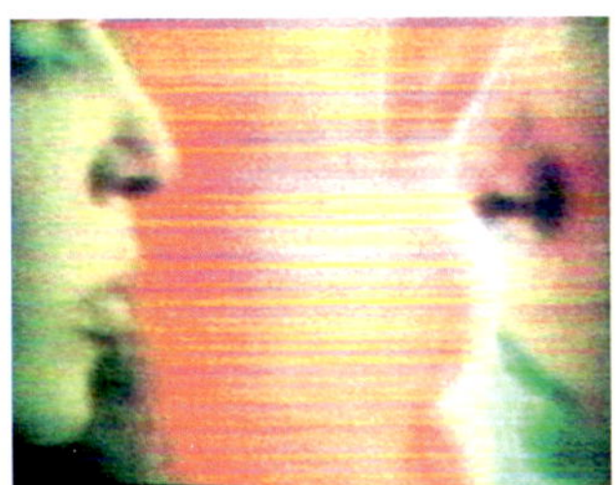
LYNDA BENGLIS

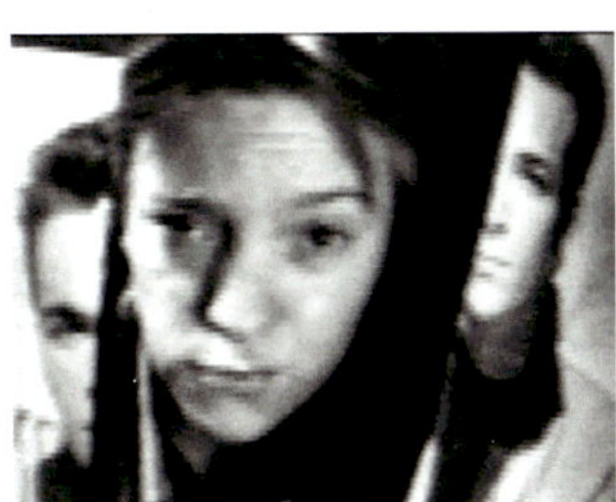
SADIE BENNING

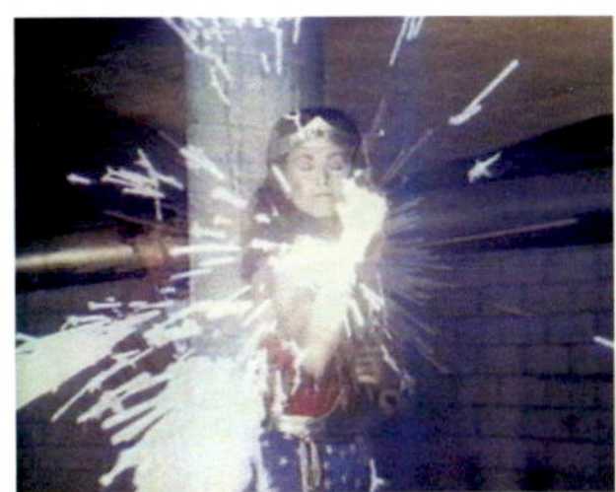
DARA BIRNBAUM

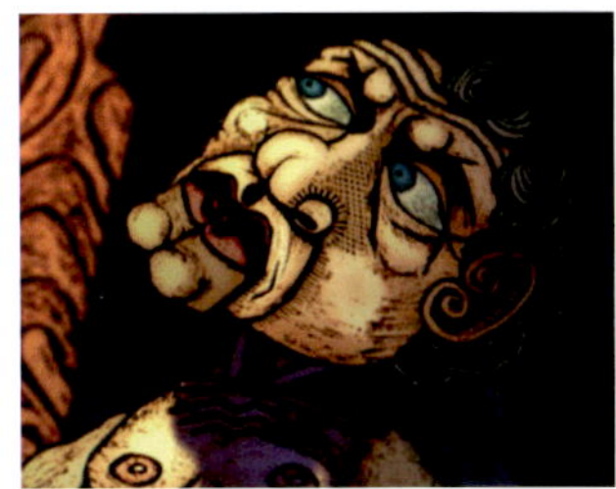
JAY BOLOTIN

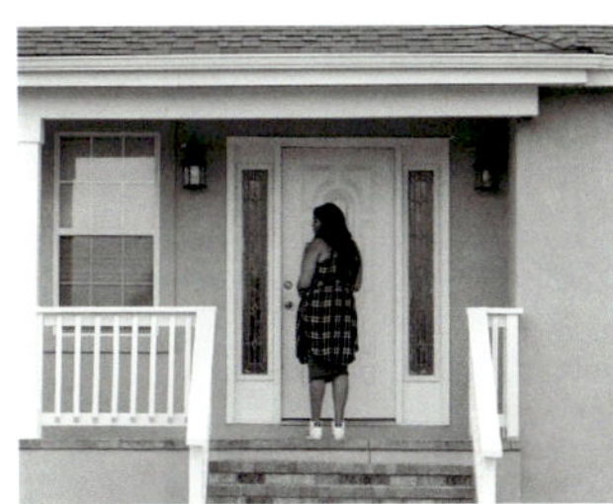
GARRETT BRADLEY

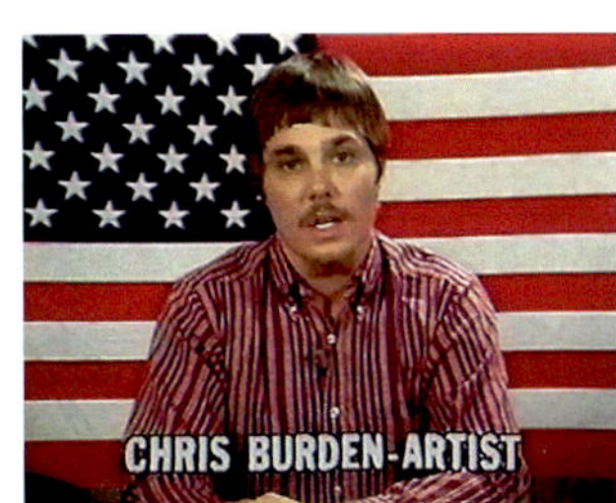

CHRIS BURDEN

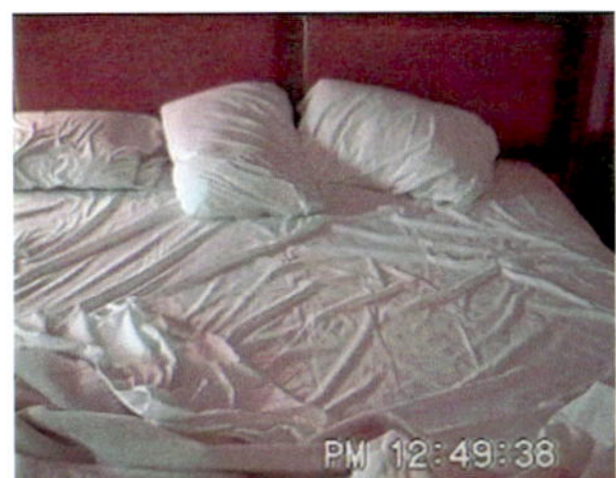

SOPHIE CALLE and
GREGORY SHEPHARD

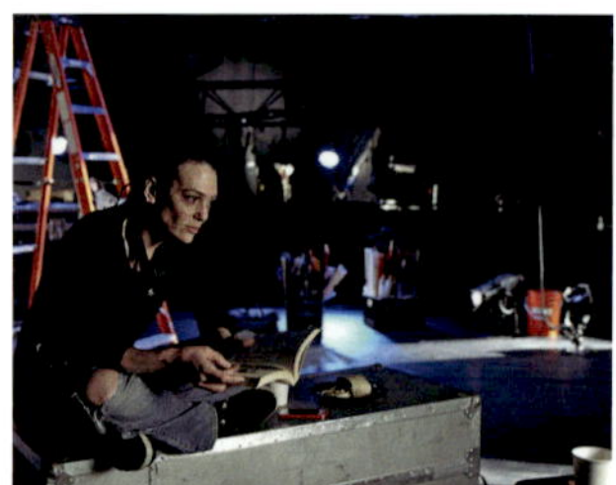
CAMEL COLLECTIVE

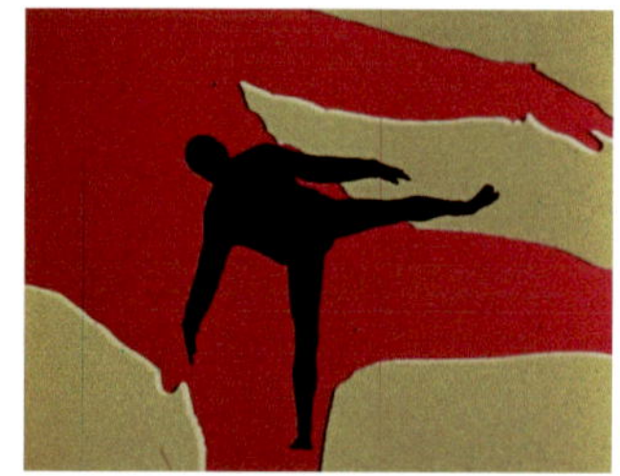
MERCE CUNNINGHAM and RICHARD MOORE

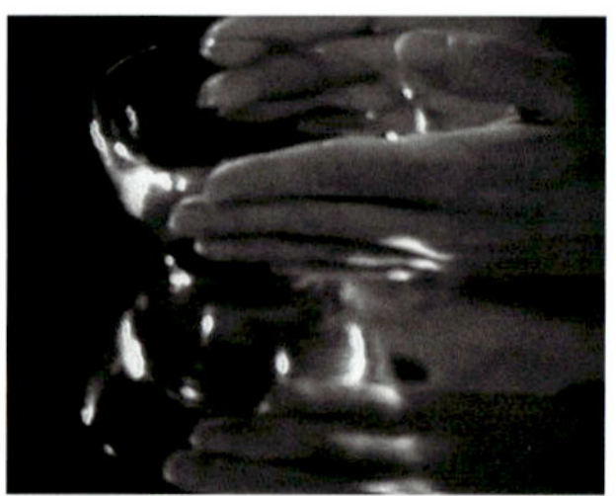
THERESA HAK KYUNG CHA

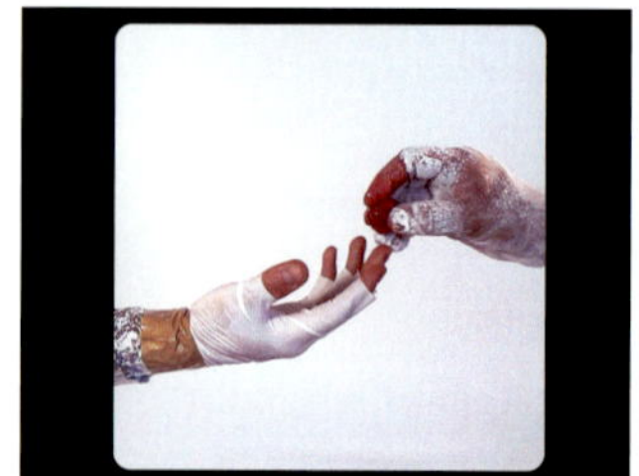
ALEX DA CORTE

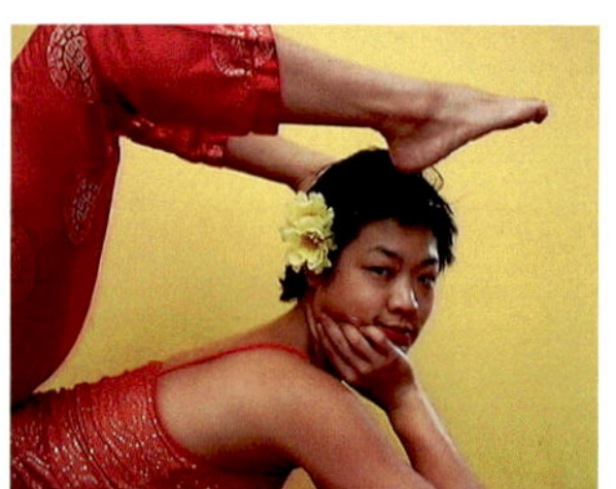
PATTY CHANG

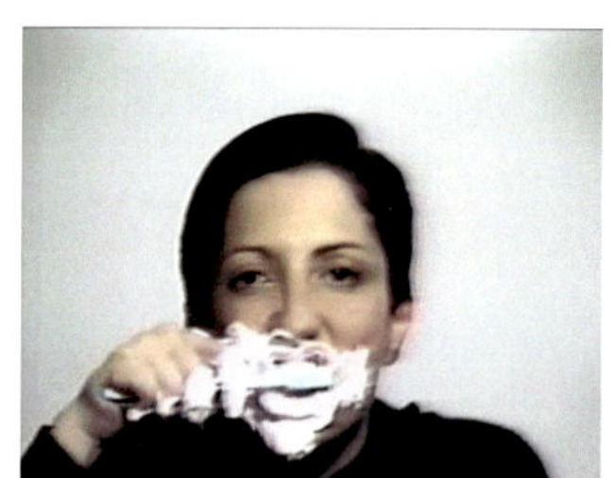
LENORA DE BARROS

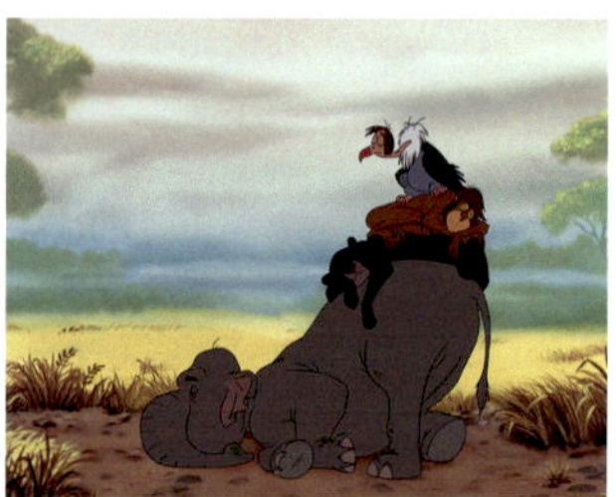
DAVID CLAERBOUT

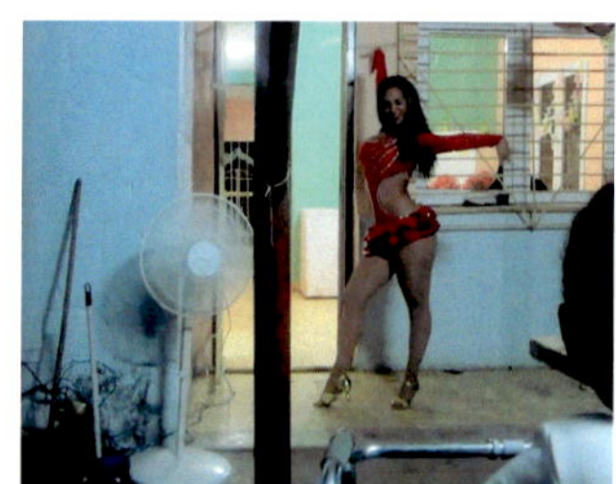
ALEJANDRO FIGUEREDO DÍAZ-PERERA

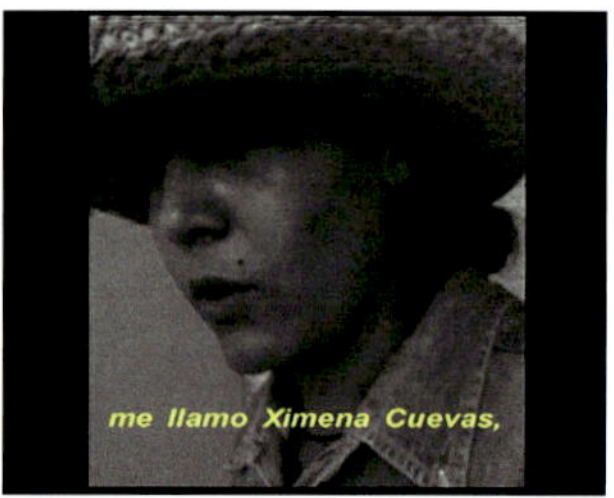

XIMENA CUEVAS

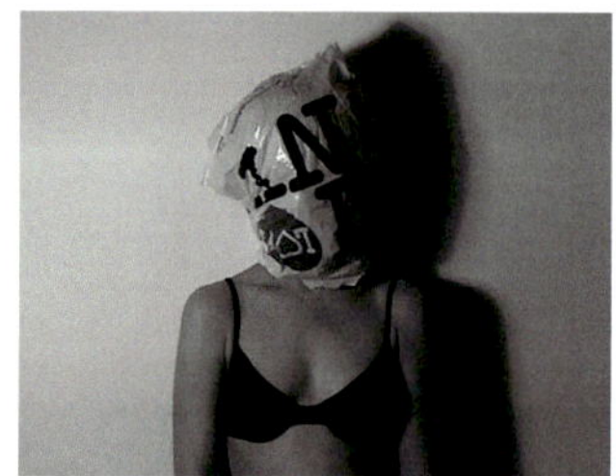
CHERYL DONEGAN

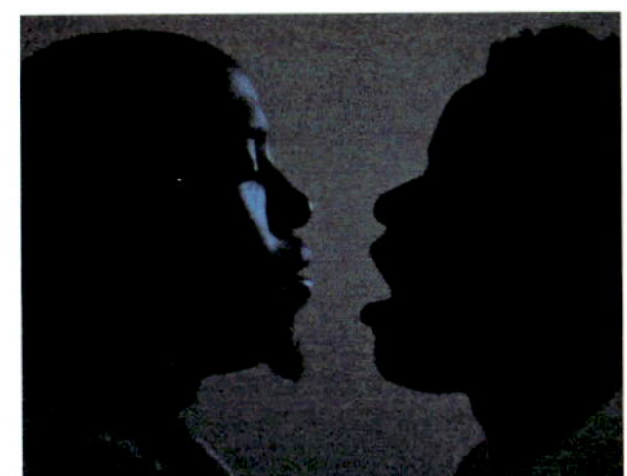
JOHN EDMONDS

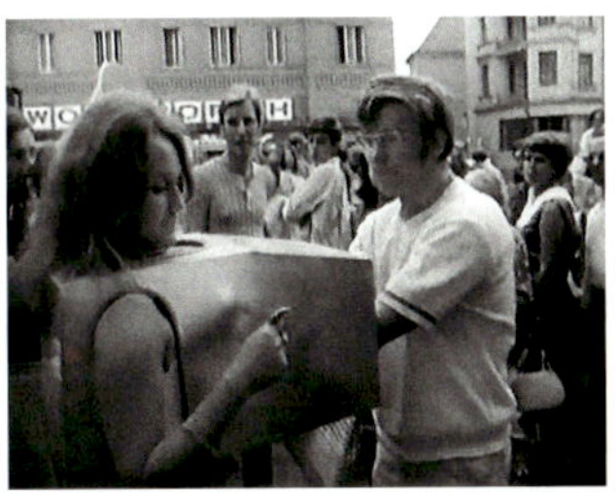
VALIE EXPORT

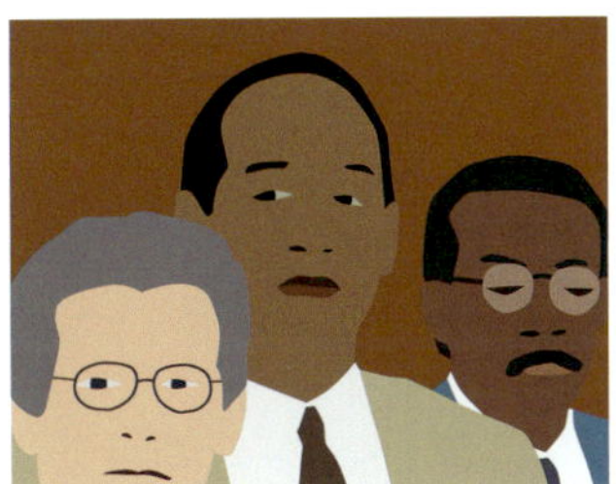
KOTA EZAWA

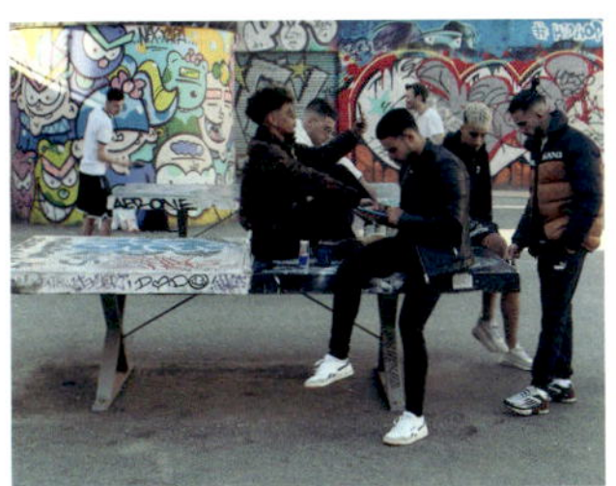
ARASH FAYEZ

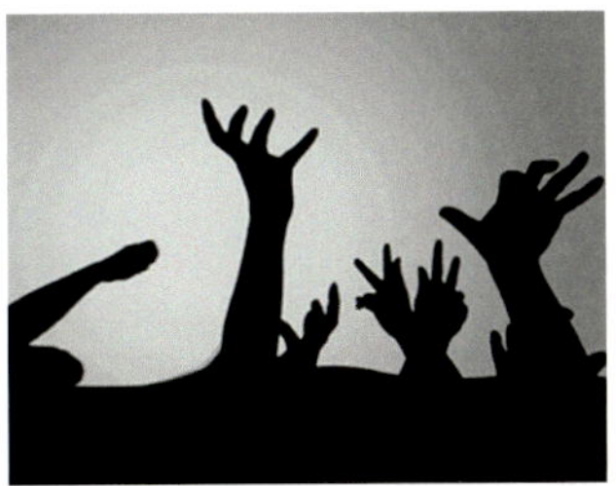
CAO FEI

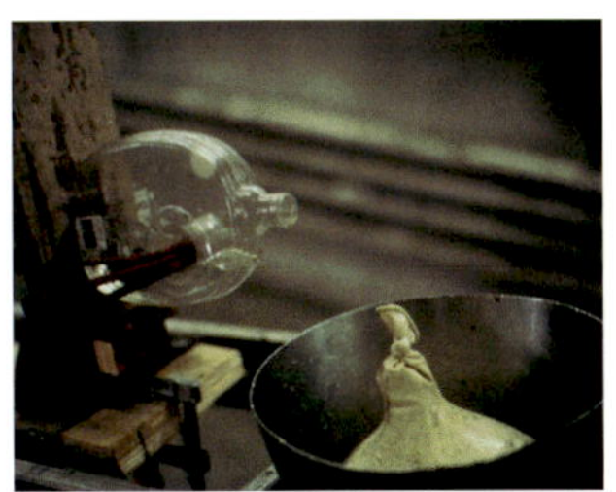
FISCHLI & WEISS

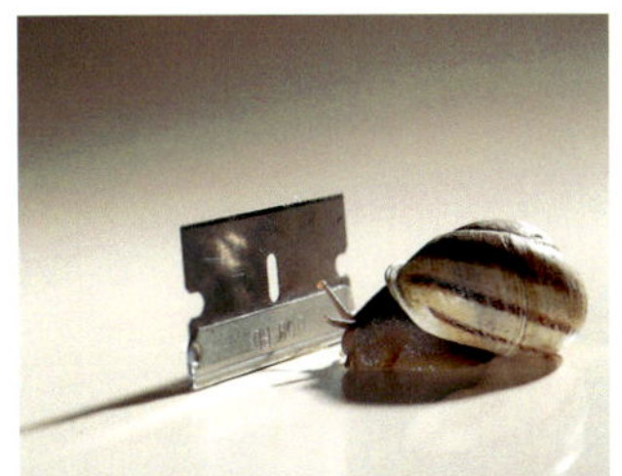
JESSE FLEMING

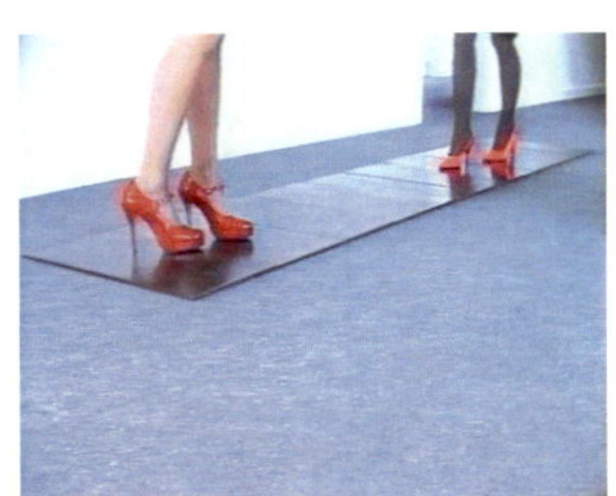
SYLVIE FLEURY

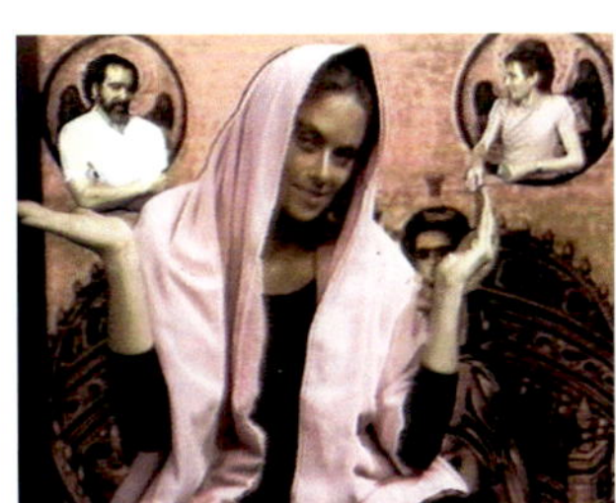
HERMINE FREED

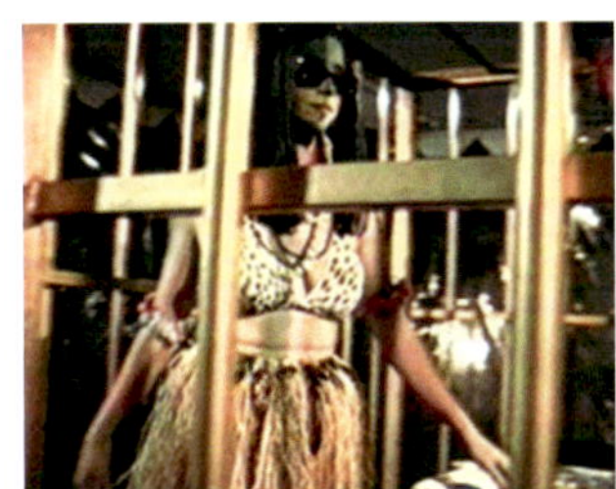
COCO FUSCO and PAULA HEREDIA

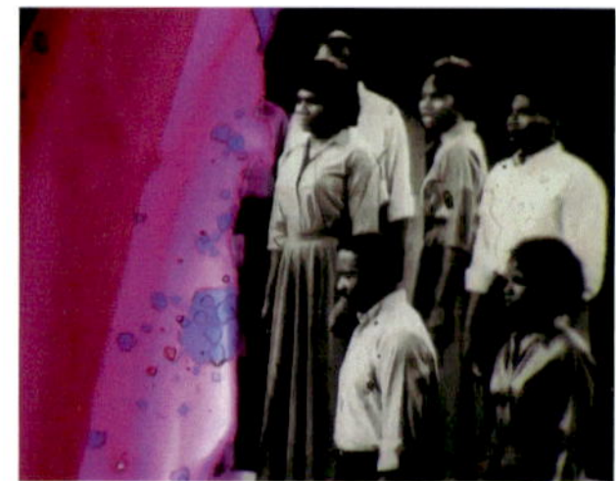
JA'TOVIA GARY

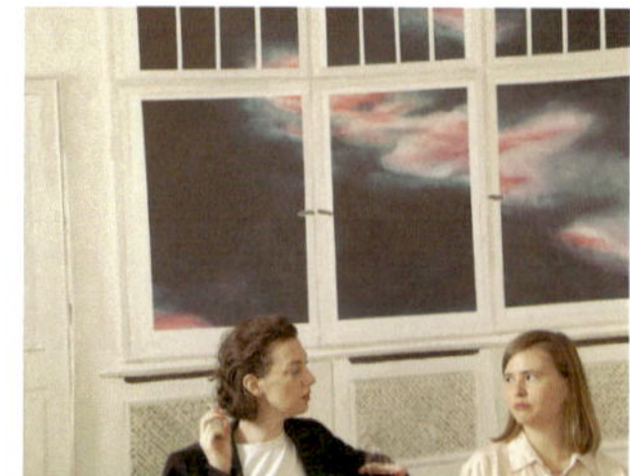
FRIEDER HALLER

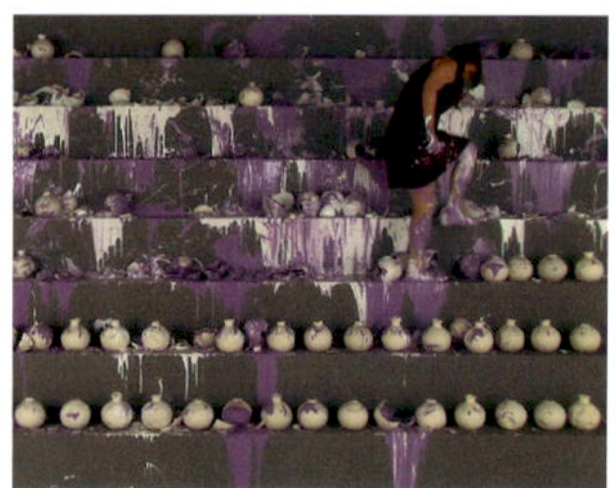
KATE GILMORE

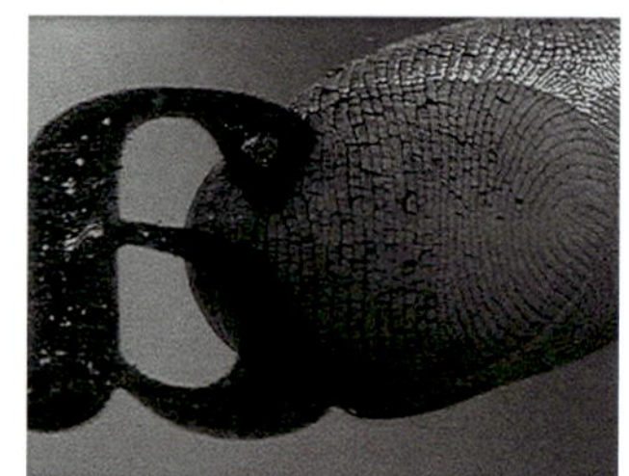
ANN HAMILTON

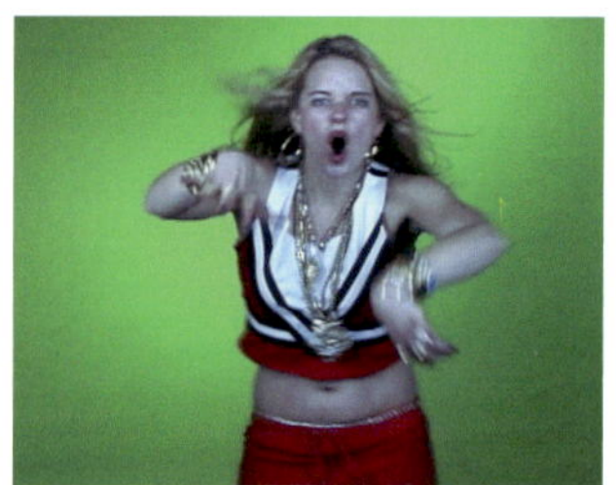
LUIS GISPERT

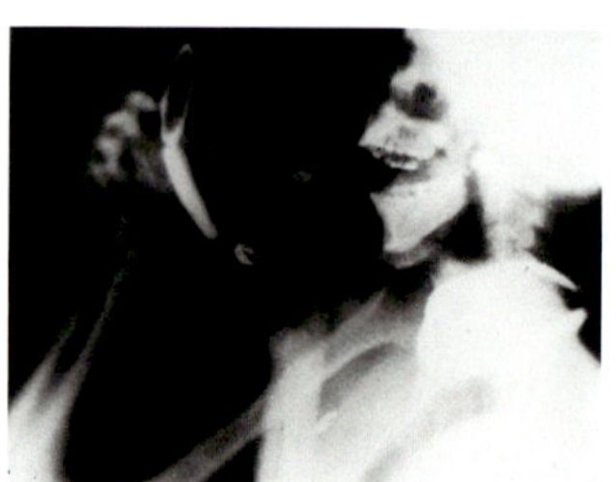
BARBARA HAMMER

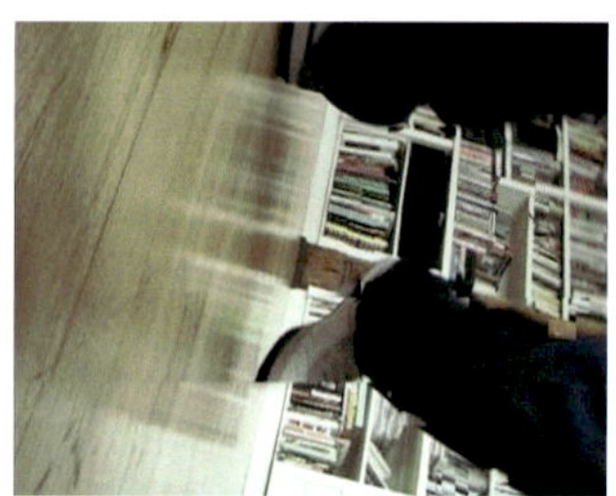
DOUGLAS GORDON

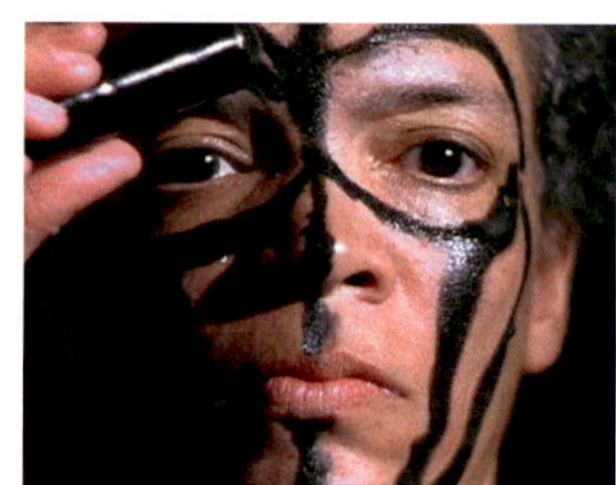
MAREN HASSINGER

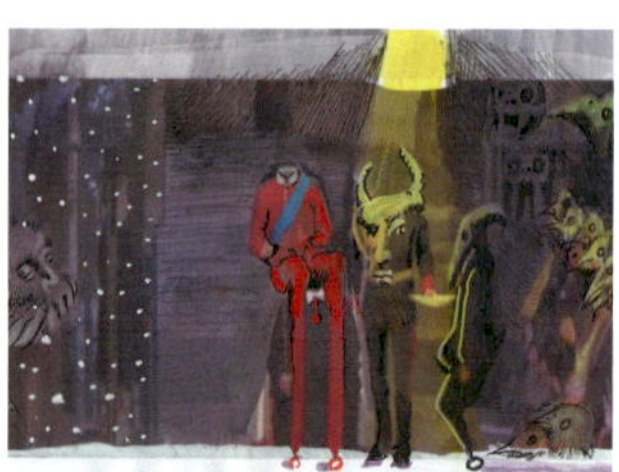
ROKNI HAERIZADEH

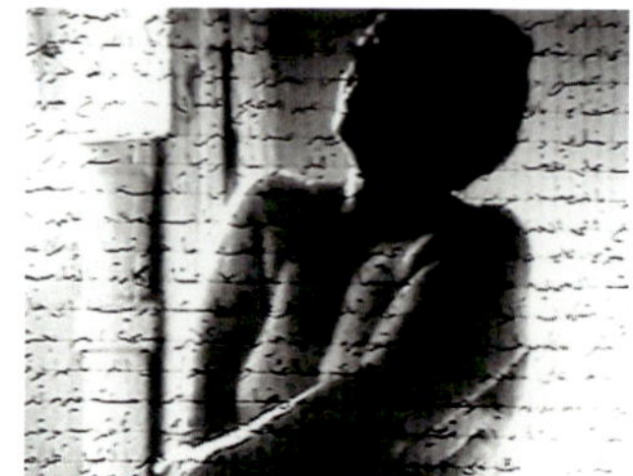
MONA HATOUM

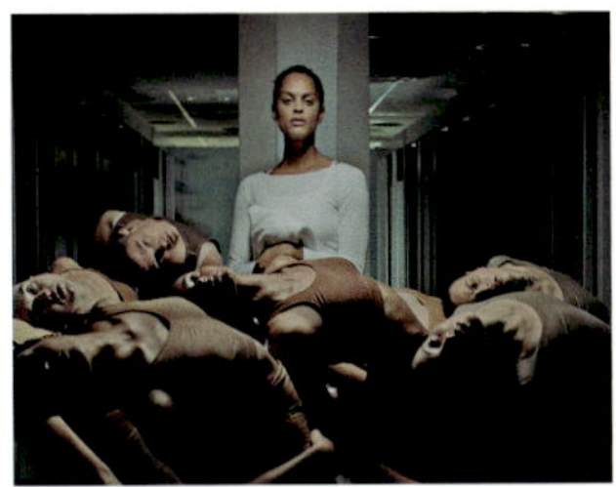
LAURA HERMANIDES

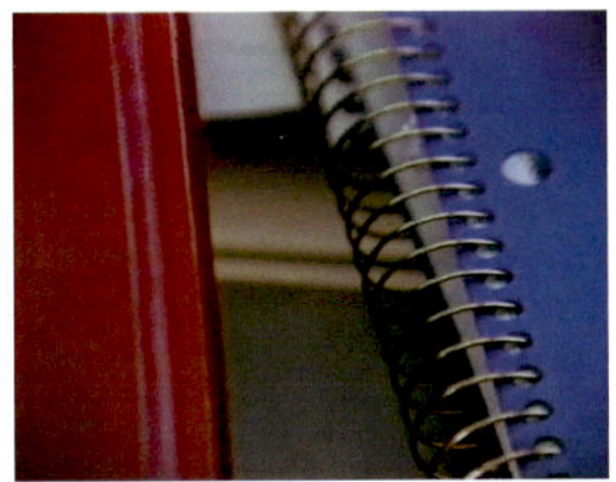
GARY HILL

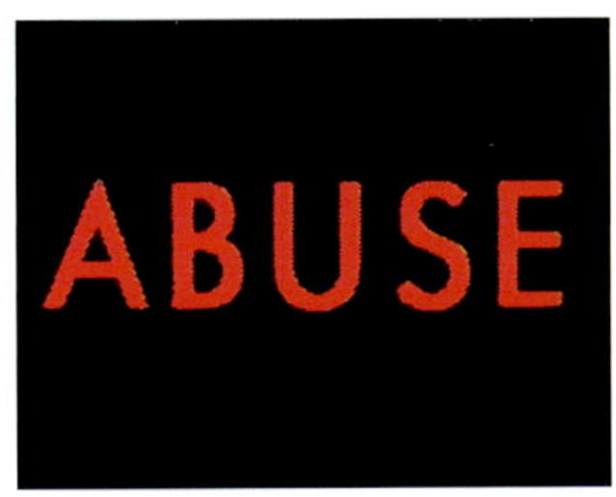

JENNY HOLZER

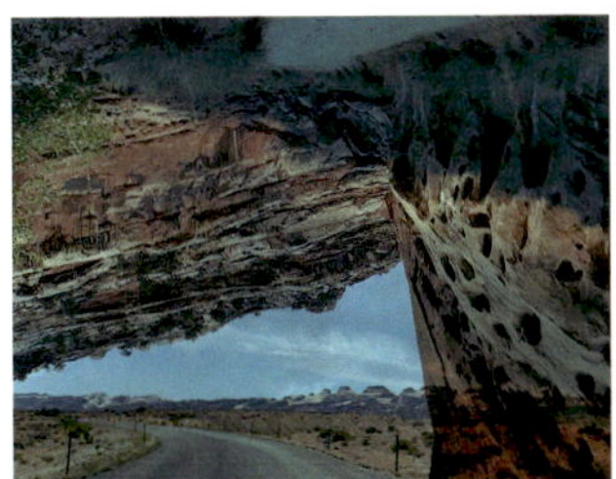
SKY HOPINKA

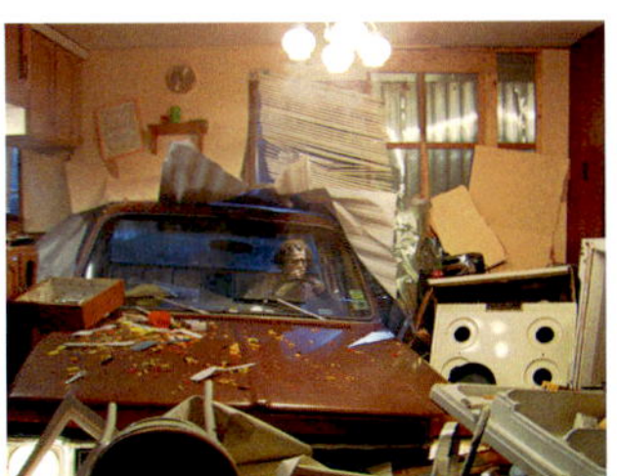
TERESA HUBBARD / ALEXANDER BIRCHLER

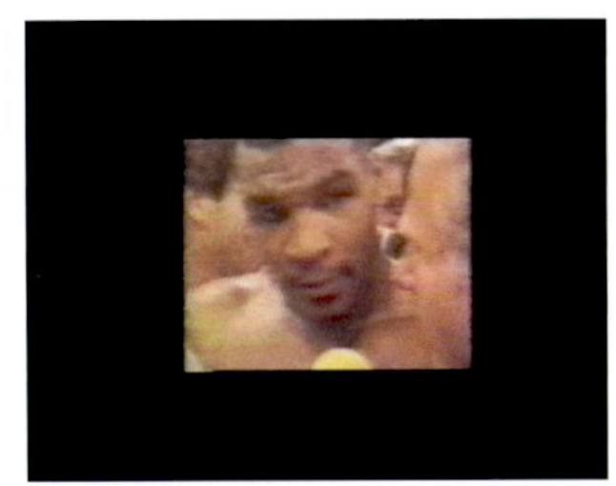
ULYSSES JENKINS

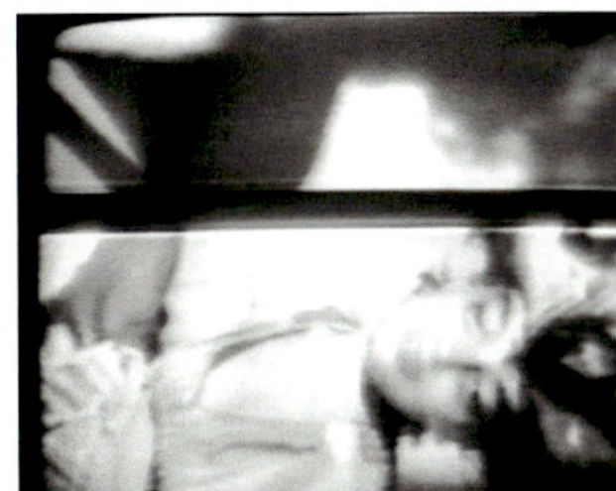
JOAN JONAS

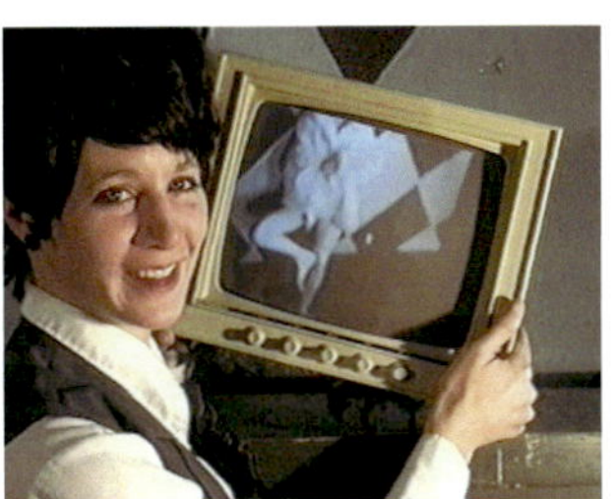
MIRANDA JULY

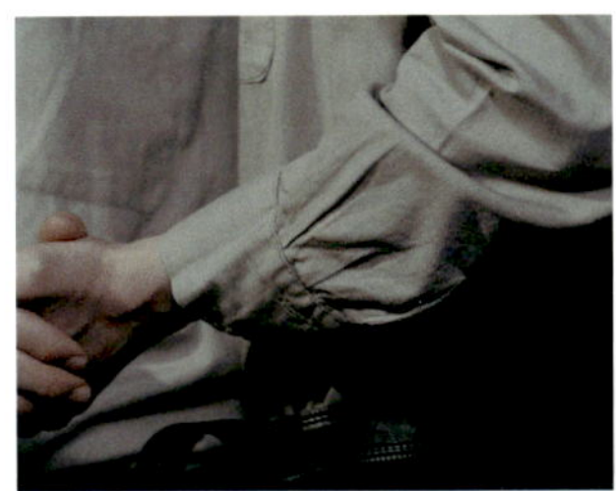
POLINA KANIS

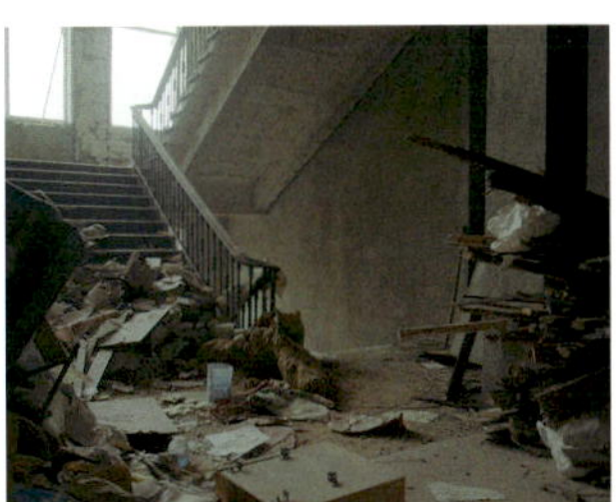
NIKOLAY KARABINOVYTCH

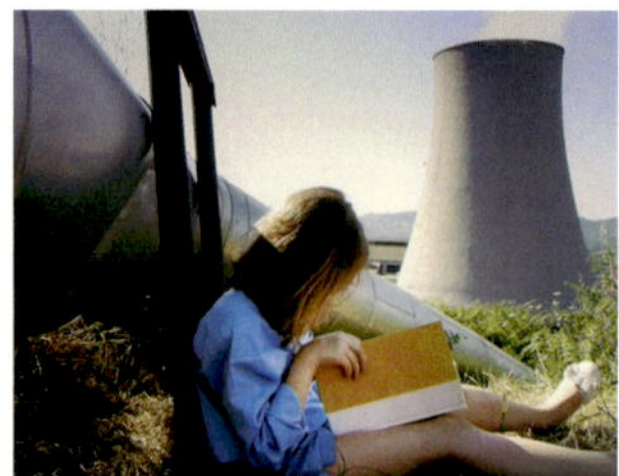

MIKHAIL KARIKIS

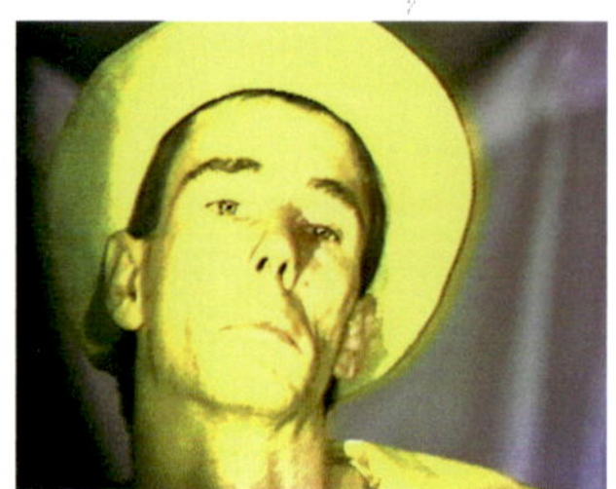

MIKE KELLEY

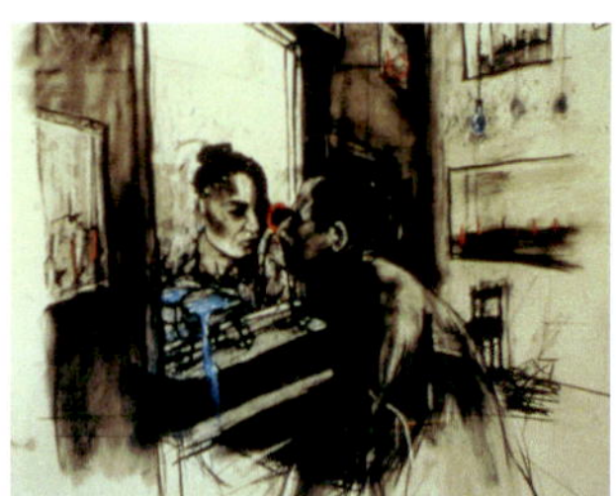

WILLIAM KENTRIDGE

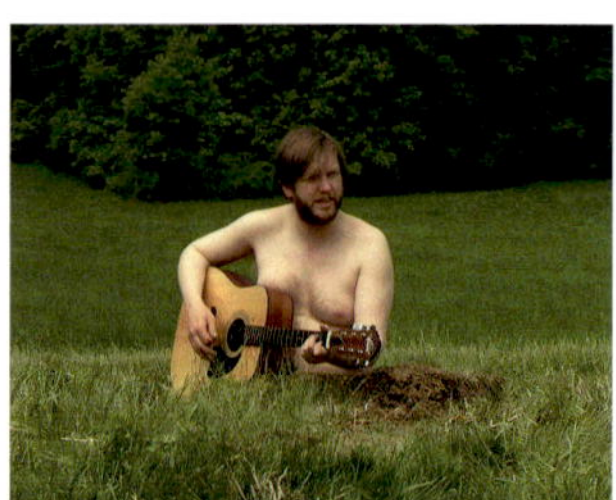

RAGNAR KJARTANSSON

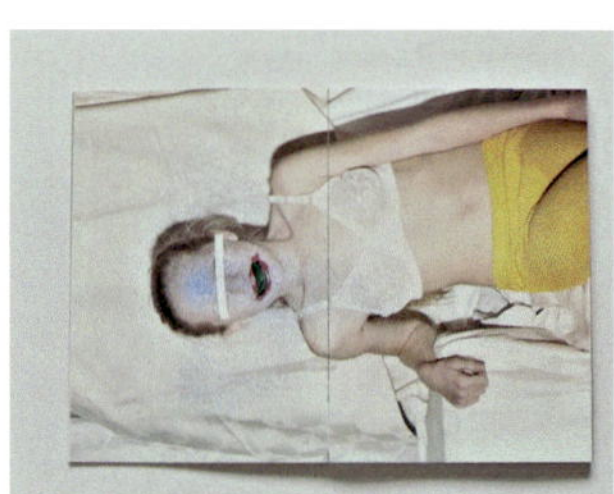

VENDULA KNOPOVÁ

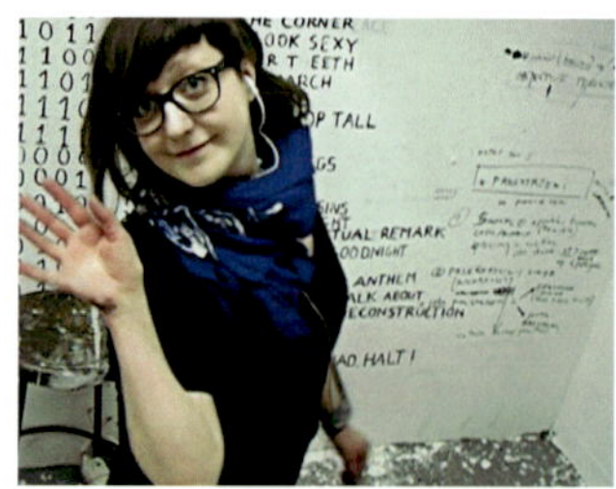

JULIA KUL

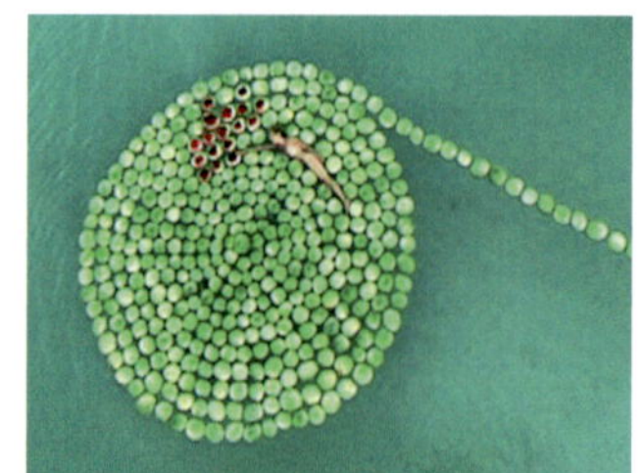

SIGALIT LANDAU

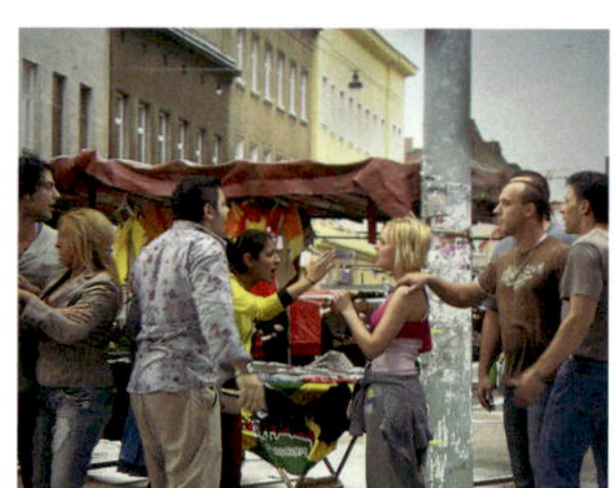

MARK LEWIS

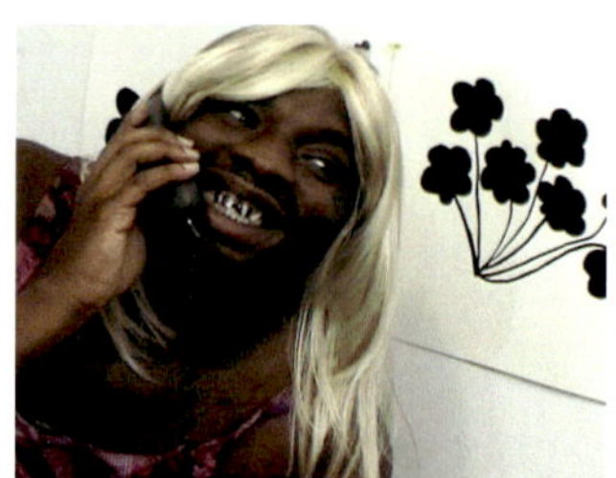

KALUP LINZY

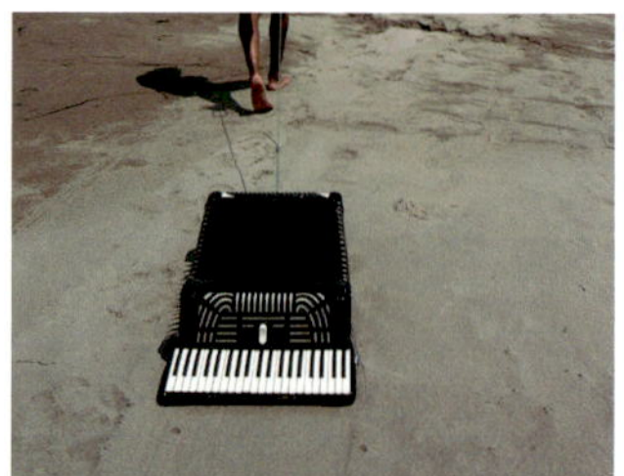

LOS JAICHACKERS

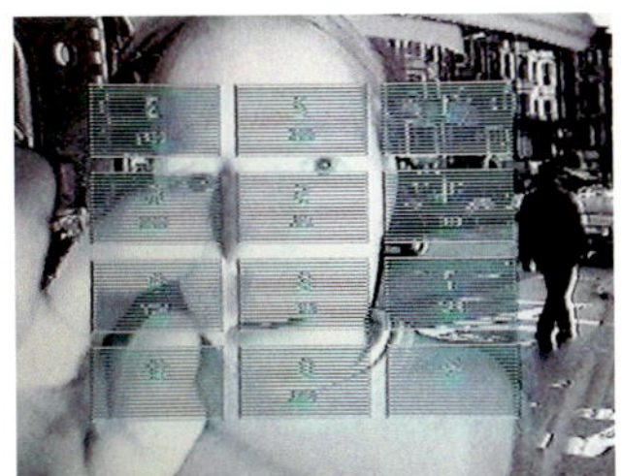
KRISTIN LUCAS

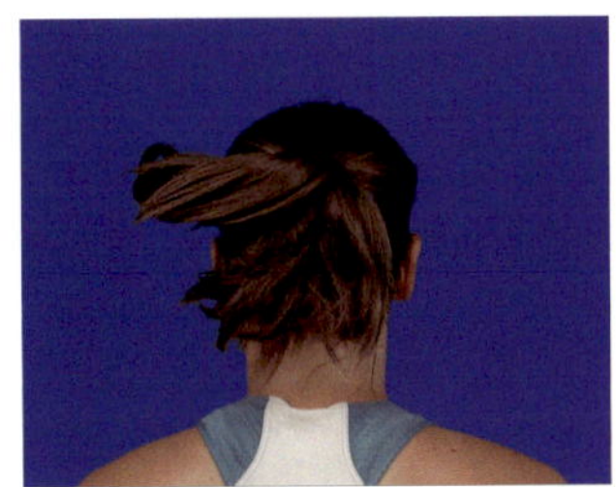
R. ERIC MCMASTER

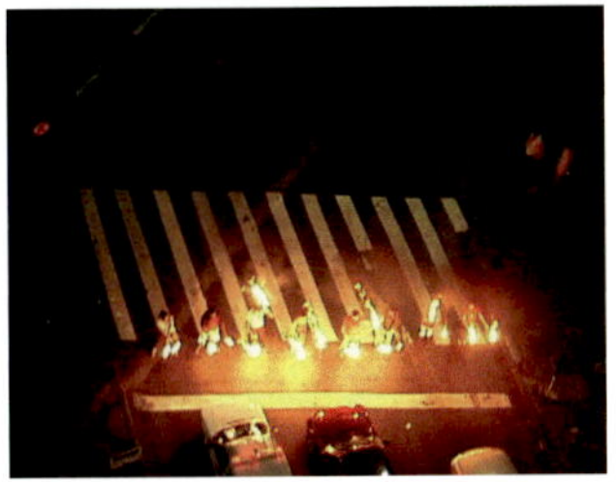
CINTHIA MARCELLE

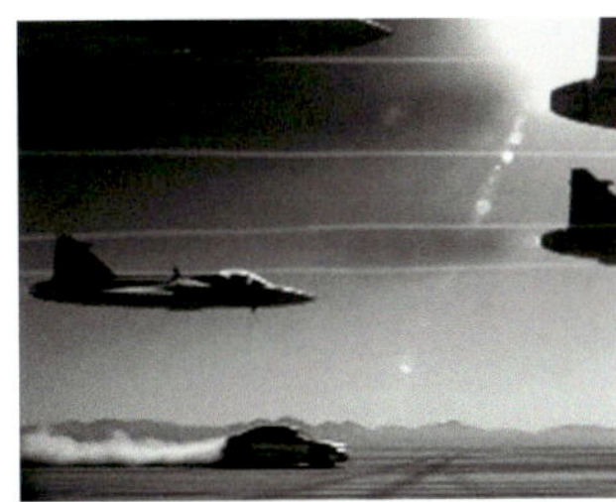
JOSEPHINE MECKSEPER

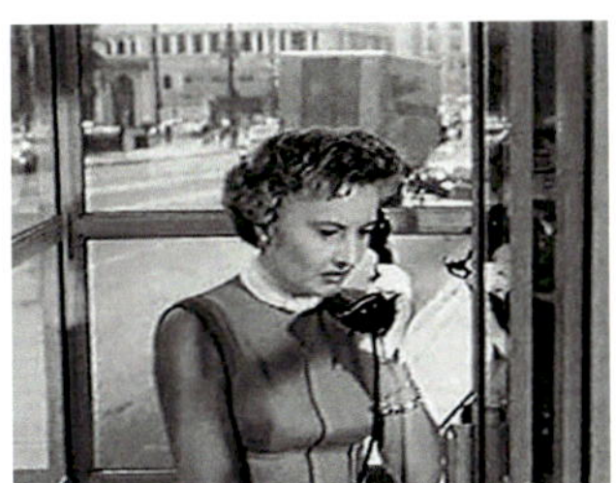
CHRISTIAN MARCLAY

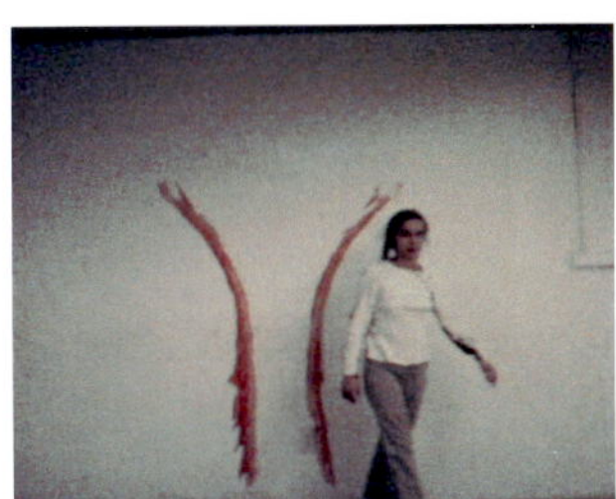
ANA MENDIETA

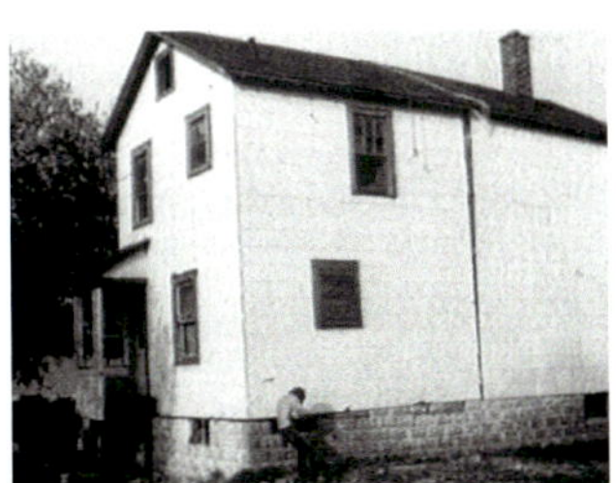
GORDON MATTA-CLARK

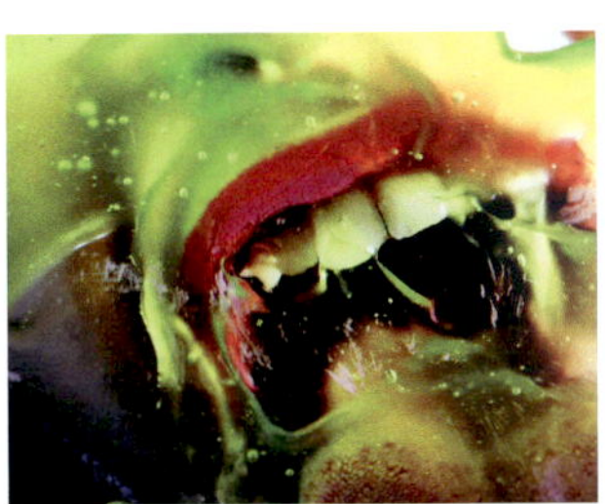
MARILYN MINTER

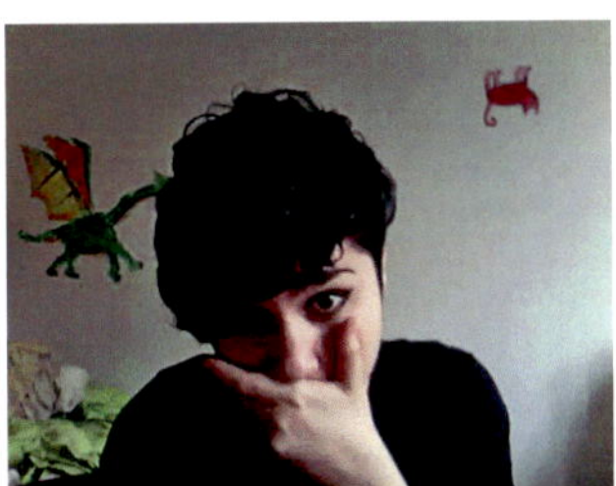
EVA and FRANCO MATTES

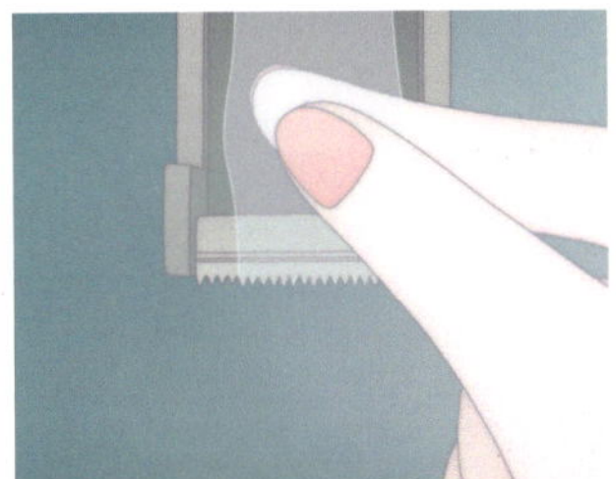
YORIKO MIZUSHIRI

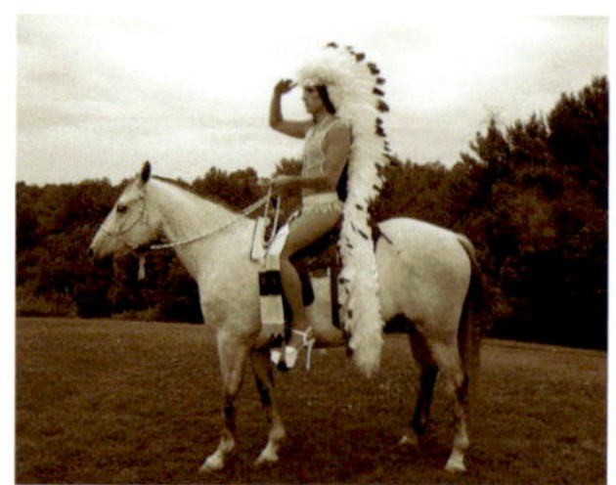
KENT MONKMAN

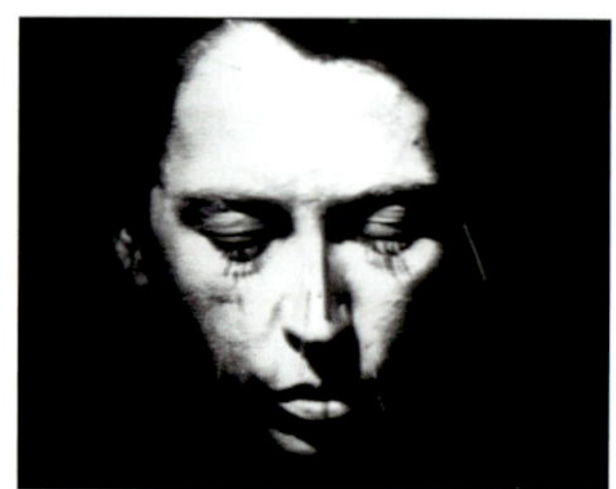
LINDA MONTANO

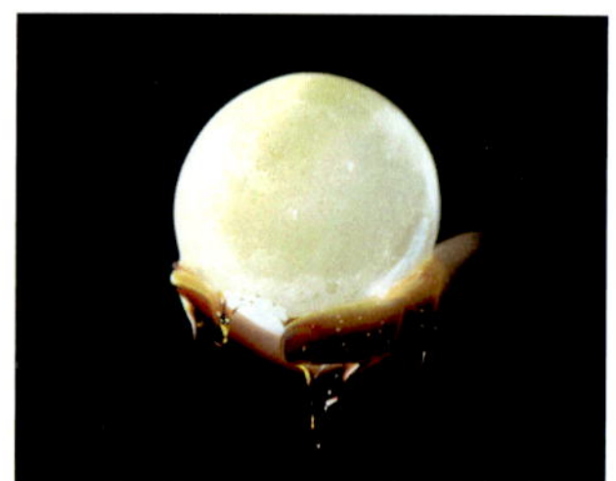
VLM

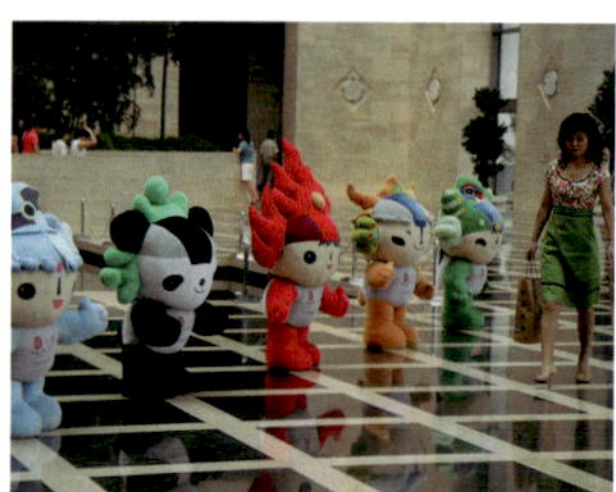
SARAH MORRIS

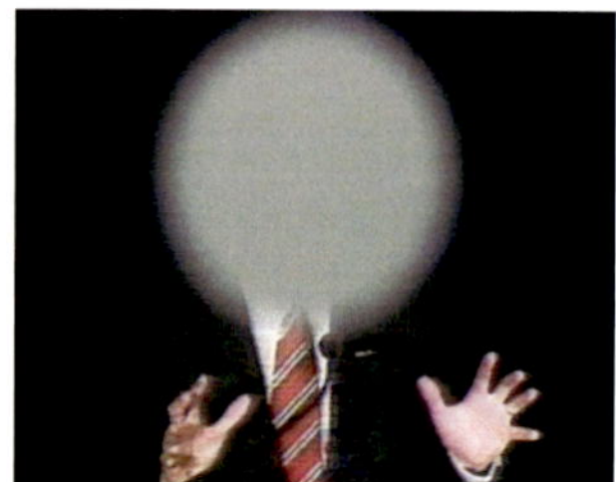
ANTONI MUNTADAS and
MARSHALL REESE

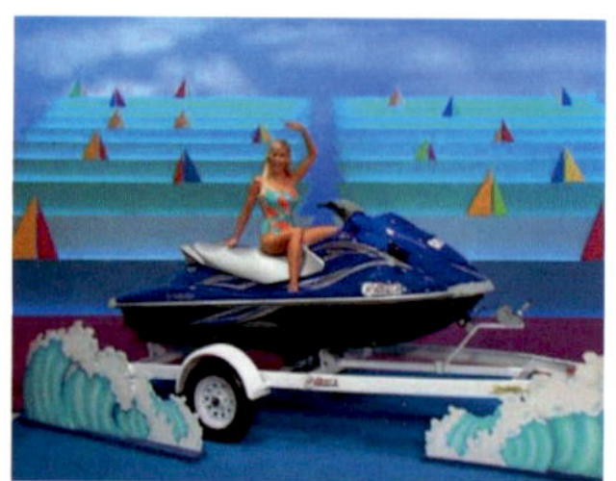
TAKESHI MURATA

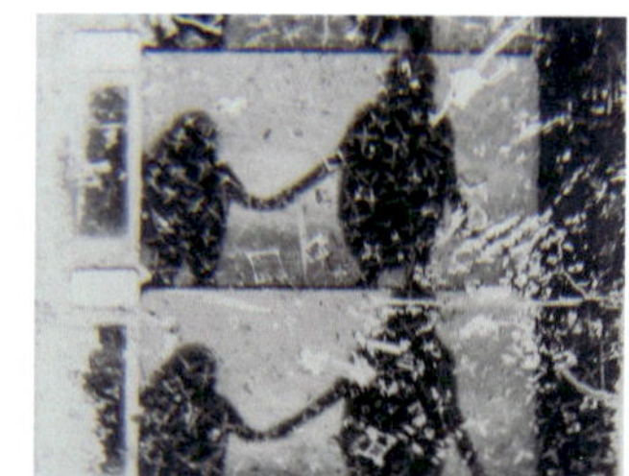
SOFÍA GALLISÁ MURIENTE

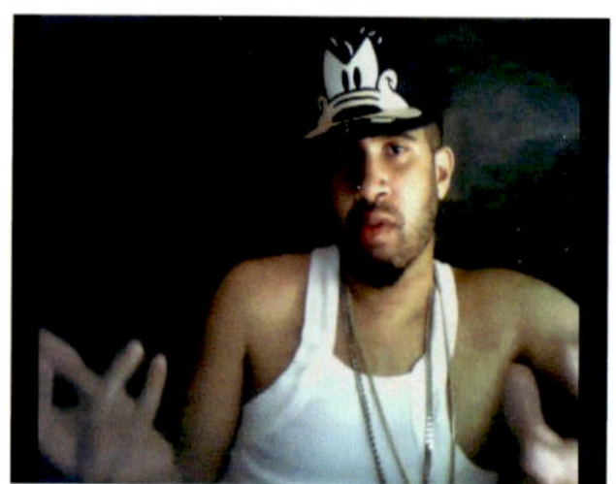
JAYSON SCOTT MUSSON

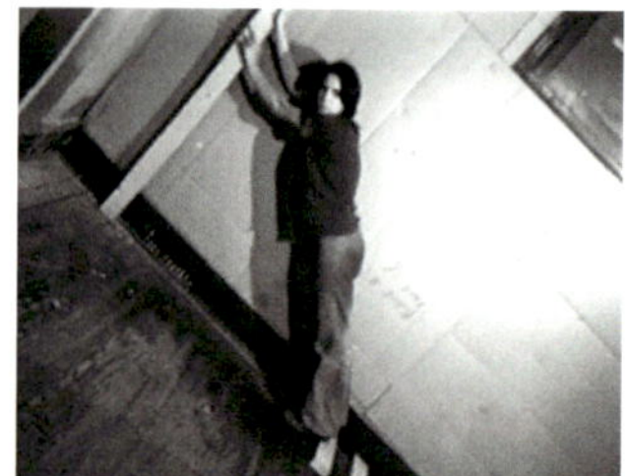
RITA MYERS

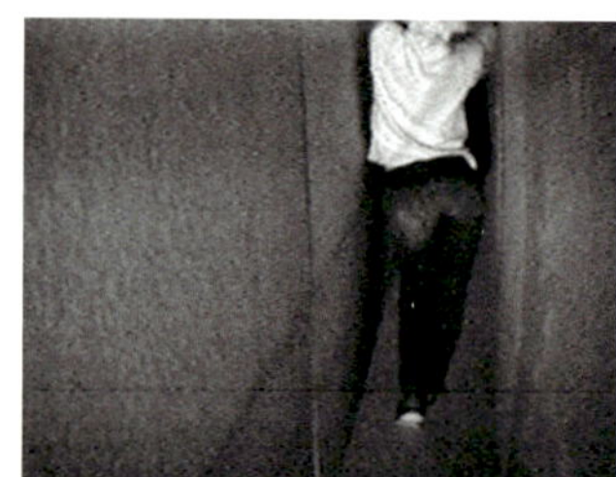
BRUCE NAUMAN

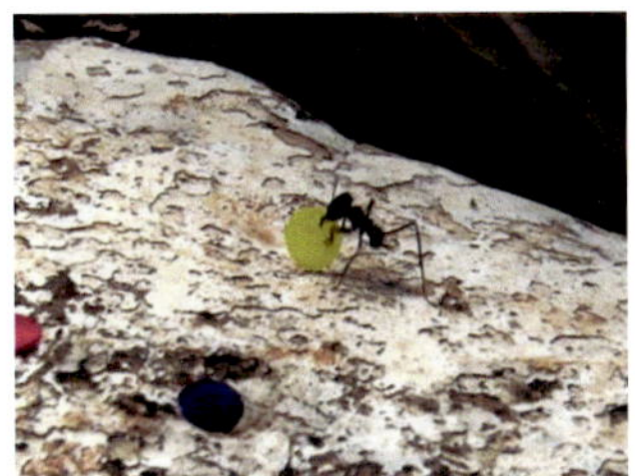
RIVANE NEUENSCHWANDER and CAO GUIMARÃES

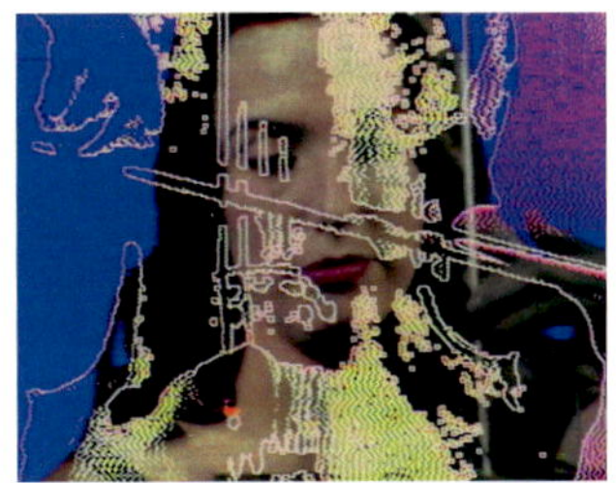
NAM JUNE PAIK and JOHN GODFREY

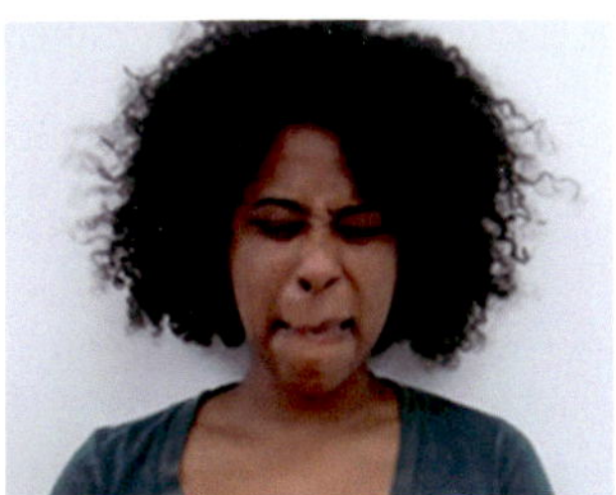
TAMEKA JENEAN NORRIS

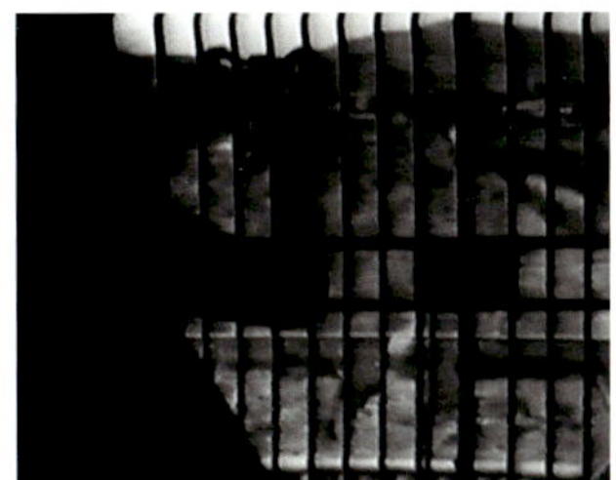
CHARLEMAGNE PALESTINE

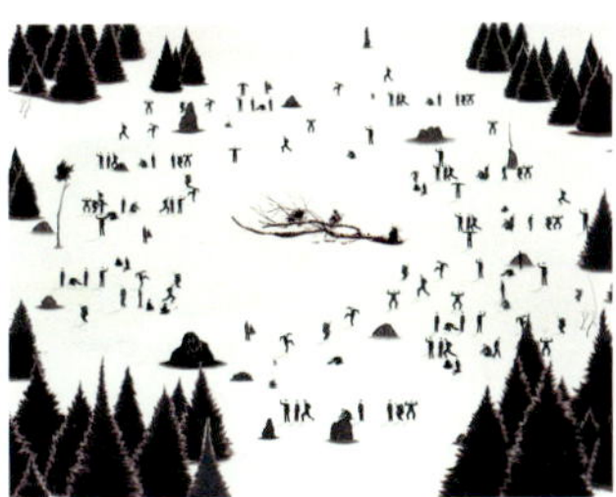
ROBYN O'NEIL

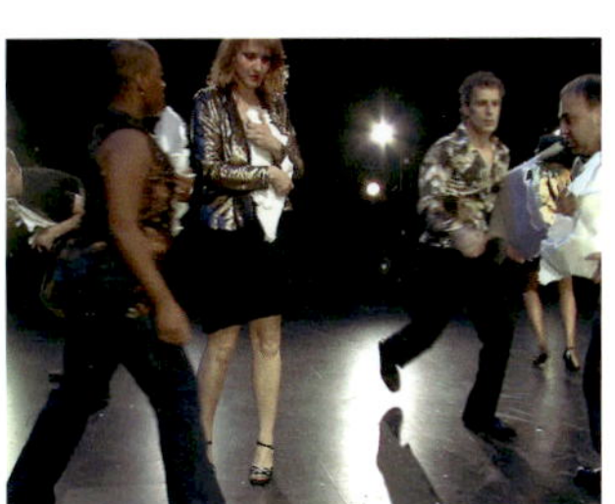
ALIX PEARLSTEIN

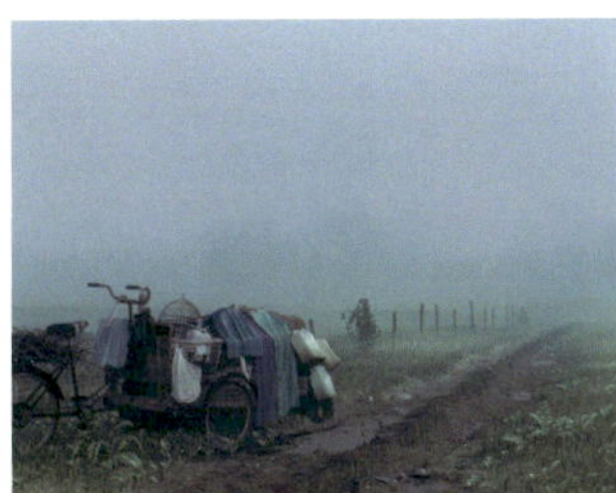
HANS OP DE BEECK

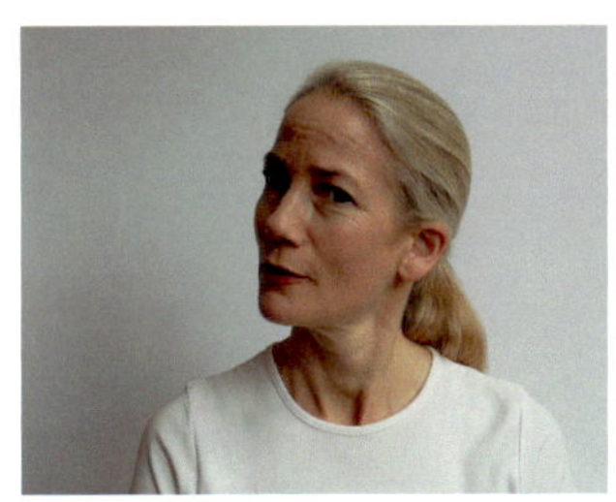
RACHEL PERRY

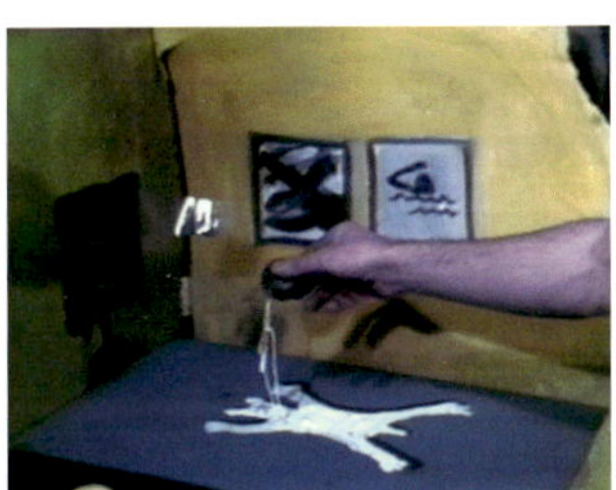
TONY OURSLER

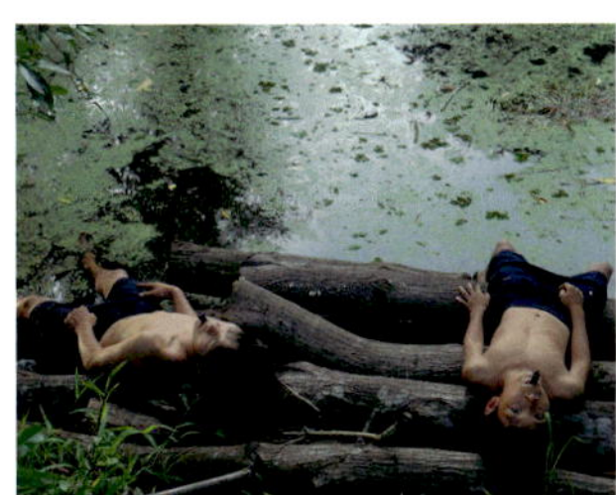
THAO NGUYEN PHAN

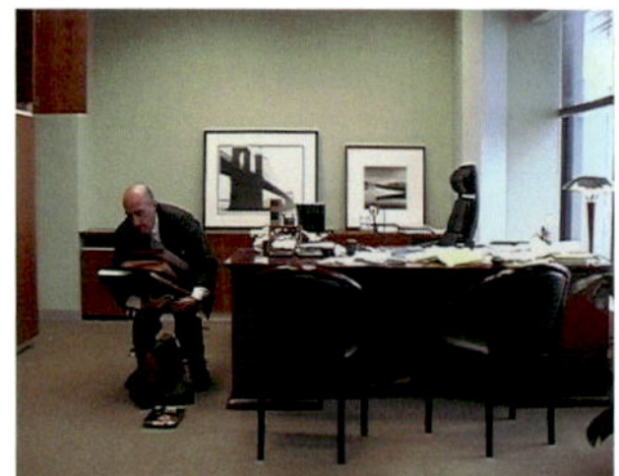
JOHN PILSON

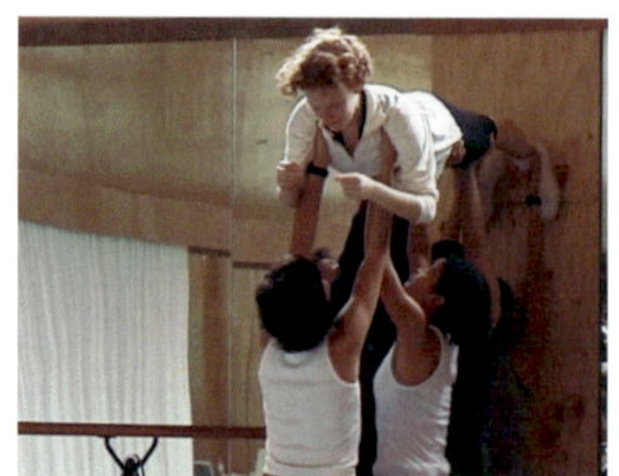
YVONNE RAINER

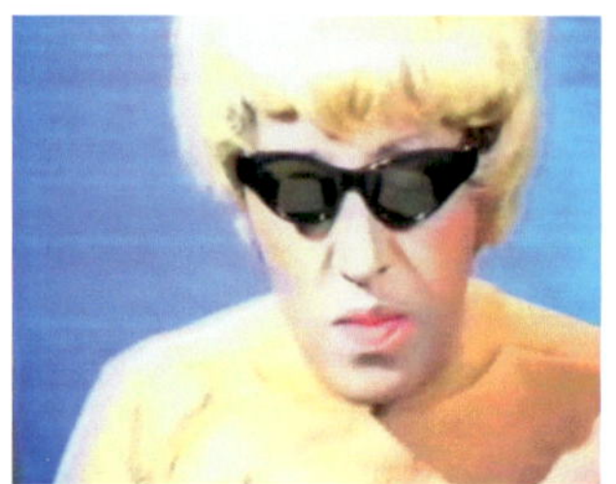
HOWARDENA PINDELL

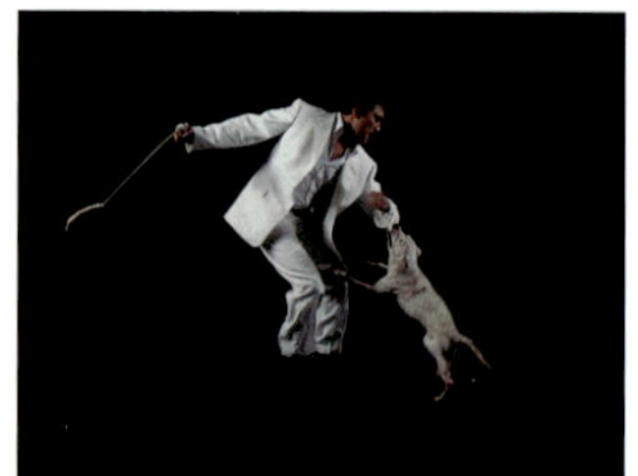
MIGUEL ANGEL RÍOS

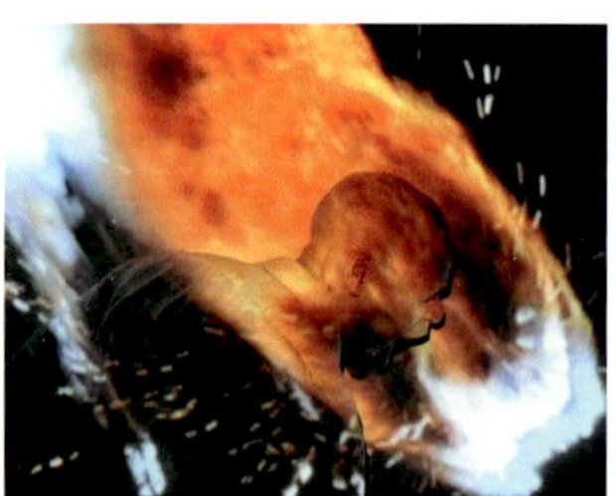
JEFFERSON PINDER

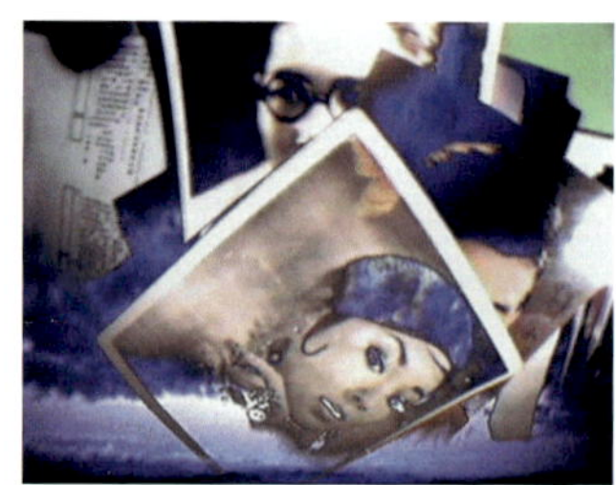
PIPILOTTI RIST

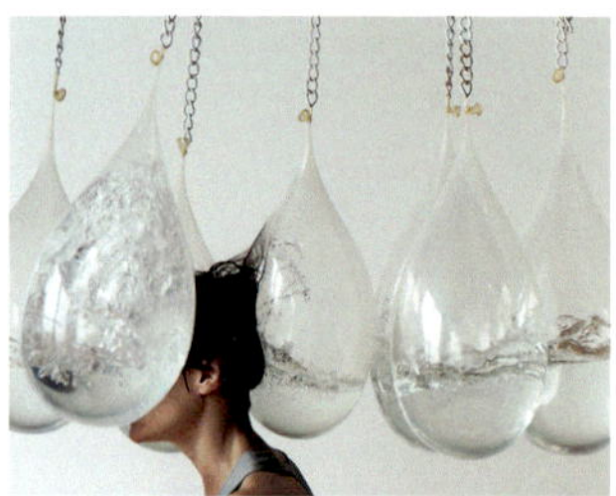
CHERYL POPE

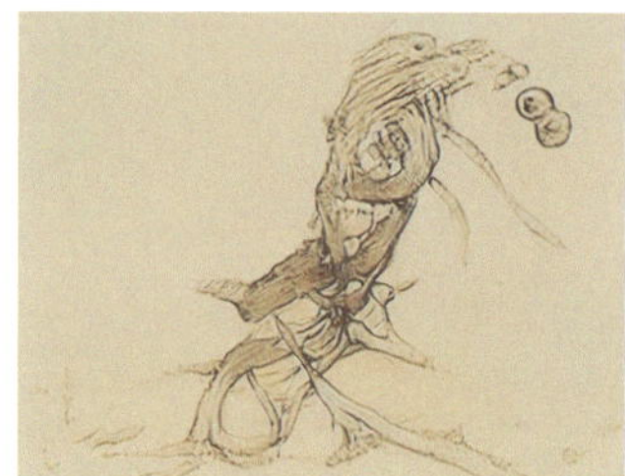
MATTHEW RITCHIE

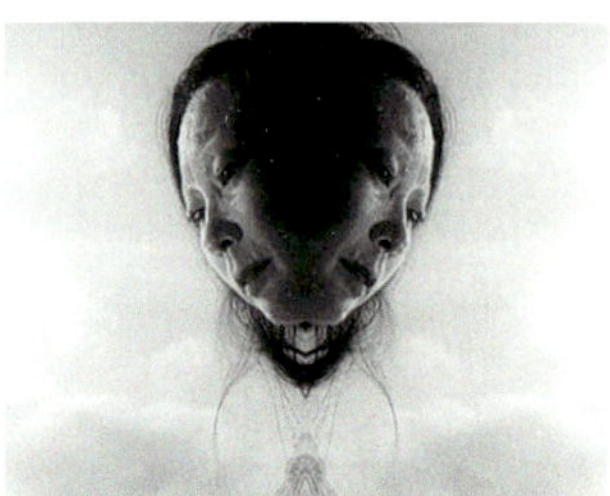
NICOLAS PROVOST

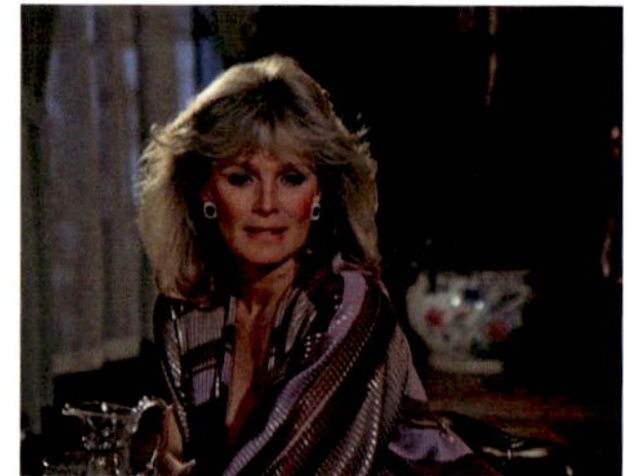
MICHAEL ROBINSON

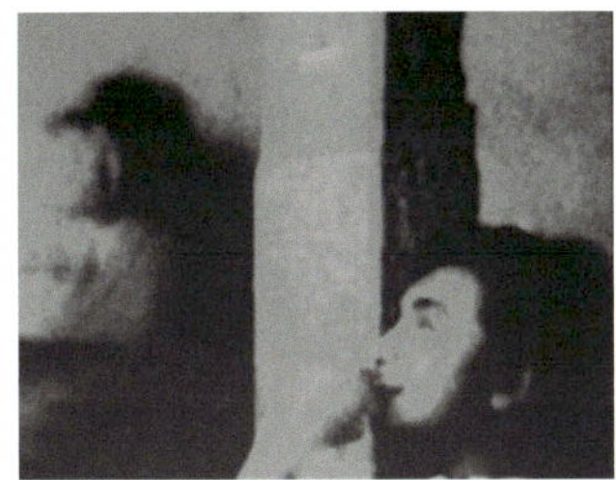

MIGUEL ÁNGEL ROJAS

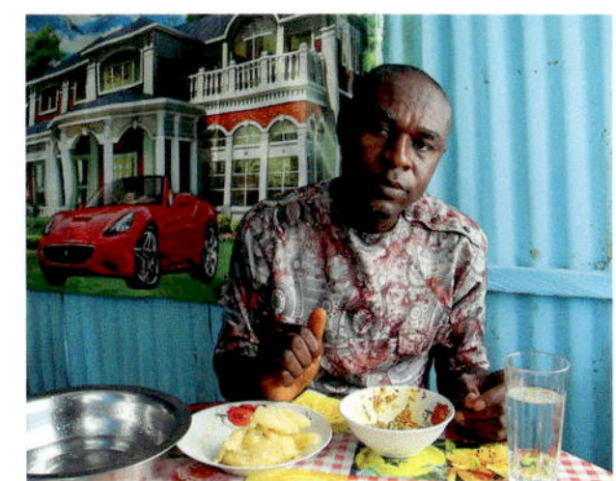

ZINA SARO-WIWA

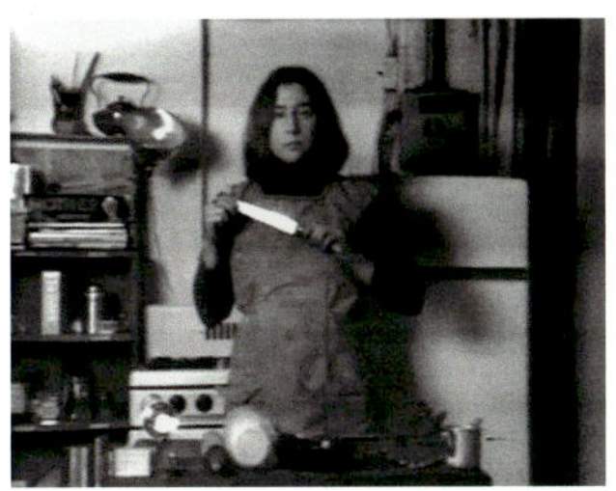

MARTHA ROSLER

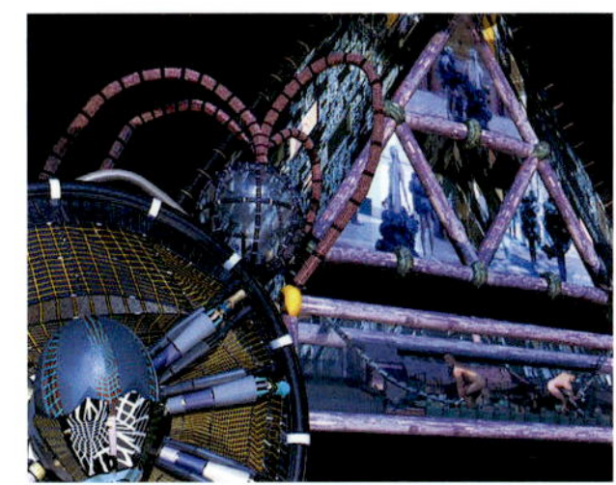

JACOLBY SATTERWHITE

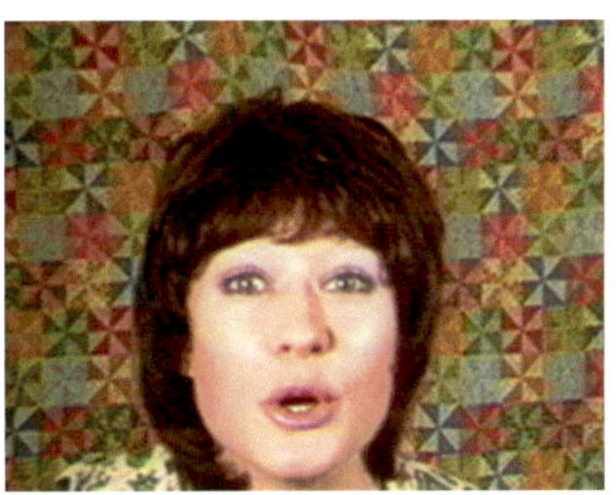

TOM RUBNITZ and ANN MAGNUSON

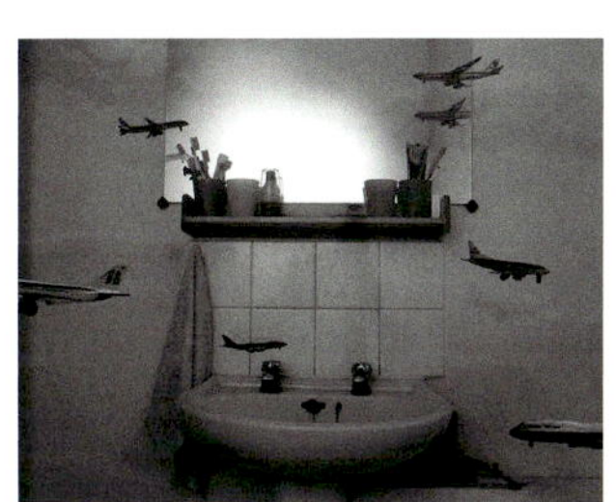

HIRAKI SAWA

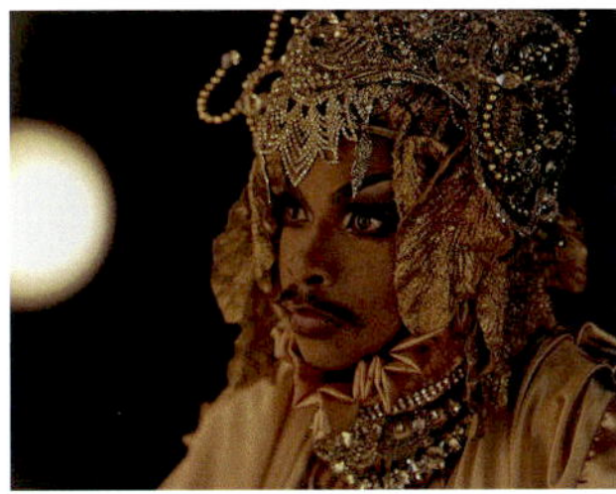

ATHI-PATRA RUGA

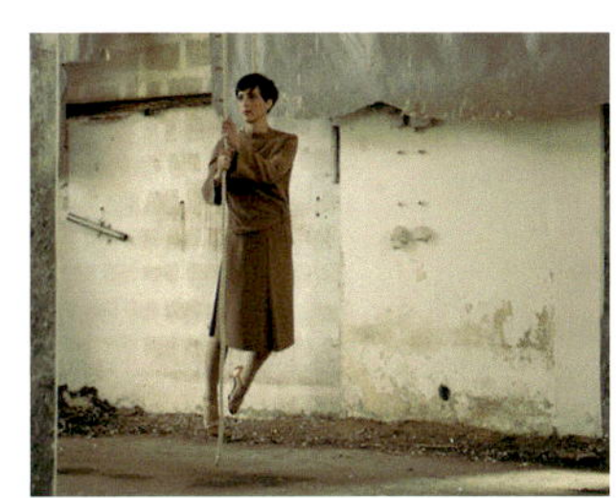

MARKUS SCHINWALD

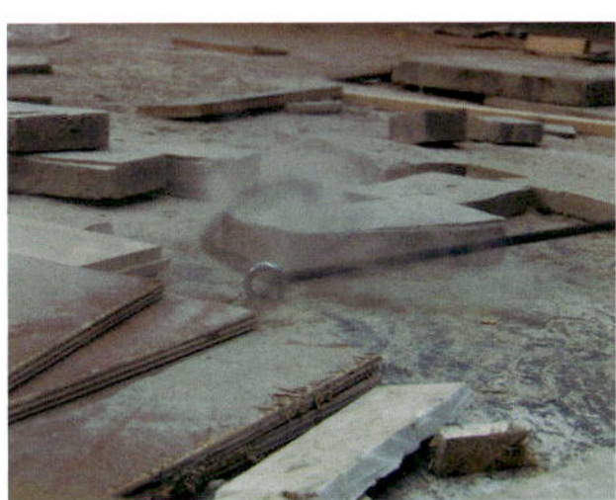

CHEN SAI HUA KUAN

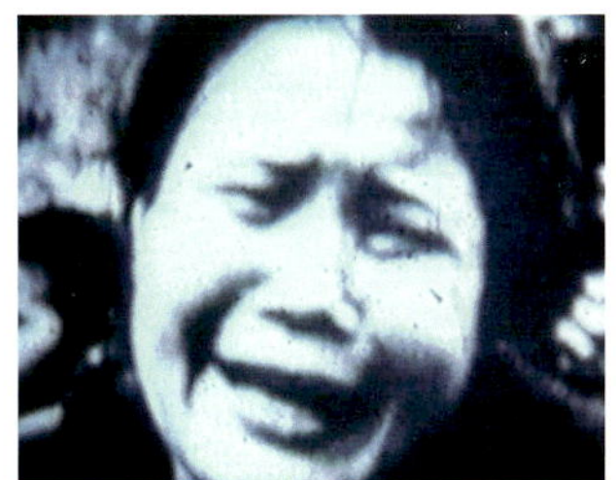

CAROLEE SCHNEEMANN

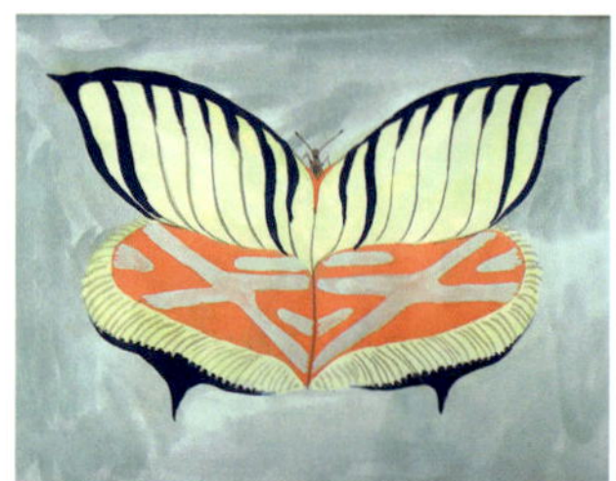
ALLISON SCHULNIK

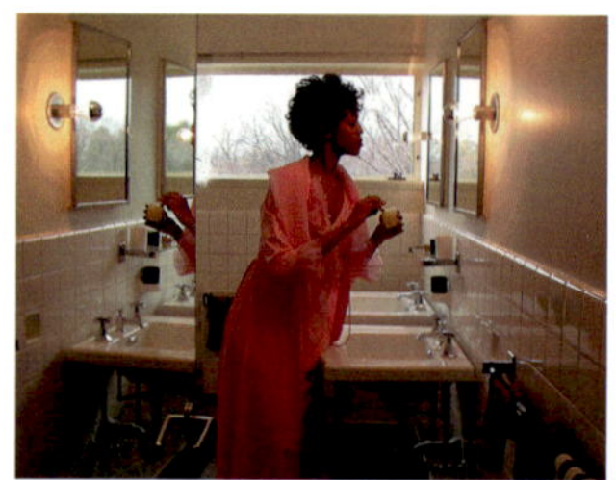
LORNA SIMPSON

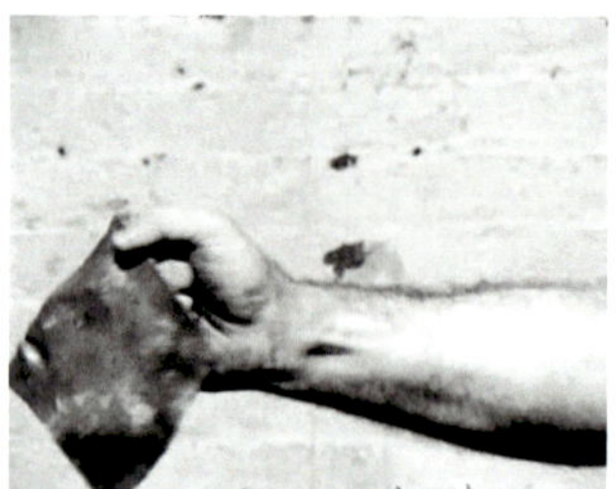
RICHARD SERRA

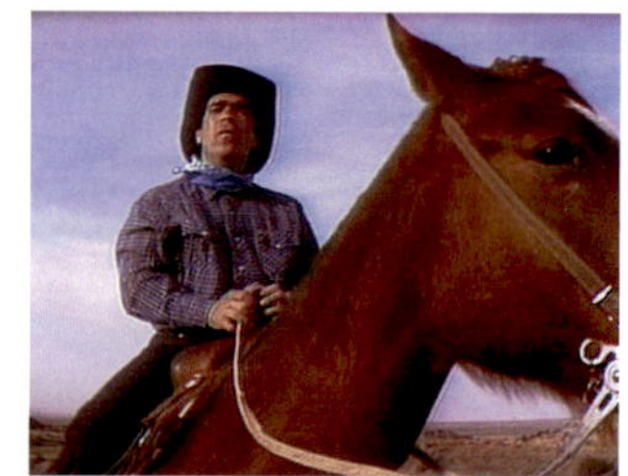
MICHAEL SMITH

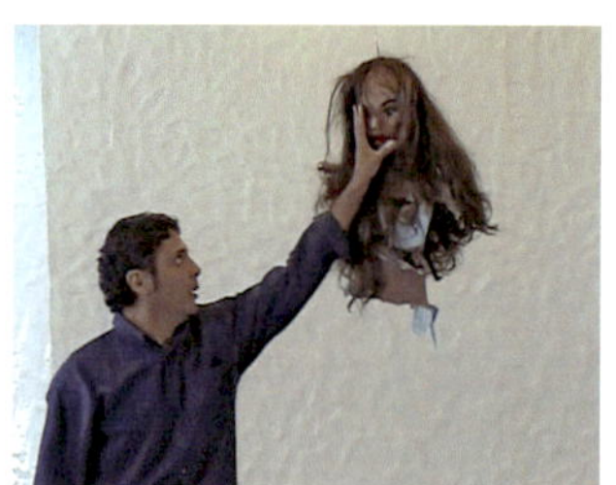
TERESA SERRANO

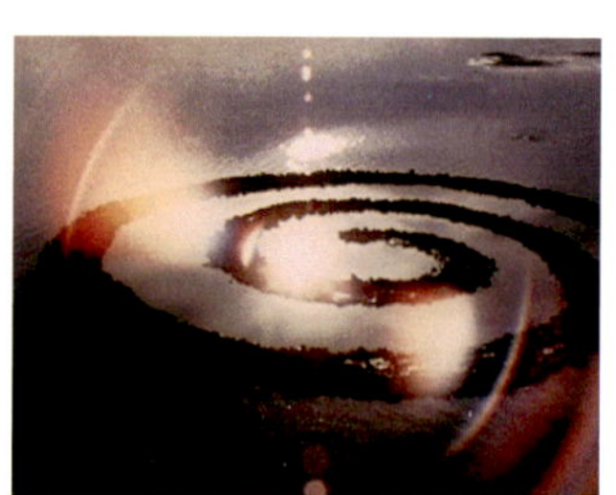
ROBERT SMITHSON

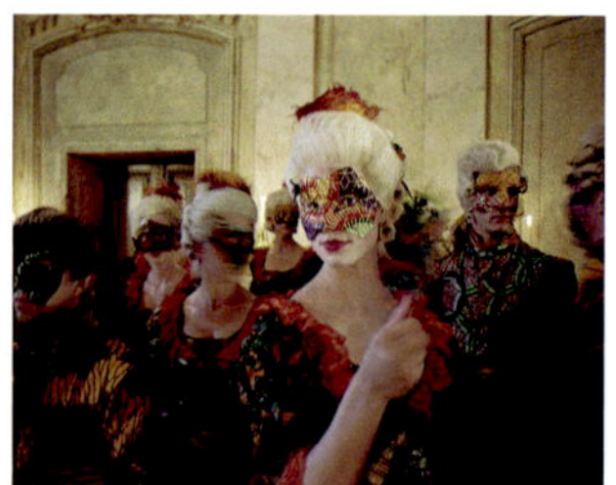
YINKA SHONIBARE MBE

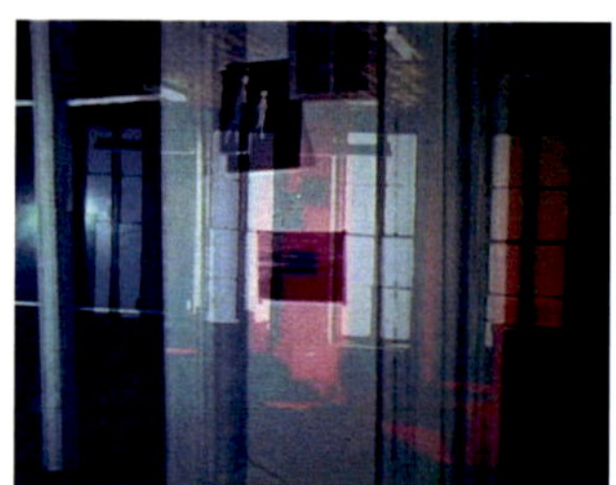
MICHAEL SNOW

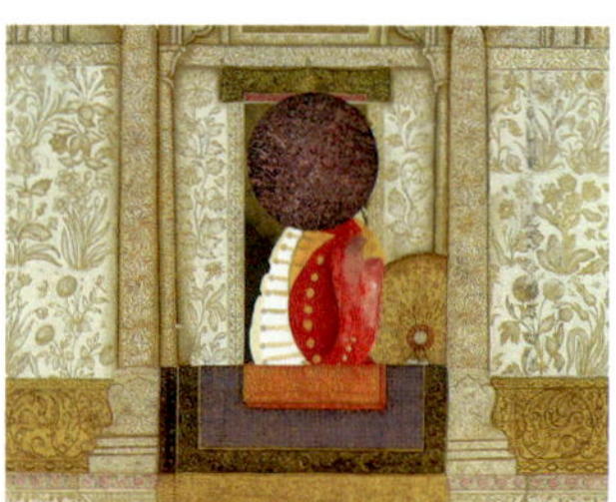
SHAHZIA SIKANDER

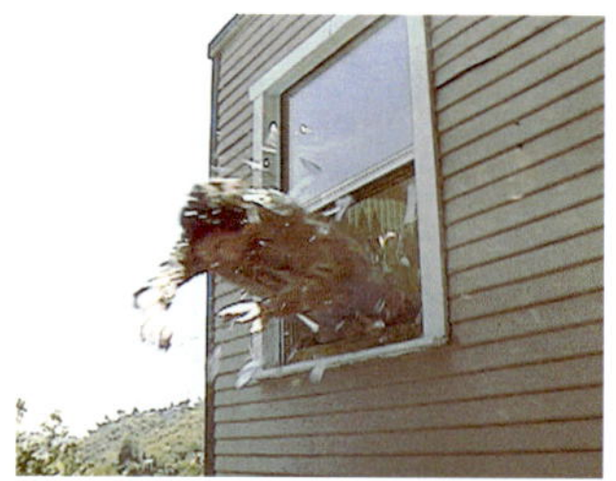
JOE SOLA

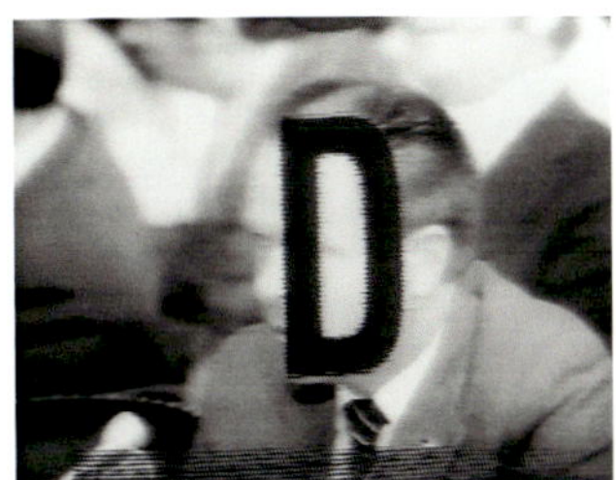

KEITH SONNIER

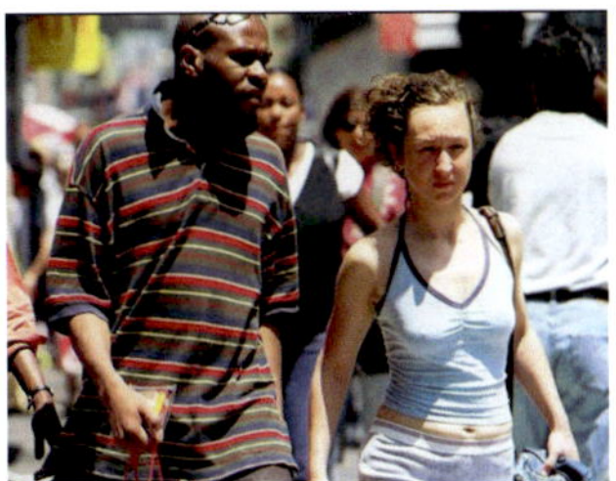

BEAT STREULI

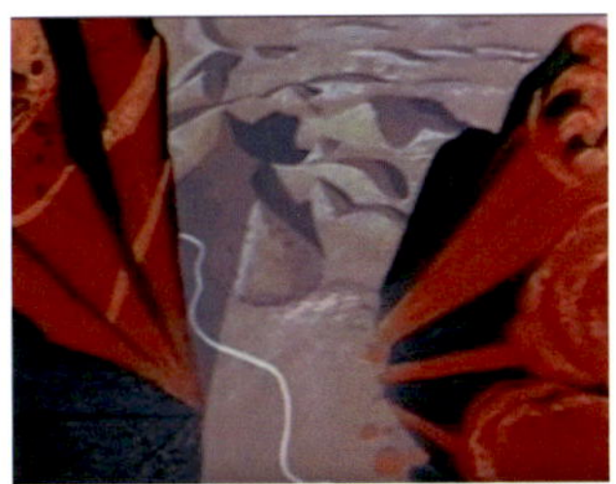

MUNGO THOMSON

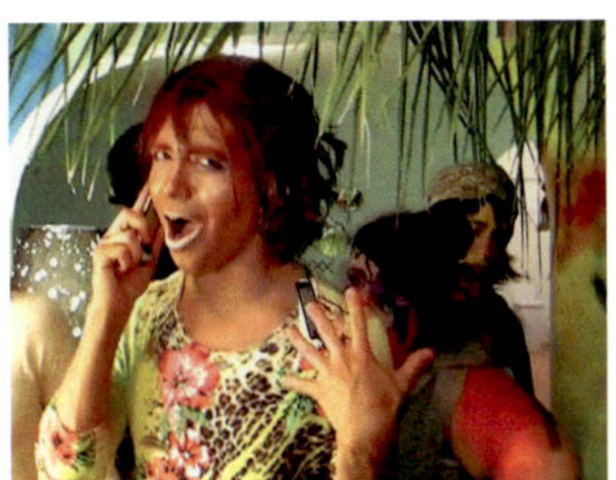

RYAN TRECARTIN

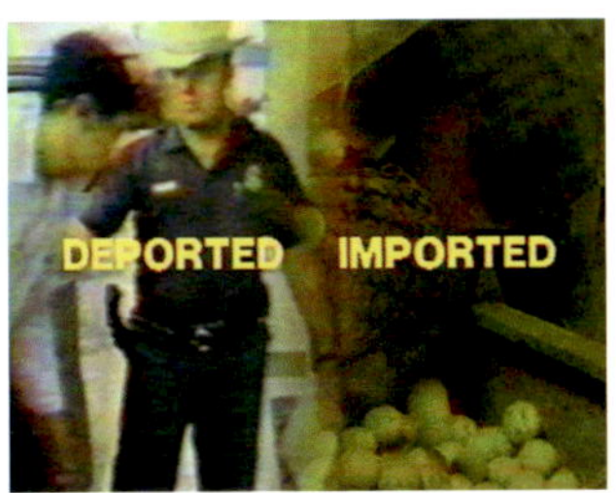

LUIS VALDOVINO

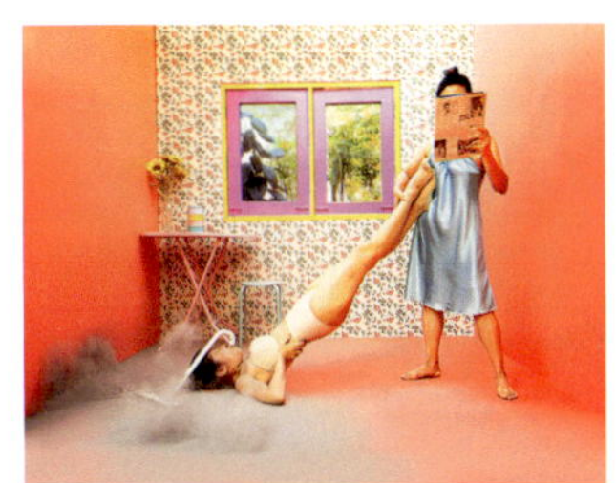

KAWITA VATANAJYANKUR

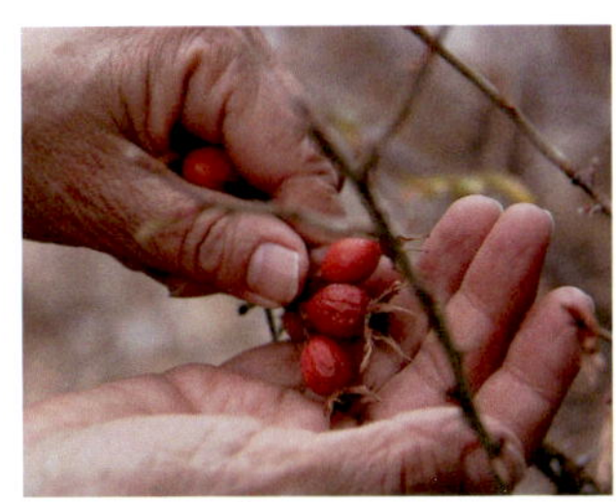

CECILIA VICUÑA

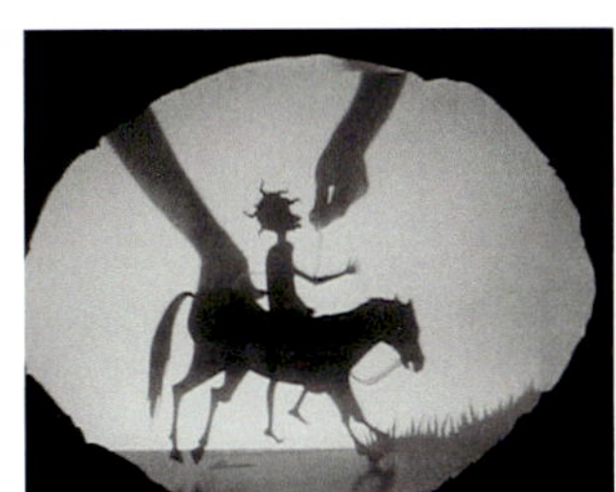

KARA WALKER

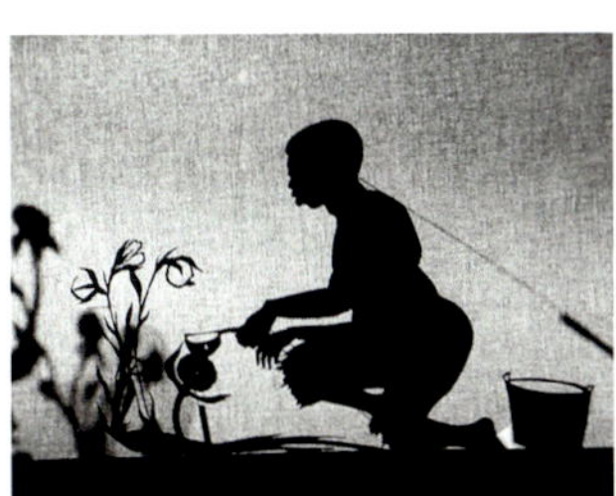

KARA WALKER

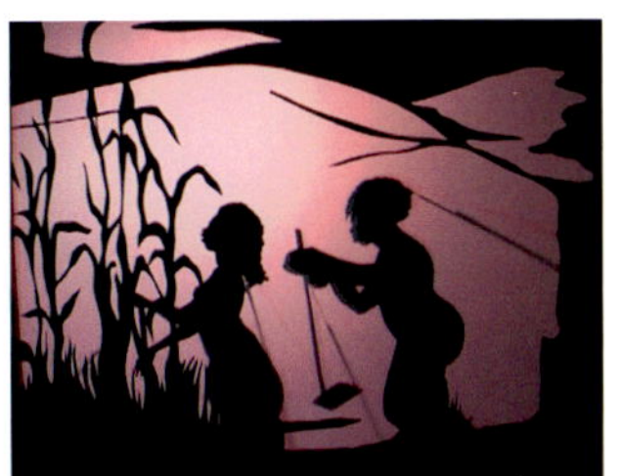

KARA WALKER

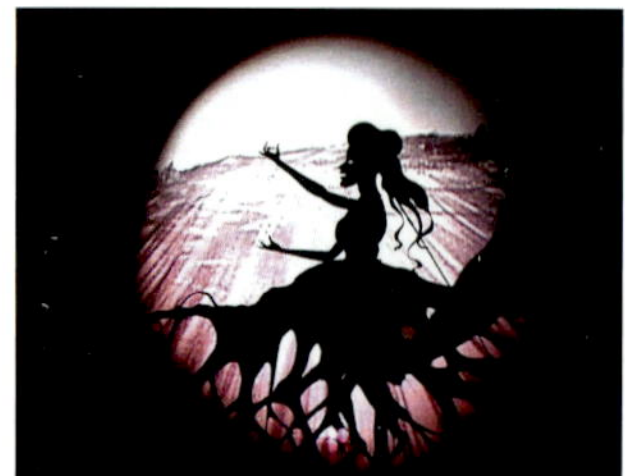
KARA WALKER

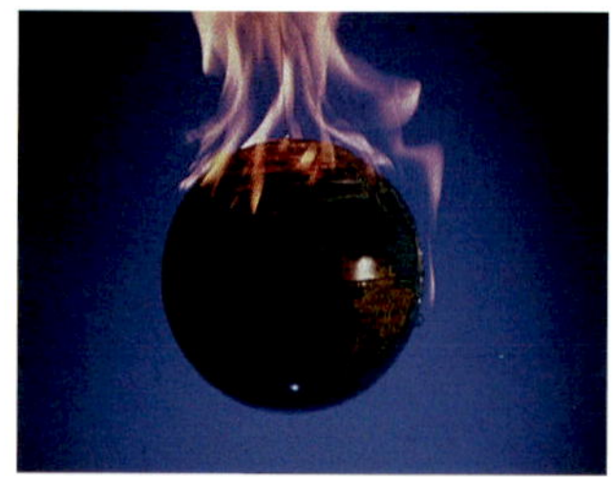
DAVID WOJNAROWICZ

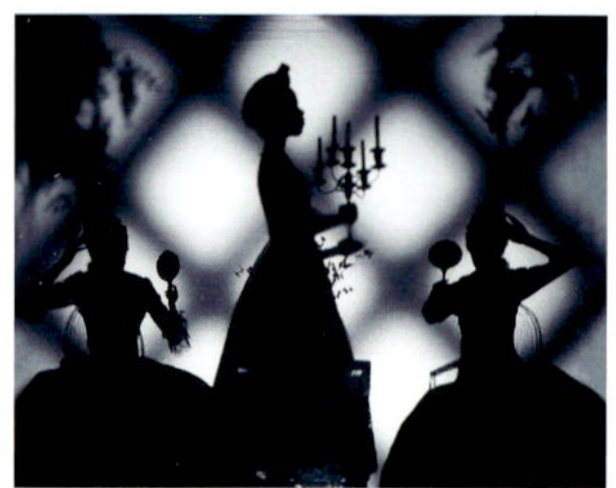
CARRIE MAE WEEMS

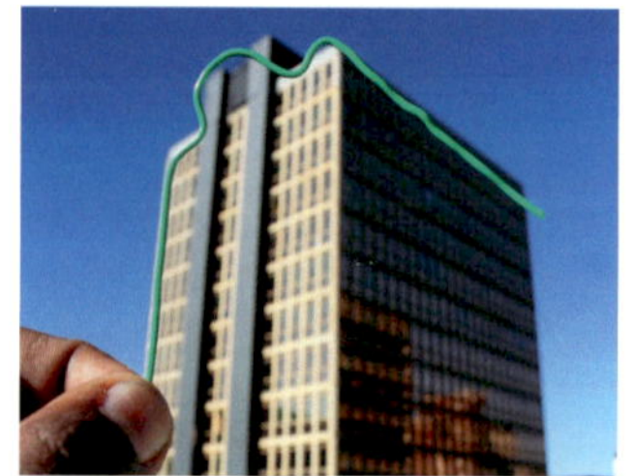
EZRA WUBE

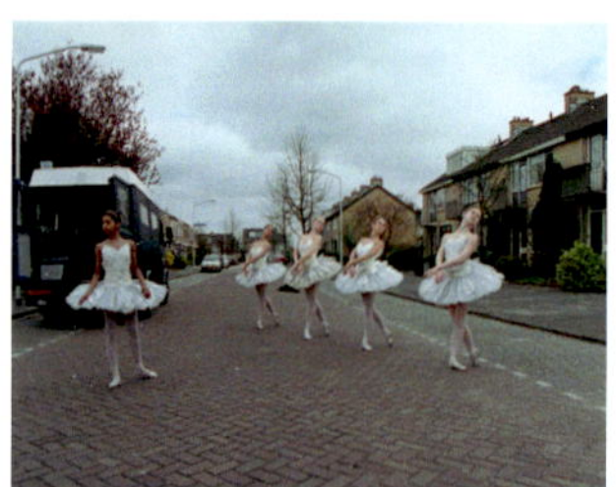
GUIDO VAN DER WERVE

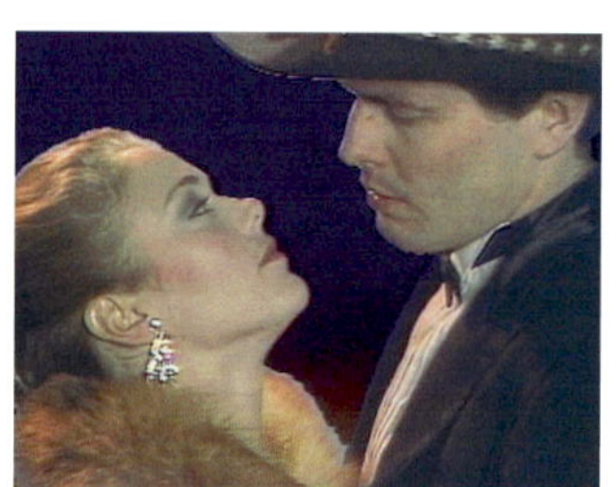
BRUCE and NORMAN YONEMOTO

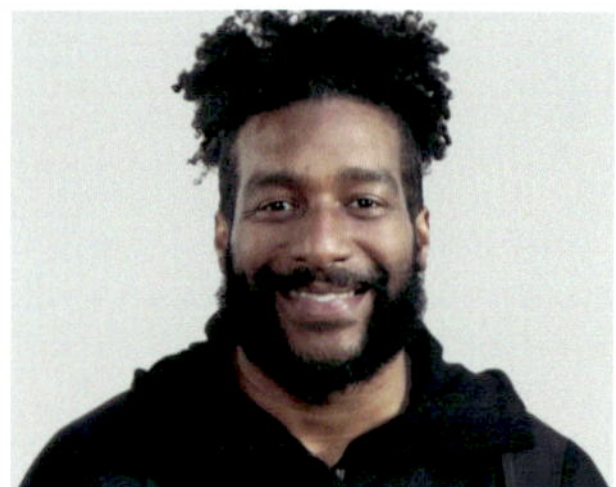
KEHINDE WILEY

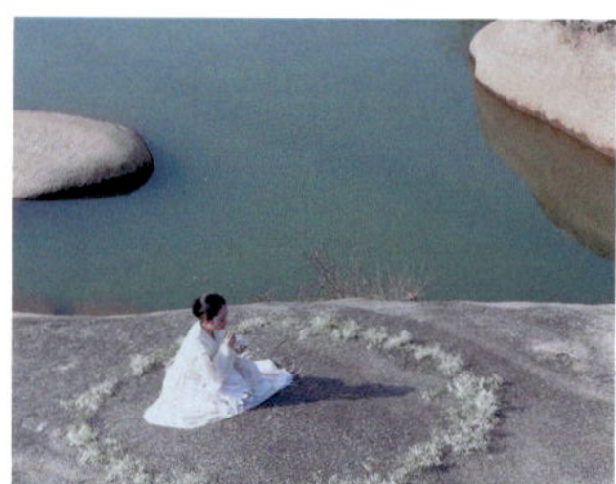
A YOUNG YU (IN COLLABORATION WITH NICHOLAS OH)

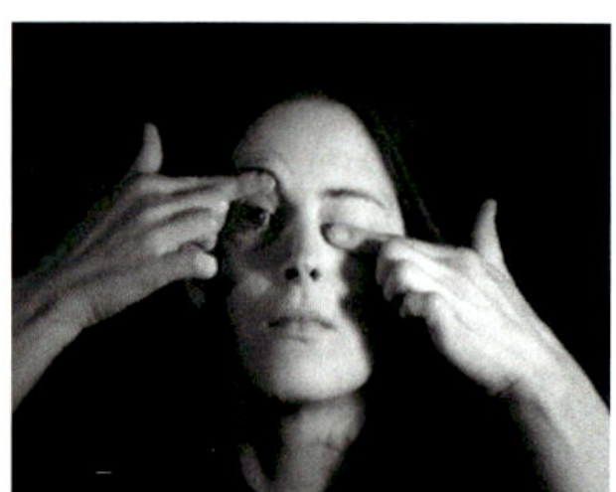
HANNAH WILKE

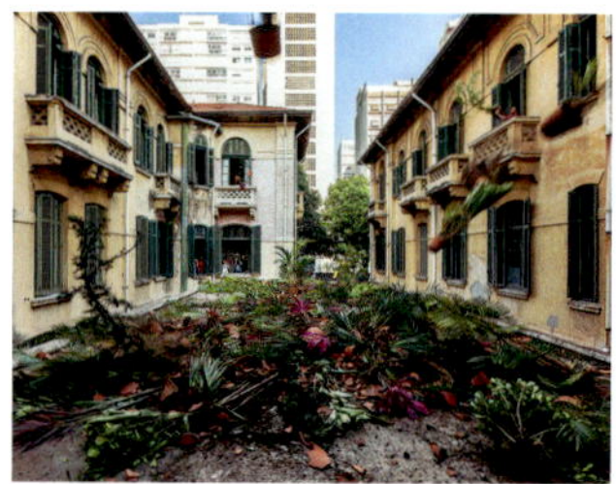
HÉCTOR ZAMORA

CAPTIONS

Abramović, Marina, and Atlas, Charles. Serbian, born 1946; American, born 1949. *SSS*, 1989. Video, 6:00 min., color, sound. Courtesy of Electronic Arts Intermix (EAI), New York. Exhibited May 2016

Acconci, Vito. American, 1940–2017. *Theme Song*, 1973. Video, 33:15 min., b&w, sound. Courtesy of Electronic Arts Intermix (EAI), New York. Exhibited January 2013

Adkins, Terry. American, 1953–2014. *Synapse*, 2004. Video, 18:01 min., color, sound. Courtesy of the Estate of Terry Adkins and Salon 94, New York. Exhibited September 2015

AES+F (Arzamasova, Tatiana; Evzovich, Lev; Svyatsky, Evgeny; Fridkes, Vladimir). Russian, born 1955; Russian, born 1958; Russian, born 1957, Russian, born 1956. *Inverso Mundus*, 2015. HD Video, 38:20 min., color, sound. Courtesy of the artists, Multimedia Art Museum Moscow, and Mobius Gallery. Exhibited November 2017

Allora & Calzadilla (Allora, Jennifer & Calzadilla, Guillermo). American, born 1974; Cuban, born 1971. *The Great Silence*, 2014. Single-channel HD video installation, 16:22 min., color, sound. © Allora & Calzadilla. Courtesy of Lisson Gallery. Exhibited November 2021

Almy, Max. American, born 1948. *Leaving the 20th Century*, 1982. Video, 11:00 min., color, sound. Courtesy of the Video Data Bank at the School of the Art Institute of Chicago. Exhibited March 2018

Anderson, Laurie. American, born 1947. *What You Mean We?*, 1986. Video, 20:00 min., color, sound. Courtesy of the Video Data Bank at the School of the Art Institute of Chicago. Exhibited June 2011

Antin, Eleanor. American, born 1935. *The Little Match Girl Ballet*, 1975. Video, 26:30 min., color, sound. Courtesy of Electronic Arts Intermix (EAI), New York. Exhibited December 2014

Antoni, Janine. Bahamian, born 1964. *Touch*, 2002. Video installation, standard projection size: 14 ft. 8 in. × 13 ft. 2 in. 9:37 min., looped, color, sound. © Janine Antoni; Courtesy of the artist and Luhring Augustine, New York. Exhibited October 2024

Baldessari, John. American, 1931–2020. *I Will Not Make Any More Boring Art*, 1971. Video, 32:21 min., b&w, mono. Image copyright of the artist, Courtesy of the Video Data Bank at the School of the Art Institute of Chicago. Exhibited June 2016

Balseca, Adrián. Ecuadorian, born 1989. *Suspensión I*, 2019. Digital 4K, 5:00 min., color, sound. Courtesy of Han Nefkens Foundation. Exhibited January 2021

Barr, Burt. American, 1938–2016. *The Elevator*, 1985. Video, 5:10 min., color, sound. Courtesy of Electronic Arts Intermix (EAI), New York. Exhibited May 2015

Ben-Ner, Guy. Israeli, born 1969. *Soundtrack*, 2013. Single-channel HD video, 11:25 min., color, sound. Courtesy of the artist and Aspect/Ratio Gallery. Exhibited December 2018

Benglis, Lynda. American, born 1941. *Now*, 1973. Video, 12:00 min., color, sound. Courtesy of Electronic Arts Intermix (EAI), New York. Exhibited September 2012

Benning, Sadie. American, born 1973. *Girl Power*, 1993. Video, 15:00 min., b&w, sound. Courtesy of the Video Data Bank at the School of the Art Institute of Chicago. Exhibited June 2018

Birnbaum, Dara. American, born 1946. *Technology/Transformation: Wonder Woman*, 1978–79. Video, 5:50 min., color, sound. Courtesy of Electronic Arts Intermix (EAI), New York. Exhibited March 2012

Bolotin, Jay. American, born 1949. *The Jackleg Testament Part I: The Story of Jack & Eve*, 2007. Woodcut motion picture, 62:00 min., color, sound. Courtesy of the artist. Exhibited November 2014

Bradley, Garrett. American, born 1986. *Alone*, 2018. HD video, 13:00 min., b&w, sound. © Garrett Bradley; Courtesy of Lisson Gallery. Exhibited February 2022

Burden, Chris. American, 1946–2015. *The TV Commercials*, 1973–77/2000. Video, 3:46 min., color, sound. Courtesy of Electronic Arts Intermix (EAI), New York. Exhibited June 2015

Calle, Sophie, and Shephard, Gregory. French, born 1953; American, dates unknown. *Double-Blind*, 1992. Video, 75:58 min., color, sound. Courtesy of Electronic Arts Intermix (EAI), New York. Exhibited August 2013

Camel Collective (Graves, Anthony, and Herrera-Prats, Carla). American, born 1975; Mexican, 1973–2019. *Something Other Than What You Are*, 2018. Single-channel version, HD video, 34:26 min., color, sound. Courtesy of the artists. Exhibited February 2020

Cha, Theresa Hak Kyung. Korean-born American, 1951–1982. *Re Dis Appearing*, 1977. Video, 2:30 min., b&w, sound. Courtesy of Electronic Arts Intermix (EAI), New York, Collection of UC Berkeley Art Museum and Pacific Film Archive. Exhibited August 2017

Chang, Patty. American, born 1972. *Contortion*, 2000. Video, 2:20 min., color, silent. Courtesy of the artist. Exhibited May 2014

Claerbout, David. Belgian, born 1969. *The pure necessity*, 2016. Single-channel 2D animation, 50:00 min., color, stereo sound. Courtesy of the artist and galleries Sean Kelly, New York, and Esther Schipper, Berlin. Exhibited October 2022

Cuevas, Ximena. Mexican, born 1963. *Contemporary Artist*, 1999. Video, 4:57 min., b&w, sound. Courtesy of the Video Data Bank at the School of the Art Institute of Chicago. Exhibited December 2024

Cunningham, Merce, and Moore, Richard. American, 1919–2009; American, 1920–2015. *Assemblage*, 1968. 16mm film on video, 58:03 min., color, sound. Courtesy of Electronic Arts Intermix (EAI), New York. Exhibited December 2015

Da Corte, Alex. American, born 1980. *Chelsea Hotel no. 2*, 2010. HD digital video, 3:04 min., color, sound. Courtesy of the artist. Exhibited September 2016

De Barros, Lenora. Brazilian, born 1953. *Homenagem a George Segal (Homage to George Segal)*, 1984. Video, 3:07 min., color, sound. Courtesy of the artist and Georg Kargl Fine Arts. Exhibited October 2023

Díaz-Perera, Alejandro Figueredo. Cuban, born 1991. *Love is a Rebellious Bird*, 2017. Single-channel video, 10:20 min., color, sound. Video donated by Dr. Scott J. Hunter. Exhibited June 2019

Donegan, Cheryl. American, born 1962. *Artists + Models*, 1998. Video, 4:43 min., b&w, sound. Courtesy of Electronic Arts Intermix (EAI), New York. Exhibited May 2017

Edmonds, John. American, born 1989. *Shotgun*, 2014. HD Video, TRT, 9:53 min., color, silent. Courtesy of the artist. Exhibited October 2020

Export, Valie. Austrian, born 1940. *Touch Cinema*, 1968. 16mm film on video, 1:08 min., b&w, sound. Courtesy of Electronic Arts Intermix (EAI), New York. Exhibited July 2014

Ezawa, Kota. German-Japanese American, born 1969. *The Simpson Verdict*, 2002. Video, 3:00 min., color, sound. Courtesy of the Haines Gallery, San Francisco. Exhibited October 2021

Fayez, Arash. Iranian, born 1984. *I Can Only Dance to One Song*, 2021. Single-channel 4K UHD video, 10:53 min., color, sound. Courtesy of the artist. Exhibited May 2025

Fei, Cao. Chinese, born 1978. *Shadow Life*, 2011. Video, 10:00 min., b&w, sound. Courtesy of Cao Fei and Vitamin Creative Space. Exhibited February 2016

Fischli & Weiss (Fischli, Peter & Weiss, David). Swiss, born 1952; Swiss, 1946–2012. *Der Lauf der Dinge (The Way Things Go)*, 1987. 16mm film transferred to video, 31:00 min., color, sound. Courtesy of Matthew Marks Gallery. Exhibited September 2024

Fleming, Jesse. American, born 1977. *The Snail and the Razor*, 2012. Single-channel video, 7:56 min., color, sound. Courtesy of Electronic Arts Intermix (EAI), New York. Exhibited October 2012

Fleury, Sylvie. Swiss, born 1961. *Walking on Carl Andre*, 1997. Video, 24:40 min., color, sound. Courtesy of the artist and Salon 94, New York. Exhibited March 2015

Freed, Hermine. American, 1940–1998. *Art Herstory*, 1974. Video, 22:00 min., color, sound. Courtesy of the Video Data Bank at the School of the Art Institute of Chicago. Exhibited December 2017

Fusco, Coco, and Heredia, Paula. American, born 1960; Salvadoran, born 1957. *Couple in the Cage: Guatianaui Odyssey*, 1993. Video, 31:00 min., b&w and color, sound. Image copyright of the artist, courtesy of the Video Data Bank at the School of the Art Institute of Chicago. Exhibited October 2015

Gary, Ja'Tovia. American, born 1984. *An Ecstatic Experience*, 2015. Film, 6:00 min., color, sound. Courtesy of the artist and galerie frank elbaz. Exhibited October 2019

Gilmore, Kate. American, born 1975. *Buster*, 2011. Video, 10:00 min., color, sound. Courtesy of David Castillo Gallery, Miami Beach. Exhibited February 2013

Gispert, Luis. American, born 1972. *Block Watching*, 2003. Digital video, 1:57 min., color, sound. Courtesy of the artist and OHWOW Gallery, Los Angeles. Exhibited March 2016

Gordon, Douglas. Scottish, born 1966. *Domestic*, 2002. Video, 13:58 min., color, silent. Courtesy of the artist and Gagosian Gallery, New York. © 2016 Studio lost but found / Artists Rights Society (ARS), New York / VG Bild-Kunst, Bonn. Exhibited January 2017

Haerizadeh, Rokni. Iranian, born 1978. *Reign of Winter*, 2012–13. Video, 6:00 min., color, silent. Courtesy of the artist and Gallery Isabelle van den Eynde, Dubai. Exhibited September 2014

Haller, Frieder. German, born 1987. *Scum Scam Scum*, 2021. HD, single-channel video, 25:19 min., color, sound. Courtesy of the artist and 14a Gallery. Exhibited December 2023

Hamilton, Ann. American, born 1956. *(abc · video)*, 1994/1999. Video, 30:00 min., b&w, silent. Courtesy of Ann Hamilton Studio. Exhibited February 2017

Hammer, Barbara. American, 1939–2019. *Sanctus*, 1990. 16 mm film on video, 18:16 min., color, sound. Courtesy of the artist and Electronic Arts Intermix (EAI), New York. Exhibited January 2019

Hassinger, Maren. American, born 1947. *Daily Mask*, 2004. 16mm film, 3:30 min., color, sound. Courtesy of the artist. Exhibited November 2018

Hatoum, Mona. British-Palestinian, born 1952. *Measures of Distance*, 1988. Video, 15:30 min., color, sound. Image copyright of the artist, Courtesy of the Video Data Bank at the School of the Art Institute of Chicago. Exhibited July 2015

Hermanides, Laura. The Netherlands, born 1988. *Anahit*, 2022. HD, single-channel video, 8:51 min., color, sound. Courtesy of The Curators Room, Barcelona/Amsterdam. Exhibited September 2023

Hill, Gary. American, born 1951. *Around & About*, 1980. Video, 5:00 min., color, sound. Courtesy of Electronic Arts Intermix (EAI), New York. Exhibited August 2015

Holzer, Jenny. American, born 1950. *Televised Texts*, 1990. Video, 13:00 min., color, sound. Courtesy of the Video Data Bank at the School of the Art Institute of Chicago. Exhibited April 2012

Hopinka, Sky. American (Ho-Chunk Nation), born 1984. *Mnemonics of Shape and Reason*, 2021. HD video, 4:13 min., color, stereo sound. Courtesy of the Video Data Bank at the School of the Art Institute of Chicago. Exhibited January 2025

Hubbard, Teresa / Birchler, Alexander. Irish, American, Swiss, born 1965; Swiss, born 1962. *Single Wide*, 2002. Single-channel video installation, 6:07 min. loop, color, stereo sound. Courtesy of Burger Collection, Hong Kong, China, Zürich. Exhibited September 2022

Jenkins, Ulysses. American, born 1946. *Secrecy: Help Me to Understand*, 1994. Video, 8:00 min., color, sound. Courtesy of Electronic Arts Intermix (EAI), New York. Exhibited December 2022

Jonas, Joan. American, born 1936. *Vertical Roll*, 1972. Video, 19:38 min., b&w, sound. Courtesy of Electronic Arts Intermix (EAI), New York. Exhibited August 2011

July, Miranda. American, born 1974. *The Amateurist*, 1998. Video, 14:00 min., color, sound. Image copyright of the artist, Courtesy of the Video Data Bank at the School of the Art Institute of Chicago. Exhibited January 2014

Kanis, Polina. Russian, born 1985. *Celebration*, 2014. Video, Loop, HD, 13:27 min., color, sound. Courtesy of the artist and Galerie C Neuchâtel-Paris. Exhibited January 2022

Karabinovytch, Nikolay. Ukrainian, born 1988. *Something Happened this Spring*, 2021. 4k digital video, 6:35 min., color, sound. Courtesy of the artist, produced with support by Dzherelo. Exhibited November 2023

Karikis, Mikhail. Greek/British, born 1975. *Children of Unquiet*, 2014. Single-channel video, 15:36 min., color, sound. Courtesy of the artist. Exhibited September 2019

Kelley, Mike. American, 1954–2012. *The Banana Man*, 1983. Video, 28:15 min., color, sound. Courtesy of Electronic Arts Intermix (EAI), New York. Exhibited January 2012

Kentridge, William. South African, born 1955. *Felix in Exile*, 1994. 35mm film transferred to DVD, 8:43 min., color, sound. Courtesy of the artist and Marian Goodman Gallery, New York. Exhibited March 2011

Kjartansson, Ragnar. Icelandic, born 1976. *Satan is Real*, 2004. Single-channel video, 63:40 min., color, sound. Courtesy of the artist, Luhring Augustine, New York, and i8 Gallery, Reykjavik. Exhibited November 2019

Knopová, Vendula. Czech, born 1987. *Tutorial*, 2015. Video, 4:51 min., color, sound. Courtesy of the Gandy Gallery, Bratislava, Slovakia. Exhibited September 2020

Kul, Julia. Polish, born 1983. *Passport Reading*, 2011. Single-channel video, 8:44 min., color, sound. Courtesy of Postmasters Gallery, New York. Exhibited April 2013

Landau, Sigalit. Israeli, born 1969. *DeadSee*, 2005. Video, 11:39 min., color, silent. Courtesy the artist and Kamel Mennour, Paris. Exhibited February 2012

Lewis, Mark. Canadian, born 1958. *The Fight*, 2008. HD Video, 5:27 min., color, silent. Courtesy and copyright of the artist and Monte Clark Gallery, Vancouver, Clark & Faria, Toronto. Exhibited April 2011

Linzy, Kalup. American, born 1977. *Conversations Wit de Churen V: As da Art World Might Turn*, 2006. Video, 12:10 min., color, sound. Courtesy of Electronic Arts Intermix (EAI), New York. Exhibited July 2013

LOS JAICHACKERS (Morales, Julio César, and Ore-Giron, Eamon). Mexican, born 1966; American, born 1973. *Subterranean Homesick Cumbia_Remix*, 2018. HD Video, 17:11 min., color, stereo sound. Courtesy of the artists. Exhibited April 2023

Lucas, Kristin. American, born 1968. *Host*, 1997. Video, 7:36 min., color, sound. Courtesy of Electronic Arts Intermix (EAI), New York. Exhibited March 2023

Marcelle, Cinthia. Brazilian, born 1974. *Confrontation (Unus Mundus Series)*, 2005. Video, 7:49 min., color, sound. Courtesy of the artist and Sprovieri Gallery. Exhibited March 2024

Marclay, Christian. Swiss-American, born 1955. *Telephones*, 1995. Single-channel video, 7:30 min., b&w and color, sound. From The Collection of Jereann and Holland Chaney. Exhibited February 2019

Matta-Clark, Gordon. American, 1943–1978. *Splitting*, 1974. Super 8mm film on video, 10:50 min., b&w and color, silent. Courtesy of Electronic Arts Intermix (EAI), New York. Exhibited November 2013

Mattes, Eva and Franco. Italian, born 1976. *Emily's Video*, 2012. Video, 15:52 min., color, sound. Courtesy of Postmasters Gallery, New York. Exhibited October 2013

McMaster, R. Eric. American, born 1979. *Pendulum*, 2014. 1080p digital video, 5:12 min., color, silent. Courtesy of the artist. Exhibited February 2023

Meckseper, Josephine. German, born 1964. *0% Down*, 2008. Video transferred to DVD, 6:00 min., b&w, sound. Courtesy of Elizabeth Dee Gallery, New York. Exhibited October 2011

Mendieta, Ana. American, born in Cuba, 1948–1985. *Untitled (Blood Sign #2/Body Tracks)*, 1974. Super-8mm film transferred to DVD, 1:01 min., color, silent. Courtesy of Galerie Lelong, New York. Exhibited August 2014

Minter, Marilyn. American, born 1948. *Green Pink Caviar*, 2009. HD digital video, 7:45 min., color, sound. Courtesy of the artist and Salon 94, New York. Exhibited April 2017

Mizushiri, Yoriko. Japanese, born 1984. *Anxious Body*, 2021. 2D digital animation, 5:32 min., color, sound. Courtesy of the artist and MIYU & New Deer. Exhibited April 2025

Monkman, Kent. Canadian of Cree Ancestry, born 1965. *Group of Seven Inches*, 2005. Video, 7:35 min., b&w, sound. Courtesy of Vtape.org. Exhibited December 2016

Montano, Linda. American, born 1942. *Mitchell's Death*, 1977. Video, 22:20 min., b&w, sound. Image copyright of the artist. Courtesy of the Video Data Bank at the School of the Art Institute of Chicago. Exhibited January 2015

VLM (Montgomery, Virginia L.). American, born 1986. *Honey Moon*, 2019. 4K digital video, 3:00 min., color, sound. Courtesy of the artist. Exhibited May 2024

Morris, Sarah. British, born 1967. *Beijing*, 2008. 35mm/HD, 84:47 min., color, sound. © Sarah Morris. Courtesy of White Cube. Exhibited January 2018

Muntadas, Antoni, and Reese, Marshall. Spanish, born 1942; American, born 1955. *Political Advertisement X 1952–2020*, 2020. Video, 98:04 min., b&w and color, stereo sound. Courtesy of the Video Data Bank at the School of the Art Institute of Chicago. Exhibited November 2024

Murata, Takeshi. American, born 1974. *Infinite Doors*, 2010. 16 mm film on video, 18:16 min., color, sound. Courtesy of the artist and Electronic Arts Intermix (EAI), New York. Exhibited April 2019

Muriente, Sofía Gallisá. Puerto Rican, born 1986. *Asimilar y destruir (Assimilate & Destroy) I and II*, 2018–19. 16mm film rephotographed to video, 2:38 min., b&w, silent/6:42 min., color, sound. Courtesy of the artist. Exhibited November 2022

Musson, Jayson Scott. American, born 1977. *ART THOUGHTZ with Hennessy Youngman (video series)*, 2010–12. HD video, various times, color, sound. Courtesy of the artist and Electronic Arts Intermix (EAI), New York. Exhibited May 2019

Myers, Rita. American, born 1947. *Tilt 1*, 1973. Video, 6:50 min., b&w, sound. Courtesy of Electronic Arts Intermix (EAI), New York. Exhibited June 2017

Nauman, Bruce. American, born 1941. *Walk with Contrapposto*, 1968. Video, 60 min., b&w, sound. Courtesy of Electronic Arts Intermix (EAI), New York. © 2010 Bruce of Nauman/Artist Rights Society (ARS), New York. Exhibited May 2011

Neuenschwander, Rivane & Guimarães, Cao. Brazilian, born 1967; Brazilian, born 1965. *Quarta-Feira de Cinzas/Epilogue*, 2006. Video, 5:48 min., color, sound, with soundtrack by O Grivo. Courtesy of the artists, and Tanya Bonakdar Gallery, New York / Los Angeles; Fortes D'Aloia & Gabriel, Brazil; Stephen Friedman Gallery, London. Exhibited March 2019

Norris, Tameka Jenean. American, born 1979 in Guam. *Untitled (Say Her Name)*, 2011–15. Video, 4:47 min., color, sound. Courtesy of the artist and Jane Lombard Gallery, New York. Exhibited November 2016

Robyn O'Neil, American, born 1977. *WE, THE MASSES*, 2011. Video, 14:00 min., b&w, sound. Courtesy of the artist and Talley Dunn Gallery. Exhibited December 2021

Op de Beeck, Hans. Belgian, born 1969. *The Girl*, 2017. HD animation film, 16:00 min., color, sound. Courtesy of the artist and Marianne Boesky Gallery. Exhibited October 2018

Oursler, Tony. American, born 1957. *The Weak Bullet*, 1980. Video, 12:41 min., color, sound. Courtesy of Electronic Arts Intermix (EAI), New York. Exhibited December 2010

Paik, Nam June, and Godfrey, John. Korean, 1932–2006; American, born 1943. *Global Groove*, 1973. Video, 28:30 min., color, sound. Courtesy of Electronic Arts Intermix (EAI), New York. Exhibited November 2011

Palestine, Charlemagne. American, born 1947. *Body Music I/Body Music II*, 1973–74. Video, 20:30 min., b&w, sound. Courtesy of Electronic Arts Intermix (EAI), New York. Exhibited August 2018

Pearlstein, Alix. American, born 1962. *Goldrush*, 2008. HD video, 3:05 min., color, sound. Courtesy of Electronic Arts Intermix (EAI), New York. Exhibited June 2014

Perry, Rachel. American, born 1962 in Tokyo, Japan. *Karaoke Wrong Number*, 2001–04 and 2005–09. Video on DVD, 7:14 and 5:46 min., color, sound. Courtesy of the artist and Yancey Richardson Gallery, New York. Exhibited March 2014

Phan, Thao Nguyen. Vietnamese, born 1987. *Becoming Alluvium*, 2019. Single-channel color video, 16:50 min., color, sound. Courtesy of Galerie Zink Waldkirchen, Germany. Exhibited May 2021

Pilson, John. American, born 1968. *Mr. Pick Up*, 2001. Three-channel video, 17:00 min., color, sound. Courtesy of Nicole Klagsbrun Gallery, New York. Exhibited May 2012 and August 2012

Pindell, Howardena. American, born 1943. *Free, White and 21*, 1980. Video, 12:15 min., color, sound. Courtesy of the artist, The University of Texas Libraries, and Garth Greenan Gallery, New York. Exhibited February 2021

Pinder, Jefferson. American, born 1970. *Afro-Cosmonaut/Alien (White Noise)*, 2008. Stop-motion animation video, 5:47 min., color, sound. Courtesy of the artist. Exhibited February 2025

Pope, Cheryl. American, born 1980. *Up Against*, 2010. Single-channel HD video, 10:00 min., color, sound. Courtesy of the artist and Mark Moore Gallery, Culver City. Exhibited September 2013

Provost, Nicolas. Belgian, born 1969. *Papillon d'amour*, 2003. Video, 4:00 min., b&w, sound. Image copyright of the artist. Courtesy of the Video Data Bank at the School of the Art Institute of Chicago. Exhibited April 2014

Rainer, Yvonne. American, born 1934. *After Many a Summer Dies the Swan*, 2002. Video, 31:00 min., color, sound. Courtesy of the Video Data Bank at the School of the Art Institute of Chicago. Exhibited January 2011

Ríos, Miguel Angel. Argentinian, born 1943. *Crudo*, 2008. Video, 3:14 min., color, sound. Courtesy of the artist and Sicardi Gallery, Houston, TX. Exhibited October 2016

Rist, Pipilotti. Swiss, born 1962. *I'm a Victim of This Song*, 1995. Video, 5:06 min., color, sound. Courtesy of Electronic Arts Intermix (EAI), New York. Exhibited September 2011

Ritchie, Matthew. British, born 1964. *Caudex*, 2022. Looped digital animation with choral soundtrack by Shara Nova, 10:54 min., color, sound. Courtesy of the artist and James Cohan, New York. Exhibited January 2024

Robinson, Michael. American, born 1981. *The Dark, Krystle*, 2013. HD Video, 9:34 min., color, sound. Courtesy of the Video Data Bank at the School of the Art Institute of Chicago. Exhibited June 2022

Rojas, Miguel Ángel. Colombian, born 1946. *Corte en el ojo*, 2003. Video, 6:47 min., color, sound. Courtesy of Sicardi Gallery, Houston, TX. Exhibited October 2014

Rosler, Martha. American, born 1943. *Semiotics of the Kitchen*, 1975. Video, 6:09 min., b&w, sound. Courtesy of Electronic Arts Intermix (EAI), New York. Exhibited June 2013

Rubnitz, Tom, and Magnuson, Ann. American, 1956–1992; American, born 1956. *Made for TV*, 1984. U-matic video, 15:00 min., color, sound. Image copyright of the artist. Courtesy of the Video Data Bank at the School of the Art Institute of Chicago. Exhibited January 2016

Ruga, Athi-Patra. South African, born 1984. *Over the Rainbow (Queens in Exile Series)*, 2016–17. Single-channel HD video, 9:27 min., color, sound. Courtesy of the artist and WHATIFTHEWORLD Gallery, Cape Town, SA. Exhibited April 2021

Sai Hua Kuan, Chen. Singaporean, born 1976. *Space Drawing No. 7*, 2010. Digital film, 60 sec., color, sound. Courtesy of the artist and Osage Gallery, Hong Kong, China. Exhibited February 2015

Saro-Wiwa, Zina. Nigerian, born 1976. *Table Manners*, 2014–16. Video, 61:22 min., color, sound. Courtesy of the artist and Tiwani Contemporary, London. Exhibited April 2018

Satterwhite, Jacolby. American, born 1986. *Healing in My House*, 2016. 3D animation and video, 9:26 min., color, sound. © Jacolby Satterwhite. Courtesy of the artist and Mitchell-Innes & Nash, New York. Exhibited April 2022

Sawa, Hiraki. Japanese/British, born 1977. *Dwelling*, 2002. Digital single-channel video, 9:20 min., b&w, sound. © Hiraki Sawa. Courtesy of James Cohan, New York. Exhibited November 2020

Schinwald, Markus. Austrian, born 1973. *Orient*, 2011. Looped, two-channel HD video, 9:00 min. each, color, sound. Courtesy of the artist and Yvon Lambert Gallery, Paris. Exhibited March 2013

Schneemann, Carolee. American, 1939–2019. *Viet Flakes*, 1965. Film on video, 7:00 min., toned b&w, sound. Courtesy of Electronic Arts Intermix (EAI), New York. © Carolee Schneemann/Artist Rights Society (ARS), New York. Exhibited July 2011

Schulnik, Allison. American, born 1978. *Moth*, 2019. Gouche-on-paper animated video, 3:15 min., color, sound. Courtesy of Allison Schulnik and P•P•O•W, New York. Exhibited March 2022

Serra, Richard. American, 1938–2024. *Hand Catching Lead*, 1968. 16mm film transferred to DVD, 3:02 min., b&w, silent. Courtesy of Museum of Modern Art, New York. © 2010 Richard Serra/Artist Rights Society (ARS), New York. Exhibited February 2011

Serrano, Teresa. Mexican, born 1936. *La piñata*, 2003. Video, 5:45 min., color, sound. Courtesy of the artist and EDS GALERIA, Mexico City. Exhibited October 2017

Shonibare MBE, Yinka. British, born 1962. *Un ballo in maschera (A Masked Ball)*, 2004. HD Video, 32:00 min., color, sound. Courtesy of the artist and James Cohan, New York. Exhibited September 2017

Sikander, Shahzia. Pakistani-American, born 1969. *The Last Post*, 2010. HD video animation, 10:00 min., color, sound. Courtesy of the artist. Exhibited September 2018

Simpson, Lorna. American, born 1960. *Corridor*, 2003. Double-projection video installation; video transferred to DVD, 13:45 min., color, sound. Courtesy of Salon 94. Exhibited December 2013

Smith, Michael. American, born 1951. *Go For It, Mike*, 1984. Video, 4:40 min., color, sound. Courtesy of the artist. Exhibited April 2024

Smithson, Robert. American, 1938–1973. *Spiral Jetty*, 1970. 16mm film on video, 35:00 min., color, sound. Courtesy of Electronic Arts Intermix (EAI), New York Art. © Estate of Robert Smithson/Licensed by VAGA, New York, NY. Exhibited May 2013

Snow, Michael. Canadian, 1928–2023. *WVLNT (Wavelength for Those Who Don't Have the Time)*, 1966–67/2003. Video, 15:00 min., color, sound. Courtesy of Electronic Arts Intermix (EAI), New York. Exhibited July 2022

Sola, Joe. American, born 1966. *Studio Visit*, 2005. Digital video, 8:00 min., color, sound. Courtesy of Blackston, New York and Tif Sigfrids, Los Angeles. Exhibited November 2015

Sonnier, Keith. American, 1941–2020. *Animation I*, 1973. Video, 13:52 min., color, sound. Courtesy of the Video Data Bank at the School of the Art Institute of Chicago. Exhibited December 2019

Streuli, Beat. Swiss, born 1957. *8th Avenue/35th Street*, 2002. Video, 20:00 min., color, sound. Courtesy of the artist and Jochen Hempel Gallery. Exhibited July 2019

Thomson, Mungo. American, born 1969. *The American Desert (for Chuck Jones)*, 2002. Video, 34:00 min., color, sound. Courtesy of the artist and galerie frank elbaz. Exhibited March 2020

Trecartin, Ryan. American, born 1981. *Sibling Topics (section a)*, 2009. HD video, 50:00 min., color, sound. Courtesy of Electronic Arts Intermix (EAI), New York. Exhibited July 2016

Valdovino, Luis. Argentinian, born 1961. *Work in Progress*, 1990. Video, 14:00 min., color, sound. Courtesy of the Video Data Bank at the School of the Art Institute of Chicago. Exhibited May 2022

Vatanajyankur, Kawita. Thai, born 1987. *Tools (video series)*, 2012–14. Video, various times, color, silent. Courtesy of the artist and Nova Contemporary. Exhibited September 2021

Vicuña, Cecilia. Chilean, born 1948. *Semiya (Seed Song)*, 2015. HD video, 7:43 min., color, sound. Courtesy of Electronic Arts Intermix (EAI), New York. Exhibited January 2023

Walker, Kara. American, born 1969. *Testimony: Narrative of a Negress Burdened by Good Intentions*, 2004. Video, 8:49 min., b&w, silent. Courtesy of the artist and Sikkema Malloy Jenkins, New York. Exhibited September–October 2020

Walker, Kara. American, born 1969. *8 Possible Beginnings or: The Creation of African-America, a Moving Picture by Kara E. Walker*, 2005. Video, 15:57 min., b&w, sound. Courtesy of the artist and Sikkema Malloy Jenkins, New York. Exhibited October–November 2020

Walker, Kara. American, born 1969. *...calling to me from the angry surface of some grey and threatening sea.*, 2007. Video, 9:10 min, color, sound. Courtesy of the artist and Sikkema Malloy Jenkins, New York. Exhibited October-November 2020

Walker, Kara. American, born 1969. *Falling Frum Grace, Miss Pipi's Blue Tale*, 2011. Video, 17:00 min, color, sound. Courtesy of the artist and Sikkema Malloy Jenkins, New York. Exhibited October-November 2020

Weems, Carrie Mae. American, born 1953. *Meaning and Landscape*, 2003-04. Video, 12:31 min., b&w, sound. © Carrie Mae Weems. Courtesy of the artist and Jack Shainman Gallery, New York. Exhibited February 2024

Werve, Guido van der. Dutch, born 1977. *Nummer Twee: Just because I'm standing here doesn't mean I want to*, 2003. 35 mm film, 3:08 min., color, sound. © Guido van der Werve. Courtesy of the artist, Luhring Augustine, New York, GRIMM, Amsterdam, and MONITOR, Rome. Exhibited March 2021

Wiley, Kehinde. American, born 1977. *Smile*, 2003. Digital video, 90:00 min., color, sound. Courtesy of the artist and Roberts & Tilton Gallery, Los Angeles. Exhibited March 2017

Wilke, Hannah. American, 1940-1993. *Gestures*, 1974. Video, 35:30 min., b&w, sound. Courtesy of Electronic Arts Intermix (EAI), New York. Exhibited April 2016

Wojnarowicz, David. American, 1954-1992. *A Fire in My Belly (A Work in Progress)*, 1986-87. Super 8mm film on video, 20:55 min., color and b&w, silent. Courtesy of Electronic Arts Intermix (EAI), New York. Exhibited May 2018

Wube, Ezra. Ethiopian, born 1980. *Mela*, 2011. HD Video, 1:43 min., color, silent. Courtesy of the Video Data Bank at the School of the Art Institute of Chicago. Exhibited May 2023

Yonemoto, Bruce and Norman. American, born 1949; American, 1946-2014. *Vault*, 1984. Video, 11:45 min., color, sound. Courtesy of Electronic Arts Intermix (EAI), New York. Exhibited November 2012

Yu, A young (in collaboration with Nicholas Oh). Korean-American, born 1990. *Mourning Rituals*, 2020-22. Digital video, 21:47 min., color, sound. Courtesy of the artist. Exhibited March 2025

Zamora, Héctor. Mexican, born 1974. *O abuso da história (The Abuse of History)*, 2014. Video, 1:52 min., color, sound. Courtesy of the artist and Luciana Brito Galeria, São Paulo, Brazil. Exhibited February 2018

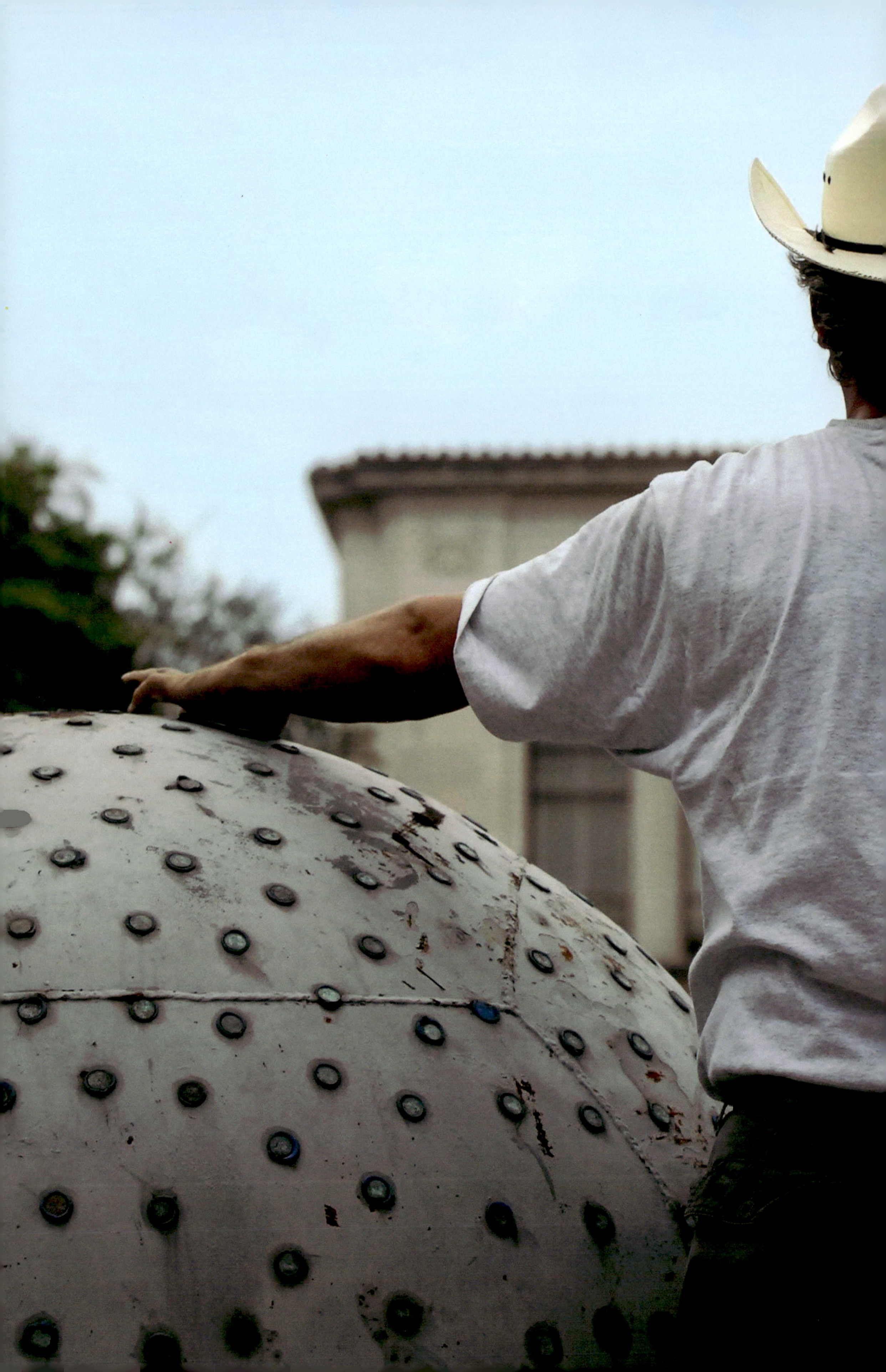

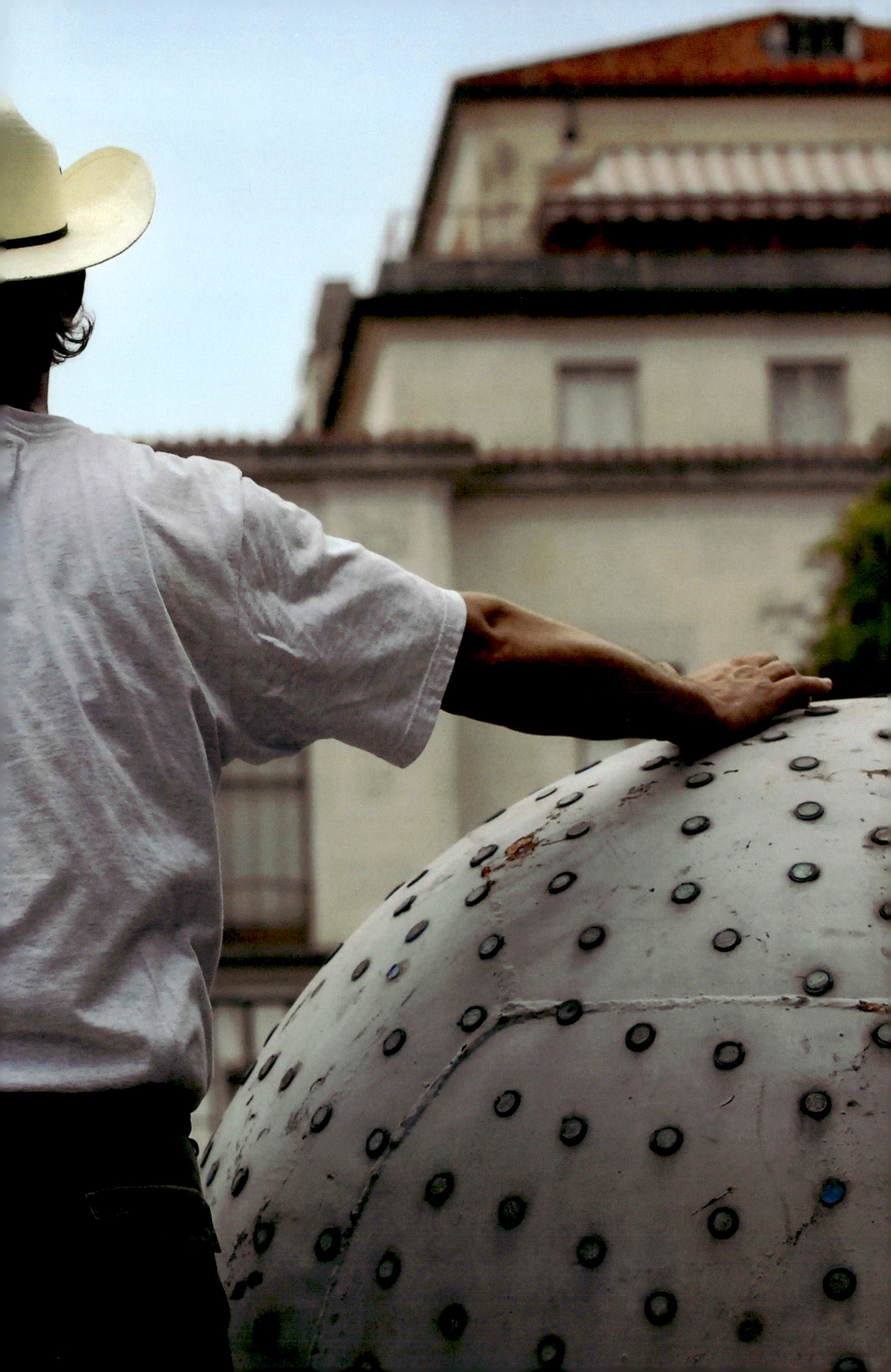

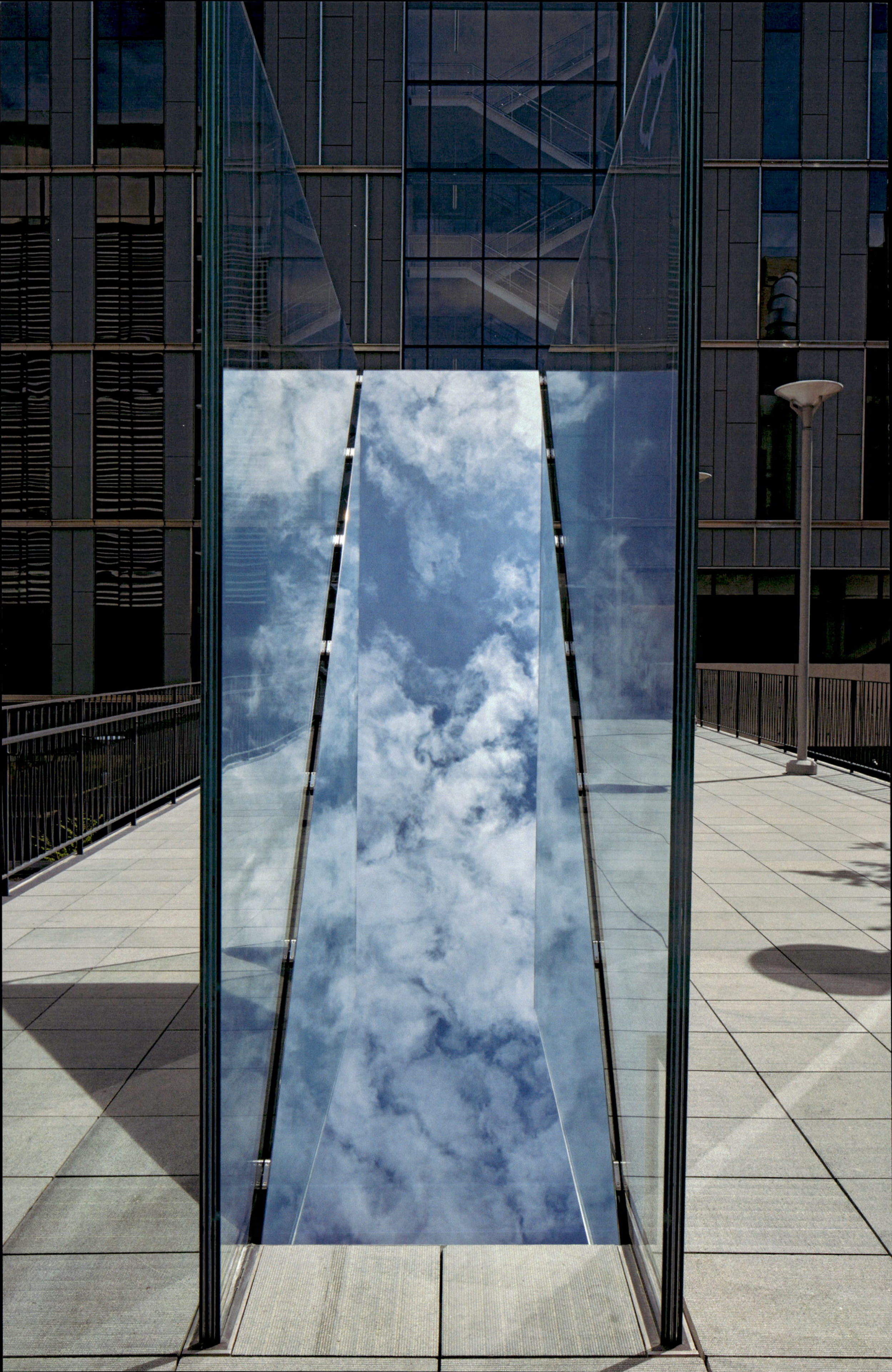

THANKS

Landmarks is grateful to the following contributors for believing in our mission to make great art free and accessible to all.

DONORS

Anonymous Contributors
Estate of Kirby Attwell
Suzanne Deal Booth
Hiram Carruthers Butler
Meta Alice Keith Bratten Foundation
Sara Carter
fd2s
The Felvis Foundation
Estate of Judith E. Fruchter
GSD&M
Sheri Clark Henriksen
Emily and Douglas Jacobson
Jeanne and Michael Klein
KMFA, Austin's Independent Classical Radio Station
KUT/KUTX
Joe R. Long
Tom and Charlene Marsh Family Foundation
Elisabeth and Brian McCabe
James A. Miller
Jenny F. Mullen
National Endowment for the Arts
Dian Graves Owen Foundation
Page
Resnicow + Associates
Rachel and Arnon Rosan
Stedman West Foundation
Still Water Foundation
The Tapeats Fund
Texas Commission on the Arts
Emily Hall Tremaine Foundation (EHTF)
Susan Vaughan Foundation
David Wescoe
Jill and Stephen Wilkinson

UNIVERSITY LEADERSHIP

Andrée Bober and Landmarks
Katie Brock and the Office of the Vice President of Operations
James Davis and the Office of the President
Douglas Gilpin and Construction Operations
David Vanden Bout and the Office of the Executive Vice President and Provost
Planning, Design & Construction
Ramón Rivera-Servera and the College of Fine Arts
Brian Smith and Financial and Administrative Services
Brent Stringfellow and Campus Operations

LANDMARKS ADVISORY COMMITTEE

Kevin Alter, 2023-present
Francesa Balboni, 2017-2023
Mirka Benes, 2008-2010
Sarah Canright, 2008-2010
Annette Carlozzi, 2008-2013
Edward Chambers, 2012-2013; 2019-2025
Ondine Chavoya, 2025-present
John Clarke, 2008-2011
Amanda Douberly, 2008-2009
George Flaherty, 2017-present
Scherezade Garcia-Vazquez, 2023-present
Lauren Hanson, 2009-2012
Amy Hauft, 2013-2019
Jana La Brasca, 2023-present
Beili Liu, 2021-present
Juan Miró, 2010-2016
Ann Reynolds, 2011-2017
Veronica Roberts, 2013-2019
Igor Siddiqui, 2018-2023
Michael Smith, 2010-2022
Jason Sowell, 2016-2017
Mackenzie Stevens, 2019-2023
John Stoney, 2017-present
Phillip Townsend, 2023-present
Robin K. Williams, 2012-2017

STAFF

Sonya Berg, Assistant to the Director
Andrée Bober, Founding Director and Curator
Kathleen Brady Stimpert, Deputy Director
Anoush Crane, Event Coordinator
Kanitra Fletcher, Landmarks Video Curator
Bill Haddad, Technology Manager
Lindsay Hamm Havekost, Assistant Director for Collections
Logan Larsen, Digital Content Coordinator
Dorothy Lin, Graphic Designer
Stephanie Taparauskas, Assistant Director for Development
Thao Votang, Business Coordinator
Michelle Voss, Assistant Curator
Catherine Whited, Education Program Coordinator

UNIVERSITY PARTNERS

African and African Diaspora Studies
Art Galleries at Black Studies
AT&T Executive Education and Conference Center
Blanton Museum of Art
Business Contracts Office
Sarah and Ernest Butler School of Music
Campus Operations
Center for American Architecture and Design
Center for Mexican American Studies
Cockrell School of Engineering
College of Education
College of Fine Arts
College of Liberal Arts
College of Natural Sciences
Dell Medical School
Department of Art and Art History
Department of Computer Science
Department of Design
Department of Mexican American and Latina/o Studies
Department of Psychology
Dolph Briscoe Center for American History
Facilities Services
Fine Arts Library
Fitness Institute of Texas
Harry Ransom Center

Humanitas
Humanities Institute
Institute for Urban Policy Research and Analysis
Jackson School of Geosciences
John L. Warfield Center for African and African American Studies
Lady Bird Johnson Wildflower Center
Landscape Services
LBJ Presidential Library
Legal Affairs
Longhorn Wellness Center
McCombs School of Business
Moody College of Communication
Office for Community Engagement and Public Practice (OCEPP)
Orange Bike Project
Planning, Design and Construction
Risk Management
School of Architecture
School of Design and Creative Technologies
School of Information
William C. Powers Student Activity Center
Women in STEM (WiSTEM)
Texas Advanced Computing Center
Texas Parents
Texas Performing Arts
Texas Science and Natural History Museum
Undergraduate College
University of Texas Libraries
University of Texas Press
University Unions
UTeach Outreach
Visual Arts Center

COMMUNITY PARTNERS

ArtTable
Austin Classical Guitar
Austin Film Society
Austin Foundation for Architecture
Austin LGBT Chamber of Commerce
Austin Museum Partnership
Austin Soundwaves
Austin Studio Tour
Austin Ukestra
Blue Dog Rescue
City of Austin Art in Public Places (AIPP)
Co-Lab Projects
Conspirare
The Contemporary Austin
dadaLab
Davis Gallery
Design Austin
Flatbed Press
Frank & Victor Design
Fusebox Festival
Future Front Texas
GalleryLog
HOPE Campaign
Imagine Art
KOOP Radio
LOLA (Local Opera Local Artists)
Lookthinkmake
The Loren Hotel, Austin
Luna Music
RC Creative
Resnicow + Associates
St. Edward's University
Texas Association of Museums
The Trail Conservancy
The Vortex
Waterloo Greenway

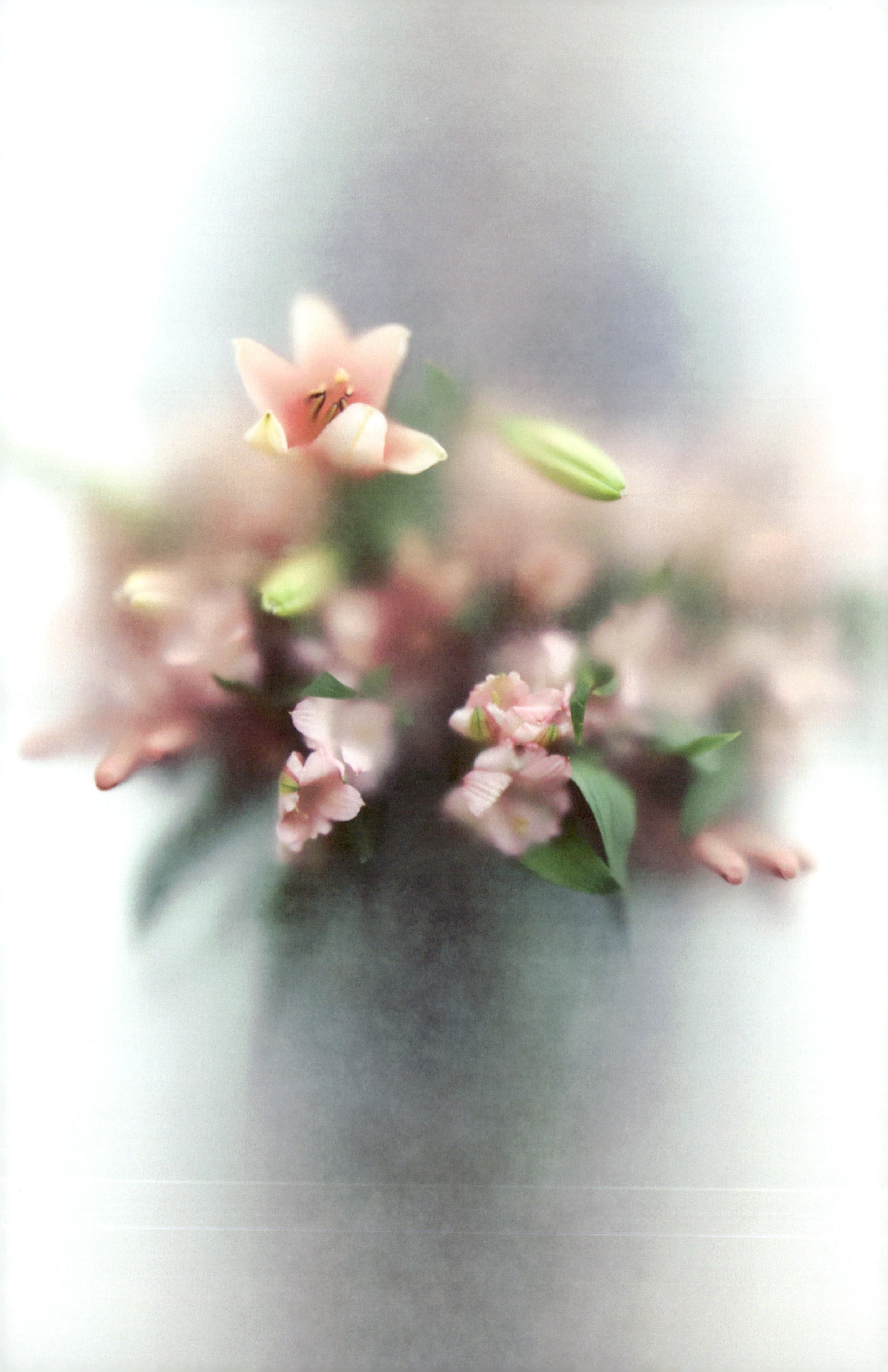

PHOTOGRAPHY CREDITS

Ben Aqua: 13, 65, 85, 133, 171
Dror Baldinger: 55, 81, 99, 105, 107, 109, 129, 131, 136
Paul Bardagjy: 4/5, 14/15, 38/39, 41, 45, 47, 51, 52, 53, 57, 58, 59, 61, 66/67, 69, 75, 78, 113, 119, 120, 125, 135, 137, 139, 140, 141, 143, 145, 146/147, 149, 150/151, 153, 154, 155, 164, 165, 167, 169, 172, 206/207
Richard Barnes: 16, 115, 116, 117, 200
Maggie Calton: 34
Sandy Carson: 32, 96 (lower), 97 (upper), 101
Ann Hamilton: 22, 77, 204
Serena Hayden: 163
Florian Holzherr: 6, 166
Mark Menjivar: 43, 63, 83, 87, 89, 95, 96 (upper), 97 (lower), 111, 123
The Metropolitan Museum of Art: 49
Marsha Miller: 2/3, 103, 198/199
Christina Murrey: 8/9, 10, 21, 35, 37, 71 (upper left, lower left, middle right; remainder are film stills from *Animal*), 91, 92, 93, 157, 159, 161, 174
Ismael Quintanilla III: 28, 36
Rey Parlá: 126/127
Lawrence Peart: 26/27
Catherine Zinser Mandel: 100

Cover image: Jennifer Steinkamp, detail of *EON*, 2020
Inside front cover: Eamon Ore-Giron, detail of *Tras los ojos (Behind the Eyes)*, 2023

To read complete essays from curatorial contributors, please visit landmarksut.org.

Library of Congress Cataloging-in-Publication Data

Names: Landmarks (Program : University of Texas at Austin), author. | Bober, Andrée, editor. | Brady Stimpert, Kathleen, contributor. | Knudson, Rainey, contributor. | Fletcher, Kanitra, contributor.
Title: Landmarks : the public art program of the University of Texas at Austin : 2008–2025 / edited by Andrée Bober ; essays by Rainey Knudson, Kathleen Brady Stimpert, Kanitra Fletcher ; with texts adapted from contributions by Sana López Abellán [and 20 others].
Description: [3]. | Austin : Landmarks, The University of Texas at Austin, 2025.
Identifiers: LCCN 2025007057 | ISBN 9781732821491 (paperback)
Subjects: LCSH: Landmarks (Program : University of Texas at Austin) | Public art—Texas—Austin.
Classification: LCC N8836.T4 L36 2025 | DDC 707.4/76431—dc23/eng/20250220
LC record available at https://lccn.loc.gov/2025007057

Production Editor: Kathleen Brady Stimpert
Image Editors: Logan Larsen and Dorothy Lin
Proofreader: Kathleen Garrett
Content Editor: Mariah Keller

Published by Landmarks
landmarksut.org

Distributed by University of Texas Press
utpress.utexas.edu
Requests for permission to reproduce material from this work should be sent to: permissions@utpress.utexas.edu

Produced by Marquand Books, Seattle
marquandbooks.com

♾ The paper used in this book meets the minimum requirements of ANSI/NISO Z39.48-1992 (R1997) (Permanence of Paper).

Printed and bound in China by Artron Art Group

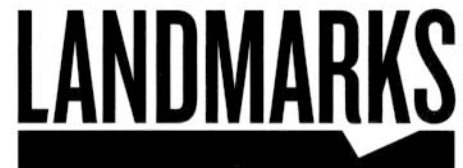

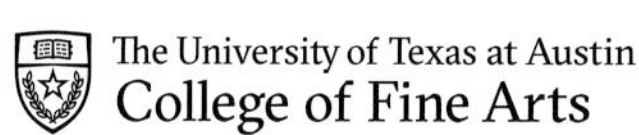

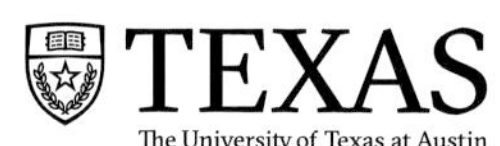